# Top Federal Tax Issues for 2019 | CPE Course

Mark Luscombe, J.D., LL.M., CPA
Annette Nellen, CPA, CGMA, Esq.
Jane Searing, CPA, MST
James R. Hamill, Ph.D., CPA
Jennifer Kowal, J.D.
John Hanning, CCSP, MBA
Steven G. Siegel, J.D., LL.M. (Taxation)

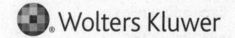

Wolters Kluwer

## Contributors

Contributing Editors . . . . . . . . . . . . . . . . . . . . . . . . . . . . . . . Kelen Camehl, CPA

Greg White, CPA

Lorraine Zecca, CPA

Technical Review . . . . . . . . . . . . . . . . . . . . . . . . . . . . . . . . . Lorraine Zecca, CPA

Production Coordinator . . . . . . . . . . . . . Mariela de la Torre; Jennifer Schencker;

Ranjith Rajaram

Production . . . . . . . . . . . . . . . . . . . . . . . . . Lynn J. Brown; Anbarasu Anbumani

This publication is designed to provide accurate and authoritative information in regard to the subject matter covered. It is sold with the understanding that the publisher is not engaged in rendering legal, accounting, or other professional service. If legal advice or other expert assistance is required, the services of a competent professional person should be sought.

ISBN: 978-0-8080-5088-9

No claim is made to original government works; however, within this Product or Publication, the following are subject to CCH Incorporated's copyright: (1) the gathering, compilation, and arrangement of such government materials; (2) the magnetic translation and digital conversion of data, if applicable; (3) the historical, statutory and other notes and references; and (4) the commentary and other materials.

Printed in the United States of America

SUSTAINABLE FORESTRY INITIATIVE

Certified Sourcing

www.sfiprogram.org

SFI-01681

# Introduction

Each year, a handful of tax issues typically require special attention by tax practitioners. The reasons vary, from tax legislation, a particularly complicated new provision in the Internal Revenue Code, to a planning technique opened up by a new regulation or ruling, or the availability of a significant tax benefit with a short window of opportunity. Sometimes a developing business need creates a new set of tax problems, or pressure exerted by Congress or the Administration puts more heat on some taxpayers while giving others more slack. All these share in creating a unique mix that in turn creates special opportunities and pitfalls in the coming year and beyond. The past year has seen more than its share of these developing issues.

*Top Federal Tax Issues for 2019 CPE Course* identifies those recent events that have developed into the current "hot" issues of the day. These tax issues have been selected as particularly relevant to tax practice in 2019. They have been selected not only because of their impact on return preparation during the 2019 tax season but also because of the important role they play in developing effective tax strategies for 2019 and beyond.

This course is designed to help reassure the tax practitioner that he or she is not missing out on advising clients about a hot, new tax opportunity; or that a brewing controversy does not blindside their practice. In addition to issue identification, this course provides the basic information needed for the tax practitioner to implement a plan that addresses the particular opportunities and pitfalls presented by any one of those issues. Among the topics examined in the *Top Federal Tax Issues for 2019 CPE Course* are:

- Tax Legislation Update: *Tax Cuts and Jobs Act*
- Self-Employment Tax: Today's World of Sharing, LLCs, & Tax Reform
- Tax Reform for Tax-Exempt Organizations
- Section 199A Qualified Business Deduction
- S Corp Distributions: Determining the Taxability
- Bonus Depreciation Update & Cost Segregation Tax Planning
- Determining Tax Basis of Property
- Understanding the Federal Gift Tax
- *Tax Cuts and Jobs Act:* Impact on Financial and Estate Planning

**Study Questions.** Throughout the course you will find Study Questions to help you test your knowledge, and comments that are vital to understanding a particular strategy or idea. Answers to the Study Questions with feedback on both correct and incorrect responses are provided in a special section beginning at ¶ 10,100.

**Final Exam.** This course is divided into three Modules. Take your time and review all course Modules. When you feel confident that you thoroughly understand the material, turn to the Final Exam. Complete one, or all, Module Final Exams for continuing professional education credit.

Go to **cchcpelink.com/printcpe** to complete your Final Exam online for immediate results. My Dashboard provides convenient storage for your CPE course Certificates. Further information is provided in the CPE Final Exam instructions at ¶ 10,300. **Please note, manual grading is no longer available for Top Federal Tax Issues. All answer sheets must be submitted online for grading and processing.**

**Note:** The material contained in this publication was current at the time it went to print.

**October 2018**

## PLEDGE TO QUALITY

Thank you for choosing this CCH® CPE Link product. We will continue to produce high quality products that challenge your intellect and give you the best option for your Continuing Education requirements. Should you have a concern about this or any other Wolters Kluwer product, please call our Customer Service Department at 1-800-344-3734.

## COURSE OBJECTIVES

This course was prepared to provide the participant with an overview of specific tax issues that impact 2018 tax return preparation and tax planning in 2019. Each impacts a significant number of taxpayers in significant ways.

Upon course completion, you will be able to:

- Recognize issues and status of guidance about the new tax law
- Identify possible planning ideas in response to the new act
- Recognize possibilities for additional tax legislation following enactment of the new tax law
- Identify when an individual is subject to self-employment tax
- Recognize self-employment issues in representative court cases
- Recognize the due diligence steps to avoid problems with self-employment tax
- Identify ways that the new law affects charitable giving
- Recognize how the new tax act affects not-for-profit organizations that have employees
- Recognize how Notice 2017-73 is applied to the quid pro quo values of items offered in charity fundraising activities
- Recognize what a qualified business is and how the deduction on income of flow-through entities functions
- Identify service and nonservice businesses and how the deductions differ for each type
- Recognize how the new tax law changes ancillary tax issues of qualified businesses
- Recognize rules applicable to passthrough of S corporation income and deductions
- Identify effects of S corporation income, liabilities, and loans
- Recognize how to characterize S corp distributions as salary versus income
- Recognize the percentages of the bonus depreciation deduction applicable for 2018 and subsequent years
- Identify how the new tax law affects other tax planning strategies such as Code Sec. 179 expensing and net operating losses
- Recognize the types of property held to be qualified leasehold improvements and qualified improvement property
- Recognize general tax basis rules and outcome of common "cost" basis situations
- Identify rules that apply in determining how to allocate basis or determine which basis to use when not all of a taxpayer's property is sold
- Recognize the special rules that apply to property received by gift or inheritance
- Recognize the effects of depreciation and nonrecognition exchanges on calculating basis
- Recognize the types of transfers and donors are subject to the gift tax
- Identify how to plan for exclusions for annual and lifetime gifts

- Recognize reporting requirements when gift amounts exceed the annual exclusion
- Recognize how existing assets are affected by and should transition to terms of the new law
- Identify ways the law opens favorable opportunities for taxpayers subject to transfer taxes
- Recognize how planners and wealthier clients can use financial and estate planning tools to minimize tax liabilities in the post-tax cuts environment

---

Additional copies of this course may be downloaded from **cchcpelink.com/printcpe**. Printed copies of the course are available for $2.99 by calling 1-800-344-3734 (ask for product 10024491-0006).

---

# Contents

## MODULE 2: BUSINESS COMPLIANCE ISSUES
### 4 Section 199A Qualified Business Deduction

### 5 S Corp Distributions: Determining the Taxability

## MODULE 3: TAX ISSUES RELATED TO PROPERTY
### 6 Bonus Depreciation Update & Cost Segregation Tax Planning

## 7 Determining Tax Basis of Property

## MODULE 4: FINANCIAL AND ESTATE PLANNING
## 8 Understanding the Federal Gift Tax

# MODULE 1: TAX REFORM—Chapter 1: Tax Legislation Update: *Tax Cuts and Jobs Act*

## ¶ 101 WELCOME

This chapter discusses the basic and highlighted provisions of the *Tax Cuts and Jobs Act* (H.R. 1) enacted in 2017 as the new tax law. The chapter discusses what little guidance has come out of the IRS so far with respect to the *Tax Cuts and Jobs Act.*

## ¶ 102 LEARNING OBJECTIVES

Upon completion of this chapter, you will be able to:

- Recognize issues and status of guidance about the new tax law
- Identify possible planning ideas in response to the new act
- Recognize possibilities for additional tax legislation following enactment of the new tax law

## ¶ 103 INTRODUCTION

The IRS is promising a lot of proposed regulations to address issues left unresolved by the new tax law; some proposed regulations have been released, as well as notices, information releases, and frequently asked questions (FAQs)—and some answers. A lot of those information releases and notices indicate their foreshadowing what they expect those proposed regulations to say, but the Treasury Department is saying that it is not really guidance, the government is just trying to give clients and practitioners an idea of what they expect the guidance to cover when it does come out.

Another issue that the chapter discusses is that the IRS has also been forced to enter into an agreement with the Office of Management and Budget (OMB) whereby there can be another level of review of tax regulations by a subdivision of the OMB, if criteria are met. That could further delay the process of some of these regulations before they are issued.

## ¶ 104 NEW TAX RATES

It is well known that there are new individual rates, with a new top rate of 37 percent. It is key to remember that there used to be a marriage penalty built into most of the higher brackets in which a couple's total tax bill was higher when they filed jointly as opposed to filing two returns as single filers for separate incomes, but that has been revised with the new percentages and phaseout rate. The marriage penalty now only applies at the top bracket. Table 1.1 shows the $500,000 single and the $600,000 joint return limits; it is only there where there is still a marriage penalty built into the rate brackets.

Table 1.1 Individual Tax Rates of 10, 12, 22, 24, 32, 35, and 37 Percent for 2018*

| Tax Rate Percentage | Taxable Income Range |
|---|---|
| 10 percent | Not over $9,525, single, $19,050 joint |
| 12 percent | Not over $38,700 single, $77,400 joint |
| 22 percent | Not over $82,500 single, $165,000 joint |
| 24 percent | Not over $157,500 single, $315,000 joint |

| Tax Rate Percentage | Taxable Income Range |
|---|---|
| 32 percent | Not over $200,000 single, $400,000 joint |
| 35 percent | Not over $500,000 single, $600,000 joint |
| 37 percent | Over $500,000 single, $600,000 joint |

\* New rate structures expire after 2025.

For the most part people will see some tax benefit from these new rates because they are a little lower than the rates that were in effect under prior law. The text discusses withholding and some of the issues of withholding that people are having to address to accommodate the new rate structure and some of the other issues.

## STUDY QUESTION

**1.** Which of the following identifies the new individual tax rate for those joint filers making more than $600,000?

    **a.** 32 percent

    **b.** 35 percent

    **c.** 37 percent

    **d.** 39 percent

## ¶ 105 CAPITAL GAINS

The new tax law enacted has no change for treatment of capital gains. The rate is no longer tied to specific rate brackets like it was under the old law, but Congress tried to keep the capital gain rates kicking in at approximately the same income levels as they applied under prior law, so no big changes are there for capital gains for 2018. The 0, 15, and 20 percent rates are retained: the 15 percent rate begins at $38,600 of gains for single filers and $77,200 for joint filing couples. The 20 percent rate applies to $425,800 for single filers and $479,000 for joint filers.

## ¶ 106 STANDARD DEDUCTIONS AND PERSONAL EXEMPTIONS

### Standard Deductions

Some major changes apply to standard deductions. There are major areas affecting individual taxpayers and simplification in the law. Under prior law, about two-thirds of taxpayers claimed the standard deduction, and it is estimated that half of the remaining individuals who were still itemizing will now be better off with the standard deduction under the new law, which has doubled. Roughly three-fourths of taxpayers might be claiming the standard deduction in 2018 and going forward. Table 1.2 summarizes the standard deduction amounts by filing status.

### Table 1.2 Individual Standard Deduction for 2018

| Filing Status | Deduction Amount |
|---|---|
| Single | $12,000 |
| Married filing jointly | $24,000 |
| Head of household | $18,000 |

Those changes represent significant simplification for a lot of people who are now better off not having to go through the effort of doing a Schedule A and itemization of deductions. Those amounts are, as was the old standard deduction, adjusted for inflation.

There could be a couple of reasons that individuals would not benefit from itemizing in the future. One is the doubling of the standard deduction. If taxpayers' itemizations under the old law were less than the $12,000 for single filers or $24,000 for joint filers, then they are probably going to be better off doing the standard deduction in the future. Also, the standard deduction will be adjusted for inflation after 2018.

There could also be another reason to start using the standard deduction: a lot of the itemizations are decreased or eliminated under the new law. Less itemizing may mean that there is less incentive for home ownership and charitable giving. Even if itemizations under the old law were greater than the new standard deduction, itemizations under the new law might be below the higher standard deductions, so clients might still be better off claiming the standard deductions. Planners should be proactive in advising clients whether they will still benefit from itemizing.

A major issue with this, as with many of the changes under the new law for all the individual provisions, is that it expires after 2025. The expiration has been one of the big criticisms of the legislation: the corporate provisions are on the whole permanent, whereas the individual tax breaks all expire after 2025. In some cases, that can make planning difficult, with respect to the 20 percent deduction for pass-through business owners and estate and gift planning.

## Elimination of Personal Exemptions

Along with doubling the standard deduction, the act eliminated individuals' personal exemptions. That will have a more negative effect for some taxpayers than the positive effect of doubling the standard deduction. If individuals have a lot of children for whom they formerly claimed personal exemptions, the families could well be taxpayers who end up worse off under the new law than they were under the prior law because the elimination of the personal exemptions is not totally offset by the doubling of the standard deduction.

## Child Tax Credit and New Dependent Credit

The new tax law doubled the child tax credit to $2,000, a provision that again expires after 2025. The law also made some changes for documenting Social Security numbers with respect to the child tax credit. The refundable portion of the credit did not increase to $2,000, it only increased to $1,400, it constitutes a little hit for lower income taxpayers. The beginning of the credit phaseout increases to $200,000 of income ($400,000 for jointly filing couples), eliminating the former marriage penalty in this provision of the tax law.

There is a brand-new credit for caring for a nonchild dependent, this is in addition to the child and dependent care credit and the child tax credit. It is $500 for caring for nonchild dependents (qualifying persons who are physically or mentally incapable of self-care). The IRS released guidance on who is a qualifying person.

## STUDY QUESTION

---

**2.** Which of the following identifies the new standard deduction for heads of household?

    **a.** $12,000

    **b.** $12,700

    **c.** $18,000

    **d.** $24,000

---

# ¶ 107 ITEMIZED DEDUCTIONS

## Mortgage Interest Deduction

The mortgage interest deduction has a new limit. This deduction has a retroactive date back to 2017. Most of the new tax law provisions are not effective until the 2018 tax year, but a few of them did have a retroactive effective date back to 2017. The mortgage interest deduction is one of them, where the limit dropped from $1 million to $750,000 for new mortgage debt after December 15, 2017. Form 1098, *Mortgage Interest Statement,* is now to include the amount of outstanding mortgage, address of the property, and loan origination date for the 2018 returns.

## Home Equity Loan Interest

The new law also provides no home equity deduction after December 31, 2017. Note the difference in language here. The December 15, 2017, date relates to new mortgage debt, preexisting mortgage debt up to $1 million can still qualify even after December 15, 2017, because it was not *new* mortgage debt. But changes to the home equity deduction apply after December 31, 2017, preexisting home equity loans, as well as post-December 31, 2017, home equity loans have no interest deductible after December 31, 2017.

That did raise the question, which was not clear in the law, about home equity loans when the money is used to buy, build, or improve a home. There was uncertainty about that and so the IRS did come out with Information Release 2018-32 to clarify that yes, if taxpayers use that home equity loan to buy, build, or improve a home then, to that extent, it is still deductible, subject, of course, to the mortgage interest deduction limits, just discussed. All of these rules expire after 2025.

## Charitable Contribution Deduction

The charitable contribution deduction survived intact and was even enhanced a bit, perhaps—out of concern that people who were claiming the standard deduction and not itemizing might be less inclined to give to charitable causes because they do not get a tax benefit. To help compensate for that, perhaps, Congress increased the contribution limit. Individuals can get a deduction for such contributions of up to 60 percent of adjusted gross income (AGI). Although taxpayers may be losing some charitable contributions on the lower income spectrum, maybe the hope is that wealthier taxpayers will up their charitable contributions a little because they can now deduct a greater percentage of their contributions.

One change that has gotten a lot of controversy: a lot of colleges were encouraging people to sign up at the end of 2017 for long-term contribution and athletic seating rights, because, starting in 2018, there is no deduction if the charitable contribution secures college athletic event seating rights.

## Mileage Rate for Charitable Miles

There had been talk about an inflation adjustment to the charitable mileage rate, but that did not happen. The rate for charitable miles for 2018 is 14 cents a mile.

## Substantiation of Contributions

Also repealed is a substantiation exception for contributions of $250 or more. In 2017 and later years, a donee can only take a charitable deduction for donations of $250 or more if the donor substantiates the donation with a contemporaneous written acknowledgement to the donee.

## SALT Deductions

One of the big issues that people have been talking about a lot and has been in the press is the limits on state and local tax (SALT) deductions. This has been a red state/blue state issue that some view as political. The law eliminates the SALT deduction in excess of $10,000 or $5,000 if married, filing separately. Contrary to eliminating the marriage penalty, this provision adds back to the marriage penalty because it is the same $10,000 limit whether a taxpayer is filing singly or filing jointly. There is no limit if the taxes are related to business or investment property.

## Prepaid Taxes and Contributions

A couple of issues came up at the beginning of 2018. Some taxpayers are probably aware and some advisors may have even assisted clients with prepaying 2017 property taxes before the new law took effect in 2018. The law itself prohibited prepaying 2018 state income taxes in 2017 but was silent on property taxes; many people rushed to prepay property taxes late in 2017. In Cook County, Illinois, alone, 192,000 taxpayers prepaid property taxes.

However, the IRS came out with Information Release 2017-210 saying that taxpayers cannot prepay 2018 property taxes in 2017 unless it has been assessed in 2017 by the local taxing jurisdiction. There may be people who prepaid property taxes who may not be able to meet that definition. Planners are not really sure what that definition means. In Cook County, for example, the assessor's office put online the property tax bills normally not posted until March, 2018 with the precise amount due and said the office would accept payments prior to year-end.

A lot of tax practitioners are also raising the issue, if the tax law was silent on property taxes while specifically addressing income taxes, does the IRS have it within its authority to restrict prepayment of property taxes when the law was apparently purposely silent on that issue? That might be an issue for the courts as well.

Another issue that has come up with respect to the limitation is that some states are trying to avoid the limit by drafting alternatives for taxpayers where they can, instead of paying state income taxes, they can pay into a state charitable fund or employers can pay payroll taxes and get a full deduction for the taxes on the state income tax liability for those payments. These charitable contributions and payroll taxes would still be deductible on the federal return. New York has established "a new system that allows taxpayers to convert their state income tax to a payroll tax, which companies would pay on their behalf and then deduct from their federal return."

In proposed regulations, the IRS has said it will disallow charitable deductions to the extent a taxpayer receives state income tax credits in return. Some states, such as California, New Jersey and New York, have already implemented such provisions and others were looking at it.

The IRS position may have an impact on some of those historical charitable contributions that had been on state tax returns in the past as well.

## Casualty Loss Deduction

The one itemized deduction that was repealed was the casualty loss deduction, but it was preserved for presidentially-declared federal disaster areas. There are more federal disaster declarations than people normally hear about. Media broadcast the big hurricanes and wildfires and that sort of catastrophe, but there are a lot more federal disaster declarations than get coverage in the popular press. That may not be as big a limit as everyone thinks, but it is something to discuss with clients about whether they want to increase their property insurance coverage if the casualty loss just for an individual theft or fire at their home is no longer eligible for a deduction.

## Medical Expenses

The medical expense deduction was slightly enhanced. It had been 7.5 percent of adjusted gross income (AGI) for a number of years and then increased to 10 percent of AGI, the same as it was for claiming it for the alternative minimum tax (AMT). For seniors, the percentage stayed at 7.5 percent and had increased to 10 percent just for 2017 returns.

Under the new law the floor has gone back to 7.5 percent, not only for regular tax purposes but also for AMT purposes. That is another break for itemized deductions that helps taxpayers. All of these changes to the itemized deductions expire after 2025.

## Miscellaneous Itemized Deductions

There has been some confusion about what miscellaneous itemized deductions remain to claim for 2018. The miscellaneous itemized deductions are disallowed only for deductions that are subject to the 2 percent floor, so that includes items like employee unreimbursed business expenses, investment expenses, and tax preparation fees.

Other miscellaneous itemized deductions that are not subject to the 2 percent floor still survive. One example of those would be gambling expenses. There has also been another change in the law with gambling expenses: gambling expenses as well as gambling losses can only be deducted to the extent of gambling winnings.

## Overall Limit on Deductions

Another change that is a positive for taxpayers is repealing of the overall limit on itemized deductions. The old phaseout is gone. There had been a marriage penalty built into the phaseout of itemized deductions; however, with the elimination of the Pease limitation completely, the marriage penalty aspect of that also goes away.

## Deductions for Tuition and Fees

There were a lot of proposals with respect to changes in the education area but they did not get into the final law. The tuition and fees deduction was restored for 2017 in the *Bipartisan Budget Act* (P.L. 115-123), signed into law on February 9, 2018. All of those regularly expiring provisions that were not addressed in the *Tax Cuts and Jobs Act* were restored. There were 30-plus expired tax provisions that were extended for 2017 only, and one of those was the tuition and fees deduction.

The legislation left them again expired for 2018, as discussed later, and planners still do not know what Congress is going to do for those reexpired provisions for 2018. Congress is looking at them one by one, and taxpayers and clients may have a situation similar to last year when everyone goes through the year not knowing for sure the status of all those tax breaks.

Other positive developments occurred for 2018. Code Sec. 529 plans can now distribute up to $10,000 per year per student for elementary and secondary school tuition. There is an expanded definition of what qualifies for an exclusion for discharge of student loan indebtedness to include death and disability. Although there had been talk about removing some of the tax breaks for graduate students, those were preserved as well.

## STUDY QUESTION

**3.** Which of the following tax areas generally remained the same under the new tax law?

    **a.** Education tax breaks

    **b.** Child tax credit

    **c.** State and local tax deductions

    **d.** Personal exemptions

# ¶ 108  WITHHOLDING AND ESTIMATED TAXES

## Withholding Tables

Withholding rates for tax deducted from paychecks have changed under the *Tax Cuts and Jobs Act.* The law did not get enacted until very late in the year, so the IRS was slow in revising the withholding tables and they were not issued until January 11, 2018. Obviously, employers did not have the new tables available to start with their January payrolls.

The new tables were required to be implemented by March 1, 2018. Some employers were able to do it earlier, but some employees out there spent two months of the year still having their previous year's amount withheld, and their withholding was probably a little excessive for the first couple of months of 2018.

## Adjusting Withholding Rates on Form W-4

All the tax changes and the many ways they could affect individuals prompted the IRS in February of 2018 to issue a new Form W-4, *Employee's Withholding Allowance Certificate,* and a new withholding calculator. The IRS certainly is encouraging employees to go through that withholding calculator and file new Forms W-4 now that they have their new withholding to compare with their old withholding, to see whether to change the amounts withheld.

Many IRS Information Releases that have come out from the IRS on this subject are encouraging what they call a "Paycheck Checkup" for employees to verify that withholding is a proper level for the new tax rates.

The new Form W-4 is not that different from the old one, and is somewhat anachronistic because it, in determining the withholding allowances, still basically uses one withholding allowance as equaling one exemption, even though the new tax law does not have exemptions anymore. Employees who have not adjusted their W-4s to reflect reduce itemized deductions may end up being over withheld for the year.

The draft Form W-4 for 2019 is different from the 2018 form, and it is already generating some criticism. The draft may not be what survives for 2019, but it is at least on the IRS website for practitioners and clients to view.

## Quarterly Estimated Tax Payments

IRS Information Release 2018-93 has also come out to address revised estimated tax payments for self-employed individuals, retirees, and investors because there are changes on the estimated tax front, as well as the withholding front. With lower tax rates in effect in 2018, estimated tax payments may also be adjusted downward if planners can accurately project clients' tax liability for the year.

# ¶ 109 RETIREMENT PLANS

Retirement is an area somewhat like education for which there had been talk about proposed changes. In the end not much was done. The 401(k) and IRA contribution and deduction limits remain the same.

There was a significant change with respect to Roth IRAs in terms of clients' ability to recharacterize a Roth conversion, clients can no longer recharacterize Roth conversions. For clients who had done a conversion in 2018 or later and then figured they had until October 15 of the following year to monitor the market and reverse it if fortunes changed and conversion value was now too high, that ability to recharacterize is gone. It remains available for 2017 conversions until October 15, 2018.

The law included some pro-taxpayer changes with respect to retirement plan loans outstanding when employees terminate or separate from their companies. Former employees can now contribute those loan balances to an IRA by the due date of the tax return for the next year and avoid the loan from being treated as a distribution, allowing more flexibility. The IRS has issued guidance on notice requirements to employees to make sure they are aware of their new rights with respect to plan loans, because under the old law, former employees basically had to report a distribution if the loans were not repaid when employees terminated. If the former employees were younger than age 59½, that distribution could have been subject to a 10 percent penalty.

## Employee Service Awards

The tax law included an increase in the length of service award exclusion for bona fide public safety volunteers, going from $3,000 to $6,000, with a cost of living adjustment provided.

# ¶ 110 COMPENSATION

## Nonqualified Deferred Compensation

The new law made some changes in treatment of compensation. Both the House and Senate bills had provisions that eliminated some of the exceptions to the taxation of nonqualified deferred compensation. Those provisions were removed from the final legislation, and the treatment of nonqualified deferred compensation survived intact.

## Excessive Remuneration

Excessive employee remuneration did not survive intact. The new tax law eliminated the exceptions under Code Section 162(m) for the $1 million compensation deduction limit for commissions and performance-based compensation. This is another rule that had a retroactive effect—back to November 2, 2017.

The law also revised the definition of who is a covered employee: the principal executive officer, principal financial officer, and other three most highly compensated employees. This is a major change and will affect how companies address compensation for their highly compensated employees.

## Incentive Stock Options

In the stock option area, after the dot.com crash in 1999 a lot of people had gotten stock options in the dot.com boom and, under the alternative minimum tax (AMT), they were required to pay tax on the value of the option at date of exercise. When the bust came, if they had not sold their stock by the end of 1999, they were stuck with a huge gain under the AMT that often became associated with a relatively worthless stock. Some people were forced into bankruptcy by that obligation, and there has been lobbying for Congress to do something about it ever since. The new tax act does not help completely, but it is at least a new election. Section 83(i) of the Tax Code allows restricted stock and ISO options settled after 2017 to defer gain for up to five years for employees of nonpublic companies who are granted stock options or restricted stock units, so it offers a little help in deferring that gain.

## Excise Tax on Stock Compensation

The excise tax on stock compensation of insiders of expatriated corporations was increased from 15 percent to 20 percent.

# ¶ 111 ALTERNATIVE MINIMUM TAX

There had been talk of getting rid of the AMT under the new law, but that did not happen. The AMT survives and the changes under the new law only apply through 2025. The changes go away in 2025; the AMT survives 2025 and reverts to its old requirements after 2025.

The new exemption amounts are significantly larger: $109,400 for joint filers and $70,300 for single filers. The exemption phaseout amounts are also increased to $1 million for joint filers and $500,000 for single filers. Under the old AMT, the highest percentage of taxpayers that used to be hit were those in the $200,000 to $500,000 income range, because people over that usually were paying at a high enough regular tax rate that they avoided the AMT. Despite the increased the exemption amounts here and the lowering of the regular tax rates from 39.6 percent to 37 percent, the AMT rates did not change. It is likely that those most caught by the AMT will move up the income spectrum. It is probably going to be a little larger hit; more wealthy taxpayers are more likely to be caught by the AMT at this point. Although the individual AMT survives, the corporate AMT was repealed under the law, and there are some special rules for carryforwards.

# ¶ 112 HOME SALE EXCLUSION

There was discussion of changing the home sale exclusion rule for avoiding tax on capital gains, but that did not happen. Home sellers can exclude up to $500,000 (for joint filers) or $250,000 (single filers) of gains from sale of their primary residence as long as the homeowners have owned and lived in the residence for two out of the last five years. There is no change in those exclusion rules.

# ¶ 113 OTHER PROVISIONS FOR INDIVIDUALS

## Teacher Classroom Expense Provisions

The House and Senate had very different visions of the teacher classroom expenses. One would have eliminated it, the other would have increased it, so the educator expense deduction remained the same and unchanged, with an above-the-line deduction of $250 for unreimbursed expenses for classroom materials such as books, supplies, computers and related software, or other equipment that eligible educators use in the classroom.

## Moving and Travel Expenses

The new law includes no deduction for moving expenses except for members of the Armed Forces, and that will result in a little more cost associated with frequent moves and employee-associated moves especially. Information Release 2018-127 discusses moving, mileage, and travel expense issues.

## Alimony

An interesting feature of the new law is the delay in applying the changes to payments and receipts of alimony payments. The rule changes apparently were postponed to allow individuals having a preexisting divorce or separation agreement to choose whether to be subject to the old law or modify terms to apply post-2018 under the new law. For payments required by agreements executed after December 31, 2018, the new law eliminates the deduction for payers of alimony; recipients of alimony will no longer have to include the payments in their taxable income. Recipients must continue to include in taxable income payments received as required by divorce agreements executed before 2019 unless those agreements are modified to be governed under the new law. The ex-spouses cannot live in the same household or file a joint return for payments qualified as alimony.

The changes could really affect how divorces are negotiated because of the loss of the deduction and exclusion from income.

> **PLANNING POINTER:** Whether payments are treated as alimony or child support might make less difference going forward, but clients responsible for paying alimony have incentive to expedite proceedings to become final in 2018; recipients have incentive to delay the final agreements until 2019.

Something else requiring a focus in divorces is careful planning for which spouse gets the head of household filing status. To get head of household filing status, the qualifying child must have lived in the home for more than half the year. Records must be maintained by the taxpayers to prove this.

## Wrongfully Levied Property

One pro-taxpayer provision of the new law extends the time limit for return of wrong-fully levied property and also the time to file a civil suit. The IRS has come out with some guidance on how to handle these issues, Information Release 2018-126. Practition-ers are reminded that the IRS says that its information releases are not really guidance but just a foreshadowing of guidance to come.

## Combat Zone Benefits

Grants of combat zone benefits have been extended to those serving in the Sinai Peninsula. There is a current proposal in Congress to extend it to people working in covert operations and in areas that have not been declared combat zones. That might be a result of some of the combat operations that have occurred in Africa, to give some relief to those members of the military if they are on special operations and in an area that has not officially been declared a combat zone. That is still in Congress and that has not passed yet. The only change is for those serving in the Sinai Peninsula.

## Heads of Household

Another little slap at tax return preparers is an increase in due diligence, expanded to apply to head of household filing eligibility. The IRS feels that some people have been claiming head of household status who are not really entitled to it, so the IRS is trying to put an obligation on the preparer to make sure that anyone claiming head of household status is entitled to it. IRS Regulation 103474-18 expands the scope of the tax return due diligence penalty so that it applies with respect to eligibility to file a return or claim for refund as head of household.

## ABLE Accounts

ABLE accounts are getting more attractive because the new law increases the contribution limits to $15,000 (an amount equal to the annual gift tax exclusion) per year to an ABLE account for a beneficiary. This amount can be from the beneficiary or can be from any other person. In addition, the new law allows the ABLE account's beneficiary to contribute an amount of $12,060 (this amount is equal to the poverty line for one individual and will change each year) or the amount of compensation included in the gross income of the ABLE beneficiary, whichever is lesser. ABLE accounts are tax-advantaged savings accounts for individuals with disabilities and their families. Contributions are not tax-deductible, but investment earnings remain untaxed as long as funds taken from the account are used for "qualified disability expenses," such as medical treatment or summer camps for those with special needs. The accounts were created as a result of the passage of the *Stephen Beck, Jr., Achieving a Better Life Experience Act of 2014* (The ABLE Act). The new law permits rollovers from 529 plans to ABLE accounts. Both the increased limits and rollover provisions are only available through 2025.

## Inflation Adjustments Using Chained CPI

The *Tax Cuts and Jobs Act* also came up with a new inflation adjustment system—chained consumer price index (chained CPI). The expectation is that it will lower inflation adjustments a little, and that is borne out by the fact that the IRS had, prior to the passage of the new law, come out with their usual projection of inflation adjustments for 2018. When the tax law passed, the IRS had to revise that projection, so Information Release 2018-94 gave those revised inflation adjustments. The chained CPI is a way to index spending and taxes (including Social Security benefits) to the rate of inflation. Chained CPI affects tax provisions for the standard deduction, earned income tax credit, and AMT. Critics hold that retirees are likely to get smaller monthly payments using this measure of inflation because it tends to show a lower inflation rate than the former system.

## Health Savings Accounts

One of the new law's revisions was to lower the health savings account (HSA) deductible contribution limit for 2018. That was creating problems for some people who had already started HSA contributions for 2018. The new inflation adjustments were not released until after the year had started, so Rev. Proc. 2018-107 restored the old higher HSA contribution limit for 2018, just to simplify matters for taxpayers for whom the limit was an issue. Thus, the contribution limit is $3,450 for 2018 for individual filers, an increase of $50 from 2017. Families can contribute $6,900.

## Congressional Living Expenses

Members of Congress also took a slap at themselves by repealing the $3,000 deduction for members of Congress for living expenses while in D.C.

## Disaster Relief

There was quite a bit of activity in the disaster area. The 2017 year was a big one for American disasters, with three major hurricanes and California wildfires. There was some special hurricane legislation after the hurricanes in 2017, and then it was codified further in the *Tax Cuts and Jobs Act*. Then more recently, the *Bipartisan Budget Act of 2018* expanded relief provisions further for some of the more recent wildfires in western states. Some of the general tax breaks are no 10 percent early withdrawal penalty from retirement plans for victims if funds were withdrawn by January 1, 2018, and that has been extended for individuals affected by the wildfires. There was a $100,000 limit with up to three years to repay or include in income.

The *Disaster Tax Relief and Airport and Airway Extension Act of 2017*, signed into law on September 29, 2017, also suspended the normal limit on charitable deduction contributions if the deductions were related to charities supporting certain disaster relief efforts. The law specifies only certain federal disaster areas that pertain to the act. The *Bipartisan Budget Act of 2018*, signed into law on February 9, 2018 adds additional disaster areas that qualify. A tax credit applied for employer retention of employees. With respect to the casualty loss during the federal disasters, the casualty loss does still survive in 2018 for them. The usual 10 percent of AGI limit does not apply; the normal $100 limit has been expanded to $500 on Form 4684, Casualties and Thefts. Congress has not yet extended these tax breaks to apply to 2018 disasters such as Hurricane Florence.

Those suffering casualty losses could elect to treat the qualified disaster losses as an addition to the standard deduction. That provision caused some problems for 2017 returns, because taxpayers have the option to claim the casualty loss in the prior year, and 2016's tax preparation software had not contemplated the election to treat the loss as an addition to the standard deduction. The IRS requests that the 2016 returns be filed manually with the words "Federally Declared Disaster" on the top of the page to claim a qualified disaster loss, as calculated on Form 4684, in addition to the standard deduction.

The Tax Cuts and Jobs Act of 2017 changes this area of the law for the years 2018 through 2025. No deduction is allowed for personal casualty and theft losses, but losses can be used to offset any casualty gains. What remains is casualty losses attributable to federally declared disasters.

## STUDY QUESTION

---

**4.** Which of the following statements is correct with respect to the new tax legislation and its impact on disaster zone relief?

    **a.** The relief is applicable to federal, state, and local disasters

    **b.** Casualty losses now carry a 5 percent of adjusted gross income limit

    **c.** Early withdrawal of retirement plan amounts must be repaid within two years

    **d.** There is no 10 percent early withdrawal penalty from retirement plans in certain circumstances

---

## Estate, Gift, and GSI Taxes

Estate, generation-skipping income (GSI), and gift taxes were changed by the new tax law. The estate tax was not eliminated, as some had proposed. It survives, but there is a doubling of the estate and gift tax exemption amount. A relatively few taxable estates existed out there, and the number shrinks even more. In 2018, now that the chained CPI amount is known, $11,180,000 is the estate tax, gift, and GSI lifetime tax exemption amount starting in 2018. This change expires after 2025, which creates a complication for revising estate plans to accommodate this temporary increase.

The annual gift tax exclusion of $15,000 per donee, reflects an increase from the $14,000 level in 2017.

The issue with increasing the exemption amount is that if planners are doing normal estate planning in which clients have a marital trust and a family trust and have relied on the exemption amount to determine what should go to the family trust and what should go to the marital trust. When the law changes the exemption amount, the allocations in estate plans can be skewed. The estate tax rates also still kick in at relatively low amounts.

> **PLANNING POINTER:** Allocations to trusts are items that have to be looked at whenever the exemption amount changes as drastically as it has for 2018 to ensure that the estate plan still matches the intent of the decedent.

## Kiddie Tax

One change was made by the new law with respect to the kiddie tax. It had been applied at the parents' tax rate—the children's investment income subject to tax at the parents' tax rate. The new law changes that system to tax children's investment income, not at the parents' tax rate, but at the estate and trust tax rate. That change can be a very severe hit because the trust tax rates are going to kick in at lower income levels than the parents' tax rates would. The kiddie tax could be more severe than it had been under prior law.

## Elimination of Certain Exclusions

Some exclusions were eliminated under the new law. The exclusion for qualified bicycle commuting reimbursements was suspended. It is uncertain why the government focused on that. The Code Sec. 74 exclusion for employee achievement awards and the Code Sec. 132 exclusion for employees' qualified moving expense reimbursement were cut, but the exclusion sunsets after 2025. This exclusion was tied to the elimination of the moving expense deduction.

# ¶ 114 TAX-EXEMPT ENTITIES

## Unrelated Business Income Tax

The changes to treatment of not-for-profit entities are somewhat corresponding to those for the taxable environment. Under the new law, calculation of unrelated business income tax (UBIT) has to be done separately for each unrelated trade or business. So that is a real negative for tax-exempt entities. Clients could have offset a loss in one activity against a gain in another, and now they have to be treated separately.

The law also modified UBIT requirements to include amounts paid for qualified transportation, fringe benefits, parking facility and on-premises athletic facilities, again corresponding to some changes being done on the for profit side. Previously, IRS Code Section 4958 imposed an excise tax on excess benefit transactions. Public Charities under Code Section 501(c) (3) can lose their tax exempt status in addition to the excise tax for excessive compensation to certain individuals running tax exempt entities, called intermediate sanction rules. The *Tax Cuts and Jobs Act of 2017* imposes an excise tax on exempt organization's executive compensation exceeding $1 million. The excise tax is 21 percent on compensation over $1,000.000.

What the law does on the for profit side to restrict deductions are handled on the exempt side by imposing excise taxes. The law imposed an excise tax on private foundation investment income and on private foundation failure to distribute income.

## Endowment Tax on Private Colleges

One item that has gotten a lot of attention, and still there is some lobbying going on to try to change it, is the excise tax of 1.4 percent on the net investment income of certain private colleges and universities. This tax comes from the *Tax Cuts and Jobs Act* and is modified by the *Bipartisan Budget Act*. This tax would mirror the 2 percent excise tax that private foundations pay on their net investment income. This tax applies to an "applicable college or university" that has at least 500 tuition-paying students during the preceding year and has more than 50 percent of its tuition-paying students located in the United States. The provisions have colleges debating whether colleges on the edge of the bill's cutoff should enroll more students to drive down the average value of their assets or colleges with slightly more than 500 students should cut enrollment next year to drop below the threshold. Another requirement is that the school have an aggregate fair market value (FMV) of certain assets if at least $500,000 per student at the end of the preceding year. The IRS has come out with some guidance on this issue in terms of what it means to meet the student limit or the investment limit. Universities and colleges are still lobbying to get this excise tax eliminated, but it is on the books for now.

# ¶ 115 PASS-THROUGH BUSINESS INCOME DEDUCTION

## Qualified Business Income

This deduction is probably one of the most difficult issues under the new law, however, promising a 20 percent deduction for qualified business income (QBI), is probably a pleasant thing to talk about with clients, if planners can figure it out. It is probably one of the most complicated issues in the new tax law along with the whole international tax arena, but the international arena primarily will affect larger corporations that have lots of resources to try to deal with the issue.

The 20 percent deduction for income of pass-through entities can affect small sole proprietorships, it applies to a lot of people, and they are having a difficult time getting the grasp of it. The fundamental point is a 20 percent deduction from qualified business income. The first thing one has to grapple with is whether this is a trade or business and what is QBI.

Section 199A says there will be allowed, as a deduction for any taxable year, an amount equal to the sum of the lesser of 20 percent of combined qualified business income, or 20 percent of the excess of taxable income over net capital gain and qualified cooperative dividends, plus the lesser of 20 percent of qualified cooperative dividends and taxable income, reduced by net capital gains. Unless clients have capital gains to worry about or qualified cooperative dividends, they can just ignore most of that language. Cooperative dividends are popular with farming operations and this area of 199A has recently been changed. See the cooperative dividends section below.

This deduction, like so many of them, expires after 2025. It is available to partnerships, S corporations, sole proprietorships, trusts, estates, real estate investment trusts (REITs), qualified cooperatives, and qualified publicly traded partnerships. Special rules apply to agricultural and horticultural companies.

## Phaseout Provisions

Another provision is that there is a limit on the deduction, but the limit does not apply if the taxable income of the individual is less than $157,500 or $315,000 for joint filers, then clients do not have to worry about the phaseout. They get the 20 percent deduction and all they have to worry about is what their QBI is. The exemption limitations do not apply even if their business is considered a service business if they are under the above taxable income levels.

If clients' income exceeds those income limits, then they do have to worry about a phaseout, but it is not an automatic phaseout as it is for specified service businesses. This deduction is limited to depending on W-2 wages and "qualified property." The deduction is limited to the greater of 50 percent of W-2 wages or the sum of 25 percent of W-2 wages plus 2.5 percent of the unadjusted basis immediately after acquisition of qualified properties.

The rules apply to purchase price, not depreciated basis, when they talk about qualified property. In theory, if clients meet those definitions, then they could still have a 20 percent deduction even though they are over the phaseout limits. That is not the case for a specified service business; there is an automatic phaseout for them.

This deduction applies in computing taxable income, not AGI, so it is going to come on Form 1040 after AGI. It is also available whether clients itemize or not. It is like an exemption—it comes after AGI, but clients can get it whether they itemize or not.

"Qualified business income" does not include investment income or compensation-like income. That is where planners can get into problems. Even if clients are under these income limits, is some of their income not qualified business income but investment income or compensation-like income? Investment income is maybe a little easier to grasp. The compensation-like income is a little more difficult. It includes guaranteed payments, payments to partners for services, and reasonable compensation.

## Cooperative Dividends

There has been one legislative change to Section 199A that was passed into law with the *Consolidated Appropriation Act of 2018*, signed into law on March 23, 2018. (This act is the nation's budget, the earlier *Bipartisan Budget Act* was a budget extender bill that allowed the government to operate for a few months until Congress could agree on a final budget.) Often referred to as the "grain glitch", the *Tax Cuts and Jobs Act* only gave the 20 percent deduction to qualified cooperative dividends.

Cooperatives are common in US agriculture where farmers join together often to market and sell their goods, furnish farm supplies and provide credit or other financial services, including export financing. Tax rules for cooperatives are in Section 1382 of the IRS Code.

The Tax Cuts and Jobs Act said the 20 percent deduction for Section 199A only applied to qualified cooperative dividends, or patronage dividends. This left out the large agricultural companies who also buy grain and other farm products. These agricultural giants were able to effectively lobby congress and the Consolidated Appropriation Act replaces the Tax Cuts and Jobs Act deduction for cooperative dividends with a restored prior law Code Sec.199 treatment for these payments.

## Reasonable Compensation

The statute uses the term "reasonable compensation," which is a fairly well developed concept in the S corporation context, where there has been a long-standing tradition of having to allocate between compensation and dividend-like income for S corporation shareholders who are also active in the business. There has been no such reasonable compensation concept in the sole proprietorship or partnership area, and the one question was whether this statute required the development of a reasonable compensation standard for those pass-through entities. In the proposed regulations, the IRS stated it does not intend to develop a reasonable compensation standard for sole proprietorships and partnerships.

The IRS will apply the developed reasonable compensation standard for S corporations but does not intend to expand it, which means that there is a greater likelihood that the 20 percent deduction will survive without having to be reduced for something like reasonable compensation for the partnership and sole proprietorship entities.

The partnership area still has complexities, like guaranteed payments that will be classified as compensation. There will not be an effort to expand what the rules already have developed.

## Specified Service Businesses

The new tax law has an additional issue with respect to the 20 percent deduction: what is a specified service business. For these same income limits, even if clients have a specified service business and are under those same income limits, the businesses are entitled to a full 20 percent deduction. The specified service business is an area in which planners need the IRS to provide some additional guidance. Some of it is obvious, such as for health, law, accounting, actuarial sciences, consulting, athletics, financial services, and brokerage services. The proposed regulations discuss in some detail what a specified service trade or business (SSTB) is and provide a safe harbor for de minimis amounts of SSTB income.

The law has special provisions for any business in which the principal asset is reputation and skill of employees or owners. This can mean that it could apply to a lot of businesses. The IRS has chosen in the proposed regulations a very limited definition focused on licensing of the names of well know personalities.

Also included for the QBI deduction are services of investing or investment management; trading; or dealing in securities, partnership interests, or commodities. The rules specifically do not include architectural and engineering businesses.

In terms of planning, people have been talking about shifting to adopting a different business entity to take advantage of this deduction, or splitting up entities to separate a specified service business from activities that might not be a specified trade or business. The proposed regulations permit aggregating of businesses for the deduction but generally prohibit the splitting up of businesses.

The QBI deduction is available not only to partnerships, S corporations, and sole proprietorships, but also to trusts and estates, REITs, qualified cooperatives, and qualified public trading partnerships. There are some special rules for agriculture and horticultural companies.

## Defining Trade or Business

For the 20 percent deduction, the IRS is being asked to determine what a trade or business is. One area in which that has come up is a real estate leasing business, in which clients own a building and lease it out. Is that an investment activity or is that a trade or business? The IRS has clarified that a building used in a trade or business that is held in a separate entity is part of that trade or business. We are still waiting for guidance on what other real estate rental activity might qualify as a trade or business.

# ¶ 116 CORPORATE ENTITY TAX RATE

The other possible entity change, rather than moving around among pass-through entities, is to think about shifting to a corporate entity, which business owners have not been doing in recent years. The most desired goal to achieve in the new tax law by the Congress members who passed it was to do a significant reduction in the corporate tax rate to try to put U.S. companies on a more even keel with international trading partners.

The corporate rate has been reduced from a top rate of 35 percent to a flat rate of 21 percent, starting in 2018. If business owners look at the 20 percent deduction for pass-through businesses compared to 37 percent ordinary corporate rate, that 20 percent deduction equates to a 29.6 percent tax rate that is significantly above 21 percent. The 37 percent rate is also above 21 percent. Business owners are starting to look at converting to corporate status; some have already announced that they are doing so. Of course, there is still the double tax issue to worry about if dividends are distributed.

One caveat on all those plans is that it's easy to get into corporate status but harder to get out. It is something a business owner would want to jump into with eyes wide open knowing the consequences of getting out.

Along with the reduced corporate rate, the dividends received deduction is reduced as well. Dividends received from another corporation were 70 percent excluded from income for less than 20 percent owned domestic corporations and 80 percent excluded from income for more than 20 percent owned domestic corporations. For tax years after December 31, 2017, the amount excluded from income is decreased from 70 percent to 50 percent and from 80 percent to 65 percent.

# ¶ 117 CODE SEC. 179 EXPENSING AND BONUS DEPRECIATION

A couple of other major changes in the business area relate to business expensing. On the expensing side, the less significant one is the expansion of Code Sec. 179 expensing. That has been increased to $1 million, with a phaseout increase to $2.5 million, and some changes in the definition of qualifying property. The $25,000 limit on expensing of certain heavy vehicles has now been adjusted for inflation after 2018.

Perhaps the more significant provision, is the change to business expensing. In 2017 the 50 percent first-year bonus depreciation was scheduled to decrease to 40 percent in 2018. This is another change with an effective date that reverts back into last year: September 27, 2017. The new tax law implemented 100 percent first-year bonus depreciation for new and used property. The law made the major addition of including used property placed in service after September 27, 2017.

This provision has a phase-down that starts January 1, 2023. There is a phase-down of the depreciation rate between 2023 and 2026. It includes film, television, and live theatrical productions, and it excludes businesses subject to the interest expense limitation.

There has been a major issue with respect to leasehold improvements, restaurant and retail property. Under prior law those were in a special category that was allowed 15-year depreciation rather than the standard 39 years for real estate. Due to a glitch, the law failed to properly address the status of leasehold improvements.

On August 3, 2018, the IRS announced the release of the much anticipated proposed regulation on the 100 percent bonus depreciation. It is Regulation-104397-18, Additional First Year Depreciation Deduction. The proposed regulations provide guidance on what property qualifies for the deduction and the rules for qualified film, television, live theatrical productions and certain plants.

There has been some guidance on business expensing, and on handling built-in gains and losses. The IRS issued Field Service Advice FS-2018-9 which has guidance on depreciation deductions.

A number of states have started taking a look at the provisions of the *Tax Cuts and Jobs Act* to discern whether they just want to incorporate all of its provisions into their state income tax provisions or to be selective. Some states are decoupling from full expensing, feeling it is too expensive for their state coffers. That is something planners should watch out for in this and other areas; it is likely states will decouple from some of the federal provisions and there will be a requirement for a state tax adjustment for these issues.

## ¶ 118 INTEREST EXPENSING

The interest expensing area is also to compensate for the expanded expensing of capital acquisitions. The new law dictates a cutback in deducting interest, the main one being a limit of 30 percent of adjusted taxable income. Any business interest denied can be carried forward indefinitely.

There is a small business exception that includes a $25 million gross receipts test. There are still some issues as to how that $25 million gross receipts test would apply for partnerships and consolidated groups, so planners are hoping for some more guidance in that area.

Farming businesses can elect not to be subject to the interest expense limitation and instead be subject to an alternative depreciation. If farmers forego immediate expensing and depreciate, they can avoid the interest expense limitation.

Notice 2018-28 has provided some guidance. There was some question about whether all corporate debt was to be considered business debt or whether some might be considered investment debt, but this notice clarifies that all corporate debt is considered to be business debt.

## ¶ 119 NET OPERATING LOSSES

Some interesting changes have been causing some concern with respect to net operating losses (NOLs). Prior law allowed the ability to carry back NOLs for two years and carry forward the losses for 20 years. That carryback was very helpful because it could provide an immediate benefit to businesses. If clients encountered a loss year, they could amend a couple years' returns and get an immediate benefit.

Under the changed law, there is no carryback except for a two-year carryback for farming losses and insurance companies other than life insurance companies. The carryback goes away but there is also an unlimited carryforward period. However, they can only carry forward up to and deduct up to 80 percent of taxable income.

There had been an ability to offset 100 percent of income in carryover years; now, it is an unlimited carryforward but a restriction on how much clients can deduct. That has made NOLs less favorable: they offer no carryback ability, no immediate benefit, and a limit on how much clients can carry forward and get a benefit each year. These changes also expire after 2025.

## ¶ 120 LIKE-KIND EXCHANGES

For many years taxpayers had the ability to do like-kind exchanges under Code Sec. 1031 with respect to personal as well as real property. Under the *Tax Cuts and Jobs Act,* like-kind exchanges will be limited to real property that is not primarily for sale, that is, not inventory. Personal property assets that can no longer be exchanged include intangibles such as licenses and patents; aircraft, boats, railcars, and other vehicles; professional sports player contracts; machinery and equipment; and artwork and collectibles.

## ¶ 121 CARRIED INTEREST

Carried interest has been an issue that Congress has discussed for a long time. The basic issue is that owners of hedge funds and private equity funds are able to get capital gain treatment, rather than ordinary income treatment, for their interests in the funds. Some people feel that the interests should be getting ordinary income treatment.

Rather than address that issue directly, Congress extended the holding period for getting long-term capital gain treatment for the income from more than one year to more than three years. Hedge funds typically hold their investments for less than three years, and a lot of them even for less than one year, so the funds' income was already having ordinary income treatment because they held the investment for even less than one year under prior law. Thus, they might not be severely impacted by this extended holding period. A lot of private equity funds might have held their investments for even longer than three years under the old law, so they might not be severely impacted by this either.

In spite of that, a number of funds were looking at trying to circumvent the issue by looking at an exception to this rule. The law provides an exception for corporations, and the question becomes what "corporation" means. These hedge funds were interpreting it as including S corporations and were setting up limited liability companies in Delaware and electing S corporation status with the idea that they would qualify for an exception to the three-year holding period.

The IRS has come out with Notice 2018-18, which states that they view a corporation as only referring to C corporations, not S corporations. But people looking at the tax statute say that is not a reasonable interpretation under the tax law of the word "corporation," and they may challenge that in court. It was probably not intended by Congress to let S corporations qualify to escape the three-year requirement, and the issue could also be a subject for a technical correction. It is not clear how quickly Congress could act on a technical correction.

# ¶ 122 OTHER BUSINESS PROVISIONS

## Sexual Harassment

Another business provision that is included in the legislation as a reaction to the "Me-Too" movement is no deduction for settlement subject to a nondisclosure agreement that is paid in conjunction with sexual harassment or sexual abuse cases. There has also been a concern that the law may be poorly written and may limit some entitlements to victims, which may have to be addressed in a technical correction as well.

## Paid Family and Medical Leave

On the good news front, there is a new employer credit for paid family and medical leave: 12.5 percent for up to 50 percent of normal wages, plus 2.5 percent up to 25 percent for each percent over 50 percent, for a maximum of 12 weeks.

## Alaskan Natives

Major tax changes were made that affect Alaska Native Corporations and Alaska Native Settlement Trusts.

## Florida Citrus

The law includes provisions to address blight affecting Florida citrus plants, a modification of the rule for deducting the cost of replanting citrus plants lost through a casualty. This one also relates back into part of 2017 with the hurricane relief legislation. The Tax Cuts and Jobs Act allows a 100 percent deduction in the first year instead of depreciating the cost over 14 years.

Basically the change here is that the farmer can bring in investors, raise capital for replacement trees and still claim the deduction if the ownership remains above 50 percent majority. In the past, the owner needed to bear the full cost. Revenue Proc 2018-35 discusses the expensing of certain cost of replanting citrus plants lost by reason of casualty.

## Domestic Production Activities

The old domestic production activities deduction has been repealed, replaced by the changes in the international provisions and the 20 percent deduction. Code Section 199 is gone and replaced by Code Section 199(A), the new 20 percent qualified business income deduction.

## Deduction Repeals

The new law repealed the deduction for commuting benefits. The entertainment expense deduction is disallowed, including membership dues. Meals are still limited to 50 percent. In the research and development area, there is a five-year amortization of research and experimental expenditures after 2021 instead of immediate expensing. Also included is a repeal of the 10 percent rehabilitation credit for pre-1936 buildings.

## Cash Method of Accounting and Inventories

The new law made some expansion of the ability to use the cash method of accounting and not maintain inventories when average gross receipts do not exceed $25 million over three years. The law creates a similar exemption from the UNICAP rules Code Sec. 471 in valuing inventories. There has also been a modification to the requirements for long-term contracts. The percentage of completion method may be used by companies with average gross receipts of 25 million or less (instead of 10 million or less).

The Internal Revenue Service issued guidance on August 3, 2018 with Revenue Procedure 2018-40 which outlines the process that eligible small business taxpayers may obtain automatic consent to change to accounting methods that are now permitted under the Tax Cuts and Jobs Act. As a result, more small business taxpayers will be allowed to change to cash method accounting starting after Dec. 31, 2017.

## Depreciation of Luxury Autos

The depreciation limits for luxury autos had been stuck for a long time. The new depreciation limit for the first year is now $10,000, which is a significant increase, and $16,000 for the second year, and continuing on as adjusted for later years.

## FDIC Premiums

For those involved with financial institutions, there is a limit on the deduction of FDIC premiums for financial institutions with assets over $10 billion.

## Orphan Drugs

The law imposes a limit on the credit for orphan drugs to 25 percent of the qualified clinical testing expenses. That was put in originally to encourage companies to try to develop solutions for rare diseases, and now Congress has put a limit on it.

## Depreciation of Farm Equipment

There have been some changes with respect to farm machinery and equipment as far as what is considered a five-year property.

## Tax Rules and Financial Statement Rules

There have been some changes in the tax law with respect to how the tax law provisions have to comply with what is claimed on a financial statement. Notice 2018-35 addresses how to handle some advance payments in that regard, but practitioners still need more guidance on how the tax provisions are to interact with the financial statement provisions. The law added a few more restrictions on how they can vary going forward.

## Expense Deductions Repeal

The new law disallows a deduction for fines and penalties. That rule already had been a restriction in the law but the new law refined and expanded it.

The law repeals the deduction for local lobbying expenses paid after December 22, 2017. This is just local; it is not state lobbying expenses. This also relates back to the prior year.

## Work Opportunity Credit

There had been talk about repealing the work opportunity credit, but in the end it survived.

## Self-Created Property

A number of years ago, the National Songwriters went in and serenaded Congress to get a tax break for self-created songs, to get capital gain treatment on their sale. That exception has now gone away, with all self-created property now treated as generating ordinary income going forward.

## Securities Gains

The law repeals the election to roll over tax-free taxable gains realized on the sale of publicly traded securities if the sales proceeds were used to purchase an investment in a Specialized Small Business Investment Company.

## Contribution to Capital

Definition of the "contribution to capital" for purposes of Code Sec. 118(a) is modified to exclude contributions by any governmental entity or civic group that are not made by a shareholder in its capacity as a shareholder. Practitioners have raised some concerns about the implications of that provision as well. If they are going to address it, this might have to be addressed by a technical correction, rather than IRS guidance. Code Sec 118 previously provided an exclusion from gross income for such contributions to the capital of a corporation.

## Aircraft Maintenance

Payments made by aircraft owners for aircraft maintenance services are not subject to the excise tax on transportation of persons or property by air.

## Qualified Opportunity Zones

Qualified opportunity zones have been highlighted by a number of commentators as something really worth looking into. It is an expansion of how a low-income community maybe designated as a qualified opportunity zone by a state, and then receive some tax benefits for activities within that qualified opportunity zone. Sellers may elect to exclude from gross income the gain on the sale or exchange of any property to an unrelated party in the tax year of the sale if the gain is reinvested in a qualified opportunity zone within 180 days. These provisions are being highlighted as a real opportunity for some tax benefits. IRS Rev Proc 2018-16 explains the procedures a state or territory had to follow to submit a nomination for QOZ status. On June 14, 2018 the announcement of the final designations for QOZ were made in IRS Notice 2018-48. The *Bipartisan Budget Act* expanded the QOZ incentive to Puerto Rico.

## S Corporation Provisions

Tax legislation always includes a few S corporation provisions. A nonresident alien individual may be a potential current beneficiary of an electing small business trust, a little relaxation in the rules there.

The charitable contribution deduction of an electing small business trust is generally to be determined by rules applicable to individuals and not to the rules generally applicable to trusts.

An S corporation that converts to C corporation status should take any resulting Code Sec. 41(a) adjustments into account over a six-year period.

## Partnership Provisions

In the partnership area, the new law repealed the Code Sec. 708(b)(1)(b) provisions with respect to technical termination of partnerships to avoid all the issues that came with technical termination.

The law repealed the election to defer recognition of capital gain realized on the sale of public securities. With this targeted provision; it is unclear how many people that would affect.

One provision that could affect a lot of people is the provision that the gain or loss from the sale or exchange of a partnership interest is effectively connected with a U.S. trade or business to the extent that the transfer would have effectively connected gain or loss had the partnership sold all of its assets at fair market value as of the date of the sale or exchange.

There is a new provision that states that, if partners sell a partnership interest that has a foreign entity, it can be subject to a 10 percent withholding requirement. Even if no foreign entity is involved or has ever been involved with this partnership, partners could be subject to a 10 percent withholding requirement unless they provide the certification that the transfer does not involve a foreign entity. That was going to create a major burden on partnerships transferring interest to provide these certifications.

The IRS has proposed providing some exemptions and relaxation of those withholding and certification requirements.

Code Section 704(d) was amended to provide that basis limitation and partnership losses apply to the partner's distributed share of charitable contributions and foreign taxes. How to deal with substantial built-in losses is also a change that made it into the law.

## Insurance Provisions

A number of insurance provisions became part of the new law pertaining to

- Passive foreign investment company rules;
- Net operating losses;
- Small life insurance company deduction;
- Life insurance reserves;
- Dividend received deduction;
- Property and casualty insurance pro-ration rule;
- Policy acquisition expenses;
- Pre-1984 policyholder surplus accounts;
- Reporting requirements; and
- Additional deduction and estimated tax provisions.

Planners who have insurance clients—and these affect a broad range of insurance companies, life as well as casualty insurers—will want to look into this list. The IRS has provided some guidance on some of these issues already. There are a number of changes in the tax law affecting insurance companies, and planners will want to go through those in more detail to see how they might affect particular clients.

## Excise Taxes Related to Liquor

With the beer, wine and distilled spirits industries, there have been a lot of changes incorporated in the new law. There has been some effort to help out the craft beer industry in these and a number of other changes that are less favorable, such as restrictions on transfer of beer between bonded facilities. Planners who have clients in these industries should review the rules in more detail relating to:

- Production period for beer, wine, and distilled spirits;
- Beer excise tax;
- Transfer of beer between bonded facilities;
- Wine excise tax credit;
- Alcohol content level of wine;
- Taxation of mead and certain low-alcohol by volume wines;
- Distilled spirits excise tax; and
- Transfer of bulk distilled spirits.

## Bond Provisions

There had been a proposal to repeal the tax-exempt status for private activity bonds. That did not make it through to the new law—bonds that are used for private purposes can still qualify for tax-exempt status.

There also had been a special provision seeking to disallow tax-exempt status for bonds for professional sport stadium construction specifically. A Congressman in Texas worked to get that one removed, that did not make it in either.

The law does repeal the exclusion for interest on a bond issued to advance refund another bond and also repeals the authority to issue tax credit bonds and direct payment bonds.

## STUDY QUESTION

**5.** Which of the following identifies one of the business provision changes enacted through the new tax legislation?

**a.** The entertainment expense deduction is eliminated

**b.** The 50 percent deduction for food has been eliminated

**c.** There is now a four-year amortization period for research and development expenditures

**d.** The research and development credit has been increased for qualifying small businesses

# ¶ 123 INTERNATIONAL PROVISIONS

International tax law is an extremely complicated area and even the people who spend all their days dealing with it are concerned about the complexity of changes made by the *Tax Cuts and Jobs Ac*t and how one provision interacts with another provision. If the law adjusts one facet of the intricate puzzle, it also affects another. International tax specialists are finding it very difficult to deal with the new law's proposal to move from a worldwide tax system, where U.S. taxpayers are taxed on their worldwide income, wherever it is earned, toward a territorial system, where U.S. taxpayers are only taxed on what they earn in the United States. It is a quasi-territorial system because it does not quite get there. It gives some taxes and tax breaks to try to get there, or make it appear the system is getting there, without really being just a tax on what taxpayers earn in the United States alone.

## Foreign Source Dividends Received

One of the ways to try to get there is a 100 percent deduction for foreign source portion of dividends received from a specified owner of a foreign corporation. If clients do get earnings from a foreign corporation, the law does not really say they are not subject to tax; clients get 100 percent deduction for the foreign source portion of those dividends received. The law also repealed the indirect foreign tax credit to go along with that.

## Repatriation of Profits from Abroad

As for the profit repatriation issue, a lot of multinational companies had huge sums of untaxed income held overseas because, under the old tax system, businesses were only taxed on active business income when it was repatriated to the United States. To avoid that U.S. tax, the companies never repatriated it; they held that income overseas and used it overseas as best they could.

In moving to a quasi-territorial tax system, Congress refused to let that income be completely lost, so there is a one-time repatriation tax on that accumulated foreign earnings, whether it is repatriated or not. For US corporations the tax rates are 15.5 percent on the cash or cash equivalents, and 8 percent on other types of earnings. Notice 2018-07 and 2018-13 cover the rules.

The law made it payable over an eight-year period, but it has been a hot issue because the first pay period was really due April 17, 2018 (the first 8 percent payment). Without a lot of guidance, a lot of corporations have been struggling with figuring out what to pay for 2017, and there are provisions in here that appeared to say that if businesses did not pay the proper amount in the first installment, then all the other installments were accelerated. The installment payment schedule is 8 percent of the net tax liability in years 2018-2022; 15 percent in 2023; 20 percent in 2024; and a final payment of 25 percent in 2025.

It has been a real hassle to try to figure out the intricacies of repatriation, and the IRS has tried to get out a lot of guidance trying to help corporations deal with these issues: Regulation 104226-18 Guidance Regarding the Transition Tax Under Section 965 and Related Provisions was issued by the IRS on August 1, 2018. The proposed regulations contain detailed information on the calculation and reporting of a US shareholder's section 965 (a) inclusion amount, as well as information for making the elections available to taxpayers under section 965.

One thing corporations were looking at were strategies such as electing a November 2017 year-end to delay the onset of the payment for at least 11 months. The IRS says that a change in accounting method or change in fiscal year just to delay the repatriation tax will not be allowed.

Also in the international area, the law made a lot of changes to Subpart F, many of them related to controlled foreign corporations and how they are dealt with under this new quasi-territorial system. To summarize:

**¶123**

- Repeal current taxation of previously excluded qualified investments;
- Repeal foreign base company oil related income;
- Inflation adjustment of de minimis exception threshold for foreign base company income;
- Controlled foreign corporation (CFC) look-through exception made permanent;
- Stock attribution rules for determining CFC status modified to treat U.S. corporation as constructively owning stock held by its foreign shareholder; and
- Eliminate the 30-day rule in Code Sec. 951(a)(1).

The other big area with this quasi-territorial system is trying to prevent gaming the system. If the IRS is only taxing on a territorial basis, there may still be an incentive to move businesses and assets or income to even lower tax jurisdictions than a 21 percent corporation tax rate.

To address that issue, taxpayers are required to pay a tax equal to a base erosion minimum tax, a BEAT tax. There is also a new tax on global intangible low-tax income, or GILTI, by a shareholder of a controlled foreign corporation. Both of these are intended to address the problem of moving income and assets overseas to avoid the new lower tax.

Many people are criticizing these provisions as affecting companies beyond what they are really intended to affect. Practitioners are voicing a lot of concern about their scope and unintended consequences.

On the flip side of that, there is a new deduction, the deduction for foreign-derived intangible income (FDII) to encourage activity to be retained in the United States. That deduction may be challenged in the World Trade Organization (WTO) as being an illegal trade subsidy. That is another issue planners are going to have to watch as that works its way through the WTO system.

Other tax provisions in the past have also been subjected to a WTO challenge; some have been successful; some have not. Issues remain in the whole area that are very complicated and still need to be addressed.

## STUDY QUESTION

**6.** Which of the following identifies the new corporate tax rate after 2017?
- **a.** 8.0 percent
- **b.** 15.5 percent
- **c.** 21.0 percent
- **d.** 25.0 percent

# ¶ 124 HEALTHCARE

The tax legislation did change one thing with respect to the *Affordable Care Act*. Congress never got repeal done in 2017, but lawmakers did get the individual mandate repealed after 2018. It is still around for this year but not for next year.

All indications are the IRS is enforcing the *Affordable Care Act* and requiring things like the employer penalty for failure to provide health insurance and the individual mandate penalties. Efforts continue to repeal the whole act, but for 2018, it is all intact and in effect.

As part of the *Bipartisan Budget Act of 201* 8 signed into law on February 19, 2018 there was a 2 year suspension until January 1, 2020 of the medical device excise tax, a 2.3 percent excise tax on the value of medical devices sold domestically, and a four year suspension until 2022 of the Cadillac tax, a 40 percent tax on high-quality high cost health plans. Those issues got suspended pending what happens to the underlying act itself.

# ¶ 125 SUMMARY AND NEW DEVELOPMENTS

## Summary

There were a lot of legislative bills with tax law changes signed into law in 2017 and 2018:

- H.R. 3823 Disaster Tax Relief and Airport and Airway Extension Act of 2017, 9-29-2017
- H.R. 1 Tax Cuts and Jobs Act, 12-22-2017
- Bipartisan Budget Act of 2018, 2-9-2018
- Consolidated Appropriations Act, 2018 3-23-2018

The *Tax Cuts and Jobs Act* will need a technical correction bill, but House Speaker Paul Ryan said in July 2018 that the tax law technical correction bill will not come until after the midterm elections. It is expected to be introduced into the House toward the end of 2018. Congressional members have been keeping a list of the items that need to be included in the bill.

## Proposed New Tax Changes

The House Ways and Means Committee has approved three bills constituting Tax Reform 2.0. The framework includes:

- Making permanent the individual and small business provisions of the *Tax Cuts and Jobs Act*.
- USA accounts—a new Universal Savings Account to offer a fully flexible savings tool for families.
- Expanded 529 Education accounts—education savings could be used to pay for apprenticeship fees to learn a trade, cover the cost of home schooling, and help pay off student debt.
- New Baby savings. Allowing families to access their own retirement accounts penalty-free for expenses when welcoming a new child into the family, whether by birth or adoption. Allowing families to replenish those accounts in the future.
- Growing Brand-New Entrepreneurs. help brand-new businesses write off more of their initial start-up costs, and remove barriers to growth

President Trump's Administration has not been silent either. On July 30, 2018, the New York Times reports that "The Trump administration is considering bypassing Congress to grant a $100 billion tax cut mainly to the wealthy" The Treasury Secretary said the administration "could use its regulatory powers" "to account for inflation in determining capital gains tax liabilities. The Treasury Department could change the definition of 'cost' for calculating capital gains, allowing taxpayers to adjust the initial value of an asset, such as a home or a share of stock, for inflation when it sells"

The article continues, "the decades-long push to change the taxation of investment income has spurred a legal debate over the original meaning of the word 'cost' in the Revenue Act of 1918 and over the authority of the Treasury Department to interpret the word in regulations". A 2002 Supreme Court decision, *Verizon Communications Inc v*

*FCC* (535 US 467), has been cited that seems to back up the thought that regulators have "leeway" in defining 'cost'. This debate is nothing new, the Bush Administration considered this and concluded that it would be illegal.

It is expected that charities and other entities could sue the Treasury Department if it tried to make the change and it would "create opportunities for gaming the tax code, in part because other parts of the code such as interest payments would still be unadjusted for inflation"

The Tax Reform 2.0 does not list capital gains as one of its framework items.

## Guidance Available from the IRS

The IRS has issued some 2018 Draft Tax Forms on their website, if you are trying to determine exactly how the IRS is going to interpret the Tax Cuts and Jobs Act you might want to look there. A lot of the forms are not listed yet. Final forms need to be made available to tax software vendors soon, so expect this web page to grow in the coming months.

A new memorandum of understanding for issuing Tax Regulations which over-turned the Reagan-era agreement that exempts IRS regulations from review of its regulations by the Office of Management and Budget (OMB) was reached April 11, 2018. The unit within the OMB that is responsible for review of the tax regulations is the Office of Information and Regulatory Affairs.

The IRS has been busy issuing guidance. It has issued a substantial number of Revenue Procedures, Revenue Rulings and Notices in addition to its recently proposed Regulations. As with all proposed Regulations, electronic comments and requests for a public hearing on the proposed regulation must be received within 60 days of its publication in the Federal Register.

All IRS guidance on tax reform is listed here:

### Regulations

REG-107892-18, Qualified Business Income Deduction

REG-104397-18, Additional First Year Depreciation Deduction (set to be published in the Federal Register on 8/8/2018)

REG-104226-18, Guidance Regarding the Transition Tax Under Section 965 and Related Provisions (not yet showing up in the Federal Register, the IRS news release was dated 8/1/2018)

REG-103474-18, Tax Return Preparer Due Diligence Penalty under Section 6695(g) (Expands the scope of the tax return preparer due diligence penalty so that it applies with respect to eligibility to file a return or claim for refund as head of household. (published – comments were due by 7/18/2018)

### Revenue Procedures

Rev. Proc. 2018-40, Changes in accounting periods and methods of accounting.

Rev. Proc. 2018-35, Changes in accounting periods and in methods of accounting (Expensing of certain cost of replanting citrus plants lost by reason of casualty.)

Rev. Proc. 2018-29, New automatic method changes to conform with FASB Topic 606 (Provides new automatic method changes and requests comments on those new changes and on future guidance for taxpayers changing their method of accounting to comply with amended § 451.)

Rev. Proc. 2018-27, Modifies the annual limitation on deductions for contributions to Health Savings Accounts (HSAs) allowed for individuals with family coverage under a high deductible health plan (HDHP)

Rev. Proc. 2018-26, 601 Rules and regulations—certain remedial actions that issuers of State and local tax-exempt bonds and other tax-advantaged bonds may take

Rev. Proc. 2018-25, Examination of returns and claims for refund, credit, or abatement; determination of correct tax liability (Depreciation of passenger automobiles under 280F.)

Rev. Proc. 2018-18, Modifying certain 2018 cost-of-living adjustments

Rev. Proc. 2018-17, Requests by certain foreign corporations for changes in annual accounting periods

Rev. Proc. 2018-16, Qualified Opportunity Zones

*Revenue Rulings*

Rev. Rul. 2018-13, Section 807 — Rules for Certain Reserves (This information is to be used by insurance companies in computing reserves.)

Rev. Rul. 2018-11, Section 1274A — Special Rules for Certain Transactions Where Stated Principal Amount Does Not Exceed $2,800,000 (2018 adjustment for inflation under § 1274A for qualified and cash method debt instruments.)

*Notices*

Notice 2018-63, Amplification and Modification of Safe Harbor Method for Participants in the HFA Hardest Hit Fund

Notice 2018-62, Guidance on the Contribution Limits Applicable to ABLE Accounts

Notice 2018-61, Clarification Concerning the Effect of Section 67(g) on Trusts and Estates (Clarifies the effect of newly enacted section 67(g) on the deductibility of certain expenses that are incurred by estates and non-grantor trusts)

Notice 2018-58, Guidance on Recontributions, Rollovers and Qualified Higher Education Expenses under Section 529

Notice 2018-55, Guidance on the Calculation of Net Investment Income for Purposes of the Section 4968 Excise Tax Applicable to Certain Private Colleges and Universities

Notice 2018-54, Guidance on Certain Payments Made in Exchange for State and Local Tax Credits

Notice 2018-48, Designated Qualified Opportunity Zones under Internal Revenue Code § 1400Z-2

Notice 2018-43, Public Comment Invited on Recommendations for 2018-2019 Priority Guidance Plan

Notice 2018-42, Update of 2018 Standard Mileage Rates Notice

Notice 2018-41, Information Reporting for Certain Life Insurance Contract Transactions and a Modification to the Transfer for Valuable Consideration Rules

Notice 2018-38, 2018 Fiscal-year Blended Tax Rates for Corporations

Notice 2018-37, Guidance in Connection with the Repeal of Section 682 (Tax Treatment of alimony and separate maintenance payments.)

Notice 2018-35, Changes in accounting periods and method of accounting (Transitional guidance under sec. 451 related to inclusion of income associated with advance payments.)

Notice 2018-30, Modification of Notice 2003-65 (Effect of first year depreciation on recognized built-in gains and recognized built-in losses.)

Notice 2018-29, Guidance Regarding the Implementation of New Section 1446(f) for Partnership Interests That Are Not Publicly Traded (Withholding on dispositions.)

Notice 2018-28, Initial Guidance Under Section 163(j) as Applicable to Taxable Years Beginning After December 31, 2017 (Limitation on deduction of business interest expense.)

Notice 2018-26, Additional Guidance Under Section 965; Guidance Under Sections 62, 962, and 6081 in Connection With Section 965; and Penalty Relief Under Sections 6654 and 6655 in Connection with Section 965 and Repeal of Section 958(b)(4) (Treatment of deferred foreign income including relief from estimated tax penalties.)

Notice 2018-23, Transitional Guidance Under §§ 162(f) and 6050X with Respect to Certain Fines, Penalties, and Other Amounts (Denial of deduction for fines or penalties for violation of the law.)

Notice 2018-18, Guidance Under Section 1061, Partnership Interests Held in Connection with Performance of Services

Notice 2018-15, New Clean Renewable Energy Bonds

Notice 2018-14, Guidance on Withholding Rules

Notice 2018-13, Additional Guidance Under Section 965 and Guidance Under Sections 863 and 6038 in Connection with the Repeal of Section 958(b)(4) (Guidance regarding deferred foreign income.)

Notice 2018-08, Revised Timeline and Other Guidance Regarding the Implementation of New Section 1446(f)

Notice 2018-07, Guidance under Section 965 (Deferred Foreign Income Corporations)

Notice 2018-03, 2018 Standard Mileage Rates

Notice 1036, Early Release Copies of the 2018 Percentage Method Tables for Income Tax Withholding

# MODULE 1: TAX REFORM—Chapter 2: Self-Employment Tax: Today's World of Sharing, LLCs, & Tax Reform

## ¶ 201 WELCOME

This chapter explains major taxation issues that have arisen in today's newer types of self-employment: the sharing economy and limited liability companies (LLCs). This chapter explores the effects of 2017's *Tax Cuts and Jobs Act* (H.R. 1) on self-employment taxation and new concerns about due diligence for practitioners and self-employed taxpayers.

## ¶ 202 LEARNING OBJECTIVES

Upon completion of this chapter, you will be able to:

- Identify when an individual is subject to self-employment tax
- Recognize self-employment issues in representative court cases
- Recognize the due diligence steps to avoid problems with self-employment tax

## ¶ 203 INTRODUCTION

The self-employment tax topic is one that often can be very straightforward: an individual reports business income using Schedule C, or a partnership activity is clearly a trigger business on which an individual computes self-employment tax. But forms of self-employment have actually become pretty complicated, and new issues arise in the current "sharing economy." This chapter explores some of these issues for individuals the IRS considers independent contractors or "gig workers"—whether they are renting out property or working part-time on "gigs." The *Tax Cuts and Jobs Act* also affects the way self-employment tax affects self-employed individuals, and how their income and expenses must be reported. Changes in the last few years include the additional Medicare tax that can apply to higher-income self-employed taxpayers and tax rate changes under the new tax law.

Also, there's been some confusion as to when someone is an owner of an LLC for which he or she owes self-employment tax. The confusion arose partly because there's an exception that was written before all the states had LLCs as an entity form, and LLCs became a very prominent way to do business. The exception was written into the tax code to deal with limited partners, and the code section has never been updated to show how to apply it to LLCs. The term "limited partner" doesn't necessarily make sense in the IRS description, and the ambiguities have been left to the courts. The IRS actually could issue some regulations, but Congress told the IRS years ago to pull those back. The discussion here will get into some of these more complicated areas in relevant code sections, as well as case law of important court decisions. Approximately 8 to 12 cases have arisen annually in the last few years, both in court and in IRS rulings, so obviously issues have not been settled. The chapter concludes with some due diligence reminders for practitioners and taxpayers to avoid problems with self-employment taxation.

# ¶ 204 INTERNAL REVENUE CODE CHAPTER 2

The Internal Revenue Code (IRC) contains chapters numbered from 1 to 100, although not all numbers are used. Practitioners spend a lot of time becoming familiar with Chapter 1, which deals with income taxes. Chapter 2 is relevant for self-employment tax issues. The chapter references are relevant because some code sections mention them. For example, section 199A(f)(3) provides that the 20 percent qualified business income deduction provided at section 199A is only allowed for "this chapter" referring to Chapter 1 of the IRC where section 199A is located. Thus, the deduction is not allowed in computing self-employment taxes provided for in Chapter 2 of the IRC.

Code Secs. 1401 through 1403 in Chapter 2 of the IRC describe the features of the tax on self-employment income. Code Sec. 1401 lists the rate of tax, Code Sec. 1402 gives definitions pertaining to self-employment, and Code Sec. 1403 includes miscellaneous provisions concerning self-employment. There's also a reference in Code Sec 164(f), which allows a tax deduction for one-half of self-employment taxes.

Code Sec. 1401 deals with the tax rate, including the 12.4 percent commonly known as the "FICA tax," for old age, survivors, and disability insurance (OASDI). The law describes "hospital insurance tax," which most people call the "Medicare tax." That's a rate of 2.9 percent of self-employment income. And Code Sec. 1401 mentions an additional tax that was added by the *Affordable Care Act* back in 2010, which is 0.9 percent of self-employment income and wages if individuals receive income above these thresholds:

- $250,000 for married couples filing jointly
- $125,000 for married couples filing separately
- $200,000 for qualifying widow(er)s
- $200,000 for single filers
- $200,000 for heads of household

## STUDY QUESTIONS

**1.** Which of the following identifies the rate of tax on old-age, survivors, and disability insurance (OASDI)?

    **a.** 12.4 percent

    **b.** 2.9 percent

    **c.** 0.9 percent

    **d.** 21 percent

**2.** The income threshold for applying the 0.9 percent additional Medicare tax is $200,000 for all of the filers *except:*

    **a.** Single filers

    **b.** Heads of households

    **c.** Married couples filing separately

    **d.** Qualifying widow(er)s

## Additional Medicare Tax

The threshold figures are actually laid out in Code Sec. 3101; 3101(a) is the self-employment tax, 3101(b) is the additional Medicare tax. The additional Medicare tax for higher-income individuals is computed using Form 8959, *Additional Medicare Tax,* and then transferred to page two of Form 1040 along with the individuals' other tax liabilities. Taxpayers owe the additional Medicare tax on both wages and self-employment income combined when their income exceeds the threshold. If individuals have positive wages but negative self-employment income, they still owe the tax if wages alone exceed the threshold.

**EXAMPLE:** Jeremy Haskell earns $150,000 in wages and files jointly with his wife Emily, who earns $175,000 of self-employment income. Individually each spouse's income is less than the threshold, but together they're earning $75,000 more than the threshold amount: $325,000. They calculate the additional Medicare tax of 0.9 percent on the $75,000, or $675, which they add to their other tax liabilities. If Jeremy had earned more than $200,000 in his wages, his employer would have had to withhold that additional 0.9 percent (but Jeremy, not the employer, would pay it) because $200,000 is the single threshold.

It's also possible that some individuals will have an amount withheld, but don't actually owe it. Others, like Jeremy, do owe it, but there will be no withholding on their paychecks because their wages don't exceed $200,000. It is something that will have to be factored into the couple's estimated tax payments.

Filling in Part I of Form 8959 for "Medicare wages," Jeremy records his $150,000 wage, putting his threshold in, and just on his wages, nothing is owed. But Emily records her self-employment income transferred from her Schedule SE in Part II of Form 8959. $150,000 of the Medicare tax threshold already got used with Jeremy's wages. The couple must adjust that threshold, which is no longer $250,000 but instead $250,000 less $150,000. The threshold is now $100,000 and the figure is now $75,000 above the threshold, which they must multiply by the 0.9 percent.

Part II of the form prompts the couple on how to handle the result. Jeremy considers any withholding by his employer by checking his Form W-2, and finds the Medicare rate taxes were $2,175, and he owes that as 1.45 percent of his wages. He already owed regular Medicare tax (OA), and that is actually what his employer withheld, but because his wages did not exceed $200,000, the employer did not have to withhold any *additional* Medicare tax.

The bottom line is that the couple does owe $675 in additional Medicare tax, which is recorded in Part IV of Form 1040. No credits may be used against the amount. Tax credits are usually applied only against Chapter 1 taxes (income tax), but Emily's self-employment income as covered in Code Sec. 1401 is not a Chapter 1 tax.

Code Sec. 1401 addresses the amount of self-employment tax, and it does apply to self-employment earnings. Tax return preparers must factor in crossing the thresholds—self-employment as well as wage income.

## FICA Tax

Social Security income, whether for an employee or self-employed taxpayer, has a cap on the *Federal Insurance Contributions Act* (FICA or OASDI) tax owed. Every year, the Social Security Administration sets that dollar amount, usually sometime in November, for the next year. For 2018, once an individual has crossed the wage income or self-employment income cap of $128,400, he or she will not owe any additional FICA tax on the additional income. This income limit for FICA affects about 7 percent of workers.

Taxpayers should bear in mind that the Medicare tax has no cap on income. Once taxpayers cross this threshold, they don't owe FICA tax on the additional income but will continue to owe, for the self-employed, 2.9 percent self-employment tax, which is the Medicare portion. Once individuals' income is above those thresholds, they've got the additional 0.9 percent Medicare tax added on as well. That can certainly add up.

## Code Sec. 164(f) Deduction

Code Sec. 164(f) discusses the deduction for one-half of self-employment tax. Self-employed taxpayers do not get any half deduction for any additional Medicare tax. The deduction of half for the self-employment tax is for other than taxes imposed by Code Sec. 1401(b)(2). Again, (b)(1) is the self-employment tax rule, (b)(2) is the additional Medicare tax. Congress thought about that and made it very clear that there is no deduction for any part of additional Medicare tax.

## Partnership Income

Code Sec. 1402 is a fairly long provision. Probably for most clients it's not an issue, they clearly have self-employment income, they have partnership income where they are working, and they owe this money. The tax preparation software gathers all the data, then calculates self-employment tax. There is a self-employment tax deduction, everything's done. But, given those 8 to 12 court decisions and IRS rulings a year regarding self-employment tax, there are issues out there.

Code Sec. 1401 talks about the 2.9 percent OASDI tax for the self-employed. The FICA tax applies. With 12.4 and 2.9 percent, individuals pay a total of 15.3 percent self-employment tax, which is pretty high. For some high-income taxpayers who earn more than that threshold, they can also owe the 0.9 percent additional Medicare tax.

Net earnings from self-employment defined in Code Sec. 1402 means the gross income derived by an individual from any trade or business carried on by such individual less the deductions allowed by Subtitle A, which are attributable to such trade or business, plus the distributive share (whether or not distributed) of income or loss described in Section 702(a)(8) for a partnership, "except that in computing such gross income and deductions and such distributive share of partnership income, ordinary income or loss." Various items not included in gross income or deductions subject to self-employment tax are listed in (a)(1)–(17).

Some items under the new tax law listed in 1–17 are fairly straightforward; others, are a bit more involved:

1. Rentals from real estate and from personal property leased with the real estate . . . together with deductions attributable thereto, unless such rentals are received in course of a trade or business as a real estate dealer
2. Dividends and interest
3. Gain or Loss on sale or exchange of a capital asset
4. Net operating losses (NOLs)
5. Community property rule for income derived from a trade or business
6. Resident of Puerto Rico ignores Code Sec. 933 in computing his income
7. No personal exemptions
8. Minister ignores Code Sec. 107 (rental value of parsonages)
9. Code Sec. 931 exclusion ignored (resident of Guam, American Samoa or the Northern Mariana Islands)
10. Certain partnership retirement payments
11. Code Sec. 911(a)(1) exclusion is not available (foreign earned income)
12. Self-employment tax deduction

13. Limited partner income/loss

14. Adjustment for church employee income

15. Member Indian tribe adjustment for income from fishing rights

16. No Section 199 deduction (domestic manufacturing deduction)

17. Each spouse's share of income/loss from qualified joint venture considered

On the simple end, there are no available reductions of self-employment tax from any personal exemptions formerly allowed in earlier years. Also, a Section 199 deduction isn't allowed for domestic production activities; the new tax law repealed it.

Item (a)(11), the foreign earned income exclusion, is not allowed for self-employment tax.

Item (a)12 is actually used in computing self-employment tax, so partners would get a deduction for that. That item was meant to equate to the fact that, when employers pay their share of the FICA and hospital insurance tax, the individuals get to deduct that. The thought there was, shouldn't the self-employed individual get to deduct that and calculate the self-employment tax as an adjustment? Apparently, the .9235 (100-50% (2.9 + 12.4)) is too high. There have been some legislative proposals to adjust that.

Item (a)(1) on real estate and personal property has also raised some issues. Some of these adjustments and special rules are fairly straightforward. Others give rise to litigation and IRS rulings that deal with (a)(1) on the rentals and real estate; a couple of rulings are regarding farming.

Item (a)(13) on whether or not a member of an LLC would owe any self-employment tax has prompted most of the court cases coming up. Sometimes the issue is just that the person doesn't know whether he or she is actually generating trade or business income. For example, if a taxpayer has a hobby that's not a trade or business. For a hobby the taxpayer doesn't get to deduct any expenses but also doesn't owe any self-employment tax. If the activity constitutes a business, then Code Sec. 1402 provisions apply.

In 2017 businesses could still claim the Section 199 deduction. Practitioners have wondered why the Section 199 deduction is on page one of the return rather than on Schedule C, where clients actually claim this deduction because they're producing domestic production gross income under Schedule C. The reason why the IRS set up the form to put the Section 199 deduction on page one of Form 1040 rather than on Schedule C is because the IRS wanted to have the Schedule C bottom line be the number pulled to and then transferred onto Schedule SE.

Also, practitioners might have wondered, why doesn't the gain or loss and sale of business property that's on Form 4797 get transferred over to Schedule C? Again, it's because of the special rules regarding the way this is set up—gain and loss, capital asset, and other adjustments. But there is a logic to why the IRS puts items on Schedule C versus somewhere else on the return. Part of it is trying to get these forms all tied together. But the goal is to get to the bottom line on Schedule C and that then ties over to the Form SE calculation.

## Minimum Self-Employment Income for Filing

Code Sec 1402 (b) (2) states that net earnings from a trade or business does not include that part of the net earnings from self-employment that are in excess of the contribution and benefit base effective for the taxable year minus the amount of wages paid to such individual during such taxable year.

The net earnings from self-employment do not include net earnings for the taxable year that are less than $400.

Frequently, clients ask whether they need to file a return—whether their income is high enough. Do clients have more than $400 of self-employment income? Then they would owe self-employment tax even though their income might not be high enough to owe federal income taxes. They need to file a tax return. This $400 minimum has remained the same for about 50 years.

## Trade or Business Income

Code Sec. 1402(c) defines what constitutes a trade or business for self-employment purposes:

> The term "trade or business," when used with reference to self-employment income or net earnings from self-employment, shall have the same meaning as when used in section 162 (relating to trade or business expenses), except that such term shall not include—
>
> - Various exceptions including:
>   - Public office where the employee is covered by the Federal Employee Retirement System or other government pension plan
>   - Work as employee with some exceptions such as newspaper sales if under age 18
>   - Special rule for ministers or employees of church controlled organizations

Unless some other exception applies, the net earnings are subject to self-employment tax, referring back to Code Sec. 162. That provision says a self-employed taxpayer may deduct the ordinary, necessary expenses in carrying out a trade or business. Code Sec. 162 talks about trade or business deductions but does not define what a trade or business is.

That's been left to court cases, described later in the discussion of a hobby versus trade or business. There are a few, limited exceptions there, but what's important is, this issue has come up in some rulings recently.

## Other Provisions of Code Sec. 1402

More rules of Code Sec. 1402 (a lengthy section) are quite specialized:

(f) Partner's taxable year ending as the result of death

(g) Members of certain religious faiths

(h) Special rules for options and commodities dealers

(i) Special rules for certain church employee income

(j) Codification of treatment of certain termination payments received by former insurance salesmen

The regulation for individuals who engage in more than one trade or business discusses aggregating net income and losses from all their businesses on one Schedule SE:

> 1.1402(a)-2(c) Aggregate net earnings. Where an individual is engaged in more than one trade or business within the meaning of Section 1402(c) and § 1.1402(c)-1, his net earnings from self-employment consist of the aggregate of the net income and losses (computed subject to the special rules provided in §§ 1.1402(a)-1 to 1.1402(a)-17, inclusive) of all such trades or businesses carried on by him. Thus, a loss sustained in one trade or business carried on by an individual will operate to offset the income derived by him from another trade or business.

The significance here is that a loss in one trade or business an individual operates may offset income he or she may derive from another trade or business.

## STUDY QUESTION

3. Each of the following individuals is subject to self-employment tax *except:*

    **a.** Self-employed individuals earning less than $400

    **b.** Real estate agents and direct sellers

    **c.** Certain employees of churches and church organizations

    **d.** Independent contractors

# ¶ 205 COMMUNITY PROPERTY INCOME OF MARRIED COUPLES

For married couples, there are some special rules. In a community property state, income from a business is considered to be community property income belonging to both the husband and the wife. But there is a special rule regarding community property income. Basically, if only one spouse is participating in a business that generates income, all the income is taxed to that spouse. Community property income belonging to the participating spouse is treated as the only income in the calculation of the net earnings from self-employment, *Smith v Comm* (TC Memo 2011-82). When both spouses participate, they're supposed to allocate income based on their respective distributive shares being how much effort and time each one is contributing.

The *Fitch* case, described later, deals with the husband and wife in a community property state. They were trying to apply the husband's business loss against the wife's business income, but the sources were clearly separate. This was disallowed.

Basically, spouses in a business operation report their income separately in almost all cases. Tax planners should be aware of these special rules. If a husband and wife are operating a trade or business together like a partnership rather than a sole proprietorship, the couple can make an election for what's called a "qualified joint venture."

Qualified Joint Ventures mentioned in Code Sec. 761, is an agreement for spouses to split everything. They file two Schedule Cs instead of a partnership return.

A recent case was determined in which spouses had not made the election and they had not filed partnership returns. They got dinged with the partnership penalty. There's a big penalty if a couple doesn't file each partnership return on time.

## Different Taxable Years

The regulations (Reg. 1.1402(a)–2(e)) cover a calendar year taxpayer who is a partner in a fiscal year partnership with a different year end, such as July 31. The partner caps self-employment tax just like he or she capped income; this regulation states that the partner will take the Form K-1 for the year ended July 31, 2018, and report that on his or her 2018 return. The partner doesn't have to pro-rate the partnership income to tie to the calendar year. Income that is reported, on Schedule K-1 is used to calculate the calendar year income. The whole amount is reported in the tax year of the K-1. No prorating between tax years is needed.

The IRS also has the short Schedule SE as well as the long version. There's a farm optional method and a nonfarm optional method. Taxpayers have multiple choices for filing, with help in Reg. 1.1402(a)–(15).

# ¶ 206 TYPES OF TAXPAYERS AND ACTIVITIES SUBJECT TO SELF-EMPLOYMENT TAX

Individuals subject to self-employment tax include independent contractors, people filing a Schedule C as sole proprietors, and partners (unless they are limited partners or get a guaranteed payment that is not for services). Maybe an individual receives a guaranteed payment because he or she is owed a return on capital or for use of property. That kind of activity would not be subject to self-employment tax. But a guaranteed payment for services is going to be subject to self-employment tax.

Life insurance agents and direct sellers are called "statutory employees" under Sec 6454 (d)(3) Rev Rul 90-93. As statutory employees, they don't have income tax withholding from their income because they're not considered employees. But the employers are required to withhold and pay social security and Medicare tax for these employees.

Special rules apply to certain rental income, which gets a little bit complicated in the farm context. A recent case, **Martin v Commisioner,** 149 TC 12 (9-12-17), is described later. Although, generally rentals of real property are not subject to self-employment tax, if there are substantial personal services involved, then for Code Sec. 1402 purposes, they will not be considered rental of real estate, and service providers would owe self-employment tax on that income.

## Home Rentals

The classic example today are airbnb rentals, which are being operated a bit more like a bed and breakfast. This is different than rentals where the guest gets a key, goes in, and uses the space and the space is cleaned after use. That's a pure rental for which the tenant or owner does not owe self-employment tax.

But some of these airbnb situations are different. In fact, in some cities, like Santa Monica, CA, the city law says an owner can only have shared short-term rentals. The owner of the property or long-term tenant, must be there during the guest's stay. When people provide shared rentals or short-term rentals like an airbnb, there's a good chance they'll cook the guest a meal, pick him or her up at the airport, drive the guest around, and clean the room every day. This service type of arrangement warrants self-employment tax.

The issue today is, what level of personal services need to occur for a situation *not* to be considered a rental of real estate but, instead, provision of personal services.

What activities generate self-employment income under Code Sec. 1402? Generally, if an individual has a trade or business within a meaning of Code Sec. 162 the activities are self-employment tax. Practitioners should look to case law.

Generally, rentals or real estate activities are not subject to self-employment tax unless individuals are real estate dealers or providing personal services. An activity is not considered a real estate rental but considered a bed and breakfast because of the amount of personal services being provided.

## Income from a Hobby Versus a Business

Differences apply to income from a Code Sec. 183 hobby versus a business. Businesses may declare a loss. Business expenses are deducted above the line on Schedule C. For any profit from a business, the net earnings from self-employment income is subject to self-employment tax.

A hobby's expenses are limited to the amount of the hobbyist's income. Prior to the *Tax Cuts and Jobs Act,* expenses of the hobby could only be deducted to the extent they exceeded (with all the other miscellaneous itemized deductions) 2 percent of the taxpayer's adjusted gross income (AGI). Since the act's passage and for the next eight years, 2018 through 2025, no hobby expenses are deductible because they would only be deductible as a miscellaneous itemized deduction subject to 2 percent of AGI floor. For the next eight years, individuals may not deduct anything that was subject to 2 percent of AGI floor. The salient point is, an individual won't owe any self-employment tax on this revenue because, per Revenue Ruling 55-258, self-employment tax is not owed on hobby income (because it is not a trade or business).

Hobby cases arise every year, mostly in the Tax Court. In one, a woman was informally operating a nightclub. Although she actually did have a location for this club and did charge a fee, she was generating losses, so it wasn't a self-employment case. The issue was whether she could deduct those losses because it was a hobby, not a Schedule C business. The woman did have other income that she was sheltering with her losses on the Schedule C. But when the IRS and the court looked at it, they held that the woman didn't know anything about operating a nightclub, had no experience as its operator, was not keeping good records, and didn't have a business plan to show how she would ever generate any income. Even though she had a location and was charging people, it wasn't a business; a business takes a lot more than that.

> **EXAMPLE:** Jim Woerner is a part-time Uber driver who says, "I'm just doing it for the fun of it. Helps pay my car payments." That does not describe a business. The risk Jim has is that he can't deduct any of his car expenses. Driving is an expensive activity. He also won't owe any self-employment tax. Jim will just take the total gross receipts and put it on the miscellaneous income line on page one of his tax return. He will take no deductions and owe no self-employment tax.

Issues arise for clients who are doing ride sharing as part-time work when they've got other sources of income, especially if they're going to show a loss. The IRS is really scrutinizing Schedule C losses when taxpayers have big wage income or big investment income. The IRS, as told by the Treasury Inspector General a couple of years ago, looks at those items on Form 1040, when Schedule C shows losses for one or more years and the taxpayers clearly have other income that they're living on. The IRS view is that there's a good chance the loss is from an activity that is actually not a business. Such a loss is disallowed.

It would not be surprising if the IRS started looking at returns of some part-time drivers. It might not be a high priority because the drivers are probably showing some small amount of net income. But basically, if taxpayers are really not in a business, they do not get deductions under Code Sec. 162. And, of course, they don't pay self-employment tax.

Because Code Sec. 162 doesn't define trade or business, practitioners turn to classic, older court decisions such as ***Groetzinger v Commisioner,*** 480 U.S. 23 (1987). It's a great case for defining trade or business because Groetzinger was a full-time gambler. That might get to a definition of gambling. The court's conclusion was that Groetzinger as a full-time gambler was in a trade or business because he did have a profit motive and was actually doing it full-time (he had lost his job). He devoted substantial effort to it. Plus, he was engaged in gambling on a regular basis. Also, unlike a part-time Uber or Lyft driver who only drives when he or she feels like it, Groetzinger gambled every day, when he was at the track or casino.

¶206

In contrast is another case, **Wittstruck v Commissioner,** 645 F2d 618 (8th Cir., 1981), in which the court found that the rental of a mobile home was a hobby. There was minimal rental activity and no profit objective found.

Key considerations for businesses are that individuals are engaged in these activities on a regular and continuous basis and doing it for a profit motive. They are trying to make a living from the work.

Profit motive is a key determinant of whether income is sourced to a business or a hobby. In **Bagley v US,** 963 F.Supp2d 162 (CD CA, 2013), the court found:

> The primary inquiry when determining whether a particular activity constitutes a trade or business is to ask whether the activity was undertaken or continued "in good faith, with the dominant hope and intent of realizing a profit, i.e., taxable income, therefrom." In other words, the "basic and dominant" motive behind the taxpayer's activities must be to make a profit or income from those very same activities.

The part-time gig worker might have a problem here, but he or she can overcome it by following the sound advice of a tax planner. What can individuals do to help show they're in a trade or business? Have record-keeping. Have a plan. Because even though Uber and Lyft set the prices, drivers do try and make tip money.

Serious ride sharing drivers keep their business records separate from their personal records. They actually track their mileage. And of course, there are apps for easily tracking business versus personal miles. The drivers keep up on the industry, reading blogs and articles weekly about what's going on in the gig driver economy—just as individuals would normally do when they are running a business.

The regs describe nine factors to differentiate a hobby from a business. These are factors that the part-time gig workers could do to give them the ability to deduct losses. (Taxpayers might have a problem if they *always* show a business loss.) The factors are:

1. Manner in which the taxpayer carried on the activity
2. Expertise of the taxpayer or his or her advisers
3. Time and effort expended by the taxpayer in carrying on the activity
4. Expectation that the assets used in the activity may appreciate in value
5. Success of the taxpayer in carrying on other similar or dissimilar activities
6. Taxpayer's history of income or loss with respect to the activity
7. Amount of occasional profits, if any, which are earned
8. Financial status of the taxpayer
9. Elements of personal pleasure or recreation

Years ago, there was a court case involving an artist who had 20 years of losses, but the court agreed with the taxpayer that hers was a business, not a hobby. She was actually generating income; she just had expenses that every year ended up causing losses. The court thought her intent was businesslike, looking at these nine factors.

The *IRS Audit Technique Guide, IRC Section 183: Activities not engaged in for profit,* offers guidance on activities that are not engaged in for profit and shows where in the law the rules may be found.

## STUDY QUESTION

**4.** Which of the following is a characteristic of a hobby and *not* a business under the self-employment tax rules?

   **a.** Earnings are subject to self-employment tax

   **b.** Expenses are deducted above the line

   **c.** The activity is not regularly carried on for profit

   **d.** Requirement to consider Code Sec. 469 (passive activity losses) and material participation tests

## Rental Real Estate

Rental real estate—again, depending on the nature and extent of services—might be subject to self-employment tax. That is addressed in the tax code and the regs.

On the services for occupants, Regulation 1.1402(a)-4(c)(1) says:

> (1) No services rendered for occupants. Payments for the use or occupancy of entire private residences or living quarters in duplex or multiple-housing units are generally rentals from real estate. Except in the case of real-estate dealers, such payments are excluded in determining net earnings from self-employment even though such payments are in part attributable to personal property furnished under the lease.

What about including income when the resident offers services for occupants? Code Sec. 1402(a)-4(c)(2) stipulates:

> (2) Services rendered for occupants. Payments for use or occupancy of rooms or other space where services are also rendered to the occupant, such as for use or occupancy of rooms or other quarters in hotels, boarding houses, or apartment houses furnishing hotel services, or in tourist camps or tourist homes, or payments for use or occupancy of space in parking lots, warehouses, or storage garages, do not constitute rentals from real estate; consequently, such payments are included in determining net earnings from self-employment. Generally, services are considered rendered to the occupant if they are primarily for his convenience and are other than those usually or customarily rendered in connection with the rental of rooms or other space for occupancy only. The supplying of maid service, for example, constitutes such service; whereas the furnishing of heat and light, the cleaning of public entrances, exits, stairways and lobbies, the collection of trash, and so forth, are not considered as services rendered to the occupant

Basically, if an individual earns rental income from real estate and is *not* a dealer, it's not subject to self-employment tax. But if the individual is providing services, then income is *not* considered rental from real estate for Code Sec. 1402 purposes, which means the individual does indeed have net earnings from self-employment (assuming there is income). The IRS has never given a magic formula to know whether taxpayers are providing enough services that arrangements are no longer considered rental of real estate.

Revenue Ruling 83-139 provides two scenarios:

> **EXAMPLE:** A trailer park owner and operator provides trailer lots, services, and facilities to trailer owners. He charges a monthly fee, there's a laundry facility,

**¶206**

there's city sewage, electrical connections, and a roadway. The owner cleans these premises daily.

**EXAMPLE:** The facts are the same except the trailer park owner provides additional services. The park contains a recreation hall, consisting of a card area, pool room, kitchen, auditorium, stage, and library. Employees of the owner supervise and maintain these areas. The owner also provides numerous recreational events, distributes a monthly newsletter to the tenants, and helps the tenants buy or sell their trailers. Employees of the owner will also connect and disconnect water, sewers, and electrical lines for the trailer owners.

The owner in the second case does far more personally for the tenants. The IRS concludes that in the first example income is rentals from real estate, and is not considered net earnings and subject to self-employment tax under Code Sec. 1402. However, in the second example, the owner provides many services beyond those required for occupancy. "These services are of such substantial nature that compensation for them can clearly be said to constitute a material part of the payments made by the tenants of the trailer park." Revenue Ruling 83-139 states the income is subject to self-employment tax.

Another illustrative case is *Hopper v Commissioner*, 94 TC 542 (1990). Hopper was a 25 percent partner in a partnership that rented out self-storage units. The self-storage place did have a soft drink machine, pest control, contents insurance, and locks and pallets for sale. Hopper was trying to offset that loss against his law firm's earnings. He claimed two self-employment businesses with income and losses that he netted together. He couldn't do that if one is considered rental because it's not subject to self-employment tax. He could not net it with the other sources. The court said, there was no evidence that he provided substantial services in the self-storage facility. The court decision said anything Hopper did was really just minor and incidental.

# ¶ 207 REVIEW OF RECENT CASES

In *Milligan v Commissioner*, 38 F3d 1094 (9th Cir.) termination payments were not subject to self-employment tax. In *Barrett v Commissioner*, 58 TC 284 (1972), the court found that "noncompetition does not constitute the carrying on of a trade or business."

In *Clark, Jr. v Commissioner*, Docket No. 4131-15 (5/12/16), Clark was generating revenue from ads on his blog site. He was blogging full-time, intending to make a profit. He did not produce a Schedule SE for the income, and the Tax court judge determined that clearly Clark was running the blog and generating revenue subject to self-employment tax.

In *Chai v Commissioner*, No 15-1653 (2nd cir 2017), Chai was making lots of money. He was working for someone who was just basically setting up tax shelters. Chai was signing a variety of paperwork to make all of this happen. He wasn't paying self-employment tax on it, but he was reporting lots of money. In 2003, he showed $2 million on his Schedule C from a Form 1099. Despite Chai's claim of providing "no meaningful services . . . just signed a lot of documents," the court ruled the work was continuous and regular and self-employment tax and penalties were due.

In *Wang v Commissioner*, TC Memo 2016-123 (6/21/16), Wang claimed that generating just one commission did not constitute a real estate practice. Although Wang reported the commission on Schedule C, no Form SE was submitted. The court found that the single transaction nevertheless was subject to self-employment tax.

*Methvin v Commissioner*, TC Memo 2015-81 (4/27/15), is a good example. Just because individuals generate a profit doesn't mean that they have a trade or business.

Methvin had a small interest in an oil and gas business. He didn't generate income. He wasn't a limited partner, nor was he himself personally involved in running or operating the organization. Agents or employees ran the operation. However, the court ruled:

> A taxpayer who is not personally active in the management or operation of a trade or business may be liable for self-employment tax if the trade or business is carried out on his behalf through his agents or employees or constitutes his distributive share of income from a partnership in which he was a member. Sec. 1402(a); *Cokes v. Commissioner,* 91 T.C. 222 (1988).

In *Morehouse,* No. 13-3110 (8th Cir. 10/10/14), the appellants were getting certain payments from the government's USDA Conservation Reserve Program, and they were arguing that these were real estate rental payments that would not be subject to self-employment tax due to the rental of real property exception. The Tax court (the lower court) held that the payments were subject to self-employment tax. The Tax court ruled that payments weren't for any rentals but just payments from the government. The Tax court addressed the issue of whether the defendants were really in a trade or business, interpreting Code Sec. 1402 broadly.

But when the *Morehouse* case got to the 8th Circuit, the circuit court ruled that the income wasn't subject to self-employment tax. These land conservation payments received from the government were more like real estate rentals for which the defendants were not providing any services and this income was not subject to self-employment tax

Sometimes courts interpret Code Section 1402 broadly, and sometimes narrowly. Perhaps the reason why Congress put in the exception for rental real estate was because lawmakers didn't want people renting out real estate without providing any kind of services and stating that the activities are building their Social Security wage base. Congress didn't think that these rental real estate activities should be sufficient for generating taxable self-employment income.

In *Martin,* 149 TC No. 12 (9/27/17), Martin rented substantial farm and facilities to a separate S corporation. The rent being charged was at or below fair rental. The S corp did employ people to manage that rental. The Martins themselves were not obligated to perform any farm-related activities as a condition of leasing the property to this S corporation. The Tax court ruled in favor of the taxpayer that the farm couple's rent from its S Corp was not subject to self-employment tax.

The court gave this interpretation of 1402(a)(1) because of the following review of law:

> (a) Net earnings from self-employment . . . means gross income derived by individual from any trade or business carried on by such individual, less deductions allowed by this subtitle attributable to such trade or business, plus distributive share of income or loss from any trade or business carried on by partnership; except that in computing such gross income and deductions and such distributive share of partnership ordinary income or loss—
>
> (1) there shall be excluded rentals from real estate and personal property leased with the real estate together with deductions attributable thereto, unless such rentals are received in course of a trade or business as a real estate dealer; except that preceding provisions shall not apply to any income derived by owner or tenant of land if

(A) such income is derived under arrangement, between owner or tenant and another individual, which provides that such other individual shall produce agricultural or horticultural commodities on such land, and that there shall be material participation by owner or tenant in production or management of the production of such agricultural or horticultural commodities, and

(B) there is material participation by owner or tenant with respect to any such agricultural or horticultural commodity

Specific to these (A) and (B) special rules, is that this case pertained to an agricultural lease for which the defendants had to provide services. Thus, yes, this income probably was subject to self-employment tax.

The 8th Circuit Court's review of **McNamara II v Commissioner,** 236 F.3d 410 (8th Cir. 2000), is a very similar fact pattern as the **Martin** case. There was a separate employment and a separate farm rental agreement. The appellants charged fair market rent or less for the rental. The appellants maintained that because they charged FMV or less for the rental, no services were included. The 8th Circuit said:

Rents consistent with market rates very strongly suggest that the rental arrangement stands on its own as an independent transaction and cannot be said to be part of an "arrangement" for participation in agricultural production. Although Commissioner is correct that, unlike other provisions, Section 1402(a)(1) contains no explicit safe-harbor provision for fair market value transactions, we conclude that this is the practical effect of the "derived under" language.

Though Code Sec. 1401(a)(1) contains no explicit safe-harbor provision for fair market value transactions; tax practitioners conclude that this is the practical effect of the use of the words "derived under" language..

The Tax court upheld in the **Martin** case, that regardless of taxpayer's material participation, if the rental income is set only at fair market rent that would indicate that the defendants were not charging anything for the services. The rent can't be considered self-employment income.

The circuit ruling also said that this S corp was charging fair market rent and the owners had invested $1.2 million in building up these facilities. The owners were helping in the chicken production business, by raising the chicks to some point. A lot of equipment was involved in this rental, so the agreement served as a return on investment rather than a method of income recharacterization. The IRS issued a nonacquiescence to **McNamara:**

AOD 2003-03 disagrees with Eighth Circuit's narrow construction of term arrangement because it is inconsistent with the common meaning of that term and with Congress's intent. The IRS agrees with the Tax court's analysis regarding the common meaning of the term arrangement, and how that term is construed for purposes of other Code provisions. If, under overall scheme of the farming operations it was understood that farmer would materially participate in farm production, and farmer did in fact materially participate, then income received from lessee is subject to self-employment tax. The IRS continues to believe that this is the correct result regardless of whether the material participation was explicitly called for under the written or oral lease.

## STUDY QUESTION

**5.** Which of the following cases related to self-employment tax issues involving a blogger's advertising revenue?

   a. *Clark, Jr.,* Dkt No. 4131-5

   b. *Wang,* TC Memor 2016-123

   c. *Chai,* TC Memo 2015-42

   d. *Morehouse,* No. 13-3310

---

In *Ryther v Commissioner,* TC Memo decision 2016-56 (3/28/16), an individual had some scrap metal that had been left over from a bankruptcy proceeding. It did have some value. Over seven years, Ryther had sales of $317,000. As to why it was just left behind after the bankruptcy, maybe the trustee didn't know it had such high value.

Ryther determined a pretty good market existed for the metal and he didn't have to do much to sell it. Perhaps he would post an ad and easily find people to purchase it. The court came up with eight factors to determine whether this was inventory or property held for sale in the ordinary course of trade or business. The Tax court basically tried to figure out whether the profit was self-employment income.

Tax practitioners should not think that just because clients earn a profit, they must be in a trade or business. The *Ryther* case is a clear reminder that profit and business are separate. If it's provisionary profit, it still could be a hobby. Clients and planners have to look at factors. The *Ryther* court didn't exactly go through the nine factors under Code Sec. 183-2, but the court looked at elements that are close to some of the factors under Reg. 1.183-2. The court also considered matters that come up in cases like *Groetzinger,* is the individual engaged in a trade or business?

*Frequency and regularity of sales:* If an individual were in business, he or she would probably be trying to sell items every day. Ryther was just an occasional seller. The court ruled, no, the scrap metal sale was not a trade or business.

*Substantiality of sales:* The court ruled that this factor was neutral. The court wasn't going to dig into that because sales were significant—$317,000 over seven years.

*Length of time the property was held:* Normally, if individuals were selling inventory, they would like to turn it over as quickly as possible. Ryther was just hanging onto the scrap. The court said, no, this does not look like a trade or business.

Segregation of property from business property: This factor doesn't really apply here.

*Purpose of the acquisition:* The court ruled the scrap was just leftover and did not evaluate that factor.

*Sales and advertising effort:* It's puzzling that the court left that factor neutral. Ryther spent very minimal effort. He just had to post the availability of the metal on the appropriate website. He could find buyers that would pick up the scrap. But the court found that factor neutral.

*Time and effort spent on sales:* Again, it is unclear that the factor was neutral as opposed to leaning toward not counting as a trade or business. If Ryther were in a trade or business, wouldn't he be spending a fair amount of time on it? Presumably the court felt that what he was doing didn't take a lot of time.

¶207

*How the proceeds were used:* If Ryther were really in a business, when he sold the inventory, he'd use the proceeds to buy more inventory. He wasn't doing that because he wasn't running a trade or business. The result was, yes, he had a profit, but he was not in a trade or business for Code Sec. 1402 purposes, nor Code Sec. 162. Thus, no self-employment tax was owed.

Today, this item would fall under an "activity not engaged in for profit." If he had any expenses, Ryther would not be able to deduct any of them. But he really didn't have much in the way of any expenses. Again, just because he made a profit did not mean he was running a trade or business. Other factors affected the call, as with the *Groetzinger* case, and the factors that the court was using here.

## STUDY QUESTION

---

**6.** In the *Ryther* case, the Tax court ruled that all of the following factors showed no self-employment activities *except:*

   **a.** Frequency and regularity of sales

   **b.** Substantiality of sales

   **c.** Length of time the property was held

   **d.** How the proceeds were used

---

The *Peterson* case, Nos. 14-15773, 14-15774 (11th Cir., 7/8/16), is an 87-page opinion. Peterson was a very high-earning—in the millions of dollars annually—Mary Kay distributor. Basically, once she did all she could to penetrate one large city market, she'd move to another city and penetrate that one. As a direct seller, under Code Sec. 3508, she was not an employee. Because of her level, the company had certain deferred compensation plans for her—not retirement plans, because she wasn't an employee of Mary Kay. Peterson was a contractor. When she started collecting this deferred compensation, she wasn't paying self-employment tax on the payments. The IRS and the 11th Circuit agreed her payments were subject to self-employment tax. Deferred compensation is not retirement savings; Peterson needed to pay self-employment tax on the deferred compensation payments.

The IRS wrote some regulations a couple of years ago because it was seeing an apparent abuse of practice by some partnerships, in which partners were not considered employees. An old revenue ruling, Revenue Ruling 69-184, suggested that partners of a partnership are not considered employees of the partnership. These partners were trying to get themselves a better fringe benefit arrangement. They had the partnership set up an LLC (as a disregarded entity), and the partners were all considered employees of that entity. The entity was providing the benefits. The IRS regs found this arrangement impermissible, the entity was still a partnership and individuals were partners, not employees. Such taxpayers were not going to benefit from these special benefit provisions that only apply to employees. A few court cases and chief counsel advice held the issue was an entity being an LLC whose members actively work in the LLC like law firm partners.

They're not paying self-employment tax because under 1402, it says limited partners aren't subject to self-employment tax because they are limited partners. They're in a limited liability company. What could be more limited than that?

LLC members are not the same as limited partners. A limited partner works in a "limited partnership," which is a specific term—one lacking guidance and one in desperate need of some guidance. According to Chief Counsel Advice 201436049, the LLC is an investment management company with partners that are working full-time, and they've got employees working full-time there, not as owners but employees.

Everyone, including the partners, were paid wages and given an annual Form W-2. When the owners received their Schedule K-1s, they claimed their distributive shares, not paying self-employment tax on them. They claimed their pay was for the work already listed on W-2s, and they had paid payroll taxes on the income.

The IRS held that the wages were fine, and the tax that should have been self-employment tax has been paid. The partners' distributive share of the income was active income earned because the management company and its partners generally have full authority and responsibility to manage and control the affairs and business of each fund.

The *Renkemeyer* decision, 136 T.C. No 7 (2011), was intended under Code Sec. 1402(a)(13) to apply to owners who were mere investors and not to active participants who acted as self-employed persons. The *Renkemeyer* case gets cited a lot. Renkemeyer was a limited liability entity running a law firm. The lawyers who owned the law firm were, in essence, partners of this LLC law firm, and were only paying their distributive shares of income, they were not paying self-employment tax on it. The ruling denied that the lawyers were limited partners. "Limited partner" means an individual is not involved in the management or operation of this entity. It's also a legal term applied only to a limited partnership entity.

*Riether v US*, 919 F.Supp.2d 1140 (DNM 2012), and Revenue Ruling 69-184, says that partners are not employees. The partners were paying themselves W-2 wages, and in addition partners received a distributive share of partnership income. Partners need to be paying self-employment tax on guaranteed payments received for services as well as their distributive shares of partnership earnings.

This case history continues. There have been a few cases in this area. Chief Counsel Advice 201440014 (9/5/14) applied to a situation in which the LLC operated restaurant franchises owned by a husband and a wife. The wife was inactive in the business, and her trust also owned part of it and was inactive. The husband received guaranteed payments representing compensation for his services and paid self-employment tax on them and the partnership claimed a deduction. He argued that this method separated income between that derived from capital and works of others versus his work. Any other income was just investment, like a dividend, for which he claimed not to owe self-employment tax.

The IRS position was that partnership taxation doesn't work that way. The owners of the LLC also made reference to the *Brinks, Gilson, and Lione* case, in which the IRS claimed that a C corporation law firm owner paid themselves too much, and part of it was really a dividend. The owner/employees in the Brinks, Gilson, and Lione law firm C corp were found to have received both compensation (deductible by the C corporation) and dividends (not deductible by the C corporation).

For the LLC taxed as a partnership the rules work differently than for a C corporation. Active partners of a partnership must pay self-employment tax on guaranteed payments for services as well as their distributive share of partnership income.

In the CCA, no self-employment tax was owed on the wife and trust's distributive share of partnership income because they were inactive owners. What if the ownership percentages were changed such that the active husband owned little or none of the LLC and the inactive owners owned more? Is there a flaw in the law from a policy perspective? Or is that a great tax planning activity? Would the IRS be able to argue that the husband should have been paid a guaranteed payment for services and for which

**¶207**

self-employment tax would be owed? It's kind of an oddity in the law for the husband and wife if the wife owned all of the partnership and was not involved in the operations at all. Perhaps this is an area where the IRS or Congress will provide guidance or new rules.

In *Castigliola*, TC Memo 2017-62 (4/12/17), three attorneys operated a professional LLC in Mississippi, and their tax advisor instructed them to learn what attorneys earned in Mississippi and to ensure they paid themselves guaranteed payments of that amount. The attorneys were to pay self-employment tax on that amount. The LLC deducted those amounts, so the partners' distributive share was just subject to regular income tax.

The IRS—and the court agreed—denied that arrangement. The attorneys were not considered limited partners. The only possible way the owners could pull themselves out of Code Sec. 1402 for the self-employment tax would be to claim to be limited partners. But the court and the IRS ruled against that claim. It was clear from the *Renkemeyer* case that "limited partner" means someone who's not engaged in operating this entity. In the *Castigliola* case, the court made it really clear that Code Sec. 1402(a)(13) is saying limited partners don't owe self-employment tax, and their distributive share has got to be claimed as truly limited partners.

In 1977, most states didn't have LLCs. The law just hadn't kept up with how business operates in this decades-old problem. The IRS regulations under Section 1402 for LLCs would be helpful, Congress saying something would be helpful. Litigation continues here.

The court did waive a negligence penalty. There were regs issued that were controversial. Congress said, under the *Taxpayer Relief Act of 1997,* those regs have no effect. The IRS just hasn't come back to revisit this issue.

The *Hardy* case, TC Memo 2017-16 (1/17/17), involved a plastic surgeon who had a variety of self-employment tax issues from past activities and owned his own practice. He also had a 12.5 percent interest in a surgery center. The IRS was trying to argue that all of his income should have been combined into one activity because that would have made the surgery center part of his active plastic surgery practice. The court denied that position. Hardy was supported in treating these as separate activities under Code Sec. 469.

Hardy's Schedule K-1 from the surgery center was showing trade or business income. His tax preparer may have thought Hardy had to report that under Code Sec. 469, trade or business income. Hardy did materially participate, so that income was treated as nonpassive income. The preparer determined that the revenue might be passive income but didn't go back and amend the prior years' returns even though it was the same income for which Hardy paid self-employment tax. In 2010 the return claimed the surgery center income was still passive income not subject to self-employment tax, which probably was the right answer.

The preparer was trying to use this passive loss. But the Tax court decided Hardy had passive activity income back in 2006 and 2007, which should have been changed to be passive activity income and that loss carried back. Because the preparer didn't do that, Hardy lost the loss because those years were not closed under the statute of limitations at the time of the filing of the original return. This is the only case covered here in which the owner of the LLC was found to be like a limited partner. Although he did do surgeries there, Hardy wasn't actually involved in managing the place. His patients had the choice of where they wanted their surgery done. Even if he was going to earn more income if they did it at his surgery center, where he owned 12.5 percent, there was no requirement that the patients had to do that.

The court found that he really wasn't like the lawyers in *Renkemeyer*, he wasn't actively involved in running the center. However, as a physician owning the surgery center, didn't he have some obligation? Would another court hold the same? Many issues were going on. Under Reg. 1.469-4, the court noted there can be more than one reasonable way to group activities, and the net investment income tax should be considered if the taxpayer could be subject to it. Could income be grouped for Code Sec. 469 but not for self-employment tax purposes under Reg. 1.469-1T(d)?

Finally, in the *Fitch* case, TC Memo 2013-244 (10/28/13), the husband was a CPA with his own practice, with large losses reported on Schedule C. His wife was a licensed real estate agent who worked full-time as an independent contractor, showing her income on Schedule C. The husband argued that the amounts on Schedule C should be netted so no self-employment tax would be owed. He also claimed that he "collaborated and contributed to the management and control of the [realty business] in a multitude of ways." The IRS and Tax court ruled that combining the loss and income was disallowed because the wife ran her realty business, even maintaining her own records, and the real estate business was not jointly operated. Possible future reforms to self-employment tax rules might include clarifying their application to LLCs and limited liability partnerships (LLPs), changing how the rules apply to S corp owners, and changing the calculation of the self-employment tax deduction as proposed in H.R. 1 of the 113th Congress.

# ¶ 208  DUE DILIGENCE CONSIDERATIONS AND AVOIDANCE OF SELF-EMPLOYMENT TAX PROBLEMS

The following are reminders about self-employment questions the practitioner should pose:

- Is the client self-employed?
- — In a trade or business?
- — For profit or hobby?
- — Gig workers/freelancers likely need assistance to set up proper records and to file Schedule SE and estimated taxes.
- Is the client an active partner / LLC member?
- Is residential rental income subject to SE tax?
- — Check with airbnb landlords as to what they do for tenants.
- Is the client involved with farming and leases (such as with the *Martin* case)?
- What are the proper calculations for combining income and losses of married couples?

# MODULE 1: TAX REFORM—Chapter 3: Tax Reform for Tax-Exempt Organizations

## ¶ 301 WELCOME

This chapter discusses the effects of the new tax law (*Tax Cuts and Jobs Act,* H.R. 1) signed on December 22, 2017, specific to its impact on tax-exempt organizations and donors. Charitable organizations must consider the unrelated business income tax (UBIT) provisions applicable under the tax cuts and the timeframe for how provisions of the new law are being implemented.

## ¶ 302 LEARNING OBJECTIVES

Upon completion of this chapter, you will be able to:

- Identify ways that the new law affects charitable giving
- Recognize how the new tax act affects not-for-profit organizations that have employees
- Recognize how Notice 2017-73 is applied to the quid pro quo values of items offered in charity fundraising activities

## ¶ 303 INTRODUCTION

In early 2018 massive commentary was issued on the major impact of tax cuts on charitable giving and the elimination of some popular deductions used by individuals, but guidance on the provisions has not clarified just how provisions of the *Tax Cuts and Jobs Act,* H.R.1, affect not-for-profit organizations and their donors. Both donors and recipients of charitable gifts should understand the timeframes of these provisions. The law also pertains to exempt organizations as employers under Code Sections 501(c)(3), 501(c)(7), and (c)(6). For simplicity, this chapter refers to such entities as not-for-profit organizations or public charities.

Some of the law's provisions apply to social clubs, Code Sec. 501(c)(7), organizations, their dues, and the paying members, who no longer get a deduction for those dues. All exempt organizations are still grappling with the provision which provides if the organization has unrelated business income (UBI) from more than one business activity, it now must isolate each revenue stream. Each business activity which generates losses may only deduct those losses against revenue from the same business activity in future tax periods. Net operating losses may be carried forward indefinitely, may no longer be carried back, and the net operating loss deduction for losses generated from tax years beginning after 1/1/2018 are limited to 80 percent of taxable income.

## ¶ 304 EFFECTIVE DATES FOR THE LAW'S PROVISIONS

Although the tax law was passed on December 22, 2017, most of the changes took effect for tax years beginning after December 31, 2017—that is, beginning in 2018. Because the 2018 tax returns will be filed in 2019, except for calculating quarterly estimated tax payments, most entities will apply the provisions sometime in 2019.

Under H.R.1, corporate provisions are generally permanent; they're not temporary. But the individual and trust provisions are due to sunset at the end of 2025.

The payroll provisions are effective as of January 1, 2018. There are changes that entities need to be thinking about now that affect payroll, even if the organization has a fiscal year end.

Why does the timing matter? Employee benefits are going to follow the individual's tax year, not the employer's tax year. The new unrelated taxable business income from the provision of qualified transportation benefits is effective for all benefits provided after 1/1/2018. Some adjustments to payrolls—such as individuals' tax rates—are also effective now.

Unrelated business income activity items may afford planners a little bit more time because they apply for 2018 or for the fiscal year that ends in 2019. However, organizations should pay attention to the change from graduated tax rates for corporations in 2017 to the flat 21 percent tax rate in 2018. Section 15 requires fiscal year corporations to calculate a blended tax rate between the graduated and the flat tax rate depending upon the number of days the corporate taxpayer has in each in each regime within its tax year.

Most of these provisions involve corporations because most not-for-profits are organized as corporations. However, if a not-for-profit is organized as a trust, its tax situation is affected for unrelated business income based on the trust rules. Private foundation clients may be organized as trusts subject to those implementation rules.

## STUDY QUESTION

---

**1.** Which of the following statements is correct regarding key timeframes and features of the *Tax Cuts and Jobs Act*?

    **a.** Provisions are generally effective for tax years beginning after December 31, 2017.

    **b.** The law was passed and signed on January 3, 2018.

    **c.** Corporate provisions remain temporary.

    **d.** Payroll provisions become effective on January 1, 2019.

---

# ¶ 305 ITEMIZED DEDUCTIONS AND CHARITABLE CONTRIBUTIONS

## Standard and Itemized Deductions

Planners are looking at how the tax cuts are affecting the charitable sector and its effects on giving. The new law doubles the standard deduction to $12,000 for single individual filers or $24,000 for married couples filing jointly. For 2018, the additional standard deduction for the aged or blind is $1,300. The increased deduction means that many individuals who formerly itemized deductions will not do so for 2018 returns. Those individuals formerly limited by what is known as the "Pease limitation" will benefit; if clients make large charitable gifts and have other itemized deductions of more than $24,000. Their itemized deduction is no longer subject to the Pease limitation and is 100 percent deductible but still subject to various limitations depending on the category of itemized deduction.

There are other limitations on itemized deductions. The new law imposes a $10,000 cap on deductions for state property and income taxes. If a taxpayer resides in a high-income tax state, like California or New York, that is going to be a drastic limitation for itemized deductions of state and local sales, property and income taxes paid. Some states have drafted legislation as a work around allowing taxpayers to make charitable contributions as a way to reduce the taxpayers state tax liability effectively converting a tax expense to a charitable contribution deduction which is subject to a much higher limitation. Also, donors who claimed a contribution deduction for gifts that secured preferable seating at college sporting events may no longer deduct such charitable gifts. The value of fundraising gala remains a non-deductible quid pro quo benefit to donors. The IRS also issued Notice 2017-73 providing guidance for donors with donor advised funds (DAFs) which states advising distributions out of a DAF which pays for all or part of attending fundraising galas will be an impermissible private benefit distribution from a DAF.

## Other Changes to Deductions

The provisions also limit the mortgage interest that can be taken, and taxpayers must use the home equity funds for improvements on their homes. The deduction of property-related interest moved downward from a $1 million cap to $750,000 on new acquisition indebtedness.

On the other hand, what may increase the amount of charitable contributions going into the itemized deduction pool is cash contributions to public charities. Taxpayers now have a 60 percent contribution base instead of 50 percent. The contribution base imposed taxpayers' adjusted gross income (AGI), is 60 percent which is an increase applied for both individuals and trusts. Gifts to private operating foundations, are subject to the same valuation and contribution base. Gifts to nonoperating foundations—taxpayers with their own private foundation eligible to make an out-of-corpus election—these are treated as conduit foundations. There are specific rules to be observed in making an out of corpus election. Such gifts would also get that 60 percent contribution base deduction. Code Sec. 170(b)(1)(A) drives which types of organizations gets the higher deductions. The higher contribution base does not apply to noncash gifts.

# ¶ 306  GIFTS MADE BY ESTATES

The estate exemption has doubled under the new tax law. It also has the inflation adjustment that kicked in in the beginning of 2011. For 2018, the individual transfer tax exemption is around $11.2 million ($22.4 for joint filers). Individuals still get to retain a stepped-up basis on bequeathed assets, so that's a really good tool for estates. But this provision could make high net worth individuals give more to their families instead of charities. Only time will tell.

Not all states tie their estate tax exclusion to the federal exclusion amount. This is an important concept. In the state of Washington, the estate tax exemption for 2018 is $2,193,00, not matched to the $11.2 million federal level. But there's no concept of a gift tax in Washington. Therefore, no state gift tax is imposed on inter vivos transfers which are under the annual federal limit even though the same transfer would be subject to state estate transfer tax if transferred as a bequest. For a Washington State resident, it's a great opportunity for high net worth individuals to do significant lifetime gifting. Perhaps people will be so used to doing lifetime gifting, they will also choose to do their charitable contribution gifting at the same time.

The individual and estate provisions sunset at the end of 2025. These terms apply right now, and the tax act states that "the Secretary shall prescribe such regulations as may be necessary or appropriate to carry out this section with respect to any difference between the basic exclusion . . . applicable at the time of the decedent's death, and the basic exclusion amount applicable with respect to any gifts made by the decedent." Such regulations have yet to be issued.

# ¶ 307  PROJECTED EFFECTS OF THE NEW LAW ON CHARITABLE GIVING

When economists, looked at the changes, they estimated that a third of individuals itemized prior to the Tax Act and now itemizing will decrease to 5 percent. Certain think tanks are projecting that converting itemizers to standard deduction takers whose tax rates are now lower will decrease charitable giving over time by $13 billion. The Tax Policy Center put the impact around $12 to $20 billion in 2018, and another $4 billion long-term with the increased exemption for the estate and gift tax. Only time will tell what's going to happen.

Table 3.1 gives a snapshot of plain vanilla taxpayers in 2018 who have one dependent child, are younger than age 65, don't have any income phaseouts, and various types of filing status. The table shows a $3,100 saving for a single individual. For a head of household, it would be over $12,000. Presumably taxpayers of any filing status are getting some tax savings, but again, this table is just modeling typical taxpayers.

**Table 3.1 Comparison of 2017 and 2018 Standard Deductions**

## Comparison of 2017 & 2018 Standard Deduction

| Filing Status | 2017 Standard Deduction | Exemption (Personal and Dependency) | 2017 Combined Amount | 2018 Standard Deduction | Credit* =Deduction @20% tax rate | 2018 Combined Amount | Change |
|---|---|---|---|---|---|---|---|
| Single | $6,350 | $4,050 | $10,400 | $12,000 | $300 =$1,500 | $13,500 | $3,100 |
| Married Filing Joint | $12,700 | $8,100 | $20,800 | $24,000 | $600 =$3,000 | $27,000 | $6,200 |
| Head of Household (assuming 1 child) | $9,350 | $8,100 | $17,450 | $18,000 | $2,300 =$11,500 | $29,500 | $12,050 |
| Married Filing Separate | $6,350 | $4,050 | $10,400 | $12,000 | $300 =$1,500 | $13,500 | $3,100 |

Assuming under income phase out levels, 1 dependent child, taxpayers under age 65

## STUDY QUESTIONS

**2.** Which of the following identifies one of the changes from the *Tax Cuts and Jobs Act* with respect to itemized deductions and charitable contributions that may affect charitable giving?

   **a.** Increase in individuals who itemize given change to state and local tax deductions

   **b.** Increase in the AGI limit to 75 percent on charitable contributions

   **c.** Increase of the estate and gift tax exclusion from $5 million to $10 million (not indexed for inflation)

   **d.** Preservation of the deduction for contributions to college sporting events

**3.** Which of the following identifies the standard deduction in 2018 for taxpayers who are married filing jointly?

    **a.** $9,350

    **b.** $12,700

    **c.** $17,450

    **d.** $24,000

---

# ¶ 308 NOT-FOR-PROFIT ORGANIZATIONS AS EMPLOYERS

Not all not-for-profit organizations have employees; some are very small and some involve only volunteers. This discussion focuses on organizations that have employees. Obviously, if a not-for-profit has employees, it needs to follow the *Employment Tax Law*. Formerly the organization under an IRS audit was subject to the concept of a "package audit"—basically, going through the payroll tax filings. Often, employment taxes was where the IRS found audit adjustments, rather than with any federal exempt tax issues or unrelated business income tax issues.

The *Tax Reform Act* made some changes to the taxability of certain employee benefits across the board. For-profit companies lose the deduction if they give their employees certain benefits. Congress felt it had to have a way of equalizing the tax treatment for not-for-profit organizations. This discussion talks about how the law attempts to equalize the tax treatment for the not-for-profit organizations because most organizations don't pay income tax unless they have an unrelated business income tax (UBIT) obligation.

Because of changes in the UBIT laws, some of these changes are very specific to not-for-profit employers. However, there are other provisions that are generic, and planners just need to be aware of them. Practitioners are going to be waiting for some guidance on those more generic matters as well.

Taxpayers are still waiting for guidance on the questions about how the transportation benefits and on-site athletic facilities should be applied. These benefits changed effective January 1, 2018, no matter what tax year the employer uses. If the organization uses a fiscal year, the new law's provision still applies as of January 1, 2018. Under the new law, if the employer provides qualified transportation benefits which are not taxable to the employee, the not-for-profit employer will be subject to unrelated business income. The only choice the not-for-profit has to avoid the tax is whether or not to provide qualified transportation benefits. The IRS issued Publication 15B providing guidance on employee benefits which are non-deductible to for-profit taxpayers and creating unrelated business income for not-for-profit employers. These benefits are either going to be treated as unrelated business income or taxable income if the employer is not providing the benefit as a qualified transportation benefit. Any unrelated business income is reported on line 12 of the Form 990-T. The only deductions which would be allowed would be any net operating loss carryforwards from prior tax periods, charitable contribution deductions which have not otherwise been utilized, and in future years, fees for prior year tax preparation services related to preparing the return reporting the income.

## Qualified Transportation and On-site Athletic Facilities

One major change under this provision is the creation of unrelated business income from the provision of "qualified transportation fringe benefits"—these income transit passes, bus passes, and qualified parking. These are "commuting fringe benefits" under Code Sec. 132(f). This benefit applies to transit between the employee's residence and workplace. Prior to Tax Reform, if the organization provided parking in its building and everyone received a parking pass valued under the annually indexed limit ($260 for 2018), that was typically, under the old law, qualified transportation fringe benefit. The benefit would not have been taxable to the employee if the employer paid for it and deductible to a for-profit employer and not subject to unrelated business income with respect to a not-for-profit taxpayer. That has changed.

The other piece is the provision of an on-premises athletic facility. This provision is very specific, and does not apply if, for example, the organization does not have "owners." This rule does not apply if the employer is not allowed a deduction. The employer would not be allowed deduction if the facilities is limited to use by owners of more than 10 percent of the organization. This is generally not applicable to not-for-profit organizations.

The question that arises is who pays for the benefit? If charged to the employer, costs are going to be taxable to the employee. Or the not-for-profit could pay UBIT on giving employees the tax-free benefits. If the employee pays for qualified transportation benefits using pretax dollars under a cafeteria plan, Publication 15B states on page 21, the qualified transportation benefits are non-deducible to the employer or in the case of the non-profit employer the amount paid through a compensation reduction agreement the amount would be subject to unrelated business income tax.

What information must an employer know to make a decision on how to proceed with transportation benefits? First, the value of the non-taxable fringe benefit excluded from compensation. Second, total cost paid or incurred to provide the non-taxable benefits. The organization's actual cost paid for these benefits for employees is what the law says would be actually subject to UBIT.

There has been discussion of employers providing transportation benefits as a taxable fringe benefit with the agreement of employees that it is being offered as a taxable fringe benefit and not as a section 132(f) non-taxable fringe benefit. If employees are subject to income tax on the benefit, would they choose to receive the benefit? Clients report that they have recently paid 100 percent of employees' bus passes, whether they use it or not. If the benefit constitutes taxable wages, some employees may say, "I don't need that bus pass, so I don't want that." If the benefits are currently being offered to the employees, again, who's paying for the benefits? Is the employer or is the employee financing the benefit through a payroll withholding? Figure 3.1 compares costs to the employer and employee.

> **EXAMPLE:** Clean Harvesting employs five individuals and offers $100 per month of transit card costs as a benefit to the employee. The transit cards cost $6,000 dollars for the whole year. If Clean Harvesting pays it, it's going to be taxed at 21 percent (the flat 21 percent for UBI). The total cost for Clean Harvesting, then, is $7,260; and there's no employee cost. This is the cost of granting employees that benefit.

**Option 1 Employer Pays UBI**

Corporate Employer Pays UBI

| | |
|---|---|
| Cost: Transit cards | $6,000 |
| Taxes ($6,000 × 21%) | $1,260 |
| | $7,260 |

No cost to employee

### Figure 3.1 Employer Payment of Transportation Costs

Option two is to make the benefit taxable to the employee (Figure 3.2). The employer still pays 7.65 percent for payroll tax. The figure shows there's about a $6,500 cost to the employer. The employee, assuming he or she is at a 20 percent tax rate plus payroll tax as well, means another $1,600. That total, between the employer and the employee, is more than $8,000. Thus, it would cost more to make the benefit taxable to the employee. However, some organizations that have a lot of employees may not be able to afford paying all those benefits and paying the tax on benefits.

### Figure 3.2 Option 2 Taxable Benefit to Employee

| | |
|---|---|
| Transit card | $6,000 |
| 7.65% payroll tax | 459 |
| Cost to employer | $6,459 |
| | |
| Employee (20% tax rate) | |
| Income tax | $1,200 |
| 7.65% payroll tax | 459 |
| Cost to employee | $1,659 |

# ¶ 309  HIGHLY COMPENSATED EMPLOYEES

## Excise Tax

The provisions under the new law mandate that, if an employee gets paid in excess of $1 million annually, a 21 percent excise tax applies on the excess compensation. The for-profit rule is that the organization doesn't get to take that deduction if the company pays certain covered employees more than $1 million. But the not-for-profit rules, include a countering provision: an excise tax. This excise tax just happens to be the same amount as a corporate tax on those amounts of compensation. Guidance is lacking to date for how an organization would pay this tax. However, it is likely going to be on Form 4720 as this is the excise tax form where most excise taxes are remitted by not-for-profits.

The tax is generally going to apply to the top five employees, the "covered employees." The tricky part is once an individual is classified as a covered employee for one year, he or she is a covered employee forever. Thus, an organization may wind up having more than five covered employees each year as time passes. This is just one, of many areas needing guidance. A big university system, hospital or other complex organization paying large salaries has the potential to have significant deferred compensation. Any organization with large compensation packages should track the five covered employees for all future periods. This reporting and taxation may be complicated and it will be easier to keep contemporary records of who the top five compensated covered employees were each year.

Including the filing organization, the terms also include the related organizations. Again, for big hospital systems that may encompass 60 entities. Complex organizations may have to figure out some mechanism for tracking all of the compensation across multiple entities. "Compensation" includes parachute payments and deferred compensation. The provisions do exclude certain licensed medical professionals, such as veterinarians. If the person is an administrator for a hospital and also practices medicine in the non-profit hospital, it's currently unclear how much he or she would have to practice medicine to meet the carve-out provisions excluding medical professionals from the excise tax. The rules don't specify what the limit is if a provider practices medicine regularly or went on rounds once a month, once a week, or once a year.

One of the areas that is really fascinating is that the law did not close a loophole around this benefit for quasi-governmental organizations. If an organization is tax exempt under Code Sec. 115(1)—for example, the University of Washington, Washington State University, or Ohio State, basically a governmental organization created by the state—this provision actually may not apply to the school. Thus, for college athletics, the football coaches in state schools with salaries above $1 million, the state school may not be subject to the excise tax. However, for coaches working at private schools, these salaries would be subject to the excise tax.

## Other Benefits No Longer Excluded from Income

There are other benefits that are no longer excluded from income of employees. Tax exempt organizations do not have an option to pay UBIT in lieu of treating benefits as taxable income to employees. These benefits are taxable to employees of for-profit and not-for-profit employers alike. The benefits are not subject to UBIT by not-for-profit employers.

If a business meal expense amount is an UBI expense or related to a private foundation's net investment income expense under Code Sec. 4940, the expense is going to be disallowed as a deduction if it is related to entertainment unless the expense is reimbursed under a non-accountable plan and included in reasonable compensation. The amount paid for "entertaining meals" gets excluded from allowable deductions after December 31, 2017. Business meals are still subject to the 50 percent limitation so long as they are not associated with entertainment expenses. The taxable benefits include payments for moving, relocation expenses, membership dues with social clubs, and reimbursement of certain meals which are associated with entertainment that used to be subject to a 50 percent limitation.

However, although those types of expenses are not allowed for purposes Code Sec. 4940 or under unrelated business income; they may still be qualifying distributions. If the organization is a private foundation, the benefits may still go into qualifying distributions under Code Sec. 4942, or they may still be charitable expenses. They are not a taxable expenditure; they are still charitable if they are for the benefit of employees or fulfill a charitable purpose.

## STUDY QUESTION

**4.** Which of the following statements does *not* apply to the tax impacts of the new tax law on highly compensated employees?

    **a.** It generally applies to the compensation of the top five employees.

    **b.** Exempt organizations paying compensation of more than $1 million will be subject to a 21 percent excise tax.

    **c.** It includes parachute payments.

    **d.** It includes certain licensed medical professionals.

# ¶ 310 UNRELATED BUSINESS INCOME

Unrelated business income is the hot topic for not-for-profit clients. Under the new law, a corporation is now taxed at a flat rate of 21 percent. Although it's commonly referred to as a "reduced rate of 21 percent," most organizations that are not-for-profits were able to take advantage of the graduated tax rates under the old rules. If an organization had UBI of less than $15,000 in a tax year, the not-for-profit actually had a 15 percent rate instead of a 21 percent rate. Some organizations, therefore, will see their tax rate actually go up, if the entities are corporations.

## Fiscal Year Organizations in 2018

If a not-for-profit is a corporation with fiscal year end, a blended tax rate is imposed for the fiscal year ending in 2018 because there was a change in the corporate tax rates. There is some discussion as to whether this applies to new taxes such as the new UBI income stream created from subjecting qualified transportation benefits such as parking provided to employees. However, although the income stream is new the tax is not, the blended tax rates are imposed on the unrelated business income, for the first fiscal year end rather than just using the new flat 21 percent tax rate. This may result in a higher rate, so tax is calculated pro rata, as a straddle based upon the number of months which fall in each calendar year covered by the fiscal year of the organization.

## Trusts Versus Corporations

For trusts, between 2018 and 2025, Table 3.2 goes through the graduated rates. If a trust has income of more than $12,500, it is going to pay the top 37 percent rate right away. (The trust's rate was previously 39.6 percent.) Keep in mind that trusts get the benefit of the capital gains rate. A trust that gets UBI generated from debt finance, such as alternative investments, and the income includes capital gains, does not pay tax on the entire income at the 37 percent rate but at a lower rate because of the 20 percent top capital gains rate.

Table 3.2 Comparison of Trust and Corporate Tax Rates

## Unrelated Business Income Tax - Corporation or Trust?
- **Corporate tax rate reduced to flat 21% (blended rate for FY taxpayers)**

| Trusts - 2018-2025* | | * Favorable 0/15/20% capital gains rates still apply |
|---|---|---|
| Trusts not over $2,550 | 10% of the taxable income | |
| Over $2,550 | but not over $9,150 | $255 plus 24% of the excess over $2,550 |
| Over $9,150 | but not over $12,500 | $1,839 plus 35% of the excess over $9,150 |
| Over $12,500 | $3,011.50 | plus 37% of the excess over $12,500 |

\* (0% capital gain up to $2,600; 15% up to $12,500; then 20%)

The other piece of this new tax rule for a corporation versus a trust is that the alternative minimum tax (AMT) went away for corporations but did not for trusts. Corporations are no longer subject to any AMT, but trusts are subject to AMT. Also, applicable for trusts are the passive activity loss rules, suspended, basis limitations, and suspended losses. Code Secs. 465 and 469 cover items that get lumped in under trusts. They do not apply in the corporate structure. For a not-for-profit that is a private foundation, it could be different.

Another consideration for trusts is the 60 percent charitable deduction limit for contributions. A private foundation that makes lots of grants to public charities and has lots of UBI could take a 60 percent deduction of that UBI on a Form 990-T return for the trust, but for a corporation, the deduction is just 10 percent of its taxable income.

**PLANNING POINTER:** Even though the tax rates are higher for a trust than a corporation, because of that fact, it's actually more beneficial for certain private foundations to be trusts. They'll have a significant tax savings in that trust structure. This entity choice does make the organization's Form 990-T much more complicated, but there is a benefit of more than it would cost to prepare a Form 990-T.

These changes in UBIT rules mean that organizations that elect to pay for qualified employee benefits will have UBI instead of considering them to be taxable compensation. That new UBI revenue stream must be included on Form 990-T. A lot more organizations are going to be filing 990-Ts, just because of that, than before.

## Separate Business Lines

The other rule that has been changed under the new law is the requirement to isolate income and losses from separate business lines, separate trade or businesses. The losses from one business line cannot offset the income from another. Expressed

**¶310**

another way, the losses from one business line are not going to be allowed to offset the income from the other. What does that look like?

**EXAMPLE:** Isaiah Stern runs a bagel shop and has another facility as a personal property rental. His personal property rental runs at a big loss, and the bagel shop is running out of income. In 2018 Isaiah can't net those losses together as he used to be able to do. His losses from each get isolated in each bucket. The losses may be carried forward as net operating losses (NOLs) to offset income for future periods, but they may not be able to be used for other different business activities. This whole isolation of trade or business lines is in need of IRS guidance.

The new tax law discusses a "trade or business," which for purposes of unrelated business income, is defined in Code Sec. 513 as a business regularly carried on, not for an exempt purpose but for profit. It is a Code Sec. 513 trade or business. A common example is running a shop or restaurant, which is a business under the new law. Other revenue streams are just deemed UBI. Debt finance property is covered under Code Sec. 514. Rental income that comes from leveraged assets is deemed UBI. This new fringe benefit rule is just deemed unrelated business income. Code Sec. 512(b)(13), transactions with certain related organizations, is deemed unrelated business income. The items that are just deemed UBI are not a trade or business. The question for the IRS is, can all that income be in its own bucket, and not have to be in a silo? Those items could all net with each other.

Pooling would be very beneficial for organizations that get UBI from alternative investments. For alternative investments, the only reason why they have unrelated business income is because there's some sort of debt inside of it; if it's leveraged, the individual could just pool those together. However, pooling does not help with income actually earned running a trade or business. Will a taxpayer be able to group all oil and gas income? If inside the alternative investment the taxpayer has a conglomerate of different things all rolled up or has stacked partnership, does the partnership have to tell the individual all the different business lines that are inside it to let him or her know how to silo them? How can the individual isolate them? If a client has alternative investments and has UBI coming from more than one stream, preparing the client's return is more complex. Planners will have to take a position on how to handle different trade or businesses.

## Net Operating Losses

Net operating loss rules are applicable in a corporate regime or a trust regime based on the type of entity. Here the focus is mostly on the corporate rules because they are what applies the most to not-for-profit organizations.

Corporate losses created after January 1, 2018, may no longer be carried back to the prior year's return. There are a few exceptions, but for the most part they can't be carried back. NOLs can be carried forward indefinitely. But those carry-forwards are isolated going forward to each business line. If an individual's business line is a coffee shop, the new law says an NOL can only stay with the coffee shop's profits and losses. It can't offset income somewhere else.

The NOL deduction for any business line is limited to 80 percent of taxable income. If an individual had a loss in 2018 from the coffee shop, and in 2019 the shop earns income, the owner can't offset that loss 100 percent to the income in 2019 but may be limited to offsetting 80 percent. When a taxpayer has taxable income, he or she is always going to be paying tax on something.

Having to do that math for every single business line, planners are not going to be simply able to calculate specifically what the UBI is. The other consideration is how to handle estimated tax payments for 2018, because these rules are currently applicable.

Formerly, taxpayers having large NOLs realized they had income but could just move forward and assume no estimated tax payments were necessary. But under the new law, taxpayers are likely to have some UBI.

The AMT has been eliminated, but under the AMT rules for corporations in that regime, the rule limited income to 90 percent of NOLs. Now organizations are in an AMT-esque situation, even though there is no corporate AMT. The new provisions are very similar to the old AMT rules. Taxpayers may have to carry forward the NOLs to income from future sources because of the NOL "80 percent limitation." The corporation may deduct NOLs in a single year equal to the lesser of the available NOL carryover or 80 percent of a corporation's pre-NOL deduction taxable income.

Another question that arises is what to do with losses from 2017 and prior years. Does the taxpayer have to isolate them per business? The law does not require doing so, but it doesn't explain how to allocate those losses. Planners could take a tax position that they are going to allocate old losses to revenue streams that emerge in 2018 and future years. That position would apply for losses that occurred before December 31, 2017.

# ¶ 311 DONOR ACKNOWLEDGMENT OF CHARITABLE CONTRIBUTIONS

There was a change under the *Tax Cuts and Jobs Act* related to donor acknowledgments. Before the new tax law, an older provision under Code Sec. 170(f)(8) had language requiring organizations to provide a contemporaneous written acknowledgment (CWA) letter to donors or follow an alternative method that the IRS would later proscribe. Revenue procedure rulings, guidance issued before the new law, said that the alternative method would require recipients to provide all donors with something that resembled a Form 1099. It would have the donor's Social Security number on it, how much the donor contribution was, and his or her address. The requirement created an uproar, because donors did not wish this highly sensitive information to be provided to the IRS. Organizations didn't want to ask their donors for that much data. The IRS pulled back that guidance.

## Case Law

A number of court cases involved organizations that have tried to use alternative methods and use that information as a reason to get a charitable deduction under Code Sec. 170. Congress removed this language after much confusion. The courts couldn't litigate around it, so that requirement is gone, which is good.

Currently, the new law's requirement removed the confusing language of Code Sec. 170(f)(8), providing that not-for-profit organizations must issue some sort of written acknowledgment of gifts of more than $250 if the donor wants to claim a charitable contribution. If taxpayers are itemizing charitable contributions, it is the donor's responsibility to receive documentation before filing a tax return.

The standard language of the acknowledgment, remaining basically unchanged in 2018, must state assurance that the donor received no goods or services in return for the contribution. If the organization has quid pro quo items, such as preferred meals or entertainment at a special event or raffle prizes, then the not-for-profit must provide a donor acknowledgement letter providing a description and value for the goods or services received associated with the donation. If the contribution exceeds $75 and there is a quid pro quo element, the donee is required to have an actual donor receipt that states the value of the quid pro quo items.

Why are these requirements important? The IRS is winning routinely on foot faults, and the acknowledgment requirements are basically low-hanging fruit. The court cases examine whether the payroll is done wrong, the organization doesn't provide the right donor acknowledgment letter, or they have done the letter wrong and the IRS denies the whole or the bulk of the contributor's deduction.

Some of these charitable donations are very large, and those for which donors and recipients typically commit a foot fault on are the ones that are not plain vanilla—not just the cash ones, they're the noncash items.

Table 3.3 contains a grid of some of the major court cases and the results.

### Table 3.3 Important Court Cases Involving Donor Acknowledgments

| Case | Result | Case | Result |
|---|---|---|---|
| **15 West 17th Street LLC v. Comm, 147 T.C. No. 19** | $64.5 million deduction denied due to no CWA, amended 990 does not fix issue | **McGradey, Phyllis (2016) TC Memo 2016-233** | Reduced donation because CWA didn't include returned benefit to taxpayer |
| **French Bayne, TC Memo 2016-53** | Deduction denied due to CWA dated after taxpayer return filed | **Boone Operations Co LLC (2013) TC Memo 2013-101** | Bargain sale that lacked good faith estimate over goods/ services received |
| **Izen, Joe Jr. No 5 (2017) 148 TC** | Deduction of a 40-year old aircraft donation denied due to 1098-C and issues with CWA | **Longino, John (2013) TC Memo 2013-80** | Denied deduction due to no CWA Taxpayer created acknowledgment letter and it was insufficient |
| **Betty Kendrix v. Comm, TC Memo 2006-9 (Former IRS Agent)** | Denied over "good or services" language and adequate description | **Kapadpodis, Gust (2014) TC Memo 2014-2015** | Denied deduction due to CWA, lack of dates and other required info |
| | | **Bayne French, et ux., TC Memo 2016-53** | Donor letter was dated *after* the date of their personal tax return, was therefore not "contemporaneous," and was missing quid pro quo language Deduction denied |
| **15 West 17th Street LLC v. Comm'r 147 T.C. No. 19** | CWA lacked statement "no goods or services were provided in exchange for the contribution" | **RERI Holdings I, LLC v. Comm'r 149 T.C. No. 1** | Partnership failed to provide basis information on Form 8283 Purchased remainder interest in property for $2.95 million Donated it and claimed deduction of $33 million |
| **Costello, David (2015) TC Memo 2015-87** | $5.5 million deduction denied due to significant omissions in appraisal | **Logan, Chandler (2014) 142 TC 279** | Denied deduction; relied on noncredible expert analysis |
| **Mecox Partners, LP v. U.S. (2016, SDNY)** | Conservation easement 60-day rule wasn't met and deduction denied | **Ben Alli v. Comm, TC Memo 2014-15** | Denied deduction for portion that didn't have qualified appraisal |
| **Issacs, James (2015) TC Memo 2015-121** | $245,000 deduction denied due to lack of appraisal info | **Friedman, Newton (2010) TC Memo 2010-45** | Denied deduction due to insufficient descriptions in the appraisal |
| **Zarlengo, Marco (2014) TC Memo 2014-161** | $330,000 deduction partially denied because appraisal was premature | **Reither, Robert v. U.S. (2012, DC NM)** | Contribution denied when Forms 8283 were not properly completed |

¶311

In *15 West 17th Street,* a $64.5 million deduction was denied because there was no contemporaneous written acknowledgement (CWA) letter. The taxpayer and the charity tried to amend the Form 990, adding the name of that donation on the Form 990 and claimed it constituted notification of the IRS. They were following the provision under Code Sec. 170(f)(8) that discusses use of an alternative method. The court ruled that alternative method doesn't work, as the IRS has held.

In *Big River Development LP v. Commissioner,* the developer's partnership actually won this case based on Code Sec. 170(f)(8). The developer had acknowledgment in the deed. This was a conservation easement that contained all the special language in the deed, fulfilling the substantiation requirement under Code Sec. 170(f)(8). That will not work anymore; under the new law, it's super important to have the donor acknowledgment letters. It's also really important if the donor is looking at the appraisal rules.

The IRS is winning routinely on foot faults when donors and recipients do not have the proper documentation for a big gift, especially a noncash item. For example, in *Izen, Joe Jr.,* the deduction for a donation of a 40-year-old aircraft was denied because of issues with Form 1098-C and lack of proper CWA. In *Betty Kendrix v. Comm,* the deduction was denied because the donation's paperwork failed to adequately describe the donation and provide "good or services" language. In *Reri Holdings I, LLL v. Comm'r* and *Reithner, Robert v. U.S.,* denial of contributions was due to Forms 8283 that were not properly completed. A post-date problem of CWA resulted in a denial in the *French Bayne* case.

Protection is afforded in some of these ways: if a professional appraisal is provided by a qualified appraiser, if a Form 1098-C is completed for a vehicle donation, and the timing of substantiation is done appropriately. These are all issues that the IRS has been using to win at court, especially in questions of a contribution's valuation. Courts are not sympathetic at all when donors and charities fail to have CWA. The planner who receives an appraisal for a noncash donation should consult the regulations and verify, line by line, that the form is properly completed; usually, it must be returned for updates or signatures. The new tax law, because it revised provisions of Code Sec. 170(f)(8), may make it easier for the IRS to litigate donation claims if the donor acknowledgment letter was not properly prepared.

## Responsibility of the Charity

From the charity's standpoint, the organization typically receives a Form 8283, which an officer needs to sign. All the form does is verify the description of the property received and who the donor was. The officer just looks at the form from the donor and concurs with the correct description of the condition and what the property was. The charity is not signing off on the value, just what was received. It's important to pay attention to that piece and not as much to the value. The charity may have recorded in its books a different value for an in-kind item. The organization shouldn't get into the business of providing tax advice; the deduction claimed is an issue between the individual and the tax advisor, not the charity.

## STUDY QUESTION

---

**5.** Which of the following cases resulted in denial of a deduction because the contemporaneous written acknowledgment date was listed as after the taxpayer filed the return?

    **a.** *Izen, Joe Jr. No 5* (2017) 148 TC

    **b.** *Betty Kendrix v. Comm,* TC Memo 2006-9

    **c.** *French Bayne,* TC Memo 2016-53

    **d.** *15 West 17th Street LLC v. Comm,* 147 T.C. No. 19

---

# ¶ 312 DONOR ADVISED FUNDS IN NOTICE 2017-73

Donor advised fund provisions are not part of the new tax act, but this is current event information from IRS Notice, 2017-73. What the IRS tried to do is take the temperature of how the sector feels about guidance on donor advised funds.

Donor advised funds have been around for a long time. They were defined statutorily back in 2006 under the *Pension Protection Act.* At that time, Congress issued the definition and the code section, and referred the specifics to the IRS to issue regulations. Well, the IRS has not issued regulations yet. Because the new law creates the need to revise the tax code, new regulations for the funds may come out soon. But back in September 2017 the IRS did release Notice 2017-73. That followed a notice earlier in the year that requested public commentary and feedback. The later notice examines three important issues:

- Section 3: Ticket purchase with a quid pro quo value to a donor was made impermissible

- Section 4: Satisfaction of a personal pledge out of a donor advised fund was deemed permissible

- Section 5: Change to the way Code Sec. 509(a)(1) and (2) public charities should calculate public support when they receive certain funds from a donor advised fund

In donor advised funds, the individual is giving a completed gift to a sponsoring organization of a donor advised fund. The discussion here uses the example of a community foundation. The individual actually gives the money to a community foundation that is going into a fund over which the donor, or related persons, have advisory rights. The donor has the right to dictate how the funds are invested or retains the right to direct funds.

The sponsoring organization is the community foundation, a Code Sec. 501(c)3 entity receiving the donation that actually has variance power, ultimate control. If a donor gives funds to a donor advised fund, the community foundation that rejects the use for the money that the donor prefers, the fund may do so. The fund may also reject use of the donation for noncharitable purposes.

Donor advised funds involve some dos and don'ts disallowing more than an incidental benefit to the donor. A donor can't get more than an incidental benefit from that charity.

**EXAMPLE:** Teresa Malloy gives money to the local Women's Advocacy donor advised fund. She wants to direct the funds to support the organization's gala in 2018. Directing the money is impermissible because Teresa would get more than an incidental benefit when she attended the gala and partook in the food and beverages.

Section 3 of Notice 2017-73 addresses that subject. It disallows donors to direct their contribution for the charitable portion of an event or service. This applies even when the donor offers to personally pay for a meal or service (the quid pro quo piece). Section 3 mirrors Private Letter Ruling 9021066, which applies to private foundations controlled by corporations. The notice grants donors only advisory privileges and makes all assets the property of the sponsoring organization, prohibiting more than incidental value to a donor. The IRS is trying to bring in some concepts here from the private foundation rules to the public charity sphere. The rules make it impermissible for donors to bifurcate the quid pro quo portion and the rest of the donation.

Section 4 provides that under certain circumstances, a donor advised fund can satisfy the pledges of the donor. In Notice 2017-73, the IRS allows use of a donor advised fund to satisfy the donor's personal pledge. This section actually relieves the burden on recipients of charities. For tax purposes, as long as the other conditions are met, charities may accept gifts to satisfy pledges. Donors do not attempt to claim a Code Sec. 170 deduction, because they already received one when they gave funds to the donor advised fund. If a public charitable organization is controlled by one person, it may be a private operating foundation, and any abuse should be addressed. Also, there are rules under "unusual grant" so that a gift doesn't tip a charity into private foundation status. Further guidance is forthcoming.

Section 5 is quite burdensome on public charities when a donation is not a completed gift. When the money goes in to the donor advised fund and the donor gets the deduction, the donor considers it a completed gift. But the IRS position is not to allow the donor to use a donor advised fund in order to not tip a public charity into private foundation status. The IRS wants public charities to do their public result tests to examine all the donations received from donor advised funds. If a charity can see what fund was the source of the money or from what individual it came, the charity must determine whether it tips the charity into private foundation status. Does the money make the charity fall below 33.3 percent required to be publicly supported? If it would, or if the funds would get the charity close to that level, the organization is supposed to count the donor as an excess contributor. If it's not a close call, the charity need not bother. The charity is going to have to do some sort of analysis.

On the flip side, if a charity has anonymous gifts from multiple donor advised funds, it should lump all the anonymous gifts together and treat them as one contributor. If that circumstance is going to tip the charity into private foundation status, the charity considers it an excess contributor. The IRS has stated that if the charity can prove the anonymous gifts are not from the same person, then the donations wouldn't have to be lumped together. The charity would have to perform some due diligence— again, administratively burdensome for the charity. Truly, these gifts from donor advised funds are technically coming from a public charity, a sponsoring organization, a community foundation. Most of the funds are public charities under Code Sec. 509(a)(1), and when 509(a)(1) money is given to another public charity under the same code section, it's good public charity money. It's not limited to the excess contributor limitations applied for the public support test.

When donor advised funds give to private foundations and other Code Sec. 501(c)(3) organizations, the sponsoring organization (community foundation) has to perform "expenditure responsibility" and verify that the funds were indeed used for charitable purposes. A donor advised fund may undertake foreign activity. The sponsoring organization does an equivalency determination or expenditure responsibility on behalf of donors, performing the due diligence when the funds are given to a foreign entity that is not a Code Sec. 501(c)(3) U.S. public charity.

The general rule of thumb for private foundations, public charities, or any charitable giving is that a donor should be allowed to make a contribution indirectly that he or she may make directly.

## STUDY QUESTION

**6.** Which of the following identifies a characteristic of Section 3 of Notice 2017-73 with respect to donor advised funds?

    **a.** It may be relied upon by taxpayers until further guidance is issued

    **b.** This section is burdensome on recipient charities

    **c.** Donors only have advisory privileges, and all assets are the property of the sponsoring organization

    **d.** The IRS may want to consider another solution similar to the penalty on private foundations that "tip" to a public charity

## ¶ 313 CENTRALIZED PARTNERSHIP AUDIT REGIME

The centralized partnership audit regime provision came about from the *Bipartisan Budget Act of 2015*. The 2017 budget reconciliation, approved by the Senate for 2018, came out of the 2015 act. The provision is that all partnerships are going to be taxed at the partnership level rather than looking through to tax returns of all the individual partners.

Before the 2015 act, if the IRS audit of a partnership found any adjustments to be made, the IRS would have to go to each individual partner to seek that adjustment. The 2015 act said that effective for years starting in 2018, the IRS is going to audit at the partnership level, with the ability to make an adjustment at the partnership level. Rules were forthcoming for how the partnership is going to deal with that.

In 2017 the Treasury Department proposed and final regulations were issued on partnership taxation. There have been proposed regs; there have been final regs. However, the AICPA asked for implementation of these rules to be delayed because a lot of organizations are not prepared administratively. Most partnership agreements need to be amended for these rules.

The reason this issue is important in 2018 is that partners may not be aware that they are subject to these rules. Also, if the IRS audits the partnership, examiners are going to seek to apply the highest tax rate. Now, it would be 21 percent, or it would be 37 percent for the individuals. The partners in a public charity would have owed zero. The charity needs to have an advocate that purports the entity in a partnership should not be subject to that high tax rate. Therefore, the tax liability should decrease because the partnership has different types of partners, corporate and other types.

A partnership advocate is now called a "partnership representative." Formerly, per partnership agreements, there was a tax matters partner for these issues; now, there is the partnership representative. This role has more elements to it than a tax matters partner. Only certain people can qualify as a partnership representative: a natural person, a U.S. person in the United States. The representative has to be available and able to act on behalf of the partnership to make these determinations. The representative is more powerful than the former tax matters partner.

The partnership representative should be provided for in the partnership agreement. If the partnership doesn't name one, the IRS can appoint one, but he or she should be aware of the needs of all the partners. The representative will be the sole person communicating with the IRS about the Centralized Partnership Audit Regime (CPAR).

Problematic with this regime is that partners may leave the partnership and new ones may join after returns for 2018 are filed. By the time the IRS audits the partnership's Form 1065 return, a new partnership representative may be in place with whom an exempt organization should communicate. Thus, one suggestion is for not-for-profit organizations to send customized letters to all partnerships involved to determine whether the entity is a corporation or trust or operating foundation. The organization alerts partnerships about the entity's treatment, advising partnerships on the CPAR rules. The letter requests annual notification on the current partnership representative and whether the partnership has elected out of the CPAR.

Special opt-out rules for corporate partnerships having less than a certain amount of people or a certain number of partners disallow certain types of partners. An exempt organization that's a trust can't opt out of the CPAR rules. Also, an exempt organization may not want automatic withholding of income taxes for your entity at the federal or the state tax level.

The regulations require that if there's an election made to opt out, within 30 days of making the election or filing the return, each partner must be notified. The letter's language might say, "Please notify us on the partnership representative, and please let us know if you're electing out, preferably within 30 days." If the partnership doesn't tell the exempt organization, it basically hasn't made an effective election. That actually protects the partnership from making that election.

---

**CPE NOTE:** When you have completed your study and review of chapters 1-3, which comprise Module 1, you may wish to take the Final Exam for this Module. Go to **cchcpelink.com/printcpe** to take this Final Exam online.

---

**¶313**

# MODULE 2: BUSINESS COMPLIANCE ISSUES—Chapter 4: Section 199A Qualified Business Deduction

## ¶ 401 WELCOME

This chapter discusses the principles and evolving regulations under the *Tax Cuts and Jobs Act* (H.R. 1) passed in 2017 for deductions under Code Sec. 199A that affect service and nonservice businesses other than C corporations starting in 2018.

## ¶ 402 LEARNING OBJECTIVES

Upon completion of this chapter, you will be able to:

- Recognize what a qualified business is and how the deduction on income of flow-through entities functions
- Identify service and nonservice businesses and how the deductions differ for each type
- Recognize how the new tax law changes ancillary tax issues of qualified businesses

## ¶ 403 INTRODUCTION

The Code Sec. 199A rules establish three types of limitations for deductions on qualified business income. The first is a general computation of 20 percent deduction for "qualified business income" before tax-favored gains, such as net capital gains. A second limitation is that the deduction cannot exceed 20 percent of the taxpayer's taxable income for the year reduced by any net capital gains included in that taxable income. Finally, a third limitation may apply to a taxpayer called a "threshold income taxpayer." For threshold income taxpayers, there are two branches that come off of that. There is one branch that applies to service businesses and another applies to nonservice businesses. The allowed deduction for service businesses may become zero simply based on the level of taxable income. The allowed deduction for nonservice businesses operated by threshold income taxpayers is based on the amount of W-2 wages and the unadjusted basis is qualifying property used in the business.

A "threshold income taxpayer" is one who has taxable income in excess of $315,000 if they are married filing a joint return and one-half of that, or $157,500, otherwise. The computations which we will illustrate later depend on how far past the threshold level the taxpayer is. If a married filing joint taxpayer has taxable income of $415,000 or more they will be referred to as a "full threshold taxpayer." This figure is one-half of that number, or $207,500, for any other status. Full threshold taxpayers may end up with zero deduction if they are operating a service business.

So the basic structure is that eligible businesses get a 20 percent deduction for qualified business income. What is meant by business income? Oddly enough, the statute did not provide a definitive answer to that question. Proposed regulations issued in August 2018 say that the definition of a business found in Code Sec. 162 will define a business. This is a commonly used definition, but it may still raise questions when applied to specific operations. For threshold income taxpayers, it is also necessary to identify each business as a service business or a nonservice business.

As noted above, the allowed deduction cannot exceed 20 percent of the taxable income reduced by any net capital gain. Under Code Sec. 1222, "net capital gain" is the excess of long-term gains over long-term losses. Practitioners net short-term and short-term gains and losses separately. Under Code Sec. 1231, if net 1231 gains exceed losses, those also get carried over as long-term capital gains.

So basically, if a client is going to get a 20 percent tax rate, the IRS is not going to allow double-dipping by also giving the client a 20 percent deduction from that 20 percent tax rate. So clients are going to have to deal with whatever the ordinary tax rate is to get a 20 percent deduction.

The break is available to any taxpayer other than a C corporation, because the whole purpose of this is that the *Tax Cuts and Jobs Act* passed in 2017 created a dramatic reduction, a 40 percent reduction in the corporate tax rate, from 35 percent to 21 percent in the maximum tax rate applicable to C corporations; that is a 40 percent reduction on that 35 percent base. Given these substantial tax breaks to C corporations, practitioners should realize that five out of six businesses in the United States are not C corporations. So to create some type of a benefit for business taxpayers, the tax law had to do it in some manner that does not affect just C corporations. This is what Congress did; this Code Sec. 199A set of rules is what the members devised.

This chapter explores which types of business income qualify for the deduction, how service and nonservice businesses are distinguished, and which taxpayers are considered threshold income taxpayers. Numerous examples illustrate how the rules apply to flow-through entities such as S corporations and partnerships.

# ¶ 404 QUALIFIED BUSINESS INCOME

## What Is a Business?

The number one feature of "qualified business income" (QBI) is that it has to be from a "business." Sound obvious? The problem is that the tax code provides a lot of definitions of what a business means. Proposed regulations adopt the definition in Code Sec. 162, which provides rules about ordinary and necessary trade or business expenses. Congress gave absolutely no guidance in the new tax law about what constitutes a business so the Treasury adopted the most commonly used definition. However, Code Sec. 199A does include interest income if it relates to the trade or business and excludes such income if it does not. The proposed regulations expand upon this, stating that interest on working capital is not connected to the business and will not be part of qualified business income. In contrast, interest earned on accounts receivable will be part of the qualified business income. Qualified real estate investment trust (REIT) dividends and publicly traded partnership (PTP) income are also eligible for the 20 percent deduction. QBI does not include capital gain or loss or dividend income.

The deduction limitation is taxable income before any "net capital gain" defined in Code Sec. 1211(11), and it basically constitutes the amount carried over to Code Sec. 1(h), the favorable rates are granted for net capital gains. Net capital gains qualify for the 20 percent deduction.

So if there is no change from the business definition used in the proposed regulations, the new law will require that we assess cases and other authority under Code Sec. 162. Recalling when the net investment income tax (NIIT) was enacted back in 2013, one way to avoid that tax is to show that the income in question comes from a business in which the taxpayer materially participates. The regulations under Code Sec. 1411 and Code Sec. 469 for passive activity losses (described later) use the Code Sec. 162 definition, so it is doubtful that Code Sec. 199A will deviate from it.

# ¶ 405 TAXABLE INCOME PLANNING

Two different issues pertain to planning for taxable income: what happens when the taxable income limitation applies and what happens if the threshold income limitation applies. Examples will illustrate the planning strategies for both.

**EXAMPLE:** Harry Hofmeyer is a taxpayer who has QBI of $200,000 and taxable income of $180,000. Normally, his tax planner would take 20 percent of the QBI and deduct $40,000. But because Harry is limited to 20 percent of taxable income, he can only claim $36,000.

Why is his taxable income less than QBI? Under the new tax law, this computation works by using a different-looking page 2 of Form 1040. So Harry's planner starts with adjusted gross income (AGI) just like under the old law. Taxpayers are no longer going to have personal exemptions, dependency exemptions, but under the new law there is the choice between itemized deductions or the standard deduction.

The planner ends up with a taxable income number before the QBI deduction and claims the qualified business income deduction. Harry is married filing a joint return, and he and wife Cecilia have QBI of $200,000, $4,000 of interest income, and a standard deduction of $24,000 (for married couples filing jointly). That standard deduction is bringing the taxable income down to $180,000 and the number is going to be limited to $36,000.

So what does Harry's planner do about that? Doing absolutely nothing is one option. The other possibility is if Harry can boost taxable income, the planner can actually increase that QBI deduction. As in all of the examples that explore planning ideas, when limitations apply, the experienced planner is always going to be looking for inflection points.

"Inflection points" are the points when planners flip from one limitation to another. So right now, the limitation is based on taxable income. If planners start blowing up taxable income, at some point they will reach a level where the limit becomes 20 percent of QBI.

**EXAMPLE:** Harry's planner realizes that if they can add another $20,000 of taxable income to Harry and Cecilia's taxable income, the limitation based on taxable income will be exactly equal to what it is for the QBI deduction. The planner suggests doing a traditional to Roth IRA conversion of $20,000, so the taxable income becomes $200,000, and the QBI deduction moves from $36,000 to $40,000. By boosting the taxable income, the planner increases the QBI deduction. The net effect is that the $20,000 additional taxable income for the Roth IRA after the QBI deduction is only $16,000.

Harry and the planner consider this option in more detail. Harry's taxable income prior to the qualified business income deduction in the original fact pattern was $180,000, and then the planner had a $36,000 QBI deduction. Harry would have ended up with $144,000 of net taxable income. In this situation, taxable income before the QBI deduction is $200,000. Harry gets a $40,000 QBI deduction, so he ends up with $160,000 of taxable income. The original $144,000 of taxable income becomes $160,000. By doing a $20,000 Roth conversion, Harry has increased taxable income by $16,000. Of that additional income, which is a Roth conversion, 20 percent of that additional income is tax-free. But is it qualified business income? A Roth conversion is not qualified business income, but the problem was that his qualified business income deduction had been limited by the taxable income, so by boosting the taxable income, Harry ends up effectively deducting 20 percent of the Roth conversion's funds.

# ¶ 406 LOSS FROM A QUALIFIED BUSINESS

The general 20 percent deduction of qualified business income applies to combined qualified business income. That means that individuals are going to net income and losses from different businesses. It also means that clients and planners are going to have to segregate income and loss from different businesses. If clients end up with a net loss from all of their businesses—a combined net loss—that carries forward to the next tax year.

**EXAMPLE:** Genevieve Wellsley is involved in two business activities. One of them has $50,000 of income; one of them has an $80,000 loss. She ends up with a combined business loss of $30,000 for her 2018 tax year.

She will not get a qualified business income deduction because she had a loss, she did not have income. But it is worse than that because now Genevieve has got to take the $30,000 loss and that has to roll into 2019. In 2019 she ends up with combined income of $50,000; she is only going to get the QBI deduction in 2019 on $20,000, which is the $50,000 that was generated in 2019, net of the $30,000 from 2018 that carries forward and reduces her qualified business income in the following tax year.

**EXAMPLE:** Kristen McNulty has a business that has a net loss of $50,000 in 2018. She also has different limitations based on a "threshold income." Anybody who has income above a threshold amount, which is $315,000 of taxable income if he or she is married filing a joint tax return, can be subject to another limitation. That limitation can be based on the W-2 wages that are paid out of that business or, in some cases, the unadjusted basis of depreciable property in that business.

The interesting thing here is what happens if Kristen had a loss of $50,000 in this particular business in 2018 and it had $200,000 of W-2 wages. W-2 wages were factored into the $50,000 loss. What the statute describes is that the $50,000 loss carries forward to 2019 and reduces the combined qualified business income from which Kristen and husband Randall can claim this 20 percent deduction.

What the statute does not explain is whether she and Randall also carry forward the W-2 wages from 2018 so that if in 2019 they happen to be a threshold income taxpayer and their deduction might be limited to a percentage of the W-2 wages, the only fair result here is if her qualified business income is being reduced by this carryforward loss, then logically the W-2 wages should also carry forward. That is something that is going to have to be resolved by regulation. The proposed regulations do not address this issue.

The same is true with the unadjusted basis of depreciable property, although that is less of a problem because the unadjusted basis of depreciable property lasts for at least 10 years and whatever it is automatically carries forward for a 10-year period. So clients are probably not going to have as much of a concern with the unadjusted basis of depreciable property.

But W-2 wages are period by period and so presumably, clients would be allowed to carry forward these wages. Planners do not actually know the answer to that question yet until the IRS addresses the issues in regulations. The general belief is that the regulations the IRS is issuing are going to allow taxpayers to carry forward the W-2 wages.

# ¶ 407 FLOW-THROUGH REPORTING

If clients have a flow-through entity, partnership, or an S corporation, they are now going to have more complicated tax returns. To find out how complicated the tax law has become over the years, clients do not count words. This is what the Congress members do: to point out that the law has become complicated, they will recite how many words there are in the tax code. The proposed regulations use the term "relevant pass through entity," or RPE, to describe such entities that will enter into the taxpayer's determination of qualified business income, including tiered entities.

The information required on a Schedule K-1 will be the important item for partners or shareholders to determine their RPE qualified business income. Partnerships always and S corps in general do not pay tax at a corporate level. The reason taxpayers file a Form 1065, *U.S. Return of Partnership Income,* or a Form 1120S, *U.S. Income Tax Return for an S Corporation,* is to provide information to the shareholder or the partner.

To the extent that these filings make the law more complicated, taxpayers have to give the IRS more information so that whoever is preparing the partners' tax return can incorporate all that information and make sure that they are doing the return properly.

One of the outcomes that the QBI deduction is going to have is to make partnership returns and S corporation returns more complicated because practitioners are going to have to segregate the income and the expenses by qualified business. Planners have to separately report W-2 wages by qualified business and separately report the unadjusted basis of business assets by qualified business. Practitioners are going to have to classify each business run by the partnership or the S corporation as either being a service business or not a service business.

## What Is a Service Business?

Unfortunately, it is not always clear what a "service business" is. But as a general rule, practitioners who do the partners' return or the shareholders' return for an S corporation are stuck with the way the entity has been classified at the entity level. The proposed regulations make clear that the classification of a service or a non-service business is made by the entity.

So if whoever does the return at the entity level says an entity is a service business, it could end up hurting a client in a situation in which the practitioner believes it's not a service business. That fuzzy area as to whether it is a service business or not is going to create a lot of problems in flow-through entities for which clients get a Schedule K-1 and say, "Why in the world are they classifying this as a service business?" Good luck would be necessary in trying to take an inconsistent position, because the examiner may reply, "Well, you have to do what K-1 says." At a minimum clients would be going to appeals.

Supplemental information for flow-throughs may be required to determine:

- What is qualified business income
- What is the partner or shareholder's share of W-2 wages
- What is the partner or shareholder's share of unadjusted basis of business assets
- Whether to classify the business as a specified service activity or other type
- How to define the activity as income or loss

It is not always clear whether the entity is a service business (discussed more later). As a general rule, the planner preparing the partner's or shareholder's return is stuck with the manner in which the entity has been classified in prior returns.

## Reasonable Compensation and Guaranteed Payments

The deduction is not available for reasonable compensation or guaranteed payment for services. The interesting thing is if planners research Code Sec. 199A, everybody focuses on the reasonable compensation issue. Experts will make the statement that a client cannot claim the QBI deduction for a guaranteed payment but then they just move on. Generally, however, the deduction is unavailable for reasonable compensation or a guaranteed payment for services.

There is a reason for that: practitioners and legislators at least have some guidance and have all given some thought to what is meant by reasonable compensation. For a long period of time they have had that issue with C corporations. That issue arises with S corporations, in which somebody's trying to avoid payroll tax and the question is whether the corporations are paying shareholders reasonable compensation. That is an issue that the IRS, courts, and taxpayers have actually dealt with.

Guaranteed payments are a little bit more complicated, as defined in Code Sec. 707 to be payments determined without regard to the income of the partnership. That is all it says. The basic idea is that it is akin to making a payment to a third party, because if someone is a partner in a partnership, he or she is assuming entrepreneurial risk. The only way the partner is going to make money is if the partnership makes money.

Most individuals would define "guaranteed payments" as ones that the recipient has to receive. In theory, that is what the term means, but in practice they work differently.

**EXAMPLE:** Ian Patterson is in a partnership that has $300,000 of income before a guaranteed payment, and David McCulloch, one of the partners, does some services for the partnership. The partnership agreement says that David is going to get a $75,000 guaranteed payment in exchange for the services.

Prior to the end of 2017, very likely the partnership would handle this situation by claiming a guaranteed payment of $75,000, reducing the income of the partnership from $300,000 to $225,000, because the entity would be allowed to deduct the guaranteed payment. When the partnership prepares the partners' Schedule K-1s, the $225,000 would be allocated among all the partners but then have a separately stated $75,000 guaranteed payment to David, so he would end up reporting the $75,000 on his Form 1040; nobody else would.

The idea is that the $225,000 is an entrepreneurial payment. The partnership would assume some risk, whereas the $75,000 was treated like compensating an employee. That is the theory behind it.

But in the legislative history of guaranteed payments, they came into law in 1954 as Congress responding to taxpayers whose position was that a partner cannot be an employee. Case law at the time held that partnerships could not even have a partner be a creditor. If the partnership were making payments to a partner in exchange for services or payments to a partner in exchange for the use of his or her money, there was no way of accounting for the arrangement. The partnership was not allowed to deduct it because it is not wages being paid to a service provider. It is not interest being paid to a creditor because in 1954 a partner could not be a creditor. The entity had no way to deal with it because a partnership could also not do special allocations.

So in response to practitioners' concerns, the Treasury Department devised Code Sec. 707. In many cases the amount was not really a guaranteed payment; it was determined by reference to income. So under the old regulations the partnership had $300,000 of income and was paying one of the partners $75,000 for services. That $75,000 came out of the income. If for some reason the income happened to be only $30,000 for the year, it is highly unlikely that there was a provision in that partnership agreement that required the other partners to make a capital call, so the $75,000 could be paid. In many cases, these so-called guaranteed payments really looked more like preference distributions.

**¶407**

The partnership may have wanted to reclassify by agreement among the partners guaranteed payments as preference distributions. That would increase the QBI deduction by 20 percent. So instead of making the $75,000 guaranteed payment to David, the agreement gave him a $75,000 priority distribution.

He would get it every year because the partnership got $300,000 of income, and then used target allocation so that the partnership was going to match the income to the distribution. David gets a preferential distribution of $75,000 but the partnership also carved out the first $75,000 to allocate to him, and then the other partners split the $225,000.

Flow-through calculations worked this way mechanically. The 20 percent deduction for QBI is after the entity claimed reasonable compensation or guaranteed payment. So that means that if an S corporation underpaid a shareholder the IRS could try to adjust that compensation both for payroll tax purposes but also by increasing the so-called reasonable compensation. The partnership would then argue that the entity's QBI was lower and the qualified business income deduction was in turn lower.

The same thing would be true with a guaranteed payment. The entity would have to make the argument that the shareholder should have had a guaranteed payment and did not, or alternatively, that the dollar amount of the guaranteed payment was too low.

What a guaranteed payment means, going back to the legislative history of the provision, is that there really is no specific authority defining what a guaranteed payment is other than determined without regard to income. Well, if the entity has $300,000 of income and everybody agrees to give $75,000 to one partner because he is working, the general idea in most partnerships is that that $75,000 is going to come out of income, if the partnership does not have the $300,000. There is no technical guarantee. There is no required capital call to make the payment. However, the position of the IRS has long been that a payment need not be guaranteed in any legal sense to qualify as a Code Sec. 707(c) payment. Attaching such a formality would allow taxpayers too much flexibility in classifying payments.

The same is true if a planner thinks about a law firm or an accounting firm. If the firm has a guaranteed payment, the entity has the income to make that payment. It is not like the firm is going to end up in a loss position when it makes that guaranteed payment. The regulations were very subjective in terms of defining what a guaranteed payment is, and the legislative history actually says in the Senate Finance Committee report that it is up to the partners by agreement to decide whether something is a guaranteed payment or a preference distribution.

Frequently a partnership agreement states that a particular partner is going to get paid a particular amount for services, and the attorney calls it a guaranteed payment. That is the way everybody has been reporting it. There is no reason the partners could not amend that agreement, providing that the amount is actually a priority distribution, and then use target allocations to get to the exact same result from a tax standpoint, with the difference that the entity now has a larger QBI deduction because it is not deducting a guaranteed payment. So that is the basic point. Going forward it will be a very interesting thing to see how creative, how clever entities are under the new tax law in terms of redefining guaranteed payments.

Planners should expect to see something in the regulations about reasonable compensation, because some judicial authority exists that defines what reasonable comp is. The rules really do not provide very much in the way of clarifying the difference between a guaranteed payment and a priority distribution.

The August 2018 proposed regulations also include guaranteed payments for capital and Code Sec. 707(a) payments for services as not eligible for the qualified business income deduction. Code Sec. 707(a) payments are those that are treated as made between the partnership and a non-partner. They tend to arise when the partner is performing services for the partnership that he or she also provides to third parties. In contrast, Code Sec. 707(c) payments are made because of the partner-partnership relationship and tend to be services that satisfy the specific objectives of the partnership. The distinction can be muddy at times but the proposed regulations exclude both types of payments from eligibility for the qualified business income deduction.

## What Is an Activity?

Once the Code Sec. 162 definition of business is applied, it is not clear what the scope of the business is. The next consideration is how many businesses does a client have? Five businesses? One business? Three businesses? That is going to depend on decisions made that at this point. They depend on how broadly or how narrowly the client defines a business.

When anticipating regulations under the new tax law, many practitioners thought that the scope of a business would follow the activity definition in Code Sec. 469, the passive activity loss (PAL) rules. PAL rules were written in 1986, and the regulations defining an "activity" were finalized in 1992. The rules were developed for a very specific reason: to classify income and expense by activity so that the IRS and courts could make determinations as to whether the taxpayer had materially participated in that particular activity. The rules had to segregate rental properties from nonrentals because they were treated differently under the passive loss rules.

The 1.469-4 regs provide factors used in defining what an activity is. From that point forward, taxpayers had to make a decision, including whether to employ the partnership level or S corp level.

In 2013, Congress passed the net investment income tax (NIIT), which imposes a 3.8 percent surtax on high-income taxpayers. However, they can avoid the surtax if they can demonstrate that:

- The income in question comes from a trade or business, not an investment; and
- The taxpayers materially participated in that trade or business.

When individuals claim to materially participate in that trade or business, then they have to have some classification of what the business is. How many businesses do partners have in this particular partnership, or how many businesses do individuals have at their own individual level?

For how to handle "activity" for the NIIT, legislators just piggybacked on the PAL rules because they already used the definition of material participation from the PAL regs. The NIIT regs require taxpayers to figure NIIT using whatever classification they use for passive losses. The NIIT regs gave taxpayers a one-shot opportunity to change classification of activities in the first year of being subject to the tax, because taxpayers might have wanted a different classification had they known that the net investment income tax rules were coming into being.

Beginning in 2018, a new complexity has arisen. In addition to the passive loss rules and the NIIT, taxpayers now have this QBI deduction. Taxpayers need to know how to segregate or aggregate businesses. The easiest way for rulemakers in the Treasury Department to address that issue is anticipated to be to use that same classification for Code Sec. 199A as for PAL and NIIT. However, the proposed regulations say that there are enough differences between the Code Sec. 199A purpose and that of the PAL rules that it would *not* be appropriate to use the activity definition.

Instead the proposed regulations focus on developing their own rules for aggregation and segregation of activities, including service and non-service activities. Generally, the two types of business must be segregated. However, where the income from a non-service business is incidental to that of the service business, the two must be aggregated. For example, the regulations have an example where a dermatologist (clearly a specified service business) also sells skin care products. If the gross receipts from the non-service business are 5 percent or less of the total gross receipts, the non-service operation must be aggregated with the service operation provided there is common ownership. The same is true if income from a rental to a service business is 80 percent or more of the total rental income from that property. So if a group of lawyers rents a building to the law practice, the rental income is aggregated with the service business income.

Keep in mind that the aggregation and segregation rules are, as of the writing of this course, proposed. It is possible that they will change when Treasury receives comments from practitioners and later issues temporary and final regulations.

## STUDY QUESTIONS

1. Which of the following statements about the 20 percent qualified business income (QBI) deduction is true?

    **a.** It applies to taxable income after any net gain

    **b.** It is available to C corporations

    **c.** It applies to a taxpayer's combined business income

    **d.** It is available for guaranteed payments for services

2. Under Code Sec. 199A, QBI includes:

    **a.** Short-term capital gains

    **b.** Reasonable compensation paid to owners

    **c.** Real estate investment trust (REIT) dividends

    **d.** All interest income

## ¶ 408  THRESHOLD INCOME LIMIT

Another major consideration beside the taxable income limitation is one known as the "threshold income limit," which is referred to in the statute simply as the "threshold limitation." It is really important that planners distinguish this limitation for purposes of the net taxable income limit.

In one case the deduction can never exceed 20 percent of taxable income minus net capital gain. But if clients are threshold income taxpayers—if they are making too much money—their deduction can actually get reduced below 20 percent. There are a ceiling and a floor. The ceiling is generally 20 percent of QBI. Clients will never get more than that: the ceiling. The floor is going to be the greater of two numbers, and those numbers are based on W-2 wages or unadjusted basis of property. If clients get above this threshold income level, then their allowed deduction gets pulled down from the ceiling (20 percent of QBI) down to the floor, this number is based on W-2 wages and unadjusted basis of property.

### Threshold Level

If the W-2 wage base exceeds the 20 percent of QBI, then clients lose their ceiling, do not have a ceiling; as a result, the practitioner simply deducts 20 percent of QBI. It is only when the 20 percent of QBI exceeds the wage or the wage capital base that clients' deduction could get pulled down. The basic idea is that this applies only to people who have income at or above the threshold level:

- The threshold level of $315,000 applies to taxpayers who are married filing jointly
- Taxpayers who are not married and filing a joint return have a threshold of $157,500
- A full phaseout of the threshold applies to joint filers at $415,000 or $207,500 otherwise

Service businesses get no deduction at all if income goes all the way through the threshold. In other words, after the threshold of $415,000, a service business gets no deduction whatsoever; it doesn't make any difference what its facts are with W-2 wages, unadjusted basis of property—all are absolutely irrelevant. But a nonservice business still gets some deduction. Its income gets pulled down from the ceiling to the floor proportionately.

To recap, there are three different limitations:

- The general limitation that the qualified business income deduction is equal to 20 percent of QBI, a "QBI limit"
- A taxable income limit, which is that the overall deduction cannot exceed 20 percent of taxable income, net capital gain
- This third limitation, the "threshold income limitation," which applies only to people with taxable incomes of $315,000 or more, married filing jointly

Usually the tax rules refer to high-income people based on adjusted gross income (AGI); this one is actually based on taxable income. That means that if clients are filing a joint return, they could actually have $339,000 of positive income sources before this limit kicks in, because with $339,000 of positive income and a $24,000 standard deduction, that makes $315,000 of taxable income. That is not above the threshold, which applies only to more than $339,000 positive income. So a smaller group of people is even affected by this.

For a nonservice business, the allowed deduction is limited to the greater of two numbers, either 50 percent of the W-2 wages for that particular business—which is why clients have to segregate W-2 wages business by business—or 25 percent of W-2 wages plus 2.5 percent of the unadjusted basis of depreciable business assets.

In general, the deduction is still limited to 20 percent of QBI, the overall limitation of 20 percent of taxable income. But this third limitation says in no case will taxpayers get a deduction that exceeds the greater of these two numbers. That means that anybody in that threshold income level should ensure that he or she takes W-2 wages. The W-2 wages can be paid to anybody. The wages do not have to be paid just to the owner; they could be paid to an employee. What happens if clients have a professional employer organization (PEO) that is paying the wages? The answer to that question: the proposed regulations say that wages paid by a PEO count with respect to the business in which the employees are employed. That is, we track for whom the individual performs services as an employee, not who administratively pays the wages. This was welcome news to practitioners.

## Entity Type

A flow-through entity may not have any workers other than the folks who own an interest in the entity. If it is a partnership, it does not have any Form W-2 wages because the only people working are partners, and partners cannot be paid on a W-2 basis. So at this point, the partnership does not have any W-2 wage.

Maybe the entity would be better off being an S corporation if it is a threshold income taxpayer, because S corporation status gives the entity the opportunity to generate W-2 wages. And there actually is an optimal amount of W-2 wages to be paid. The math is actually fairly simple, but it is stuff accountants can handle. The practitioner can explain the computation to an attorney and the client; everybody thinks this approach genius because the practitioner figured out the optimal amount of wages. But remember – this is a maybe and one has to be careful to avoid suggesting an entity type just to maximize the QBI deduction.

If business income exceeds the threshold, $315,000, is there an alternative calculation if we have partnerships and sole proprietorships that do not pay wages to non-owner employees? The question is, if the practitioner deducts the lesser of 20 percent of QBI or the greater of 50 percent of W-2 wages, does the client get a deduction of zero because a partnership is not paying any wages? The answer is no if the entity is in that $315,000 to $415,000 range. In that range, the entity is still going to get some deduction. Once income exceeds the $415,000, if the entity is not paying any W-2 wages, it's going to end up with zero deduction.

## Definition of a Business

Clients may claim that the activity is a business because that is the only way to get this 20 percent deduction, so clients have incentive to say it is a business. Some activities may be an investment and some may be a business.

Clients may believe they know what a business is but they cannot articulate a definition. The Fifth Circuit Court of Appeals defines a business as requiring a sufficient quantum of focused activity. That definition means absolutely nothing. It is not helpful in many cases, so there are going to be a lot of situations where the activity level is borderline. Clients want it to be a business so they can get the deduction. But if it is a business, does that mean that the entity has self-employment income for the partners? The answer is maybe yes, maybe no, because that is still an unsettled area. Some experts take the position that if the entity makes a reasonable guaranteed payment for services that is the measure of self-employment income. An April 2017 Tax Court case didn't accept that argument, but it is still a rather unsettled area.

The problem is that clients have got to make a guaranteed payment if they are trying to assess self-employment tax and using the guaranteed payment as a measure. By making the guaranteed payment, clients also lose 20 cents on the dollar of the QBI deduction.

When the NIIT regulations were issued, taxpayers could avoid the tax by claiming an activity was a business. The NIIT regulations adopted the Code Sec. 162 (ordinary and necessary trade or business deductions) test of what is a business. If a taxpayer claimed an activity was a business for one purpose, he or she had to be consistent for other purposes. The regulations made the point that if the entity claimed to be a business, the owners had better be issuing all the appropriate Form 1099s.

As mentioned earlier, the proposed QBI regulations also adopt the Code Sec. 162 definition of a trade or business. This may be the clearest definition found in the tax law, but there are many situations where it is not at all clear whether a particular operation is a business, an investment, or a personal activity. Facts and circumstances will determine the answer, but at least Code Sec. 162 provides a fairly rich base of authority in the form of judicial decisions for different fact patterns.

One issue, described later in this course, is rental income. Individuals can avoid the NIIT on rental income if they are qualified real estate professionals. But a requirement to avoid the NIIT is material participation, whereas to claim the QBI deduction, that requirement does not apply. But the same definition of a business applies to both provisions.

Clients having rental income may argue that activity is a business. The regulations under Code Sec. 1411 require clients to make all the Form 1099 filings then. If the clients say rental income constitutes a business, it is a business all the way down the line.

## STUDY QUESTION

---

**3.** What is the start of the threshold amount for single taxpayers for claiming the QBI deduction?

- **a.** $157,500
- **b.** $207,500
- **c.** $315,000
- **d.** $415,000

---

# ¶ 409  WAGE OR WAGE/CAPITAL LIMIT

W-2 wages are income as timely reported to the Social Security Administration (SSA). If not timely reported to the SSA, the wages do not count. Interestingly, a couple of deductions in the tax law require explicit substantiation. The rules are in Code Sec. 274(d) for travel expenses, business gifts, business entertainment, listed property, and in Code Sec. 170(f) for charitable contributions. Planners should ensure that clients maintain appropriate substantiation for these expenditures. Some planners manage that by including lines in return organizers for which clients confirm that they have proper substantiation. Other planners handle the issue in their engagement letter language, stating that by signing the letter, clients certify that they have the required substantiation for 274(d) and 170(f) deductions.

Planners are going to have to do something similar for W-2 wages. Clients claim a QBI deduction for threshold income taxpayers—and, again, they are the only people who care about W-2 wages. If individuals have less than $315,000 of taxable income, the W-2 wage issue is absolutely irrelevant. In that situation, planners do not need any certification. But if clients have more than $315,000 of taxable income, are married filing jointly, and their deduction is based in part on the representation that they have paid $100,000 of W-2 wages, then their planner needs to know that the Forms W-2 have been timely filed with the SSA. Planners want to ask that question, either in the organizer or the engagement letter.

# ¶ 410  UNADJUSTED BASIS OF DEPRECIABLE PROPERTY

## Code Sec. 179 Expense Election Versus Bonus Depreciation

"Unadjusted basis" means the basis of an asset before clients have reduced it. The statute says it is determined immediately after acquisition. So if clients acquire an asset on November 27, 2018, the unadjusted basis is the basis of that asset on that date. For that reason, because the statute says that, the unadjusted basis is not reduced by any bonus depreciation, and more importantly, by the Code Sec. 179 expense election. If clients acquire an asset on November 27, 2018, they have not claimed any Code Sec. 179 expense election until they file that tax return and make the election. The proposed regulations use the acronym "UBIA" for unadjusted basis immediately after acquisition.

If clients elect to use the 179 expense election, they cannot use bonus depreciation for the asset. Bonus depreciation is by default; clients have to elect out of it. If they do not have any basis to claim the bonus depreciation because they already expensed it by election, then they do not get any bonus depreciation. So clients have not done anything on November 27, 2018. Until they file their 2018 returns, the unadjusted basis of that property is not reduced by anything. For this reason, the proposed regulations agree that UBIA is not affected by Code Sec. 179 or bonus depreciation.

## Recovery Period and Purchase Price Allocations

The unadjusted basis is used for the greater of the statutory recovery period or 10 years. If clients purchase a 5-year property that property carries forward for 10 years; it is part of their unadjusted basis for purposes of the 2.5 percent of unadjusted basis. Normally most businesses that are going to use unadjusted basis are in real estate, and so the asset is something like a building. If the asset is a building, its statutory recovery period is 39 years, so clients are going to use this unadjusted basis for 39 years. The odds are clients are going to sell the asset long before then, and the unadjusted basis goes away at year-end because clients do not use the asset in a trade or business anymore.

One of the interesting aspects about this is it can affect purchase price allocations. Planners do purchase price allocations under Code Sec. 1060 using the "residual method." It is a top-down allocation. Planners start with assets like cash, then go on to marketable securities, then receivables, then inventory. There is a catchall category for anything that does not fit into another category. Planners have Code Sec. 197 assets other than goodwill, then goodwill, going concern value in category 7.

Planners prepare and clients file a Form 8594, *Asset Acquisition Statement,* along with their income tax returns. That form explains how clients and planners did the purchase price allocation. Historically, buyers would want to allocate the fast-pay assets, ones like receivables and inventory, Class III and Class IV, because the clients could essentially write those off immediately. The receivables would be collected very shortly. The inventory would be disposed of quickly. Otherwise, clients were not really interested in assets for which they would receive basis back quickly, so they preferred a Class III or Class IV allocation. They don't want Class V.

Under the new tax law, the argument now becomes whether clients want Class V allocations, as long as an asset is not a building. If clients own multiple 7-year properties, they might want to bypass receivables and inventory and go right into Class V, put it into 7-year property, and claim a Code Sec. 179 expense election and/or bonus depreciation. For 2018 clients may end up writing the whole asset off anyway, so they get exactly the same result as if the Class V property were receivables or inventory. But now, for 10 years clients have more unadjusted basis of the depreciable property and could possibly increase their Code Sec. 199A deduction by taking that position.

**EXAMPLE:** On June 12, 2018, Pierce Winston buys $300,000 of qualifying Code Sec. 179 property. He and his planner make an expense election. All the property is used in a qualifying business held on December 31, 2018. The unadjusted basis, the $300,000, is counted. On June 12, 2018, there is no expense election; the expense election is made when Pierce files his 2018 tax return. Some practitioners disagree with that position. Some competent tax advisors maintain that if a purchaser like Pierce claims a 179 expense election that will not be part of the unadjusted basis. As with other parts of the new tax law, Code Sec. 199A does not define all of the necessary terms. Regulations should resolve the issue before taxpayers file 2018 returns.

Because the rules are dealing with a flow-through entity like a partnership or an S corporation, clients' share of W-2 wages, clients' share of unadjusted basis of property is determined by reference to their share of the wage deduction and of the depreciation deduction. In an S corporation, that is pretty easy to figure out because it has to be straight up allocations per share per day. In a partnership, practitioners have the flexibility to do special allocations. Later, the text will focus on some issues specific to partnerships, including the ability to actually do a special allocation and what constraints there are on doing that.

What happens in year two, once clients take a Code Sec. 179 expense election?

**EXAMPLE:** Jessica Florez got an asset for $300,000, claimed a Code Sec. 179 expense election, and included that in the asset's unadjusted basis. She will include it for the longer of 10 years for the statutory recovery period. So if that is a 7-year property and she claims the 179 expense election, she will still include that in unadjusted basis for 10 years. And one of the actions her tax preparer is going to have to do is make sure that whatever preparation software figures her return actually does that, actually keeps this asset around even though it has no basis.

## STUDY QUESTION

**4.** The unadjusted basis of depreciable property is:

**a.** Reduced by Code Sec. 179 depreciation

**b.** Eliminated if the property is no longer used in the qualifying business

**c.** Used for a period of five years

**d.** Irrelevant for purposes of the QBI deduction

# ¶ 411 FACTORS AFFECTING CHOICE OF ENTITY

If a client is a threshold income taxpayer and the only people who work in his or her flow-through entity are the owners, partnerships can be disadvantaged relative to S corps. The reason is if it is a partnership and the only folks working are the partners, the client cannot give them Forms W-2. So the issue here is whether to convert LLCs or partnerships to S corps. This issue is generally not determinative. The point is that W-2 wages are one little factor for which an S corporation might be a preferable entity choice. However, there are probably 100 factors in determining whether a client chooses to be a partnership or an S corporation.

In 2018, relative to 2017, when clients may have those shareholders who are in the threshold income level and the entity does not have any wages paid to third parties, the S corporation may have multiple employees, and so the owners are paying millions of dollars of compensation to people other than the owners. It does not make any difference if they are a partnership or an S corporation; they have the employees. They have the ability to create wages. Is it really beneficial to change the type of entity for the sole purpose of getting an additional QBI deduction? The answer might be yes in certain circumstances, in very limited circumstances. The new tax law, tax rates, and QBI deduction have changed the choice of entity dramatically in 2018.

Are shareholder wages excluded? No, they are not. Shareholder wages are included in this W-2 base. Now, what happens is that shareholder wages are subject to a little bit more flexibility, particularly if the entity has just one shareholder; 52 percent of all American S corporations have one shareholder. And so, the shareholder has a little bit of flexibility because whether he or she pays compensation in a W-2 form or not, the income tax effect is the same. The shareholder's choice is going to have a different payroll tax effect, so many shareholders tend to want to lowball the compensation and that is, of course, an issue that the IRS has been looking at for 20 years now.

Perhaps the entity actually does want to pay W-2 wages. Again, a later example explores this issue. Particularly if a shareholder's income exceeds the OASDI base, so all wages will do is pick up some additional Medicare tax, the shareholder may decide to generate an additional QBI deduction.

However, the shareholder wages are part of the W-2 wages, so they are part of that floor, 50 percent of W-2 wages. But of course, the more wages are paid to the shareholder, the lower the QBI, and therefore the lower the QBI deduction.

As mentioned earlier, if a client uses an outside provider such as ADP, Paychex, or TotalSource to handle the payroll, the proposed regulations clarify that cost will be allowed to be included in the W-2 wages. The reason the inclusion may be allowed is because some businesses might give up using this outside payroll company solely for a tax reason. The government should absolutely not want to have tax laws that drive people to give up practices for a nontax reason that make perfect sense just to generate a tax deduction.

# ¶ 412 SERVICE BUSINESS

For clients who have a service business, it is not a good thing to be a threshold income taxpayer. If clients are not threshold income taxpayers, it does not make any difference at all. So whether clients own a service business or not, a service business is important only for those people who have taxable income above that threshold. Again, the threshold is $315,000 for those married filing jointly, half of that otherwise.

So threshold income taxpayers do not want a service business. Later, examples show that clients get a lower deduction with a service business. Once clients hit the end of that threshold level, $415,000, the deduction actually goes to zero. So clients absolutely do not want a service business if they can avoid them.

## What Is a Service Business?

A "service business" includes certain businesses, such as consulting firms, law, and accounting. It also includes any business in which the principal asset is the skill or reputations of one or more of the employees (Code Sec. 1202(e)(3)(A). Veterinarians and physical therapists are considered to be in service businesses under letter rulings, but architects and engineers are excluded. The definition of "specified service businesses" appears in Code Sec. 1202(e)(3)(A). Code Sec. 1202 covers the qualified small business stock of a C corporation in which stockholders can get a 0 percent tax rate—a 100 percent exclusion from the gain on a disposition of this qualified small business stock up to $50 million of gross asset value if it is a C corp and shares have been held more than five years. That applies to any stock acquired after September 27, 2010.

Code Sec. 1202 provision has been in the law since 1993. When Congress put it in the law, taxpayers got a 50 percent exclusion, and it then increased to 75 percent, and in 2010, it climbed to 100 percent. When it was 50 and 75 percent, taxpayers had an alternative minimum tax (AMT) preference, it was a reduction from the 28 percent capital gains rate, not the 20 percent. And as a result, it wasn't a big deal. A lot of people did not set up C corporations because they were going to be subject to two levels of tax just to hopefully get a small benefit.

So a lot of people did not get excited about this provision, and a lot of case law was not created on this issue. This is unlike development of the NIIT rules, for example, when rules were piggybacked on the PAL rules, which already had a long history and case law that interprets the very detailed regulations. When the net investment income tax borrowed from the passive loss area, there was a very rich history of what the rules meant. Provisions of Code Sec. 1202, on the other hand, borrow from a provision that has no regulations and essentially no case law. By saying that a service business is defined in Code Sec. 1202(e)(3)(a), the statute describes professions like consulting and law and accounting, they are specified service businesses.

The proposed regulations provide some clarity by type of service business. For example, the regulations note that the existence of a professional license is not important. Like "accounting" services including bookkeeping because that is ordinarily considered to be part of accounting. The fact that bookkeepers do not need a professional license is not relevant. Health care providers are limited to those people who see patients–but do not include those who do nothing but billing for medical services. Legal services include paralegals, but not court stenographers (because they can provide services outside of the legal business).

Engineers and architects are excluded by statute, perhaps because they were also excluded under former Code Sec. 199 (domestic production deduction).

## STUDY QUESTION

---

**5.** A business performing _____ services is **not** a specified service business for purposes of the new tax law.

    **a.** Physical therapy

    **b.** Engineering

    **c.** Accounting

    **d.** Veterinary

---

### Skill and Reputation Requirement

But the real problem is that there is also an antiabuse provision, and the definition includes any other business in which a principal asset of the trade or business is the "skill and reputation" of one or more employees of the business. What does that mean? There may be reasonable, different interpretations of what that means.

> **EXAMPLE:** Max Steinholm has a tax consulting practice. He also teaches seminars and webinars for accountants seeking continuing professional education (CPE) credits. Max's accounting practice is a specified service business. However, is Max's teaching a specified service business? No, it is not. But what about the skill and reputation requirements? Is a principal asset of the trade or business of teaching seminars the teacher's skill and reputation? But some CPE programs send whomever they can, qualified or not, across the country to a remote town, and that individual is not tapped because of skill or reputation, but just availability. That is not so much being part of a service business, even though the unqualified individual shows up. So there is actually nothing unique about teaching seminars; someone may get paid for the service of teaching a seminar, but that is not a service business, because the statute restricts the types of services very specifically, plus anything else where the skill and reputation is the principal asset of that business.

> The proposed regulations take a very narrow definition of the skill and reputation item. It is limited to things like endorsement income so that we would expect to see it for entertainers more so than other types of service providers.

**EXAMPLE:** Maxine Mueller is a hairdresser with many clients who are very finicky (but loyal) about which stylist is allowed to cut their hair. It would appear her clients go to Maxine's salon because of her skill and reputation. Sounds as though she has a service business. However, in some cases people just walk in to Maxine's salon and have whichever stylist is available cut their hair. That is not a skill and reputation situation under the proposed regulations.

As noted earlier, the income from an ancillary non-service business can be grouped with the service business if there is common ownership and the non-service income is 5 percent or less of the total.

**EXAMPLE:** Anastasia Comchek, an optician who has income from eye examinations, is also selling contact lenses and frames and grinding lenses. Although the non-service income may be more than 5 percent of the total gross receipts, it is expected that the income comes from sales to customers of the service business. The proposed regulations would group the two activities under the service umbrella.

Is a real estate agent considered a service business? No. This is so because the only category that they can come within is "brokerage services." The proposed regulations say that brokerage services is limited to receipt of a fee for bringing a buyer and seller together for a securities transaction. It does not include real estate sales or insurance sales. Moreover, some clients who sell real estate also invest in real estate because they think that they understand the market well, and so they have properties that generate rental income. So they are going to get the 20 percent QBI deduction on their commissions, but they are going to get it on the rental income.

Is this also applicable to rental of farmland? Yes, such a rental is also a trade or business according to the Tax Court. Other case law as to what is a trade or business concerns the issue of a sufficient quantum of focused activity. There has to be a certain amount of activity taking place in order for it to be a trade or business, but the Tax Court holds that such rentals of a single rental house or farm are a trade or business.

## Allocation Issues

If clients have one management company paying wages for many partnerships that are rental real estate, can the clients allocate the wages? Yes. It is a logical approach because the partnerships have common costs. Planners are going to have to come up with some reasonable cost driver to do an allocation. Logically, planners are going to be permitted to do such allocations.

Right now, again, all planners have is the statute, which does not provide definitive answers. The proposed regulations offer some guidance but we can expect some modifications to those regulations before they are issued in temporary or final form. When the dust settles, planners ought to end up with the same answer as if somebody actually went to the trouble of getting rid of the management company and paying the wages entity-by-entity, business-by-business. Why make taxpayers do something like that?

Again, this service or non-service debate is going to apply only to people who have income above the threshold level. For nonservice businesses, if clients are above that threshold level, they care about wage or wage capital. That creates this floor to use in some quantitative examples. If clients have a service business, the deduction can actually go to zero.

So the result of this for a service business is bad if clients have threshold income. If they do not have threshold income, they do not care. Even a nonservice business needs W-2 wages to get a deduction if clients' income is above the threshold. As shown later in the quantitative examples, if clients make too much money and have a service business, they are not getting anything from Code Sec.199A. If clients have a nonservice business, they get some break as long as they are paying W-2 wages or have unadjusted basis of depreciable assets. If clients do not have the W-2 wages, clients do not have the unadjusted basis of depreciable assets, then even in a nonservice business clients are not going to get anything.

What wages are counted? Perhaps a client has a family office. One company pays wages and bills; the other family entity is a management company. Can the other entities claim a proportionate part of the management company's wages? Yes, the rules are going to have to allow something. Clients are going to make cost allocations. The entities have to have direct and indirect costs that will have to be allocated for the different businesses that share common services.

The regulations probably don't go into a lot of detail about how clients should do that, but the approach should prove reasonable. Attorneys who are going to be drafting these regulations never went to accounting school and learned how to make allocations. The planner's role will be to instruct clients that they are going to have to substantiate why they make particular allocations as they will.

> **EXAMPLE:** Doris Clayton has an S corp with three distinct, different types of businesses. One is an ordinary operating business, one is a Schedule F type, and one is a rental activity. Her Schedule F business has income and is paying wages. Where should Doris report that income? Ordinarily her practitioner would put wages in on page 1 of Form 1120S. But then there is a consideration about reporting something like depreciation. Normally depreciation is reported on page 1 unless it is part of a passive activity. Then it must be carved out and become separately stated. And so now, if Doris is going to take the wages in question and track them by these individual businesses, then they are all going to be separately stated items.

Thus, as the tax law becomes more complicated, Schedule K-1s become more complicated. Businesses will have more separately stated items, because of returns reporting items like carryout wages and carryout unadjusted basis of property. Similar complexities will arise with depreciation. Depreciation that may have been included as part of ordinary income or loss, is now going to have to be separately stated because it is going to be allocated among different businesses. The same task will apply with W-2 wages, which may have to be separately allocated. That is something that Congress and the IRS are going to cover by regulation. The IRS is not going to be able to match that and so it is going to be more an issue if there is an audit, planners will have to be able to tie the individual allocations to Form W-3 and will also have to be able to justify whatever allocation method planners decided to use.

## STUDY QUESTIONS

---

**6.** Which of the following statements is true regarding service businesses?

    **a.** A service business has the wage or wage/capital limit as a floor on the allowed deduction

    **b.** Whether a business is categorized as a service business has no bearing on its QBI deduction

    **c.** A service business's QBI deduction can be zero

    **d.** Code Sec. 199A excludes certain types of law firms from the definition of a service business

**7.** Peter Niesen, a married taxpayer filing jointly, has QBI of $200,000. He reports taxable income of $250,000. What is Peter's QBI deduction?

   **a.** $31,500

   **b.** $40,000

   **c.** $50,000

   **d.** $63,000

**8.** Suzanne Deveroux is a married taxpayer filing jointly. Her planner considers the following income and wage amounts for her: taxable income = $450,000; QBI = $100,000; W-2 wages = $60,000; unadjusted basis of capital = $400,000; wage limit = $30,000 (50 percent × $60,000); and wage/capital limit = $25,000 (25 percent × $60,000 + 2.5 percent of $400,000). Which of the following to applies to her?

   **a.** The taxable income limit applies to Suzanne's situation

   **b.** Suzanne's QBI deduction is $20,000

   **c.** Suzanne's QBI deduction is $30,000

   **d.** Code Sec. 199A does not apply to Suzanne's situation

---

## Types of Threshold Income Taxpayers

An investment advisor who manages portfolios is running a service business. The taxable income limitation was 20 percent of taxable income minus net capital gains. There is also limitation based on threshold income. Threshold income, the terminology used in 199A, begins at $315,000, and it ends at $415,000. The following examples show what happens as clients go from the beginning point to the ending point. The rules for service and non-service businesses are the same except the (a) QBI (b) W-2 wages and (c) UBIA for a service business are first multiplied by something called the "applicable percentage." The applicable percentage is 100 percent if taxable income is $315,000 or less, zero if taxable income is $415,000 or more, and a proportional figure in between. For example, if taxable income is $335,000 it is 80 percent, $355,000 it is 60 percent, $385,000 it is 30 percent and so on.

Married couples filing jointly are not threshold income taxpayers if their taxable income is $315,000 or below. Once individuals' income exceeds $315,000, they become some type of a threshold income taxpayer. Some may be a "partial threshold taxpayer," meaning he or she is a threshold taxpayer with income exceeding $315,000 and less than $415,000. Anyone who hits $415,000 in income is a "full threshold taxpayer."

    **EXAMPLE:** The Jeffersons, who file jointly, have qualified business income of $200,000 and taxable income of $300,000, including $50,000 of net capital gain income. The couple therefore are not threshold income taxpayers because their taxable income does not exceed $315,000.

    Their deduction is going to be 20 percent of qualified business income, 20 percent of $200,000 or $40,000, but it is going to be limited to 20 percent of taxable income minus the net capital gain, $300,000 – $50,000 = $250,000. 20 percent of $250,000 = $50,000, so the deduction is $40,000, limited to $50,000. Because the 20 percent of QBI is less than 50 percent of wages, here there is no limit, the Jeffersons get the full $40,000 deduction. It does not matter whether this is a service business or not.

    The couple can easily understand what is going on. They earned $200,000 in the business, they were able to deduct 20 percent of it. When clients do not have a C corporation, it is straightforward to present the idea that they might be able to exclude 20 percent of their income with this new QBI deduction. All the different limitations can be dealt with later.

¶412

Technically, of course, the QBI deduction is a deduction, not an exclusion. But for some clients hearing it, it is easier to say 20 percent of their income is just excluded; they owe no tax on it. Effectively, that is what is happening. The key is to explain the concept to general clients without focus on tax terminology.

**EXAMPLE:** Gerry Utendahl has QBI of $200,000 and taxable income of $220,000, including a $50,000 net capital gain. He is not a threshold income taxpayer. Taking 20 percent of the QBI equals $40,000, but his 20 percent of taxable income net of the capital gain is $34,000. So Gerry's deduction is limited to $34,000. But why should he accept the limit? Perhaps the planner can devise ways to generate additional taxable income—not too much, but enough to reach the inflection point. Every dollar Gerry can add to income increases his taxable income by just 80 cents. He is limited in his deduction by 20 percent of $170,000 versus 20 percent of $200,000.

Just as in an earlier example, the planner can suggest using $30,000 in a traditional IRA to Roth IRA conversion. Gerry's income is now $250,000, $50,000 of which is a net capital gain. So $250,000 – $50,000 = $200,000, and 20 percent of $200,000 = $40,000, which is exactly equal to 20 percent of QBI. So Gerry can claim a $40,000 deduction. This approach also holds only when the taxable income limit applies, not the threshold income limit.

If taxable income exceeds the threshold, the otherwise-allowed deduction is reduced proportionately throughout the phaseout range. The reduction computation depends on whether the business is a service business. If it is, the deduction can go to zero; the nonservice limit changes to wage or wage/capital computation.

If taxable income exceeds the threshold, clients will have a reduction in the amount that they are allowed. What is that reduction going to be? The reduction is proportionate throughout the phaseout range. So in the following examples of married couples filing jointly, they become threshold income taxpayers when income reaches $315,000 and phases out if their income reaches $415,000. They do not get hit with the full extent of it between those amounts. They have a proportional share of it.

What does it mean to be a threshold income taxpayer? It means that clients' deduction goes from 20 percent of QBI down to the greater of 50 percent of the W-2 wages, or 25 percent of the W-2 wages and 2.5 percent of the unadjusted basis.

So once clients reach $415,000 of taxable income, the computation becomes relatively simple. If it is not a service business, they simply get the lesser of 20 percent of QBI or the greater of 50 percent of W-2 wages, 25 percent and 2.5 percent. The trick comes when clients have between $315,000 and $415,000. Thankfully, such computations are the perfect task for software to manage!

**PLANNING POINTER:** Planners should have conversations before year-end with clients whose income falls in the phaseout range to discern whether they have opportunities to adjust income from businesses such as rental properties or, as above, IRA conversions.

**EXAMPLE:** Martin Cadell, a married client, has a QBI of $200,000 and taxable income of $250,000. No, he is not a threshold income taxpayer because his income is less than the $315,000 threshold. So what kind of deduction does Martin get for 2018? He can deduct 20 percent of QBI because his taxable income exceeds QBI. So this is a starting point.

At this point Martin's planner does not care whether he has a service business or a nonservice business; because Martin is not a threshold income taxpayer, it does not make any difference.

**EXAMPLE:** Aidan and wife Catherine Millweather have taxable income of $450,000. They are full threshold taxpayers because their income exceeds $415,000; they have made it all the way through that phaseout range. So this becomes actually a fairly simple computation. This is going to be another base point to use to try to figure out some variations of their situation.

Their qualified business income from a non-service business is $100,000. Normally the planner would take 20 percent of $100,000 which is $20,000. Thus, the normal deduction, as defined by the statute, is $20,000. The problem is that the Millweathers are a full threshold taxpayer, so their deduction actually becomes the lesser of either 20 percent of QBI or 50 percent of the W-2 wages, or 25 percent of W-2 and 2.5 percent of capital, the greater of those two. Obviously that calculation may get confusing because it is a lesser of A or the greater of B, and B has two components to it.

In this situation, Aidan's W-2 wages are $60,000. They have an unadjusted basis of capital of $400,000. The wage limit is 50 percent of $60,000; 50 percent × $60,000 = $30,000. The wage capital limit is 25 percent of Aidan's W-2 wages; 25 percent × 60 is $15,000 plus 2.5 percent of the unadjusted basis. That 2.5 percent of $400,000 is $10,000. So $15,000 + $10,000 is $25,000. So the planner compares the greater of the $30,000 wage limit with the $25,000 wage capital limit. Of course, that's $30,000.

Here the W-2 limit actually exceeds 20 percent of QBI, and so the Millweathers do not really have a ceiling and a floor here. The ceiling would be 20 percent of QBI. That is the amount that an individual who is not a threshold income taxpayer would get. The floor is the greater of the wage limit or the wage capital limit.

Usually, if clients become threshold income taxpayers, they are pulled down from the ceiling to the floor, and planners think about raising the floor of the clients' income to get a bigger deduction.

Right now, the Millweathers do not have a ceiling and a floor, because the 50 percent of W-2 wages actually exceeds 20 percent of QBI, so the deduction is just flat out $20,000, the lesser of $20,000 or $30,000. So the couple actually did not get pulled down.

Even a "normal" taxpayer like those discussed earlier, with $250,000 of income would still get a $20,000 deduction. So the Millweathers in the example end up in the same place as an individual who happens to have $250,000 of taxable income.

If clients are in nonservice businesses, and some examples that follow concern nonservice businesses, too much taxable income causes the otherwise-allowed deduction to be pulled down: a ceiling and floor. So if the 20 percent of QBI is already below the floor, then if the floor is above the ceiling, the planner does not even think about it in those terms. Being a threshold taxpayer does not really matter in a situation like that.

Does the definition of a business include the rental of commercial and residential real estate? It should because the proposed regulations adopt the Code Sec. 162 definition of a trade or business. The Tax Court has held that even a single rental can be a trade or business. The NIIT regulations dealt with this issue and cautioned that rental real estate is not a trade or business as a matter of law. While this is a true statement, the courts have been fairly liberal in interpreting rental real estate as a trade or business.

For clients who have that issue come up, it is actually easy research for a planner to do, because the Tax Court is essentially uniform, except in bizarre fact patterns, in stating that even a single rental house can be a trade or business under the Code Sec. 162 definition. When the Treasury Department issued the NIIT regulations, it actually took a very harsh position on treating rental income as trade or business income, and the department was soundly criticized by commentators, so the department had to back off of that position. So the answer in general is yes, the business of renting commercial and residential real estate is a trade or business.

Another interesting twist is that under the NIIT rules, in order to not treat income as investment income, it has to be income from a business in which a taxpayer materially participates. Under the PAL rules, rentals are automatically passive, so a taxpayer doesn't materially participate in rentals.

Thus, the general rule under the NIIT rules is that rental income, whether it be commercial or residential, is subject to the tax if an individual is a high-income taxpayer. The exception to that is if the individual is a qualified real estate professional, because qualified real estate professionals at least get the opportunity to prove that they materially participated. A qualified real estate professional who materially participates in a rental activity can avoid the NIIT on that income.

When the planner switches to the QBI deduction rules, there is no requirement in the statute that an individual must materially participate in the business that gives rise to that income. Clients can get that 20 percent deduction for business income even if they are passive with respect to that activity. The AICPA and very likely other organizations have pointed that out to the Treasury Department and the preamble to the proposed regulations states that to be the case. If clients have income from a commercial or residential real estate operation, they can claim that 20 percent deduction. Even though that is rental income, it is treated as business income and that is the only requirement. The IRS will treat it as business income under the QBI deduction rules.

Those same clients, if they are high-income taxpayers, will then walk over to the NIIT rules and for those purposes claim not to be qualified real estate professionals but that their rental income is investment income subject to the 3.8 percent surtax on investment income. The cognizant planner might object that clients claimed the QBI 20 percent deduction on business income and then the rule says to pay a 3.8 percent surtax because it's investment income. That is exactly right, the planner will conclude, because the two rules are different. Code Sec. 1411 requires material participation, whereas Code Sec. 199A does not.

## Planning for Threshold Taxpayers

When the taxpayer's deduction will be pulled down to the "floor" because the taxpayer is a threshold income taxpayer, there are some simple planning strategies that may help.

> **EXAMPLE:** One obvious strategy is raising the floor. In previous examples, clients were not threshold income taxpayers with incomes of more than $315,000. Those situations could be helped by pulling taxable income up if the 20 percent of taxable income limit is binding. For every additional dollar of taxable income that generated, final taxable income only went up by 80 cents. Planners in those cases suggested moves like Roth conversions. Gracie McMillan's situation is different because she is a threshold income taxpayer (with a non-service business); her planner advises her to pull up the floor by paying more W-2 wages. Gracie has an S corporation with one shareholder (Gracie), and to some extent she has the flexibility to determine what the wages are. An earlier example stated QBI to be $200,000. Gracie has been paying $60,000 of wages because she does not want to

pay more payroll taxes. That must mean she had prewage business income of $260,000. Gracie's planner wants to hit an inflection point where the ceiling is equal to the floor. The ceiling is $40,000, or 20 percent of QBI including the $60,000 wages. The floor is $30,000, 50 percent of the wages. The problem is that as she starts to pay more wages, her QBI goes down, and as she pulls the floor up, she pulls the ceiling down by 20 cents on the dollar. She wants to reach the optimal amount of wages.

What happens to her deduction if she pays more wages? If Gracie pays $70,000 of wages instead of $60,000, 50 percent of $70,000 is $35,000, so her QBI deduction moves from $30,000 to $35,000. That's a pretty good deal.

If Gracie pays $80,000 of wages, 50 percent is $40,000, so she would get a QBI deduction of $40,000. But with $80,000 of wages the QBI is only $180,000, so the actual deduction is limited to $36,000. So $70,000 of wages was better than $60,000, but $80,000 of wages is too much.

To find the optimal amount of wages, Gracie's planner performs these calculations:

.50 wages = .20 ($260,000 – wages)

.50 wages = $52,000 – .20 wages

.70 wages = $52,000

Wages = $52,000 ÷ 7 = $74,286

QBI would be $185,714

20 percent of QBI = $37,143

50 percent of W-2 wages = $37,143

The QBI deduction increases by $7,143

The planner does not want to go above 74,286, because then 20 percent of QBI is going to become the limitation and Gracie will not benefit from additional wages, so she does not want to pay more than that.

She moves from $60,000 of wages to $74,286, paying the full OASDI and the Medicare—not a good idea. So thinking about overall taxes, including the payroll taxes, Gracie probably does not want to do this. If she is thinking about also making a retirement plan contribution, maybe it makes sense to adjust the wages this way. But again, there are many moving parts. Also, a smart IRS agent might question the wages being exactly equal to the optimal W-2 wages: was Gracie paying reasonable compensation? She might want to think about wages in terms of the value of services provided, not simply optimizing the deduction.

**EXAMPLE:** Jeremy Harrison has an S corporation, of which he is the one owner-employee. He can set the wages at whatever level he wishes subject to obviously having to pay reasonable compensation. The amount of wages will not affect the shareholder's income reported. So for every dollar of wages that Jeremy pays himself, it is simply going to shift the income from a Schedule K-1 report to a Form W-2. But any adjustment is going to affect his QBI deduction. In 2018 Jeremy has $800,000 of QBI. Currently his wage is $200,000, so his income exceeds the OASDI base. So if he increases the compensation in any way, the worst outcome is picking up the Medicare tax. That is not a bad deal.

His current QBI deduction, $100,000, goes all the way to 50 percent of the wages. What should his optimal wages be? Using 50 percent of the wages is equal to .2 × $1 million. That $1 million is the QBI before he pays the $200,000 in wages –

wages. So Jeremy's planner is trying to determine wages, which turn out to be $285,714. So if Jeremy increases the compensation paid from $200,000 to $285,714, he can increase the QBI deduction from $100,000 to $142,857. So increasing wages by $85,714 increases the deduction by $42,857 (50 percent of $85,714). So up to the point where he hits that inflection point, every additional dollar of wages is increasing his QBI deduction by 50 cents, so for every one more dollar of wages, he gets an additional 50 cents in deduction.

Assuming Jeremy is a 37 percent taxpayer, 37 percent of 50 cents is 18.5 cents, so he is saving 18.5 cents for every additional dollar of W-2 wages. He is paying 2.9 percent for Medicare, so that is an easy trade-off. So this is something that he should do. Jeremy should think about boosting the wages in a situation like this.

The computation of the deduction is more complex when the taxpayer is within the phaseout range for a threshold taxpayer. The 20 percent of QBI is a ceiling and the greater of the wage or wage/capital limit is the floor. As one moves through the phaseout range he also has the allowed deduction lowered from the ceiling to the floor.

**EXAMPLE:** Salvo Bertini has a 2018 taxable income of $385,000, which makes him a partial threshold taxpayer; he is not all the way through the threshold ($415,000) for the deduction. He operates a non-service business. His income places Salvo at 70 percent of the way to the threshold. His ceiling is $40,000 (20 percent of his QBI) because QBI is $200,000. His floor is $30,000 because W-2 wages are $60,000. The 50 percent of W-2 wages is more than 25 percent of the W-2 wages and 25 percent of the unadjusted basis. So Salvo's planner starts at the $40,000 ceiling but does not go all the way to the floor, just 70 percent of the way, moving from $40,000 to $33,000, because the spread between the ceiling and floor is $10,000. Salvo's not all the way through the phaseout.

**EXAMPLE:** Margie and Theo O'Rourke are married filing jointly on their real estate business, and they have taxable income of $4 million. Their QBI is $2 million. The starting point is taking 20 percent × $2 million to get $400,000 as a ceiling. Their W-2 wages are zero, but their unadjusted basis of capital is $40 million on a building the couple owns. It is depreciable property, so 2.5 percent of that $40 million = $1 million. Their planner compares options: the lesser of $400,000, 20 percent of QBI, or $1 million. The couple does not have a ceiling apply here so they will simply deduct 20 percent of QBI.

**EXAMPLE:** It turns out that everything is the same for the O'Rourkes, except that the unadjusted basis instead of being $40 million is only $8 million. Now, 2.5 percent of $8 million is $200,000. In this situation they have a ceiling and a floor: the ceiling is $400,000, which is 20 percent of QBI; the floor is 2.5 percent of the unadjusted basis of the property, $200,000.

Where are the O'Rourkes in the threshold? They are all the way through. So what their planner advises them to do is go from $400,000 all the way down to $200,000. So their deduction is going to be $200,000.

If that taxable income was only $385,000 they would be 70 percent of the way through the phaseout, so instead of going from $400,000 to $200,000, they are going to go 70 percent of the way from $400,000 to $200,000. That is a $200,000 spread. So 70 percent × $200,000 = $140,000; they are going to go from $400,000 to $260,000. Here, that is not the case.

Comparing the two scenarios for the O'Rourkes, in the first case they had no taxable income limit because the capital was so high that 20 percent of QBI applied. It did not matter what their taxable income was. In the second case, they had a taxable income limitation, but a deduction was still allowed based on that significant capital base. Theirs is a real estate operation: they do not have any wages, but they have a lot of capital. And a huge number of real estate lobbyists—perhaps as many as 5,547—worked on the new tax law!

Planners working with real estate operations should bear in mind that such scenarios are most common with real estate operations that have a large capital base. However, the operation must be a business.

## STUDY QUESTION

**9.** Quincy Washington is a married taxpayer who files jointly. He has taxable income of $450,000, and his QBI from a non-service business = $200,000. His W-2 wages = $60,000, and his unadjusted basis of capital = $400,000. Quincy's wage limit = $30,000 (50 percent × $60,000), and his wage/capital limit = $25,000 (25 percent × $60,000 + 2.5 percent of $400,000). Which of the following does Quincy's planner find to be true?

   **a.** The taxable income limit applies to Quincy

   **b.** Quincy's QBI deduction is $30,000

   **c.** Quincy's QBI deduction is reduced by 70 percent

   **d.** Quincy's taxable income is below the threshold limit

## When Is Real Estate a Business?

As mentioned earlier in instances a single rental property or rental farm was deemed a trade or business by the Tax Court for DBI deduction purposes—even when management duties are minimal, it constitutes a trade or business. Different tests have been applied to the requirements for business treatment. During the Great Recession, many rental houses were sold at a loss, and clients did not want the losses to have capital treatment but Code Sec. 1231 treatment. The Tax Court allowed sale of a single rental house to be treated as a trade or business. However, for the NIIT, the material participation requirement applies.

Is the unadjusted basis of property the original purchase price? Yes. The only difference is for real estate, clients have to exclude the land. In part, the deduction depends on how much is allocated to the land. Planners do a cost segregation. Everything but the land still qualifies. The only difference is that the unadjusted basis of the property continues for the greater of 10 years or the statutory recovery period. So any property that falls into 27.5 or 39 years for recovery, clients can use that unadjusted basis for 27.5 or 39 years, or until the disposition of the asset, whereas anything that falls into a 5-year recovery, 7-year, that is going to be for 10 years. But owners are going to get it for 10 full years.

If a $40 million building is nine years old, does the planner use the 2.5 percent for 10 years beginning in 2018 for just one more year? Clients can use it for 39 years, so that is not really an issue. When the deduction begins this year, 2018, planners can go back and check acquisitions made in 2011 and include them as part of the unadjusted basis of depreciable property. So it is not just property that is placed in service beginning in 2018; planners must go back to earlier acquisitions also.

Consideration of a triple net lease rental is definitely harder. If it is a triple net lease property, it is more difficult to argue that it is a trade or business. However, the Tax Court has been generous in this regard.

**¶412**

Typical cases in the Tax Court where the ruling said rental properties are not a trade or business were situations in which an individual had inherited a rental house from parents and had a tenant there, so the individual just waited out the lease. After the tenant left, the individual sold the property. The reason the individual wanted to argue it was a business is because there was the basis adjustment at date of the parents' death, and the individual had all the selling costs for the property, ending up with a loss on the sale that the individual wanted to claim as a Code Sec. 1231 loss. The Tax Court typically ruled that such an individual never held that property in any way and had no intent to hold it for rental.

There are other cases in which the property in question was essentially a vacation home that was rented out casually and intermittently. The owners were not charging fair rental value. That was not a trade or business. Those are the cases that the taxpayer lost.

## STUDY QUESTION

---

**10.** Under which statutory definition of a business has a single rental property been held to be a trade or business?

    **a.** Code Sec. 199A

    **b.** Code Sec. 162

    **c.** Code Sec. 355

    **d.** Code Sec. 1231

---

# ¶ 413 LIMITATION FOR SERVICE BUSINESSES: APPLICABLE PERCENTAGE

Everything discussed so far is a nonservice business. So a couple's deduction got reduced from $40,000 to $30,000 in the facts of the above examples because they went all the way from the ceiling ($40,000 with assumed QBI of $200,000) down to the floor ($30,000 with W-2 wages of $60,000) due to their taxable income of $450,000. They were full threshold taxpayers.

Another example showed a couple who had income of $385,000, so they were partial threshold taxpayers. The ceiling of $40,000 was dragged down to $33,000. They did not go all the way down to the floor because they did not have income of $450,000 or more. They went 70 percent of the way down.

What happens in a service business? Why are service businesses inherently evil in a situation when clients are threshold income taxpayers? There is only one reason. There is only one difference that affects the otherwise-allowed deduction. There is something called the "applicable percentage." The applicable percentage is 100 percent, minus the percentage determined by the quotient of taxable income minus the threshold income exceeding $100,000. In other words,

100 percent – (Taxable income – Threshold income) ÷ $100,000

**EXAMPLE:** Sean and Laura Everton have $385,000 of taxable income from their service business. They are 70 percent of the way through the threshold. So the applicable percentage becomes 30 percent: 100 – 70. Basically, what that is saying is that they still have 30 percent left. It resembles a gas gauge: at $315,000 it is full and at $450,000 it is empty. At $385,000, the Evertons' tank is still 30 percent full—30 percent is left. ALL relevant figures are adjusted to 30 percent of their actual figure before the computation of the QBI deduction is done. So if QBI is $200,000 as in our earlier examples, it is adjusted to $60,000.

There are three numbers that are relevant: qualified business income, W-2 wages, and unadjusted basis of capital. Previous examples looked at 20 percent of QBI, 50 percent of W-2 wages, 25 percent of W-2 wages, and 2.5 percent of unadjusted basis. We continue to do this for a service business, but only after adjusting the figures by the applicable percentage.

Treatment of the service business is exactly the same thing, with the only difference being redefinitions of the terms qualified business income, W-2 wages, and unadjusted basis of capital. It is going to be whatever the right number is multiplied by the applicable percentage.

For $385,000 of taxable income, the applicable percentage is 30 percent. The W-2 wages become 30 percent of the real W-2 wages. The unadjusted basis of depreciable property becomes 30 percent of the real unadjusted basis, and the qualified business income becomes 30 percent of the real qualified business income. Once the formula reduces it from what it really is down to 30 percent, then the planner just goes forward and does the calculation exactly the same as for a nonservice business.

Considering what that means, planners can see that if clients' taxable income is at $415,000, the applicable percentage is zero (100 percent − 100 percent). In the calculation of an allowable deduction, QBI becomes zero, as does the unadjusted basis of capital and the W-2 wages. Thus, the deduction is zero, too. That is how a service business can lose the deduction. If clients' income is between $315,000 and $415,000, they will get some deduction amount, but it will be less than the nonservice business because the applicable percentage is used in addition to the other limitation shown in previous examples.

**EXAMPLE:** The McMasters are married, filing jointly, in a service business: a law firm. Their taxable income is $450,000 so they are full threshold taxpayers. Their QBI is $200,000, but now the business, the law firm, is definitely a service business. In this situation, the normal QBI deduction, 20 percent of $200,000 = $40,000. That is their ceiling. They have W-2 wages of $60,000, and 50 percent of that is $30,000. In the earlier example of Gracie McMillan's nonservice business, she went from $40,000 to $30,000. The McMasters have the problem that theirs is a service business. So what their planner needs to do first is to determine the applicable percentage.

Their income is above $415,000, so the applicable percentage is zero (100 percent − 100 percent). That means that their qualified business income is now treated as if it is zero ($200,000 × 0). Their W-2 wages are zero, ($60,000 × 0). Their unadjusted basis is also zero ($400,000 × 0). When all those three numbers are zero, the deduction becomes zero: very simple. That is how the McMasters get to a zero deduction above $415,000. The planner first has to use the applicable percentage.

**EXAMPLE:** Craig and Jean Campbell are partial thresholder taxpayers with a service business income of $385,000. That means that they are 70 percent of the way through the threshold. What happens to them if they are 70 percent of the way?

Comparing their situation with Salvo Bertini's in his nonservice business, Salvo's allowed deduction was $33,000. That was the ceiling of $40,000, or 20 percent of his QBI. His floor was $30,000, 50 percent of the W-2 wages. He was 70 percent of the way through that phaseout. He went 70 percent of the way from $40,000 to $30,000, and that got an answer of $33,000 for Salvo.

The Campbells' planner is going to do exactly the same computation for their service business, but first is going to have to reduce everything by the applicable percentage. The applicable percentage here, like the gas gauge, is 30 percent, because at $315,000 it is 100 percent full, at $450,000 it is empty. They are all the way down to 30 percent from empty.

So the Campbells' QBI is now not $200,000, it is $60,000. Their W-2 wages are not $60,000, they are $18,000. Their unadjusted basis of capital is not $400,000, it is $120,000. The planner will multiply everything by the applicable percentage first and then do the normal computation.

Well, the normal computation says to use 20 percent of QBI. That is the ceiling. But now QBI has been redefined from $200,000 to $60,000. Multiplying 20 percent of $60,000 gives $12,000, so the Campbells' ceiling is now $12,000 and their floor is 50 percent of W-2 wages, just like it was back for Salvo. The difference is that the W-2 wages are redefined from $60,000 to $18,000, so 50 percent of $18,000 is $9,000. They now have a ceiling of $12,000 and a floor of $9,000. They are 70 percent of the way through the phaseout, so they go 70 percent of the way from $12,000 to $9,000. That gets the result of $9,900.

Salvo's deduction was $33,000. Here for the Campbells, it is $9,900, which happens to be 30 percent of $33,000, so the service business deduction is 30 percent of the deduction that the Campbells would have had had theirs been a nonservice business. The reason it becomes 30 percent is because their planner is doing the funky thing with the applicable percentage.

Comparing these two situations, their income situations are exactly the same. One is a service business, one is a nonservice business. The only figuring performed differently is before the planner does the calculation, the Campbells' numbers are reduced by the applicable percentage, getting down to a deduction that is 30 percent.

This comparison reflects the earlier analysis of what constitutes a service business. There will be many cases for taxpayers in this situation: their taxable income is above the threshold, so it makes a difference whether it is a service business. Planners will be in the position of discussing with clients whether to consider a trade or business to be a service versus a nonservice one. Is the planner's professional standard that he or she can sign a tax return if there is substantial authority—meaning 40 to 45 percent chance of success if challenged.

The proposed regulations expand upon the definition of a service business but leave some unanswered questions. For example, "consulting" is a service business. Consulting is said to be helping clients to achieve their goals. There are many well-known "consulting" firms, but there are also many individuals who would call themselves consultants. Let us say that a tax planner evaluates the language of the regulations and decides that, for a particular client, there is a 50 percent chance that the business is a consulting service business.

Given that this is a toss-up, planners may believe they have substantial authority for treating it as a service business and substantial authority for treating it as a nonservice business, so this year planners may go either way on this in signing a return. When clients are posed with this dilemma, they are going to want numbers to help them determine if they should take an uncertain position. The planner may respond that if it is not a service business, taxpayers will take that position for a deduction for $33,000. If it is a service business, taxpayers may get a deduction for $9,900, 30 percent of what they otherwise would get.

Clients will look at an additional $23,100 of deduction if they take the position that theirs is not a service business. But understanding the IRS could challenge that position and they could possibly lose, most planners would be okay signing returns having met their professional standards. Some clients, who if faced with a situation like that, are going to decline the higher deduction because they want no trouble with the IRS. Other clients may absolutely decide to claim the higher deduction. It is really their call to make.

# ¶ 414 ANCILLARY ISSUES

## Adjusted Gross Income Versus Taxable Income

Threshold income is based on taxable income. Planners may become fixated on adjusted gross income. Everything that planners are used to is AGI. This case for service businesses is based on taxable income.

The new tax law increased the standard deduction to $24,000 for married couples filing jointly. When planners talk about $315,000 of taxable income, they are not talking $315,000 but $315,000 plus deductions, which under the new law for couples is at least a $24,000 deduction. Couples could actually push it to $339,000. A ballpark for 2018 is $350,000 for couples with no mortgage interest deduction who are using the standard deduction. Non-QBI deductions can help increase the QBI deduction, but they can create a benefit of more than that 20 percent. Previous examples showed taxpayers who have QBI of $200,000 and taxable income of $170,000. They are limited to $34,000 unless they increase their taxable income from $170,000 to $200,000. Then they could increase the QBI deduction by 20 percent of the additional income. Planners show it makes sense to aim for 20 percent: that is the amount of the deduction. It is very easy to say if clients earn $315,000 of taxable income, they would bet if they had an additional dollar of deduction, that that would actually reduce their taxable income by $1.20—an additional 20 percent. But that is not the way it works. When clients are in that phaseout range, it is not the case that they boost the deduction by 20 cents per dollar.

**EXAMPLE:** Sophie and Jacque Duquette both work, but only Jacque works in a nonservice business. Jacque files a Schedule C for his self-employment income of $200,000 as listed on the Schedule C. Sophie is an employee with a W-2 job, and her income is $189,000 on a W-2, so she will not get the QBI deduction because she has salary income. Their taxable income is $200,000 plus $189,000 minus their $24,000 standard deduction, so they are at $365,000 of taxable income. That is exactly halfway through the phaseout. The question is what is Jacque's qualified business income deduction? Normally it would be 20 percent of $200,000, or $40,000. Jacque would normally get a $40,000 deduction. He is a Schedule C filer and he does not have any employees, so he has no W-2 wages. There is no capital in Jacque's business either. So he is going from a ceiling of $40,000 to a floor of zero, and he is going to go halfway from $40,000 to zero, meaning $20,000. The base point is for Jacque with $200,000 of Schedule C income and Sophie earning $189,000 from her W-2 employment. The family is going to get a $20,000 QBI deduction.

Now Jacque gets an opportunity to make a $20,000 retirement plan contribution to a closed-end fund (CEF). What happens? Normally he would assume he is going to deduct $20,000, and their taxable income would go down from $365,000 to $345,000. That is kind of the first step, but the second step is instead of being 50 percent of the way through the phaseout, the Duquettes are now only 30 percent of the way through, so that they are going to get 70 percent instead of 50 percent. Their ceiling is $40,000, the floor is zero, but they are going to go only 30 percent of the way from $40,000 to zero, so the QBI deduction is going to be $28,000.

Jacque's QBI deduction goes up by $8,000 because he added $20,000 of deductions. His benefit essentially means that for every dollar of deductions that he generates, he is actually reducing taxable income by $1.40. The figure depends on where he is in that phaseout range. What if he claims more deductions, or he makes a larger retirement plan contribution? He likes the idea of getting 140 percent deduction for every dollar contributed to the retirement plan. It is almost like having a match except that the match is coming from the government instead of the employer.

Jacque doesn't want to go below $315,000; he could if he really wanted to make that much of a retirement plan contribution, but in terms of getting extra bang for his buck, once he hits $315,000, he is out of the phaseout anyway. Jacque decides to make a $50,000 retirement plan contribution to bring him down from $365,000 to $315,000 in taxable income. Now he gets a full $40,000 QBI deduction because he is now out of the phaseout range. By making that $50,000 contribution, his QBI deduction goes up by $20,000, from $20,000 to $40,000, and the net benefit is $70,000, which is 140 percent of the $50,000. As long as Jacque stays within that phaseout range, bringing him from $365,000 all the way down to $315,000, every additional dollar of deduction that he can generate actually reduces his taxable income by $1.40. That is a pretty hot deal. So Jacque and Sophie start looking for other types of deductions.

Their planner looks at the same scenario, $365,000 of taxable income, but if Sophie does not work, all of the income comes from Jacque's qualified business. In the first situation, because of the taxable income Jacque loses 50 percent of his otherwise allowed QBI deduction. 20 percent of $389,000 is $77,800. The ceiling is $77,800. The floor is zero because Jacque has no W-2 wages; he has no depreciable property.

What if Jacque makes that $20,000 retirement plan contribution? What is that going to do to his QBI deduction? It is going to give him a $20,000 deduction, but for his QBI deduction, which is $77,800 as a ceiling, zero as a floor, instead of affording him 50 percent, he is now going to get 70 percent of that. He is going to get 20 percent more.

Calculating 20 percent more on a $77,800 base, Jacque will get another $15,600. Add that to the $20,000 deduction that he is already going to get, and he is actually going to get a 177.8 percent benefit. Every dollar of deductions he generates, is going to reduce taxable income by $1.78.

Jacque ponders going all the way down to $315,000 if he makes a $50,000 retirement plan contribution. He has a different issue: if he goes all the way down to $315,000, the QBI deduction is 20 percent of $389,000, which is $77,800. Except now he has brought the taxable income down so low that the 20 percent of taxable income kicks in and he can only deduct $63,000.

He does not want to make a $50,000 retirement plan contribution strictly because he will get a 177.8 percent benefit. But if his planner tells Jacque that by making a $20,000 contribution, he will get a 177.8 percent benefit, the planner must ensure that Jacque's income does not go too low because then the taxable income limitation kicks in, and he will not receive that 177.8 percent anymore.

## Pending Issues and Future Actions

Congress knew that regulations to pin down many of the vagaries of the new tax law are necessary, so legislators are granting the Treasury Department the authority to write legislative regulations. Legislative regulations are directives from Congress. When the regulations are written in temporary or final form, they have the force of law. They are like the passive loss regulations. The August 2018 proposed regulations are not authoritative, but the Treasury Department has said that taxpayers may rely upon them until they are issued in temporary or final form. Passive loss regs, by the way, are legislative regs because Congress thought that people would try to game the system with the passive loss rules, so the laws give the Treasury Department the authority to write the rules while the game is being played, knowing that Treasury would write the rules in a way that the government wins. That is why businesses ended up with incredibly complicated passive loss regulations.

Consolidated return regs are legislative regulations. That is why they are so long. Congress gives the Treasury Department the authority to write the regs, so Treasury can listen to comments that people submit and can prohibit taxpayers from claiming deductions based on people's ideas.

In 1982, Congress created something called the "substantial understatement penalty," Code Sec. 6662, in response to tax shelters. Tax shelters were running amok at the time, so Congress created an additional 20 percent penalty to taxpayers' tax liability if they take a position on their returns that lacked substantial authority and reduced their tax liability by 10 percent of the proper amount. That code has been in the law since 1982, all the way to 2018. It is still in the law, but Congress changed it. In 2018 if the item in question relates to the Code Sec. 199A deduction, the threshold, instead of being 10 percent of the proper amount of tax, went to underpayments of just 5 percent of the proper amount of tax generating the 20 percent penalty.

One of practitioners' responsibilities in the professional standards is if the taxpayer might be subject to a penalty, planners have a responsibility to inform them that they might be subject to the penalty. All the subjects of this chapter create the need for planners to have substantial authority for clients' claims; any understatement is going to be a substantial understatement because Congress lowered the bar. Planners have to inform clients that particular positions might be subject to a substantial understatement penalty.

Additionally, page 2 of Form 1040 for 2018 returns will look substantially different. There will be taxable income before the QBI deduction, the deduction, and taxable income after the deduction. Early indications are that the Form 1040 will be shorter with more schedules. Any state that piggybacks on the federal system and uses AGI will not allow taxpayers to get the benefit on their state returns unless their state modifies the state's laws.

## Shifting Allocations and Transitory Allocations

How will an entity like a partnership allocate wages? The general rule for partnerships is to do so by agreement, but the agreement has to have a substantial economic effect. The same rule applies to depreciation.

What happens if clients are threshold income taxpayers and the planner wants to allocate W-2 wages to them? The planner advises allocating unadjusted basis to them. The other folks do not need it. There are four partners: one is the threshold, the other three are not threshold, and the partnership decides to do a special allocation to the threshold partner. Can the entity do that? In theory, yes; in practice, perhaps no. The reason is whether the other three partners would accept allocation of all of the wages and all of the depreciation to one partner. Perhaps the other three would demand some other benefit in lieu of wages and depreciation. That situation creates a "shifting allocation." It lacks substantiality because partners are using an item of a different character to essentially offset the allocation that is made to the threshold partner.

¶414

Allocation of W-2 wages, allocation of depreciation can work, but they can work only if partners are not going to offset them within the same time period with different types of items.

If partners are going to offset allocations in a subsequent period, the issue is with what. If they do so with income that they know year-by-year exists, it is a "transitory allocation." It happens within five years, it lacks substantiality. If partners do it with gain on the sale of the property, it is okay. If a specific partner is going to get more deductions but the others are going to make him whole by giving him more gain on sale of the property, that is okay because rulemakers always assumed in the substantiality rules that the value of the property equals its basis, so there will not be any gain to allocate. But it is not a simple thing.

## STUDY QUESTION

**11.** Partnership RST has four partners. One is a threshold taxpayer; the other three are not. Under the new tax law, how should RST allocate the W-2 wages?

    **a.** RST should allocate all of the W-2 wages to the threshold taxpayer

    **b.** RST should allocate the W-2 wages among all four partners

    **c.** RST should not do an allocation in this case

    **d.** More clarification is needed from the IRS, but RST can adopt a reasonable position

## Basis Adjustments

Planners and clients should be very careful about special allocations in a partnership. They have to ensure they clear the substantiality hurdle. Partnerships can also have issues with Code Sec. 734 and Code Sec. 743 adjustments that are allocated to depreciable property. Right now, the tax code is silent on whether taxpayers can use Code Sec. 734 adjustments, which affect the basis of partnership property, and Code Sec. 743 adjustments, which affect the basis only of the partner who purchases an interest in the partnership. The proposed regulations say that these adjustment do not affect the UBIA for Code Sec. 199A purposes. The preamble to the regulations said that Treasury was concerned that such adjustments could result in double counting basis.

## STUDY QUESTION

**12.** Which of the following statements is true regarding Code Sec. 743 and Code Sec. 734 adjustments?

    **a.** Neither one affects the UBIA for Section 199A purposes

    **b.** Section 199A requires that Code Sec. 734 adjustments be used to allocate depreciable property

    **c.** Only Code Sec. 734 adjustments affect the capital base

    **d.** Negative Code Sec. 743 adjustments affect unadjusted basis

## Depreciation Schedules

Practitioners are going to have to see how this fleshes out with software, but the software is going to have to continue to carry property. If clients have property from 2009 that was expensed under Code Sec. 179, where it has been fully depreciated and clients do not have the property on the books anymore, it has to go on the books because clients will keep that on their returns for 10 years.

Property from prior acquisitions are still going to come into play, so planners must have fixed asset schedules, whereas now clients have this generous Code Sec. 179 100 percent bonus depreciation, even if there is no basis. Planners are going to want to keep that original basis because it might impact the Code Sec. 199A deduction.

# MODULE 2: BUSINESS COMPLIANCE ISSUES—Chapter 5: S Corp Distributions: Determining the Taxability

## ¶ 501 WELCOME

This chapter discusses how taxation applies to distributions from S corporations, a commonly used entity of choice for various types of small businesses. S corps are a commonly used pass-through structure that individuals prefer. When S corps commonly make distributions to shareholders, the issue arises of whether the distributions are taxable or are a return of shareholders' basis. Additionally, it may be difficult to determine whether a distribution is a loan, a loan repayment, or a distribution of income.

## ¶ 502 LEARNING OBJECTIVES

Upon completion of this chapter, you will be able to:

- Recognize rules applicable to pass-through of S corporation income and deductions
- Identify effects of S corporation income, liabilities, and loans
- Recognize how to characterize S corp distributions as salary versus income

## ¶ 503 INTRODUCTION

This chapter provides training on how the intersection of rules about S corporation taxation affects the taxability of distributions of cash and property by an S corporation. Examples illustrate how rules apply in the federal tax regime. Individuals are partial to pass-through taxation, and the idea that if they want to cease using the S corp entity, they are able to switch to C corporation status. For example, if the company wanted to go public, and is an S corp, they can switch it back to a C corp before the IPO. This is more straightforward in terms of stock ownership, than an LLC or partnership structure. LLC and partnership interests can be a little bit tricky and require agreements as to what happens if the entity desires to go public in the future. In this regard, some people are more comfortable with being an S corp.

There are still a lot of S corps out there and they commonly make distributions to shareholders. Unlike a situation in which a client has a C corp that is making distributions, the S corp distributions are typically dividend-type distributions. The type of S corp distribution can vary, thus determining whether they are taxable or are a return of basis largely depends on shareholder basis.

Part of what this chapter examines are the rules regarding shareholder basis and how to determine the purpose of the distributions. This chapter will help practitioners understand how the shareholder gets basis, what increases basis, and what reduces it. Also, the text looks at determining whether a distribution might be a loan, a loan repayment, salary, or a distribution of income. Detailed discussions explore how the intersection of all of these rules affects the taxability of distribution from S corps, both distributions of cash and distributions of property.

The first discussion is about the rules regarding the pass-through of S corp items of income and deductions. It describes how shareholders have additions to S corp basis, including the effects of S corp liabilities, which generally do not affect the shareholder basis, and then shareholders' S corp loans. The chapter also discusses the characterization of distributions as salary versus distributions as income. It is a little tricky to determine just the right amount of salary income for S corp shareholders versus income distributions to the owners. Next the chapter discusses loans between S corps and their shareholders. Finally, it discusses taxable distributions.

# ¶ 504 THE UNIQUE FEATURE OF S CORPORATIONS

An S corp is a regular corporation for state law purposes that makes a special election to be treated as an S corp entity under the Internal Revenue Code. There is no such thing as an S corp for state law purposes. It is just a regular corporation that makes a special tax election. If the election is made at the outset—essentially as soon as the corporation is formed or within the short deadline thereafter—then the corporation will generally be treated as a pass-through entity for tax purposes.

If an entity that had been a C corp at one point in time and then switched over to become an S corp, a few different rules come into play that can cause complications. For most purposes today, practitioners can assume the discussion is talking about S corps that have always been S corps.

## Flow-Through of Profits and Losses

Generally speaking S corps profits and losses flow through to shareholders whether or not the profits and losses are distributed. The virtue of that pass-through structure is that income is not taxed at the corporate level like a C corp is. Instead, everything flows through to the shareholders—the income flows through to them; the deductions and losses flow through to them. All flows through, whether the corporation makes any distributions or not.

## Advantages and Disadvantages of the Structure

The advantage of that structure is that, generally speaking, distributions of cash are not going to be taxed because shareholders consider those cash distributions to be out of the previously taxed earnings. The corporation is sending the earnings through. And as long as that is the cash being distributed, it has already been taxed. In which case, shareholders need not do anything. The corporation makes basis adjustments when it distributes those profits and losses so that the income is not taxed a second time when it is actually distributed. The flow-through of S corps is similar to the rules for other pass-through entities, such as partnerships and limited liability companies (LLCs).

There are some key disadvantages to S corps that are summarized here. There are several restrictions on the ability to select an S corp entity status and to maintain it:

- It is only allowed to have single class of stock, which can be voting and nonvoting, but preferred stock or distribution preferences for certain shareholders are not allowed;

- Ownership is generally restricted to U.S. individuals, estates, and certain types of trusts;

- Inadvertent violations of these requirements result in termination of S corporation status and treatment as a C corporation; and

- An S corporation that was formerly a C corporation has to keep track of built-in gains at the time of conversion and is subject to corporate-level tax.

Thus, an S corp cannot have preferred stock and is not permitted to have distribution preferences for certain shareholders. If the entity needs different owners to have different economic interests outside of their proportional ownership differences, an S corp cannot do that.

Another important restriction is that S corp ownership is generally restricted to U.S. individuals, estates, and certain types of trusts. An S corp cannot have foreign shareholders, for example, and cannot have an entity be an owner of the S corp stock other than certain types of trusts. If the S corp inadvertently violates the S corp's requirements—for example, getting an ineligible shareholder—the entity's status automatically terminates, and the entity will default back to being a C corp.

Also, the maximum number of shareholders for an S corp is 100.

C corps are very easy to get into and hard to get out of. If owners have an entity that absolutely would not want to be a C corp because shareholders do not want that double level of tax—if they have appreciated property inside, it is hard to get it out without paying tax on that appreciated property at the C corp level—then it can be risky to have an S corp. If the owners fail to adhere to any of these restrictions, the entity will become a C corp subjected to double tax. In this case, the entity will not be able to get the appreciated property out again without paying tax on whatever corporate-level gain is on the assets.

If the S corp was formally a C corp, it needs to keep track of built-in gains at the time of its conversion because C corps do require a corporate-level tax on built-in gain on those corporate assets and corporate properties. A C corp cannot avoid that by converting to S status. The built-in gains tax requires the S corp to keep track of what that built-in gain was at the time of conversion. That is then subject to corporate-level tax when the assets are sold if the sale is done within a particular timeframe.

To summarize, the requirements for being an S corp are that the entity is limited to 100 shareholders, it may offer only one class of stock, and distributions of appreciated property may be taxable if the company was formally a C corporation.

## STUDY QUESTIONS

---

1. Which of the following is an advantage of forming an S corporation?
   a. Distributions of cash are generally not taxed
   b. A single class of stock is allowed
   c. Ownership is generally restricted to U.S. individuals
   d. Basis adjustments for distributed profits are similar to those for C corporation rules

2. Each of the following identifies a requirement for forming an S corporation *except:*
   a. There can be only one class of stock
   b. It must be owned by only individuals or certain trusts
   c. There may be an unlimited number of shareholders
   d. Owners must be U.S. citizens or residents

---

# ¶ 505 ADDITIONS TO S CORPORATION'S SHAREHOLDER BASIS

What kinds of additions typically occur with an S corp shareholder's basis? Such additions will ultimately affect which distributions are taxable and which are not. This basis is going to be a very important number, so it is vital to understand it. Items of income and deductions of the S corp pass through to the shareholders, and then these amounts get reflected in the stock basis. Because they are not taxed at the corporate level and flow through to the shareholders, those income flow-throughs increase the shareholder basis if they are income. Generally, distributions are not taxed to the extent of the shareholder's stock basis.

This basis in S corp stock is quite important for determining the gain or loss on the sale of stock. Basis is also important for determining whether losses are deductible. Basis figures in determining the taxability of distributions of cash or property from the S corp. Knowing the basis is important for determining what happens if shareholders actually sell the stock and incur losses, and whether those losses are able to pass through.

## Figuring Cost Basis and Carryover Basis

The taxability of those distributions of cash or property from the S corp will be indicated by that basis. To know the basis at distribution time, shareholders have to know what the initial shareholder basis is. What is the initial basis that shareholders start with for the S corp? For the initial basis, the starting point is the normal rules for basis in Code Sec. 1012, which says that basis is "cost basis." So if the stock was purchased, it had cost basis under Code Sec. 1012.

If the stock was received in exchange for a capital contribution, then the stock basis will be the amount that was contributed to capital. In that case, the basis rule for nonrecognition transactions essentially says that the basis will be the amount contributed to the capital of the corporation—that "carryover basis" of whatever was contributed plus any gain recognized minus any money received.

Basis is going to be the basis of whatever was contributed. And if that was cash, it will be the fair-market value of that cash plus any gain recognized minus any money received that would be "boot." Later, if a shareholder makes any additional cash contributions, it will increase the stock basis.

## Upward and Downward Adjustments to Basis

Once shareholders have the initial basis—essentially, either the amount paid to purchase the stock or the amount contributed to capital—now shareholders need to know about adjustments to basis. And adjustments to basis are going to be:

- Positive adjustments (increases) to basis because of additional capital contributions and when the income flows through to the shareholder. Income that flows through to the shareholder will increase the basis; or

- Negative adjustments (decreases) to basis because of losses and deductions that flow through to the shareholder; any cash distributions will also decrease basis.

Some special ordering rules apply in order to know when to reduce the basis as shares have distributions and losses, events that are negative adjustments to basis. Positive adjustments to basis are essentially done as they happen. Capital contributions increase basis as they are made. Income flow-through will increase basis as of the end of the year (typically). Shareholders need some special ordering rules to know what to do when the S corp has losses in a particular year and it is also making distributions. Shareholders need to be able to determine whether the loss that passes through is deductible, whether there is sufficient basis for it, and whether the distribution that is being made is taxable. Perhaps, if shareholders use up the basis on letting a loss flow through, it is going to make a distribution taxable.

**EXAMPLE:** Nathaniel Howard is a shareholder with a basis of $1,000 in an S corporation's stock. The S corp makes a $500 distribution in October and has a

$700 loss for the year. How should these numbers be treated for Nathaniel's tax reporting? His basis is only $1,000, but the distribution and loss total $1,200. The distribution reduces basis for purposes of determining loss, but the loss does not reduce the basis for determining consequences of the distribution. In this example, the ordering rules essentially say that distributions are taken into account first. This means that the basis of $1,000 would be reduced by the $500 distribution. Additionally, that $500 distribution would not be taxable. That takes Nathaniel's basis down to $500, and then the $700 loss would only be allowed to the extent of the remaining $500 basis. The remaining $200 loss would have to be suspended.

When losses are suspended, there are different places where shareholders keep track of the suspended losses. Essentially, the suspended losses under Code Sec. 1366(d)(2) are the losses not claimable in a particular year because shareholders do not have sufficient basis to absorb them; they are saved. Shareholders can use them in a future year. It is not that they are gone forever, shareholders have to wait until they have sufficient income or basis to use them.

How exactly do upward adjustments apply shareholder basis in the S corp stock? First, there are basis increases from items of income. The rules say that the increase is both basis increase for "separately stated" items of income and "nonseparately stated" items of income. Generally, the S corp rules in Code Sec. 1366 describe these definitions. Essentially they say items are separately stated if their consequences will depend on the situation of the shareholder. For lots of situations, the S corp income and deductions will just flow through as a net item as nonseparately stated items, just either net income or net loss. Shareholders do not need to review every single item of income and every deduction if the consequence is not going to matter in terms of which shareholder is receiving it.

For certain kinds of activities, their consequences will depend on the shareholder receiving income or losses, and those are going to be separately stated. But both the flow-through of separately stated and nonseparately stated items of income will increase shareholder basis. Again, just by definition, an item is considered to be separately stated if its consequences depend on the situation of the shareholder.

Now interestingly enough, upon further thought the rule starts to make sense. Shareholders will increase basis for items of income that are tax exempt. No one is supposed to get taxed on this income, right? It flows through, and it is not taxed. But it should increase the shareholder basis, because if it did not, when the S corp actually distributed it, it would be taxable. To make it truly tax exempt, shareholders need it to flow through and not be taxed, but also increase the shareholder basis.

Shareholders do not increase basis by income that was excluded under Code Sec. 108(d)(7)(A), which are the rules regarding exclusions for "cancellation of indebtedness income." Exclusions are not the same as tax-exempt items; they are just excluded under Code Sec. 108. The idea there is that because that income is actually phantom income (noncash income), shareholders do not need to account for that in basis. There should not really be any of that cancellation of indebtedness income to distribute because it is phantom income. Shareholders are just concerned with the cash income that is tax exempt. We need it to get out to the shareholders without being taxed because it is truly tax exempt.

What causes some of the reductions to stock basis? The brief introduction to this was provided in the previous example of the stock basis of $1,000 and then both the loss and the distribution. Shareholders make downward reductions in stock basis for both losses and cash distributions.

¶505

What are the circumstances that generate downward reductions in stock basis? First are distributions that are nontaxable. If shareholders have sufficient basis to absorb a distribution, then that is going to go through. It is not going to be taxed to the shareholder, but it will reduce basis.

Second, separately stated loss and deduction items are going to flow through. This is the same as the income piece of it. Under a similar rule to what applies for the income, a "separately stated item" is an item that will have a different treatment depending on who the shareholder is. If S corps have separately stated losses and deductions, those will flow through to the shareholders and reduce their basis. Similarly, nonseparately stated loss items when the S corp has a net loss after all the nonseparately stated items are aggregated together flow through. Presumably, the shareholders can use that loss if the rules allow. As a result, that net loss will reduce their basis.

Also, nondeductible expenses should reduce the shareholder's basis unless he or she elects otherwise (Treas. Reg. 1.1367-1(g)). This is a similar flipside to the tax-exempt income. Even if this expense was not deductible from a tax standpoint, it did reduce income in terms of what should flow through without being taxed. Meaning that those nondeductible expenses will also reduce shareholders' stock basis.

**NOTE:** Keep in mind that the stock basis cannot be reduced below zero. If shareholders are in a situation where they are getting close to reducing basis below zero because of losses and deductions, those losses have to be suspended until there is sufficient stock basis to claim them. If distributions exceed basis, those distributions are taxable. Losses or deductions that would dip the shareholders below zero are suspended until the shareholders have the sufficient basis. In future years, the losses or deductions can be netted against the current year's income to use in that future year when shareholders do have sufficient income.

What is the character of excess distributions? The character, generally speaking, will be capital gain because it is not income that is flowing through. It is as though the shareholders folded their stock in exchange for that distribution. The character is similar to a redemption transaction in the corporate area, as discussed later. Generally speaking, the character is capital gain similar to when there are nondividend distributions in the C corp context. Shareholders get to use their basis, and the excess is capital gain. So shareholders treat it like a sale of the stock.

The ordering rules that dictate the order of adjustments to be made when multiple items occur in one particular year are:

1. Required increases to basis;
2. Reductions for nondividend distributions;
3. Reductions for nondeductible expenses; and
4. Reductions for losses and separately stated deductions

In terms of the order of adjustments, first are required increases to shareholder basis. Those would be for items of income that flow through, both separately stated and nonseparately stated and tax-exempt items. Next, shareholders make any reductions for nondividend distributions. That would be distributions that are able to be claimed to the extent of basis. Third, shareholders make reductions for nondeductible expenses. Finally shareholders make reductions for losses and separately stated deductions.

**NOTE:** The fact that distributions adjust the basis prior to adjustments for losses means that the S corp can make tax distributions out of the current year's income. In S corps that typically do not make a lot of cash distributions, it's important that they make tax distributions so that shareholders can pay their taxes on the income that flows through. The order of adjustments for losses means S corps should be able to make distributions necessary for shareholders' tax payments out of sufficient basis from income that flows through.

**EXAMPLE:** On January 1, 1997, Agatha Beaton, the full shareholder of an S corp, has a zero-stock basis. Halfway through the year, the S corp distributes $70,000 to her. At the end of 1997, her nonseparately stated income is $50,000. She also has a long-term capital gain of $20,000 and a Code Sec. 1231 loss of $75,000. What does her tax practitioner do with all this in terms of determining the taxability of the distribution because it happened halfway during the year? Is that $75,000 suspended Code Sec. 1231 loss only offset by future 1231 gain? No, that is just a suspended loss. The 1231 gain, is a separately stated item, and so it would remain a separately stated item. That loss would just depend on Agatha's treatment. It would retain its character as a 1231 loss, and it would have to be netted with other 1231 gains if there were any. However, Code Sec. 1231 net losses can be used as ordinary losses.

In order to figure out the taxability of the distribution, the practitioner considers the ordering rule. Its mandate is to figure taxation not necessarily based on time but on the ordering rule. The ordering rule says that the first calculation is to adjust the stock upward for any nonseparately stated and separately stated items of the income. As a result, Agatha's basis is going to increase by the $50,000 and by the $20,000 long-term capital gains. Is the long-term capital gain from the distribution taxable? Yes, absolutely: any distributions in excess of basis are taxable to the shareholder. This means that Agatha's basis has increased to $70,000.

At this time, the practitioner takes out distributions. Agatha received a distribution of $70,000. That will not be taxable, but it will take her basis down to zero. Now, the $75,000 Code Sec.1231 loss is not deductible because she does not have sufficient basis to absorb it. This means that the loss will be suspended, and will be carried forward until Agatha has sufficient income or stock basis to claim it in a future year.

That suspension rule is the one set forth in Code Sec1366-2(a)(3).

**EXAMPLE:** Andrew McClellan owns 100 percent of the stock of CPM Enterprises, an S corp. On January 1, Andrew has a stock basis of $30,000. During year 1, the S corporation allocates $20,000 of ordinary income to Andrew, and $30,000 of long-term capital loss, and then distributes $60,000 to him. In this case, Andrew had a stock basis of $30,000. There is $20,000 of ordinary income that passes through to Andrew, increasing the basis of $50,000. When the distribution of $60,000 is made, that is going to be used against his basis to the tune of $50,000. The remaining $10,000 will then be treated as long-term capital gain.

This relates to the issue of what happens when an S corp makes distributions in excess of basis. These distributions are generally going to be long-term capital gain because they are treated as though Andrew sold the stock. When that happens, the $30,000 of capital loss cannot be used because Andrew does not have sufficient basis, and that loss will end up being suspended.

To recapitulate, the only time items end up as taxable is when an S corp distributes more than a shareholder has earned. The idea there is that perhaps the shareholder has already taken too much in the way of distributions. This excess is going to be taxable because it is as if the shareholder only had a certain amount invested in the S corp, and that is what his or her basis tracks. However, if the shareholder ultimately has more cash than that, he or she has actually had a gain on the S corp transaction. In which case, that gain absolutely is taxable.

¶505

## STUDY QUESTION

**3.** With respect to ordering rules, which of the following identifies the first step?

    **a.** Reductions for nondividend distributions

    **b.** Reductions for nondeductible expenses

    **c.** Reductions for losses and separately stated deductions

    **d.** Required increases to basis

# ¶ 506 ACCUMULATED EARNINGS AND PROFITS AND THE ACCUMULATED ADJUSTMENT ACCOUNT

If an S corporation was previously a C corporation, it has to keep track of the accumulated earnings and profits (E&P) that it essentially brought over when electing S corp status. On the taxation of distributions from C corporations, generally speaking, if an item is a "dividend distribution," it will be taxed as a dividend to the extent of the corporation's E&P.

If the C corp converts to an S corp status and then makes distributions that exceed what the S corp earnings have been, the entity is, in actuality, distributing previously untaxed E&P of the C corp. That distribution will need to be taxed as a dividend. In the past, this practice was more complicated when there was such a difference between the dividend rate and the capital gain rate. At that time, it would have been undesirable to have something taxed as a dividend. Currently, if this distribution is going to be taxed as a C corp dividend, at the dividend rate, the difference is minimal. This is a concept that practitioners should be aware of.

The "accumulated adjustment account" (AAA) keeps track of previously taxed undistributed earnings that are earned while an entity is an S corp. Once this account balance goes to zero, any further distributions are treated as taxable dividends. The AAA tracks what is happening to the S corp shareholder basis but at the corporate level, so shareholders can know whether they have started to dip into accumulated E&P or not.

Once shareholders have gone through all of the AAA, any further distributions are going to be treated as taxable dividends even if the shareholders do have shareholder basis because these are actually out of C-corp corporate earnings. This is a bit more of an unusual case because it involves C corps that have converted over to S corp status.

When an S corp is distributing cash that is not in excess of the shareholder's basis but there's not enough AAA, should the distribution reduce additional paid-in capital on the balance sheet, with the issue being whether it would cause AAA to go negative? If the entity has never been a C corp, the S corp really does not even need the AAA. It is fine to keep track of the balance, but it does not really serve any additional purpose. If the AAA is different than what the shareholders' basis was, then maybe the S corp has made some sort of error or miscalculation; those amounts are supposed to go hand in hand. So if the entity has never been a C corp, the S corp really should not be overly focused on the AAA.

If the S corp is making a distribution that exceeds AAA, the entity is likely making a distribution that is exceeding the shareholder's basis. If it does not exceed that basis, perhaps it is because the shareholder put in additional cash contributions. If the shareholder put in additional contributions of cash or property to increase the basis, that will not be taxable to the shareholder when the S corp essentially is returning that piece to him or her.

# ¶ 507 ADJUSTMENTS MADE ON A SHARE-BY-SHARE BASIS

Adjustments are made on a share-by-share basis. Even if the S corp shareholders would want to keep track of an aggregate basis for all of their shares—and indeed, many of them do that—instead technically, under the rules, they are supposed to track the basis of each individual share. When adjustments are made to shareholder basis, if shareholders have different blocks of stock that were bought at different times and for different prices, the shareholders do need to make a share-by-share adjustment. The way that the S corp makes the share-by-share adjustments is by making them in a prorated manner based on the length of the time the shareholders owned the stock during the year and the prorated amount of income or loss.

The calculations are relatively simple if all of the stock has been owned the entire year.

> **EXAMPLE:** Bethany Johnston owned 25 shares of stock for 10 years and 75 shares of stock that she has owned for 6 years. When her S corp makes the income flow through, she has to know which shares of stock are getting their basis reduced. In this instance, the income flow-through will go 25 percent to the 25 shares and 75 percent to the 75 shares.

If part of the stock has only been owned part of this year, then the shareholders have to prorate a little bit further, which makes calculations a bit more confusing. Prorating is done so the entity does not get to benefit one group of stock more than another, in terms of that basis increase or basis reduction. S corps do generally respect that difference in shares of stock in a corporation.

# ¶ 508 EFFECT OF S CORPORATION AND SHAREHOLDER DEBT ON SHAREHOLDER BASIS AND DISTRIBUTIONS

S corporation debt and shareholder debt may increase the shareholder stock basis and then, as a consequence, affect the treatment of distributions. One big principle to keep in mind—and this is a big disadvantage of S corps compared to partnerships or LLCs—is that there is no shareholder basis credit for S corp debt. Contrast that with a partnership or an LLC, in which the partner's share of the partnership's debt, particularly nonrecourse debt, gets allocated to the basis of the partners or LLC members and allows them to take distributions or losses to the extent of that.

## No Basis Credit for S Corporation Debt

That rule is not true with respect to S corporations. S corp shareholders do not receive basis credits for debts that are owed by the company to third parties. So if debt is attributed to the S corp, no individual shareholder gets stock basis for that. This is something that is often forgotten, as many tend to believe that S corps and partnerships are treated equivalently.

For shareholders to receive basis for debt, they would only get debt basis, not stock basis. And the shareholder has to be making a direct loan to the corporation. This is going to be a loan from the corporation to the shareholder, and then the shareholder will acquire a basis in that debt, not a basis in the stock.

> **NOTE:** Personal guarantees by the shareholder will not create shareholder basis, either debt basis or stock basis.

## Loans from Shareholders to the S Corporation

A loan from a shareholder to an S corp gives the shareholder basis in the debt—that is, the loan itself—but not a basis in stock. The debt basis can be used to absorb *losses* that pass through, but it cannot be used as basis to absorb any *distributions* that pass through. To absorb distributions passing through, the shareholder needs to have a stock basis.

To get the debt basis, to take losses—because sometimes, shareholders loan money to the corporation to get sufficient basis to take losses—the arrangement needs to be a bonafide loan from the shareholder to the corporation. To ensure it is viewed as a bonafide loan, the shareholder should make as many indicia as possible that the debt is true debt, such as: a written promise to pay, an interest rate set at or above the applicable federal rate, and an indication of the intent to repay the loan (the latter of which is the most important test in terms of true debt).

For the debt/equity factors, there are common law factors used in determining whether a situation is debt or equity. There are also new regulations under Code Sec. 385 in helping to determine whether the transaction constitutes debt or equity. Those factors may come into play to recharacterize the holding as equity that formerly was debt.

## Shareholder as Conduit

In the case in which the shareholder is loaning to the S corp, it may be better to have it reclassified as equity; the shareholder then gets basis credit in the stock because it will be treated like a capital contribution. In that case, the shareholder will then have stock basis rather than debt basis.

This applies to loans in which the S corp shareholder lends the money to the corporation and the bonafide loan gives the shareholder basis in that debt, in that note from the corporation to the shareholder. That debt basis can then be used to absorb losses—not distributions, just losses. One approach to give the shareholder sufficient basis to claim losses is to give the shareholder debt basis, the shareholder may try to borrow money from a bank or other third party and then do a wraparound loan to the corporation. This means that the shareholder may attempt to obtain the third-party borrowing, obtain the funds, and then loan those funds to the corporation. If the corporation had borrowed the money directly from a lender, the shareholder would not be able to get any basis for that. However, if the shareholder borrows the money and then loans the funds to the corporation, the shareholder does receive debt basis.

Generally speaking, that strategy is fine and will work for tax purposes, but the shareholder needs to take care to act as the lender. The shareholder must not merely act as a conduit in the sense that the corporation is just paying the bank directly. The shareholder needs to maintain the minutes, the notes, and all those items of substantiation to reflect that he or she is the lender, rather than indicating that the third-party lender is actually the lender to the corporation.

Does that strategy work for related parties? It is trickier and riskier to have the loan be with related parties. If the shareholder borrowed money from another related entity and then made a loan to the corporation, the S corp and shareholder would have two levels of involvement in proving there was bonafide debt. However, if the shareholder has cash to loan to the corporation, that type of loan should be permitted.

When related parties are involved, the IRS tends to take a closer look at whether substance over form applies in some way to recharacterize the transaction as something else. A shareholder may run into that view if related-party debt is used. However, if a conduit-type of loan like that with a related party applies, there are no specific statutory rules that would cause problems. The issue that arises for this purpose is whether the shareholder is truly intending to make a valid loan.

Does this setup ever increase stock basis, or only debt basis? A shareholder's loan to the S corp will only create debt basis, which can be used to absorb losses. The shareholder will not get stock basis for this. If the corporation borrows from a third party, the shareholder does not get either a stock basis or debt basis. This kind of scheme is done to give the shareholder enough basis to take losses that are flowing through. That is really the purpose of it. The related party question is only making the situation a little murkier.

## Using Debt Basis for Loss Pass-Through

If a shareholder's interest in the corporation is terminated during the year, the basis reduction is applied with respect to the indebtedness held immediately before the termination of the shareholder's interest. In this case, any indebtedness acquired by the shareholder after the last day may not be taken into account.

> **EXAMPLE:** Terence Rigby owns stock in X, an S corporation, at the end of its calendar year. He held no indebtedness during any part of the year up to December 31, but on December 31 he loaned the corporation $15,000 and received a note in return. This $15,000 in additional basis may be taken into account in determining Terence's loss deduction for that year. If he had sold all of his stock in the corporation on June 30 of that year, then he could take into account only indebtedness he held as of the close of June 30, i.e., none. Therefore, in that case, any net operating losses allocated to him would be limited to his stock basis on June 30.
>
> Even if Terence sells as of June 30th, he is going to still be getting some losses and some income passing through to him. If he wants sufficient basis, he needs to make the loan while he is still a stockholder as well.

At what point can a shareholder take back the loaned amount from the corp, and would it be taxable? The shareholder would not necessarily want to take the funds back one day later because it would appear that the loan was never intended to be made; it can be seen as a type of deposit. Authorities do say that if the corporation had the right to do with the money what it pleased, then it was not obligated to return it the very next day. Such an action does not present a problem, but some respectable amount of time gives a better appearance. Presumably, when the loan is made, the lender probably wants the timing to be specified. Even if it is a short-term loan, the lender would likely want to put that timing in the agreement. If it is a demand loan, the shareholder should probably wait at least a little while to take funds back. Also, it would not be taxable because the shareholder has made a loan, and the intent was to have it repaid. In this instance, that is just repaying the loan that was made to the company.

For a loan, the shareholder may make it to get some debt basis to be able to take a loss. And when the loan is repaid, it is not taxable. And that is true even if the loan was made to get the debt basis to be able to take the losses. So when the loan is repaid, the loss flow-through itself would reduce the debt basis. And so if the shareholder had no other way to increase basis in the meantime, then the repayment of the loan would indeed be taxable because the debt basis would have gone down to zero. If the flow through losses were fully reducing the debt basis, and the losses flowed right through in the full amount of the debt basis, then the shareholder would have a zero basis in the debt. And then when the debt was repaid, that would in fact be taxable.

## No Use of Debt Basis for Tax-Free Distributions

Even with that debt basis, shareholders cannot take any tax-free distributions. Additionally, that basis is only good for taking a flow through loss. The basis of stock is going to be reduced by distributions that are not includable in income. With distributions for which shareholders have sufficient stock basis to absorb the losses, then you would reduce stock basis; debt basis is not reduced by that. Once the basis in stock has been reduced to zero and before shareholders can reduce basis of the indebtedness, they have to reduce their stock basis to zero. Any distributions at that point will be includible in income.

## STUDY QUESTION

---

**4.** Which of the following statements is correct relating to an S corporation and shareholder debt on shareholder basis and distributions?

    **a.** The S corporation rules are consistent with partnership rules

    **b.** S corporation shareholders do not receive basis for debts owed by the company to third parties

    **c.** Personal guarantees by a shareholder creates shareholder basis

    **d.** A shareholder is not required to make a direct loan to the corporation in order to receive a debt basis

---

# ¶ 509 DISTRIBUTIONS OF SALARY VERSUS INCOME DISTRIBUTIONS

Distributions of salary versus distributions of income always raise a tough question for a closely held S corp in which the key owners provide services to the corporation. How do such distributions work, and are they really distributions of S corp income or are they taken out as salary?

Determining whether an owner provides substantial services to any business entity, including an S corp, can be pretty difficult. It is often more likely for owners who provide services to a corporation to be treated as employees rather than as owners. The default is to treat owners as employees because, if they are providing substantial services, they would likely need, at least in some regard, to be treated as employees. It is often necessary to determine what is "reasonable". What is reasonable compensation for the work they are doing?

In other contexts, the concern is that maybe the compensation is too high—say, stripping out corporate earnings when the C corp rate was still so high and practitioners would try to get big deductions for compensations paid to shareholder employees. With S corps, practitioners worry about making the salary income too low because they want to ensure that sufficient employment taxes and other withholding will be collected as well. So the S corp needs to determine what "reasonable" compensation is.

## Employment Taxes

With respect to the employment tax issues, S corp officers and employees providing services generally need to be paid some salary. That is going to be subject to employment taxes because it is an exchange for their services. Just like other employees, if shareholders perform services, they have to pay their share of employment tax, and the employer has to pay its share. The same rules apply for S corp owners who are providing some services.

Now contrast that with distributions of S corp earnings, which are not subject to income tax at the shareholder level, provided they have sufficient shareholder basis. Those are not taxable from an income tax standpoint if they have enough basis. They are also not subject to employment taxes because the distributions are from company earnings rather than payable as salary. Shareholders that own 2 or more percent of an S corp are required to include the value of any fringe benefits that they get as part of their S corp status in gross income. They are not considered to be employees for purposes of those fringe-benefit rules. It is kind of a hybrid being both an employee and owner.

## Self-Employment Tax

Self-employed individuals, of course, have to pay self-employment tax at the FICA rate. Although certain amounts are nontaxable—particularly if they are getting rental income or dividend income—most of their earnings are going to be taxable at a rate of 12.4 percent for the Social Security tax and 2.9 percent for the Medicare tax. For S corporations, the S corp owners do have a distinct advantage with respect to these self-employment taxes because instead of being self-employment income, payments are a distribution of earnings to the owner not subject to those employment taxes. The corporation has to withhold payroll taxes only from amounts that are deemed to be wages or salary for any employee-shareholder. The standard is based on the value of that employee's services. However, the remainder of any distribution or undistributed profits will not be subject to self-employment or payroll taxes. This can, obviously, save a lot of money, which is likely why a lot of entities are set up as S corps.

> **EXAMPLE:** John Edwards, the presidential candidate a few years ago, got in trouble over this position; as did Newt Gingrich. They set up their businesses as S corps. The entities were essentially just personal service businesses. John Edwards ran his legal practice through his S corp, so there was not a lot of capital involved. It was, basically, just his services, he treated the income as though it was earnings from his corporation, did not pay self-employment taxes on it, and took a very bare minimum. It was thought that was unseemly, particularly from someone who was running for president. However, there are a lot of people who are definitely doing the same thing.

## STUDY QUESTION

**5.** Related to employment tax issues, shareholders owning at least what percent are required to include the value of fringe benefits income?

   **a.** 1 percent

   **b.** 2 percent

   **c.** 5 percent

   **d.** 10 percent

## Reasonable Compensation

How does the S corp know whether compensation being paid is adequate or inadequate? In order to avoid payroll taxes, the S corp may be tempted to underpay the shareholder-employees for the services that they perform and make up the difference in the form of distributions. The shareholder owners could say that the entity is their company, in essence they are just taking the money out of their own company. If they're successful in doing this, the shareholders can avoid the employee share of *Federal Insurance Contributions Act* (FICA) and Medicare taxes. The employer may avoid the employer's share as well.

Addressing this situation, the IRS made rules and standards. Rev. Rul. 74-44 provides that the IRS may recharacterize as wages a corporate distribution to a shareholder in lieu of wages and thus assess whatever employment taxes would have been due. If the IRS sees what looks like an S corp calls a "distribution" is actually wages, that will initiate further scrutiny by the IRS. That will include a look at the impact of the individual shareholder on S corp earnings. How valuable were those services to the total earnings of the business? In answering that question, practitioners and the IRS need to look at whether the business is capital intensive or labor intensive. Especially if the entity is labor intensive, the people who are performing the labor should receive a fair salary.

> **EXAMPLE:** A husband and wife owned an S corporation in which the husband did not work and the wife only worked 12 hours per month on clerical work. The IRS failed on attempting to collect any payroll taxes, because the wife was not an employee; her work was too infrequent.

> **EXAMPLE:** Contrast a closely held, personal-services S corporation, an S corp accounting firm, in which the shareholder took no salary. No activity was going on except the performance of the accounting services, so it does not seem reasonable to take no salary.

One factor that sometimes comes into play if there is capital in the business is determining a fair rate of return on the capital. If shareholders have equity in the business, what is a fair rate of return? What is a fair rate of return on capital? Shareholders cannot say the entirety should be salary if there is also capital in the business. Some state tax agencies, like California, tend to ignore basis rules or debt structure and take unreasonable positions on many issues

Is there abuse of this situation? A Treasury Inspector General Report, issued in July 2002, had data that summarized the average shareholder wages and distributions of 84 S corps that were at that time under audit. The data indicated that the average shareholder wage of those S corps was $5,300, whereas the average distribution was $350,000. If those shareholders were performing services, that does appear to be abusive. The report recommended to the IRS that it aggressively review S corp shareholder-employees to ensure reasonable compensation is reported along with appropriate FICA and Medicare taxes.

The issue for federal purposes is a fair salary for the work performed. In an S corp the choices involve salary versus income. There is a distinct possibility of family-income shifting. Treasury Regulation 1366 provides that in determining what is a reasonable allowance for services rendered for the S corp, all facts and circumstances must be considered. One of those facts and circumstances is the amount that ordinarily would be paid in order to obtain comparable services from a person who is neither a member of the family nor a shareholder in the corporation. For instance, if a senior family member receives inadequate consideration for services rendered or for capital provided (money lent to an S corporation), his or her gross income, consisting of compensation will be increased. The income of the S corp that flows through to the shareholders will be correspondingly decreased. If the entity is closely held in that context, a shareholder can attempt to shift income from one family member to another who may be able to afford to declare more, and is in a lower tax bracket.

**¶509**

**EXAMPLE:** All the stock of MaxShift, an S corporation, is owned in equal portions by a father, Emory Redgrave, and his three children. Only Emory is active in the business, and his salary for the taxable year is $100,000. After deducting such salary, the corporation's taxable income for the year is $100,000, and each of the four shareholders reports $25,000 of income from the corporation.

On audit, the IRS determines that a reasonable salary for Emory would have been $160,000. If such salary had actually been paid, the corporation's taxable income would have been reduced to $40,000, and each shareholder would have reported $10,000 of income from the corporation. Emory's total income from the corporation would have been $170,000 rather than $125,000. Therefore, to place the shareholders in the position they would have been in if a reasonable salary had been paid to Emory, the IRS can attempt to reallocate $15,000 of income from each of the three children to Emory.

Noteworthy is that if an S corp pushes a bigger salary for a particular shareholder, the amount that flows through to all the shareholders is reduced.

Reasonableness is ultimately determined on the basis of all the facts and circumstances if a case goes to court. In *Roob v. Commr,* the court examined the nature of the services performed, the responsibilities involved, the time spent, the size and complexity of the business, prevailing economic conditions, compensation paid by comparable firms for comparable services, and salary paid to company officers in prior years. Other courts also consider: the employee's qualifications, general economic conditions, and, in the case of small corporations with a limited number of officers, the amount of compensation paid to the particular employee in previous years.

# ¶ 510 LOANS VERSUS INCOME DISTRIBUTIONS

Previously, the text examined circumstances of a shareholder making a loan to the corporation. What about the reverse: when the corporation distributes cash to the shareholder? The issue is whether the corporation just loans the money to the shareholder or makes an actual distribution. There are times that shareholders withdraw cash from their closely held S corps without truly knowing the character of the cash payment. How should a practitioner advise the client?

**EXAMPLE:** In preparing client Clive Grant's tax return for 2017 in February 2018, his accountant noticed a $200,000 cash distribution from an S corporation to Clive in October 2017. The accountant asks Clive what the payment was, and he asks, "What should it be?"

Can the accountant advise Clive that a loan would be best treatment, because Clive does not have sufficient basis for a tax-free distribution? Can a lawyer prepare a note from Clive to the corporation dated as of October 2017? Did the corporation really make a loan to him? It is hard to support that something is debt if there is no indicia of the fact that it is debt. What are some of the indicia of debt? When an instrument contains a written, unconditional promise to pay on demand or on a specified date a certain sum of money and to pay a fixed interest rate, it more closely resembles debt. Being subordinate to other debt indicates that an instrument represents equity. If the corporation makes a loan to Clive but he already has several debts, it looks less likely to be true debt. A high debt-to-equity ratio suggests that most creditors might consider it too risky to make a loan. If practitioners look at a loan from a corp to a shareholder, they might be trying to consider whether the shareholder could get a loan on similar terms from a third-party lender. Additionally, if distributions are made to all shareholders in proportion to their equity holdings, it is going to be very unlikely they are considered to be loans because those look like proportional distributions of income.

What about the question of backdating the note to October 2017? Backdating assigns an event to a date prior to that of the actual occurrence. Clive's practitioner finds out in 2018 that a distribution was made in late 2017. What documents are needed to give this its proper characterization? There is a negative connotation to backdating, due to the legal trouble of others who backdated stock options. In that case, that type of backdating was definitively fraudulent.

If there are enough facts to support that the transaction may have indeed been a loan intended to be paid back (other loans made to the shareholder were paid back), then the practitioner may backdate the agreement or note to October 2017, if that was concluded to be the intent of the parties.

It is trickier where there was no clear intent of the parties; if Clive just took out $200,000 cash and did not really know why. In that case, there is not a true characterization.

Consider the difference between backdating that memorializes something that actually happened—a type of backdating that is appropriate—versus backdating that fabricates. Obviously, backdating that fabricates is the kind that is fraudulent because it makes up something that never happened. An entity might want to memorialize past actions, like minutes from a meeting that were not typed until later. The document may be dated as of that earlier date. Ratifying past actions, an attorney may sign an LLC agreement as of January 1st because it took the party several months to agree on final terms. Or finally, backdating may be used for clarification of terms, this is the one discussed here. The note clarifies whether the distribution to the S-corp shareholder is a salary payment, a distribution of profits, or a loan. Maybe that is a valid reason to backdate. If a practitioner can determine what it actually was, the note needs to clarify that.

## STUDY QUESTION

---

**6.** Each of the following identifies an acceptable reason for backdating *except:*

   **a.** Memorialization of past actions

   **b.** Ratifying past actions

   **c.** Backdating an invoice to reflect it in an earlier period

   **d.** Clarification of terms

---

# ¶ 511 TAX DISTRIBUTIONS

Tax distributions provide a means for S corporation shareholders to pay the tax liabilities resulting from allocations of income. If the S corp. is required to make monthly or quarterly distributions of its net available cash flow under a shareholder agreement, or makes regular distributions of its cash flow, there generally is no need for it to make tax distributions.

## Third-Party Debt

However, when the S corporation owes debt to a third party, providing for tax distributions in the shareholder agreement or loan agreement can be important. In that case, including a tax distribution provision in the shareholder agreement ensures that the shareholders receive enough distributions to pay their tax liabilities. The practitioner should ensure there is consistency between the terms of the tax distribution provisions included in the loan agreement and the partnership agreement.

## Frequency and Timing of the Distributions

One consideration in drafting tax distributions is the frequency and the timing of those distributions. When will they be made and how often? Ideally, tax distributions are made to coincide with the due date of quarterly estimates for the shareholders. However, determining each shareholder's share of income for each quarter may be administratively burdensome. Perhaps practitioners do not necessarily get that amount fine-tuned on a quarterly basis. Sometimes, tax distributions are only made annually prior to April 15th of the next taxable year.

Are distributions of appreciated property to shareholders valued at fair market value and cause shareholder gain? Yes. Basically, it is the same idea as if a C corp was distributing appreciated property. When the appreciated property comes out of the S corp, that transaction triggers gain. Then that gain will flow through to the shareholders and increase their basis. When the property is then distributed, the distribution will be equal to whatever the fair market value of that property is.

> **EXAMPLE:** The RiteInk corporation had a basis of $10,000 in the property, and its value had gone up in value to $100,000. The shareholder, Ashley Jorgensen, had actually contributed that property to the corporation. Her basis in the S corp stock was also $10,000. Currently, it has gone up to $100,000. Ashley wants the property back. The distribution she receives will trigger a gain of $90,000. That will increase her basis to $100,000, and then the $100,000 distribution, which is the fair market value of the property, will again reduce her basis down to zero. The gain is taxable, the distribution is not, as long as there is sufficient basis. Generally, that is the way the tax distribution works.

What is the fair market value of the shareholder's basis? Generally, the rule says that the fair market value of the distributed property being distributed to the shareholders should be determined as if it were sold in its entirety. What would the shareholder get if he or she sold it to a third party? To the extent that shareholders do not know that, they look for comparables or try to get an appraisal.

Now when shareholders are distributing built-in loss properties—depreciated property—the corporation does not recognize loss. This is similar to the C corp level under Code Sec. 311. Shareholders do not get to take losses on distributions of depreciated or built-in loss properties, and the same thing applies here for the S corp. If the S corp distributes built-in loss property, no loss is recognized.

In that case, the stock basis is reduced by losses that are not deductible. One question that comes up with the S corp is if shareholders are distributing built-in loss property, should they be reducing stock basis by that unrecognized loss? Most practitioners seem to think the answer is yes. Even though shareholders cannot recognize the loss and it cannot flow through to the shareholders, it should reduce the basis.

---

**CPE NOTE:** When you have completed your study and review of chapters 4-5, which comprise Module 2, you may wish to take the Final Exam for this Module. Go to **cchcpelink.com/printcpe** to take this Final Exam online.

---

# MODULE 3: TAX ISSUES RELATED TO PROPERTY—Chapter 6: Bonus Depreciation Update & Cost Segregation Tax Planning

## ¶ 601 WELCOME

This chapter discusses the changes to tax deductions for bonus depreciation of new and used qualified business property made by the *Tax Cuts and Jobs Act* (H.R. 1) passed in 2017. Proposed regulations were published August 8, 2018. The proposed regulations are "reliance" regulations; taxpayers may choose to rely on them, and if so, the IRS won't challenge the taxpayer. However, taxpayers aren't bound by the regulations until the tax year that final regulations are published. Rules under the new tax law apply to acquired property in addition to self-constructed property. The decrease after 2018's 100 percent bonus depreciation in coming years is reviewed. The discussion includes the self-rental rule, grouping election, and strategies for maximizing bonus deductions using cost segregation. The chapter concludes with a description of the regulations for tangible property.

## ¶ 602 LEARNING OBJECTIVES

Upon completion of this chapter, you will be able to:

- Recognize the percentages of the bonus depreciation deduction applicable for 2018 and subsequent years
- Identify how the new tax law affects other tax planning strategies such as Code Sec. 179 expensing and net operating losses
- Recognize the types of property held to be qualified leasehold improvements and qualified improvement property

---

## ¶ 603 INTRODUCTION

"Bonus depreciation" is a tax deduction for trades and businesses that enables them to take an immediate first-year deduction on the purchase of qualified business property in addition to other depreciation. The rules are applied to specific types of property with a general depreciation system (GDS) recovery period of 20 or fewer years under the modified accelerated cost recovery system (MACRS). This property is often referred to as "short-life property" for which costs are recovered under the GDS. Under the new law, bonus depreciation also applies to qualified used property acquired for trades and businesses but only if the property wasn't acquired from a related person, inherited, received by gift, previously owned and used by the taxpayer, and its basis isn't determined with respect to other property of the taxpayer.

Water and utility property are subject to some special rules, as are computer software and long production period property. "Qualified property" includes qualified restaurant property and qualified retail improvement property that are placed in service prior January 1, 2018 if they also meet the requirements of qualified improvement property. However, "qualified property" doesn't include qualified restaurant property or qualified retail improvements placed in service after 2017, even if it meets the requirements of qualified improvement property. This has changed under the new tax law, and this chapter provides a timeline of current rules. Bonus depreciation does not apply to anything recovered using the alternative depreciation system (ADS), so a property that is being used outside of the United States and for which taxpayers are forced to use ADS, it does not qualify for bonus depreciation.

Longer production period assets are defined under Code Sec 168 (k). Longer production period property is property that:

- Meets the general requirement for qualifying property
- Is subject to Code Section 263A Uniform Capitalization Rules
- Has a production period greater than one year and a cost exceeding $1 million and has a MACRS recovery period of at least 10 years or is used in the trade or business of transporting persons or property for hire, such as a commercial aircraft.

# ¶ 604 BONUS DEPRECIATION CRITERIA UNDER THE NEW TAX LAW

## Phasedown of Rates

The new rates for bonus depreciation are:

- 100 percent depreciation (a rise from the previous rate of 50 percent) is applicable for assets acquired after September 27, 2017, through the end of the year 2022;
- The rate phases down by 20 percent each year after 2022 for the next five years; and
- The rate for 2027 is 0 percent.

The *Tax Cuts and Jobs Act* provided businesses with a lot more clarity, so over the next 10 years companies know what the bonus rules are going to be. The rates for those years make bonus depreciation much more of a planning tool when businesses want to purchase either eligible new property or eligible used property. That is a significant change in tax rules and something very important to understand. Table 6.1 lists the specific rates with their inclusive dates.

Table 6.1 Bonus Depreciation Rates (inclusive dates)

| | |
|---|---|
| 9/11/01 – 5/5/03 | 30% |
| 5/6/03 – 12/31/04 & 1/1/08 – 9/8/10 | 50% |
| 9/9/10 – 12/31/11 | 100% |
| 1/1/12 – 9/27/17 | 50% |
| 9/28/17 – 12/31/22 | 100% |
| 1/1/23 – 12/31/23 | 80% |
| 1/1/24 – 12/31/24 | 60% |
| 1/1/25 – 12/31/25 | 40% |
| 1/1/26 – 13/31/26 | 20% |

Personal property and land improvements are now fully expensed even for buildings that had already been previously occupied when the taxpayer acquired them.

Some very large real property trades or businesses (trailing three-year gross receipts greater than $25 million) and real property trades or businesses that are "tax shelters" are subject to new interest limitation rules of Section 163(j), beginning in 2018. The term "real property trade or business" is defined in Code Sec. 469(c)(7). Real property trades or businesses that are subject to the new interest limitation rules may elect out. However, the election out comes with a price: Businesses that elect out must use ADS depreciation for residential real estate (27.5-year property), nonresidential real estate (39-year property), and qualified improvement property "QIP" (see discussion below). Property subject to mandatory ADS depreciation isn't eligible for bonus depreciation. However, none of the foregoing property will qualify for bonus depreciation in 2018. It's possible that Congress will make a technical correction that will allow QIP to qualify for bonus depreciation, and if that happens, real property trades or businesses will have to weigh the loss of bonus depreciation against the limitation of interest expense.

Most real estate trade or businesses won't be subject to the 30 percent interest limitation of § 163(j), and therefore won't need to consider making the election out of the interest limitation rules. These businesses therefore won't be subject to ADS treatment in the case of residential real estate, nonresidential real estate and qualified improvement property.

Bonus depreciation was developed after the September 11, 2001, terrorist attack. The federal government decided to encourage building using the bonus depreciation write-off of part of new building construction immediately in year one of the building's useful life. The table shows a spike in the rate in 2003, eventually rising to the 100 percent rate in 2010 and 2011. Bonus depreciation disappeared briefly but changed to 50 percent in 2012 through the date of passage of the new tax law in 2017. The 100 percent rate is set to apply through 2022, then phase down 20 percent per year until it disappears again in 2027 (unless Congress revises the law again).

> **EXAMPLE:** In 2018 Master Management Corp is acquiring a $10 million building. Master Management does a cost segregation study (described later) in which it's noted that $2 million of that is personal property and $1 million is land improvements, anything outside of the footprint of the building. That $3 million will get 100 percent bonus depreciation on in year one. Which is a significant deduction. Because it's an acquired (used) property, it's a significant change from previous law allowing zero bonus depreciation.

A trade or business can opt out of claiming bonus depreciation at all or elect to use a 50 percent rate if the company makes the election with its timely filed tax return. The 50 percent bonus depreciation election only applies to the taxpayer's first tax year ending after 9/27/2017. A taxpayer may elect out of bonus depreciation on a class-by-class basis for the tax year. Why would a taxpayer choose such an election? The answer, described in more detail later, concerns net operating loss (NOL) carryforwards that mitigate the need for deductions using bonus depreciation.

However, a lot of clients simply miss taking bonus depreciation without electing out formally. Once made, the election is irrevocable. Taxpayers file Form 3115, *Application for Change in Accounting Method,* to get bonus depreciation in its applicable timeframe.

## Qualified Improvement Property

The law states that qualified improvement property in 2018 and onward is a 39 years useful life with no bonus depreciation allowed. Everything is subject to change with additional guidance or technical corrections, but this discussion is built on how the law reads now.

## Written Binding Contract Rule

Under bonus depreciation eligibility through the new tax law's written and binding contract rules, the rules apply to acquisitions after September 27, 2017. Proposed regulations provide that property acquired under a written binding contract is treated as acquired at the time the contract is entered into. The written and binding contract rules apply to bonus depreciation if a building went into contract prior to September 28, 2017.

The written and binding contract rule that was incorporated into some of the 2003 tax law was not included in current tax law. That's one of the issues about which the American Institute of CPAs (AICPA) and other organizations sought immediate guidance.

> **EXAMPLE:** Ed Kowalski made an acquisition that closed on October 1, 2017, but he entered into the contract to purchase that facility on September 1, 2017. Under the proposed regulations, the property won't qualify for bonus depreciation.

Recall that used property did not get bonus depreciation until the new tax law approved it for use after September 27, 2017. Clients should be aware of the risk.

## Auto Dealers

Bonus depreciation is not available to certain taxpayers with floor plan financing, such as the Toyota and the Ford dealerships, boat dealerships, or the John Deere dealership. Floor plan financing is used to finance the acquisition of motor vehicles (car, boat, farm machinery or equipment) held for sale or lease and secured by the inventory acquired. But only if the floor plan financing indebtedness was taken into account under the new rules that limit the business interest deduction to 30 percent. If the company qualified for the exception to the interest deduction limitation by having annual average gross receipts under $25 million for the last three years, bonus depreciation would still be available. Note that those operating entities are the ones with floor plan financing. Oftentimes, such businesses are owned in a separate limited liability company (LLC), but even if they're wholly owned, with Mom and Dad owning the operating entity along with the real estate holding company, or maybe their children are involved in owning some of the real estate but they're not involved in the ownership entity or operating entity.

If the operating entity leases from a related party or holding company, clients may say that the holding company is not under floor plan financing and therefore should get bonus depreciation. Brand-new car dealerships go up all over the country. Many dealerships have to remodel their showrooms these days to conform to the new dealer specs. This could be quite impactful to those owners that have not done that and are embarking on a major remodel, and would get carved out of qualifying for bonus depreciation. Planners should ensure that they understand that maybe there's a difference between the operating entity and the real estate holding company, and that they potentially should or would get bonus depreciation.

## STUDY QUESTIONS

**1.** Which of the following specified property types with respect to bonus depreciation is *not* classified as qualified property for property placed in service **after** December 31, 2017?

    **a.** New or used property

    **b.** Water utility property

    **c.** Qualified restaurant and retail improvements

    **d.** Long production period property

**2.** What is the bonus depreciation rate for the year 2026?

    **a.** 20 percent

    **b.** 40 percent

    **c.** 60 percent

    **d.** 80 percent

# ¶ 605 INTERPLAY OF BONUS DEPRECIATION AND CODE SEC. 179 EXPENSING

Taxpayers can elect to expense certain property by completing Form 4562, *Depreciation and Amortization,* and attaching it to their tax returns. Code Sec. 179 allows businesses to deduct the purchase of qualified equipment and software. Qualified property for the Section 179 deduction is tangible section 1245 property (new or used) depreciable under MACRS acquired by the purchaser for use in an active trade or business. The deduction limit is $1 million, and there's a capital investment limitation of $2.5 million and then a dollar-for-dollar reduction after that. In 2018, Code Sec. 179 was expanded to include a new category of assets called "qualified real property" which includes additional items such as a roof; heating, ventilation, and air conditioning (HVAC); as well as improvements to the interiors; fire protection; alarm systems; and security systems of nonresidential properties. Later, this chapter describes how cost segregation studies apply here.

These new items should seem familiar to practitioners. Over the last several years, planners have all been educated about the tangible property regulations, those tangible property regulations that dropped in 2013, that these were the units of property or the major components. These are for commercial buildings only, not residential, and for improvements made after the building was first and originally placed into service.

> **EXAMPLE:** Pieter Knudsen, a client, purchased an existing 10-year-old structure in 2018 for $4 million. *Before* placing it in service, Pieter's workers put on a new roof, HVAC, fire protection and security system for $500,000. All of it is eligible for Code Sec. 179 immediate expensing.

> Expensing is allowed only for improvements after the original building was placed in service. The issue is the original building. Because it is a used building, a 10-year-old building used before Pieter placed it in service in 2018, is still eligible for Code Sec. 179 expensing.

> That answer would be different if Pieter were going to capitalize it. If he were forced to capitalize it and didn't have the Code Sec. 179 rules, it would be an amelioration of an existing condition and so therefore he couldn't take it as a current year expense from the tangible property regulation. He would have to take it as depreciable asset, and those depreciable assets are very likely going to have a useful life of 39 years. The difference is because Code Sec. 179 improvements are covered all in one year but depreciated over 39 years, Pieter would rather take it under Code Sec. 179.

Code Sec. 179 expensing now includes personal property used for furnishing lodgings, such as furniture and appliances, hotel rooms and student housing, and apartment buildings. There's no benefit in taking Code Sec. 179 expensing on tangible personal property when clients have 100 percent bonus depreciation applied. Clients are trying to avoid the $2.5 million cap with this play. If clients acquired more than the $2.5 million of capital expenditures, then Section 179 deductions start being reduced. Planners tell clients they are going to get to the same answer: expense the cost or depreciate it and apply the 100 percent bonus depreciation. Clients are going to take all of it in the current year, so there's no difference at the end of the day.

> **NOTE:** There's no benefit in taking a Code Sec. 179 expense on tangible personal property when bonus depreciation is 100 percent. Bonus depreciation is preferable to use by very large businesses that spend more than the $2.5 million spending cap for the year.

Be aware that both Code. Sec. 179 and bonus depreciation are subject to recapture as well. If clients are creating massive deductions with bonus depreciation that could come back and catch up with them if they're going to sell it within, perhaps, three to five years, another route is preferable. Taxpayers should consider Code Sec. 179 expensing on items ineligible for bonus depreciation, such as roofs, to avoid hitting the Code Sec. 179 cap.

For certain noncorporate lessors, Code Sec. 179 expensing should not apply as per Code Sec. 179(d)(5). There are two criteria exceptions to that. Individuals and partnerships who are not corporations and lessors of commercial real estate may not be able to claim Section 179 expensing for qualified purchases. Caveats apply and clients and planners should understand the rules.

## ¶ 606 PURCHASED PARTNERSHIP INTERESTS

Proposed regulations published August 8, 2018 provide that purchases of interests in partnerships may result in bonus depreciation, beginning with purchases after September 27, 2017. Bonus depreciation applies only to the "stepped-up" portion of qualified property.

> **EXAMPLE:** On September 28, 2017, Buddy pays David $100 for a 50 percent interest in Celtic Properties, LLC. Celtic Properties, LLC owns an apartment building. Buddy and David aren't related, and Buddy hasn't previously owned an interest in the LLC. David's share of the underlying basis in the LLCs property is $50, so the step-up is $50 ($100 minus $50). The LLC has a Code Sec. 754 election in place. The purchase price and step-up are allocated as follows:

| | Purchase price allocation | Seller's share of net tax basis | Step-up | Bonus depreciation |
|---|---|---|---|---|
| Land | $20 | $10 | $10 | $0 |
| Building | $50 | $30 | $20 | $0 |
| Land improvements | $15 | $10 | $5 | $5 |
| Personal property | $15 | $0 | $15 | $15 |
| Total | $100 | $50 | $50 | $20 |

In the above example, neither land (not depreciable) nor building (recovery period is greater than 20 years) qualify for bonus depreciation. Further, the carryover basis of land improvements and personal property ($10 and $0, respectively) don't qualify for bonus depreciation. Only the "stepped-up" portion of land improvements and personal property qualify ($5 and $15, respectively).

Note that step-ups that occur under Code Sec. 1014 (date of death step-ups) do not qualify for bonus depreciation.

## ¶ 607 LIKE-KIND EXCHANGES

Proposed regulations published August 8, 2018 provide that replacement property acquired in a Code Sec. 1031 exchange can qualify for bonus depreciation. The amount of bonus depreciation depends upon whether the replacement property is new property or used property.

Property acquired in a like-kind exchange comes in two varieties: "exchanged basis property" (this is the carryover basis from the relinquished property), and "excess basis property" (this is the increase in basis which typically results from acquiring a more valuable piece of property).

In the case of new replacement property, both the exchanged basis and the excess basis property qualify for bonus depreciation.

**EXAMPLE:** Seth has a like-kind exchange in 2018. He exchanges two duplexes for a small apartment building. Seth is increasing his investment by borrowing $100,000 of "new money" to increase his investment in real estate. The replacement property (i.e., the apartment building) is brand new. Bonus depreciation is as follows:

| | Carryover basis | Excess basis | Total | Bonus eligible |
|---|---|---|---|---|
| Land | $50 | $10 | $60 | $0 |
| Building | $50 | $50 | $100 | $0 |
| Land improvements | $20 | $30 | $50 | $50 |
| Personal property | $0 | $10 | $10 | $10 |

In the above example, personal property no longer qualifies for like-kind exchange treatment for exchanges completed after 12/31/17. Therefore, this property is treated as purchased, and is outside the like-kind exchange rules, and it qualifies under the general rules for bonus depreciation. Land improvements qualify for like-kind exchange (since they're real property) and since the replacement property is new, both the carryover basis and "excess basis" qualify for bonus depreciation.

In the case of used replacement property, only the "excess basis" property qualifies for bonus depreciation.

**EXAMPLE:** Same facts as above, except that Seth acquires a used apartment building as a replacement property.

| | Carryover basis | Excess basis | Total | Bonus eligible |
|---|---|---|---|---|
| Land | $50 | $10 | $60 | $0 |
| Building | $50 | $50 | $100 | $0 |
| Land improvements | $20 | $30 | $50 | $30 |
| Personal property | $0 | $10 | $10 | $10 |

In the above example, since the property is used, only "excess basis" qualifies for bonus depreciation. As discussed above, the personal property is no longer covered by the like-kind exchange rules and is therefore allowable as purchased used property eligible for bonus depreciation. Land improvements qualify for bonus depreciation, however since the replacement property is used, only the "excess basis" portion qualifies. The carryover basis in land improvements doesn't qualify for bonus depreciation.

# ¶ 608 NET OPERATING LOSSES UNDER THE NEW TAX LAW

The landscape for net operating losses (NOLs) has changed since the enactment of the *Tax Cuts and Jobs Act* in 2017. This is important because of the deductions that 100 percent bonus depreciation is going to create.

**PLANNING POINTER:** NOLs can no longer be carried back to a previous tax year. A little planning opportunity exists for fiscal year taxpayers for whom the

2017 tax year is still open. For NOLs created in 2017 the carryforward can offset 100 percent of taxable income into the future. Planners now need to track pre-and post-2018 NOLs because clients are carrying those NOLs forward post-2018 at 80 percent, whereas clients are carrying forward the 2017 or pre-2017 NOLs at a 100 percent rate.

**EXAMPLE:** CostSave Company, which has a fiscal year ending in 2017, did not need deductions in 2017, but paid $100,000 in taxes in the prior year. If CostSave does a cost segregation study for the 2017 year, the company can create $500,000 of NOLs that they can carry back to get a refund on that $100,000 tax paid.

Because it's CostSave's fiscal 2017, the company can carry the remaining NOLs forward at a 100 percent offset for taxable income in future years. The opportunity is no longer available for 2018. The company will be limited to 80 percent in offsets it cannot carry back. This is another planning tool, but has just a few months left to use for some taxpayers. If clients fit that scenario, planners might want to check whether it makes sense to do a cost segregation now and implement in 2017, as opposed to waiting until 2018.

# ¶ 609  COST SEGREGATION TO CAPITALIZE ON BONUS DEPRECIATION

## What Is Cost Segregation?

Cost segregation takes a lump-sum payment for property and splits it up into many different parts. The technique is applicable for acquired property, new construction, even a remodel of a significant size, or buildouts. If a client owns a major discount store chain and is doing a million-dollar buildout in every mall across the country, maybe the technique will work well because the planner can go as far back as 1987 for the client's properties.

## Types of Property Analyzed

Cost segregation is a time-valued money concept. Would a client pay a practitioner's fee to go back as far as 1987? Likely no, but the benefits analysis will determine that. Clients don't have enough time left to recover any fees that may be incurred per a cost segregation analysis. At the very bottom, the practitioner is looking at building structures, both commercial and residential, and splits them up between the 39-year, 27.5-year, 15-year categories for anything in the exterior footprint of the building, the asset class called land improvements. Land improvements involve curbing, drainage, that kind of project.

Seven-year property is applicable to a lot of manufacturers. This is personal property that's used in manufacturing. Five-year property, again a lot of trade or business properties are recovered over 5 or 7 years, is personal property. Cars and office equipment would be recovered over five years. Details of the cost recovery system are discussed in Code Section 168.

The planner takes the lump sum of those expenses from over the years and breaks the costs down, or "componentizes" them. The planner, considering the time value of money, tries to take deductions earlier to increase the client's cash flow. A dollar the client receives today is worth a whole lot more in a deduction than it will be 39 years from now. The planner uses a discount rate or rate of return that holds that a dollar saved today can be applied from a cash flow or savings standpoint to recover and have more money 39 years from now, recovering the fees associated with it.

## Dispositions

The secondary goal is to establish depreciable lines for each major building component that is likely to be replaced in the future. This pertains to dispositions, which now are allowed for anytime that the owner removes something from the building, including the roof, windows, doors, or bathroom fixtures. The focus is on anytime something is removed from the building, or a renovation that takes place. For example, 10 years after the building was constructed.

It's determined that a client needs to depreciate that new asset. The planner can take an allowable disposition, but to do so has no better way than understanding what the value of that is than to go back to records of cost segregation for the asset. The tax preparers need this information to claim a retirement loss or a partial disposition.

Cost segregation deductions are more valuable for fiscal 2017 tax returns than starting in 2018 under the new tax law. The permanent deductions or permanent tax savings could be realized by claiming deductions before the 2018 rates apply; it's a rate arbitrage. If the planner can shift income to tax years with lower rates, that may or may not be more valuable to the client.

Taxpayers who opt not to perform a cost segregation study because it only represented a timing difference should possibly reconsider. Sometimes clients look at a planner's offer to prepare a cost segregation study to create additional deductions in the current year and inquire whether the study would create any more deductions. The approach would just frontload those deductions. Clients cognizant of planners' fees might decide against the study.

Clients may be reconsidering if their deductions are at a higher tax rate. With tax rates are falling, those deductions will become less valuable into the future. Why not pull them forward, frontloading them?

**EXAMPLE:** Magnetic Photos, a C corporation, purchases a building in 2014 for $1 million. The corporation's planner applies a cost segregation to the corporation's 2017 return, accelerating $100,000 of future depreciation in this 2017 return. The corporation is trading an immediate tax savings of $35,000. Under the new tax rate of 21 percent for corporations in 2018, there's a $14,000 permanent tax savings because of the rate arbitrage, the old 35 percent corporate rate versus the current 21 percent, or $35,000 versus $21,000.

That's in addition to traditional benefits of accelerated cash flow and time value of money that a cost segregation study will allow. Planners should discuss with clients who are in a tax-paying situation. Those deductions, if they can be used or even if they can't with NOLs, are more valuable for 2017 returns.

At some point the benefit flips. If Magnetic Photos has a lot of 5-year and 15-year property associated with the purchased building, the corporation will have used up a lot of the deductions in the earlier years and get fewer in the future.

One of the most common tax planning tools for anyone involved with real estate is cost segregation. It can be done any time after a building is purchased. Many people believe they unfortunately missed the time window because it was placed in service a year or even several years ago. Those old numbers could be ideal candidates for study. Perhaps the clients didn't need the deductions then. The planner can remind clients that within the first couple of years, returns can be amended.

The IRS allows a taxpayer to apply for a change in accounting method on form 3115. A change in accounting method usually requires an adjustment when the IRS approves the taxpayers request. This adjustment is booked in the year of change. It's an easy Code Section 481(a) calculation that taxpayers are allowed to catch up and adjust for the missed depreciation. Clients can take the missed depreciation all in the year of change. Practitioners complete Form 3115 and claim any missed deductions in that year of change.

# ¶ 610  THE SELF-RENTAL RULE AND GROUPING ELECTION

## The Self-Rental Rule

The self-rental rule holds that clients can't use losses from a *separate* real estate entity (if it's a passive activity) against active income. A planner's client is an S corporation involved with a nonpassive activity from which it earns business taxable income of $100,000. The client also owns a real estate LLC, a passive activity (client has little involvement other than ownership) that has $100,000 in losses the same tax year. The client should marry those businesses together for tax purposes so there is no tax liability (the loss offsets income). The S corporation cannot net (offset) the income with the LLC's passive losses. In such an instance, the client must assume a 40 percent tax rate and send the IRS $40,000.

## Grouping Election

The opposite is true using the grouping election. Under Sec. 469 (and Reg. Sec. 1.469(c)(1)), the deduction of losses from a passive activity is limited to the amount of passive income from all passive activities, until there is a fully taxable disposition of the taxpayer's entire interest in the activity. A "passive activity loss" is generally the excess of the aggregate losses from all passive activities for the tax year over the aggregate income from all passive activities for that year. When a taxpayer's passive activity loss deduction is disallowed, it is treated as a deduction for the next tax year and can be carried forward indefinitely. It allows the client to net income and losses between the S corporation and LLC. The rules are that both entities must be 100 percent owned by the same individuals and that the grouping election is made in the first year those entities coexist. The result for the S corporation and LLC in this situation is zero tax due. The tax preparer elects grouping on its Form 1065, *U.S. Return of Partnership Income,* or Form 1120S, *U.S. Income Tax Return for an S Corporation.*

Reg. Sec. 1.469-4(c)(2) provides a facts-and-circumstances test for determining whether a grouping of activities results in an appropriate economic unit. Therefore, whether activities constitute an appropriate economic unit under this test and may be treated as a single activity depends on all the relevant facts and circumstances. A taxpayer may use any reasonable method of applying the relevant facts and circumstances in grouping activities. The factors given the greatest weight in the regulation are:

- Similarities and differences in types of trades or businesses;
- The extent of common control;
- The extent of common ownership;
- Geographical location; or
- Interdependencies between or among the activities.

Reg. Sec. 1.469-4(e) provides that once a taxpayer has grouped activities, the taxpayer cannot regroup those activities unless "it is determined that a taxpayer's original grouping was clearly inappropriate, or a material change in the facts and circumstances has occurred that renders the original grouping clearly inappropriate."

## Cost Segregation Developments

A study was published by AICPA on March 31, 2016, about estate planning using cost segregation. In decades past, if a client had a building with a basis in excess of $1 million, planners would by default suggest performing a cost segregation study and never really consider anything else. With today's tangible property regulations, planners discuss performing a comprehensive fixed asset review, not just a cost segregation study. The tangible property regulations affect cost segregation studies for retirements, identification of repairs, and deductible property refreshes versus capitalized improvements.

The cost segregation might be included in that review, but why not take a look at some of the retirements or dispositions? Maybe tax planners are depreciating items that otherwise through the tangible property regulations should have been a repair expense. A comprehensive fixed asset review is really what was brought on by the tangible property regs to take a holistic view of the depreciation schedule rather than applying the default of doing a cost segregation study and accelerating one asset's recovery period.

# ¶ 611 QUALIFIED REAL PROPERTY

Earlier the text discussed qualified leasehold improvement (QLI) property and how is that different from qualified improvement property and qualified restaurant property and qualified retail property. These all have been around for quite some time, other than the qualified improvement property. Qualified Leasehold Improvements was released with the *Protecting Americans from Tax Hikes Act* (PATH Act) and then all of these were modified again through the 2017 tax law. All of these distinctions pertain to nonresidential properties only.

## Qualified Leasehold Improvement Property

Qualified leasehold improvement property has been around for quite some time. It was the first qualified real property that was described under the rules. It's includes Code Sec. 1250 property that constitutes an improvement to a nonresidential property. It covers improvements to the interior portion of the building that was exclusively occupied by the lessee, so it excludes common areas or anything like that.

QLI property must have been placed into service at least three years after the original structure was placed into service. QLI property was pursuant to a lease.

> **EXAMPLE:** Nathaniel Berens, a taxpayer, couldn't own a building for three years and then decide to open a professional practice inside that building, redo the inside of the building, and claim it was qualified leasehold improvement property. The three-year for the related-party lease would kick Nathaniel out. There is some 80 percent common ownership rule. So planners should just know that there's a clause for that.

Under the old law after 2015 and prior to the Tax Cuts and Jobs Act, Qualified Leasehold Improvements were depreciated over 15 years. They did not qualify for bonus depreciation unless they also qualified as "QIP". The new Tax Cuts and Jobs Act of 2017 makes some changes here. QLI has been eliminated for property placed in service after December 31, 2017. For property placed in service prior to January 1, 2018, the QLI rules exclude some improvements. QLI excludes costs to enlarge the building, elevators, escalators, or internal structural framework. Owners who have to replace the structure of the roof could not claim QLI. Any structural components would not be QLI if they were for the benefit of a common area, such as a redoing the elevator bay area. These activities would not constitute qualified leasehold improvements.

Many taxpayers make the mistake of claiming bonus depreciation (assuming it meets the definition of QIP) on all tenant improvement property and leasehold improvement costs, assuming all the costs qualified. The representative of the builder says to the tax planner that the activity was just related to the building's interior fit-out. The rep doesn't explain that the builder did some roofing, moved some walls around, and in short there was some significant structural work that was done. The builder installed some new storefront glass and made a couple of upgrades to the elevators and common hallways.

The builder's rep says the builder did the interior fit-out and the tax planner takes that information and applies bonus depreciation and qualified leasehold improvement property to all of it when it's not applicable. The planner doesn't know and have the details behind the costs, which could come back to haunt the builder when the IRS disallows some of the depreciation because it's clearly not QLI property. The tax planner needs to know more than that the activities involved just an interior fit-out. The planner wants to know the actual assets and the scope of what occurred.

Improvements don't qualify if the property leased is between commonly controlled parties. For this purpose, common control means 80 percent or more common ownership.

**EXAMPLE:** A qualified leasehold improvement on property occurred between related parties in 2017. Jerry and Kramer are business partners who own a research and development business called Serenity Now. And they lease the space from a real estate holding company, Monks Café, LLC. The R&D business ownership is split evenly, with Jerry owning 50 percent and Kramer, 50. Monks Café, though, is 35 percent owned by Jerry, and Kramer at 35 percent. George Evans is in on the action, and then Elaine Dawson gets 10 percent.

This involves the 80 percent rule. Monks Café's ownership is 70 percent common owned with the R&D business, so the owners are not related parties because it's below the threshold of 80 percent, and the improvements are done in July as a QLI property, and they will get the 15-year recovery period.

It's a situation in which just because it appears that the owners are related parties, Jerry's, an owner in both and there's some small ownership owned by some other people. It's clearly going to be common ownership. This scenario, knowing the details, was certainly fruitful for Jerry and Kramer because they were able to take those improvements and have them treated as 15-year property.

# ¶ 612 QUALIFIED IMPROVEMENT PROPERTY UNDER NEW TAX LAW

The treatment of qualified improvement property ("QIP") has changed over time:

- It was enacted in the PATH Act, which was effective for property placed in service after December 31, 2015. Initially, QIP qualified for 50 percent bonus depreciation.

- The rules involving QIP were modified by the Tax Cuts and Jobs Act ("TCJA") for property placed in service after 9/27/2017: Proposed regulations provide that QIP acquired and placed in service after September 27 and before January 1, 2018, is eligible for 100 percent bonus depreciation.

- However, QIP placed in service after December 31, 2017 isn't eligible for bonus depreciation. As discussed below, this appears to have resulted from a drafting error that was a part of the Tax Cuts and Jobs Act, and Congress may enact a technical correction to fix the problem.

**EXAMPLE 1:** The client, Michelle, purchased an office building in 2015. In February 2017, she replaced all the light fixtures and wiring inside the building. This qualifies as QIP and for 50 percent bonus depreciation.

**EXAMPLE:** Same facts as above. In November 2017, Michelle replaced all the plumbing fixtures in the building. This qualifies as QIP and for 100 percent bonus depreciation.

**EXAMPLE:** In 2018, Michelle replaces all of the interior doors in the building. This qualifies as QIP, but bonus depreciation won't be available, unless Congress enacts a technical correction (see discussion above).

There are no more separate definitions for qualified leasehold improvements, qualified restaurant property, or qualified retail property. That history of what specific types of qualified property is gone. After December 31, 2017, planners can no longer use the treatment for qualified restaurant property, qualified retail property or qualified leasehold improvement property. It's been replaced by QIP. The Conference Report says the QIP will have 15-year bonus treatment, but the Internal Revenue Code doesn't reflect that. Earlier, the text said qualified improvement property was 39-year property with no bonus depreciation. That's how the tax law is written now. A technical correction is needed here. IRS proposed regulations published on August 8, 2018 also indicate that QIP won't qualify for bonus depreciation for improvement placed in service after December 31, 2017. On August 16, 2018, several members of the Senate Finance Committee sent a letter to Treasury and the IRS asking the IRS to fix the QIP glitch. However, it's unlikely that the IRS will act unless and until Congress passes a technical correction.

QIP includes owner-occupied real estate, whereas QLI property could not be. QIP did not contain a three-year rule, whereas QLI property had to be at least three years old. In 2017, builders would construct a building's shell at the very onset of the year and place it into service. Their business was leasing the structure out as they looked for tenants. The owners would place that original structure in service and provide a tenant allowance a year later. That process would be eligible now, with the new law, to be QIP to build out the interior space without waiting three years.

## Improvements Not Considered to Be QIP

Qualified improvement property only covers nonresidential real property and does *not* include:

- Costs for the enlargement of a building;
- Elevators or escalators; or
- The internal structural framework of a building.

**EXAMPLE:** Mike Swenson spends $1 million on upgrades to an office building. Of the total, $150,000 is for rooftop HVAC units, windows, and interior seismic upgrades. None of the $150,000 in expenditures will result in QIP.

Mike's planner must truly understand what the work is for and its scope.

## Elimination of Qualified Restaurant Property

Qualified restaurant property (QRES) was defined as any Code Sec. 1250 property that is a building or an improvement to a building in which more than 50 percent of the square footage is devoted to the preparation of, and seating for on-premises consumption of, prepared meals. Proposed regulations provide that QRES that also qualifies as QIP is eligible for 100 percent bonus depreciation if placed in service after September 27, 2017 and before January 1, 2018. Proposed regulations provide that the restaurant building won't qualify for bonus depreciation, just the qualified improvements to the building.

Restaurants didn't fare well under the new law. It eliminated QRES, under which restaurant structures were depreciated over 15 years for property placed in service after December 31, 2017. This wasn't just the interior improvements but the whole structure itself. The changes present a significant issue for restaurants, very brick-and-mortar, very capital-intensive. They need a place for people to sit down and eat. Many restaurateurs are not going to be able to purchase those restaurants in the future.

## Elimination of Qualified Retail Improvement Property

Qualified retail improvement property (QRET) is similar to qualified restaurant property. It too was extended through the PATH Act, but no longer exists due to changes in the 2017 tax law for property placed in service after December 31, 2017. Proposed regulations provide that QRET placed in service after September 28, 2017 and before January 1, 2018 qualifies for 100 percent bonus depreciation. QRET represented any improvement to the interior portion of a nonresidential building; if such, the portion was open to the general public and used for selling tangible property to the general public. QRET had to be some brick-and-mortar store in which individuals would potentially go shop.

QRET did not include any enlargement of the building, elevator, escalator, or structural framework.

## STUDY QUESTIONS

**3.** Which of the following property placed in service after 2017 is now depreciated over 15 years (versus the prior 39-year life) and remains eligible for bonus depreciation?

    **a.** Qualified improvement property

    **b.** Qualified leasehold improvement property

    **c.** Qualified restaurant property

    **d.** Qualified retail property

**4.** Which of the following is an example of qualified improvement property?

    **a.** Costs for the enlargement of a building

    **b.** Nonstructural interior common area improvements

    **c.** Elevators or escalators

    **d.** The interior structural framework of a building

# ¶ 613 SELF-CONSTRUCTED VERSUS ACQUIRED PROPERTY

Proposed regulations provide that there are two types of self-constructed property: Property constructed by a third party for the taxpayer, and property constructed by the taxpayer itself.

A lot of property is built this way. For example, if Amazon wants a property built, such as another headquarters in Boston or Atlanta, and Amazon finds a contractor that will build what it's looking for to its specs, that's self-constructed property constructed by a third party. No construction outfit is going to build that size project on spec in the hope that somebody moves into it. This type of construction arrangement is referred to as "property constructed by a third party for the taxpayer." Such arrangements are subject to the "binding contract" rules. If, however, Amazon constructed the property itself, different rules apply.

Some residential properties are built on spec, such as developments in new neighborhoods, but most often when something is built, it's financed. The builder is engaged with the taxpayer who entered into a written and binding contract. If the client signs the written and binding contract before construction begins, it is property constructed by a third party for the taxpayer, and this is the most common method.

## Date Rules for Property Constructed for the Taxpayer by Builder

Proposed regulations published August 8, 2018 provide that the written binding contract rules apply to property constructed for the taxpayer, by another person. Such property is treated as acquired on the date that a written binding contract is entered into.

> **EXAMPLE:** Amazon picks Atlanta as its new headquarters. It signs a written binding contract with a construction company on September 1, 2017. None of the property covered by the contract will qualify for 100 percent bonus depreciation (including personal property and land improvements that is covered by the same contract). However, if otherwise eligible, personal property and land improvements will qualify for 50 percent bonus depreciation.

## Date Rules for Property Constructed by the Taxpayer

Proposed regulations published August 8, 2018 cover the treatment of property constructed directly by the taxpayer for its own use. Under these regulations, the date that construction begins is controlling. If construction begins after September 27, 2018, qualified property will be eligible for 100 percent bonus depreciation.

However, construction isn't considered to begin prior to the time that "physical work of a significant nature" begins. "Physical work" doesn't include planning, site clearing, test drilling or excavation to change the contour of the land. However, it does include beginning work on the excavation for footings, pouring the pads, or driving foundation pilings into the ground.

The proposed regulations also provide a safe harbor to determine when production begins: It begins when the taxpayer pays or incurs > 10 percent of the total cost of the property (not including the cost of land and preliminary activities). See further discussion below.

> **EXAMPLE:** Amazon picks Boston as its new headquarters. Amazon chooses to use its own construction department to construct a new building, rather than hiring a builder. On September 30, 2017, Amazon begins physical construction of a significant nature, including excavation for footings, and driving foundation pilings. The qualified property associated with the building (personal property and land improvements) will qualify for 100 percent bonus depreciation.

### Table 6.2 Acquired and Self-Constructed Properties Compared

| Property Constructed by a Third Party for the Taxpayer | Property Directly Constructed by the Taxpayer for Its Own Use |
|---|---|
| Client hires a builder to construct property. | Client constructs its own property. |
| Date of the written binding contract to acquire the property is highly relevant to bonus depreciation eligibility. | Date when "physical construction of a significant nature" has begun is highly relevant. |
| Assets qualifying for the 100 percent bonus must meet both the placed in service rules and the acquisition rules.<br>Property acquired pursuant to a written binding contract entered into before 9/28/2017 is subject to the 50 percent bonus rate if placed in service in 2017, to the 40 percent bonus rate if placed in service in 2018 and to the 30 percent bonus rate if placed in service in 2019.<br>Qualified property acquired pursuant to a written binding contract entered into after 9/27/2017 and placed in service after 9/27/2017 and before 1/1/2023 get the 100 percent bonus depreciation rate. | In order for assets to qualify for the 100 percent bonus, physical work of a significant nature must begin after September 27, 2017 and be placed in service after 9/27/2017. There is also a 10 percent safe harbor (see discussion below). |

The practitioner wants to know the property's placed- in-service date as well as when it was acquired and when substantial construction was started on the project.

> **EXAMPLE:** A developer begins construction of a building on November 1, 2017. Jason Hampton, the taxpayer signed a written and binding contract on December 28, 2017, to buy it when construction was completed. The property was completed and Jason placed it in service in 2018. The eligible costs are subject to 100 percent bonus depreciation under the written and binding contract, which was signed after 9/27/2017.

Starting with contracts signed after 9/27/2017 through those signed in 2022, bonus depreciation is 100 percent! A practitioner's understanding of when the written and binding contract was signed is very important.

## Construction Safe Harbor

Another issue to understand is the 10 percent safe harbor, related to having more than 10 percent of the work completed. The purchaser may have paid for more than 10 percent of the work, but perhaps more than 10 percent of the work has not yet been completed. Under the safe harbor, construction is not considered to have begun until the purchaser pays for or incurs more than 10 percent of the total cost of the property, excluding land or property clearing or building design costs. Purchasers are always paying in arrears. Some lag time may exist between when concrete went into the ground and the builder received final payment for that step.

> **PLANNING POINTER:** If a client signs a written and binding contract after construction begins—that is, the building is an acquired or on spec property—the practitioner can check whether any substantial changes to the contract were made during a bonus-eligible period. There may be an opportunity to claim 100 percent bonus depreciation because the contract terms underwent a substantial change. Change orders of any size may constitute a significant change. "Significant change" does have a definition around it, but the practitioner should not assume that it might not apply because perhaps the builder just applied a few change orders. It could create a new bonus-eligible period.

Thus, for self-constructed property:

- The construction begins when "physical work of a significant nature" begins under a factors and circumstances test; and
- The construction does not include preliminary activities such as planning, designing, securing financing, exploring, or researching the property.
- The safe harbor rule means:

- Construction begins after the purchaser pays or *incurs* more than 10 percent of the total cost of the property, excluding land and preliminary activities such as planning and designing;
- An accrual basis applies, so even if the taxpayer hasn't yet paid 10 percent of the cost but 10 percent of construction is completed, construction is considered to have begun; and
- It is important to document whether the safe harbor is relied upon by using a cost segregation study.

## STUDY QUESTION

---

**5.** Which of the following identifies a characteristic of acquired property?

   **a.** Client signs a contract to acquire the property before construction begins

   **b.** Date of contract is not determinative for bonus depreciation eligibility

   **c.** Date of contract is highly relevant to bonus depreciation eligibility

   **d.** Consideration of when construction began and the 10 percent safe harbor

---

# ¶614 MAXIMIZING BONUS DEDUCTIONS USING COST SEGREGATION

To recap, clients can take a deduction of 100 percent of the cost of qualified property (e.g., land improvements and personal property) incurred in year one for 2018. Why do clients do that? They want to maximize their bonus depreciation eligibility. The Realtor tells clients who bought a $3 million building that it's a $3 million building. Some of the price is tied up in personal property; some of it is tied up and attributed to land improvements. How does a practitioner get that split apart?

## Segregating Costs

Cost segregation enables the taxpayer to take full advantage of the bonus depreciation rules. It identifies every building component that is eligible—special piping and fixtures. That means a lot of people ask to have an explanation of them. Special piping and fixtures are 5-year property in a medical office. Medical offices may have a small surgical center, and they need piping for air and vacuum and water that's used during the outpatient surgery. That is considered special piping, as well as personal property and recovered in most cases in fewer than 5 years. Certain finishes in carpentry, like millwork, built in cabinets and desktops, and a reception area are recovered over 7 years. It is all millwork.

In an apartment complex there is cabinetry for the kitchen. In most cases, that would be deemed as personal property and recovered over 5 years. Distinguishing types of improvements is what cost segregation does. It splits up the building in very different ways. Separation goes as far as in a kitchen in an apartment complex, the wall plugs for a refrigerator or a toaster or a coffee maker, maybe for eight of the outlets in that kitchen are deemed to be supporting equipment or are personal property.

Certainly the refrigerator that's movable, but the wiring, the Romex that goes back to the panel and then a portion of that panel would be deemed 5-year property. Cost separation is very in-depth. It's engineering-based, and a cost segregation study can certainly split up a $3 million cost into many, many different components.

Costs of certain exterior land improvements are recovered typically over 15 years, the drainage, the asphalt, curbing, maybe a pool at an apartment complex or some fencing or lighting in a parking area. All of those are land improvements. The exterior footprint of the building would be recovered over an accelerated period of 15 years, it is sometimes bonus depreciation applicable. Prior to 2018's changes in the law, it was bonus applicable on newly constructed property. After the tax law changes, it is bonus depreciation eligible at 100 percent for new and used or acquired property. The deductions are going to be significant.

Planners are seeing an uptick in cost segregation studies that are being requested because of the power of bonus depreciation, using cost segregation to find out what that accelerated property is so the builders can be bonus eligible and they can take those deductions quickly through a cost segregation planning strategy moving forward. When a building owner dies and a property is inherited, any gains built up during that decedent's life are forgiven. The beneficiary receives a step-up in basis, which means the property tax basis is reset to the current year's fair market value on the date of the death and the depreciation starts all over.

This process provides an opportunity to apply the cost segregation study on the decedent's prestepped-up basis, creating a permanent tax savings. As shown in this next example, not only is doing a cost segregation study for the new owner but perhaps also for the deceased owner is advisable. The planner just applies the cost segregation twice.

**EXAMPLE:** The decedent's gain is forgiven for Bess and Lizzie McNamara, who are mother and daughter. Bess purchases a $1 million investment in an apartment complex during 2008. The mom depreciated it from 2008 to August 2015, when Bess dies. Now Lizzie receives this property, and the new fair market value is $2 million. The gain forgiven is the $1.2 million. It's the fair market value less any depreciation already taken, so $728,000 is the undepreciated amount of the investment.

Thus, when Lizzie receives the complex, its fair market value is $2 million. Now most CPAs already know that $2 million is a great candidate for cost segregation. They know there's enough basis here to make cost segregation work to their benefit and their client's benefit. But the original, prestepped-up basis on the undepreciated basis is the most valuable candidate. Again, Bess made the purchase in 2008. Her undepreciated basis is $728,000. What they Bess and Lizzie are doing is probably recovering that over 27.5 years—$1 million over 27.5 years, leaving in 2015 an undepreciated basis of $728,000.

Building on that, the date of Bess' death is August 2, 2015. Lizzie must file a tax return for income generated from the short period January through August. A cost segregation is done on a Form 3115. The planner is filing it because the property was originally placed into service in 2008 and the planner is going to generate through the catch-up deduction, in which the Code Sec. 481(a) calculation is the catch-up of missed depreciation, a better way to say it. Let's say that this will generate $174,000 of catch up depreciation. The undepreciated basis with the cost segregation has now been moved down from $728,000 to $554,000.

The permanent tax savings of $68,904 is against the tax rate of almost 40 percent. That is $174,000 of additional depreciation that the planner was able to take for Bess, not Lizzie. It must be done on a Bess' final tax return. The planner has created permanent tax savings for Bess because the step-up is forgiven, but now the planner has reused the same study; it's the same building.

Bess hasn't really renovated it significantly from 2008 to 2015, when Lizzie received it, so the planner can apply it to Bess' estate in a timely filed return, and the planner can file or implement that cost segregation for Lizzie. The planner gets a two-for-one there. The most significant part of all of it is that this move is creating permanent tax savings of $68,000, rather than just the time-valued money concept of accelerating depreciation.

After all of this, the property gets stepped up to fair market value. The planner performs a cost segregation study for Bess' heirs. The additional cost to refresh the original cost segregation is nominal. It's almost the same study just being applied to, instead of a basis of $1 million dollars, the same building; the planner is just applying it to $2 million. This same planner placed the property in service in August of 2015, with the implementation. There is no Form 3115 that needs to occur in this scenario; Lizzie just applies it as the new owner on her depreciation schedule.

Another reason to complete a cost segregation study or the reason a cost segregation study might be valuable for clients who are going to hold a building and/or need to drive down income facilitates future partial dispositions. It does denote what the important major building categories are. It states what the units of property are, so that repairs in the future can be deemed or looked at, at whether or not they should be expensed in the current year.

**EXAMPLE:** If Joseph Eberley bought a building and did a cost segregation study and found out he has $1 million of HVAC to deal with, and he did just a ton of work for $50,000. Does that greatly affect the unit of property? Does it often affect the unit of property by more than 30 to 40 percent? No, it does not, so therefore that's going to help Joseph determine that most likely that cost, even though it seems like a big cost, is really not a big cost as compared to the HVAC components that are determined in the cost segregation. Joseph would likely be able to expense that.

Practitioners should ensure study results are provided within a depreciation schedule format for easy upload. Oftentimes clients make these additions for which practitioners are not sure they've been treated properly. Once the practitioner has done a cost segregation, he or she would know that the specialist in depreciation has looked at the numbers and given the determination. Most often the specialist is going to say whether bonus is applicable or not. Those are factors for high-dollar amounts that have a great impact on a return and the deductions, plus they certainly give the analyst comfort in knowing he or she got it right.

In previous years, planners and clients were only concerned about taking that commercial building over 39 years and splitting it out among accelerated property. Now they're concerned about the accelerated property and the major building components or and the units of property.

Continuing forward with the understanding of more detailed depreciation schedules that are yielded from cost segregations, the electrical systems, the fire protection systems, and HVAC systems are all units of property that will be properly displayed in the results. These all have the same in-service date, but all have different lives, methods. The cost segregation study also shows whether or not bonus depreciation should be applied.

As the practitioner digs further and further into completing a quality cost segregation study, what he or she will find for most quality vendors is that these depreciation schedules are provided. Some of these depreciation schedules are even in an uploadable form to the practitioner's depreciation system. That is a factor to look out for as the planner chooses a provider.

¶614

## Predemolition Study

The cost segregation may be performed before a building is demolished. This is a strategy that should be reviewed by the tax planner. Building basis must be capitalized when anything is demolished, it's going to be capitalized to the land. It might be worth the client's while to have a planner do a cost segregation study on that building just before it's demolished.

> **EXAMPLE:** Giuseppe Malroni, a client, buys a property for $2 million 10 years ago. His company never did a cost segregation study. However, he demolished it this year. His planner's cost segregation study finds $400,000 of personal property and land improvements that can be written off. The remaining basis goes to land.

When a client is demolishing a building, that entire basis that is 39-year property will go to land unless the client can identify personal property or land improvements that otherwise can be written off in that year.

> **CAUTION:** This strategy does not work if a building is purchased and immediately demolished.

## General Asset Account Election for Demolished Buildings

The tangible property regulations provided an opportunity to avoid rolling over a demolished building's remaining basis to land. A taxpayer who anticipates a possible demolition of a newly acquired building might want to elect to put that building into a general asset account (GAA). The GAA rules allow clients to continue to depreciate the building after it has been demolished, so as under the old rules of Code Sec. 280(b), clients don't lose the future deductions that they otherwise would have had.

If a new building is constructed, the taxpayer still can take depreciation on the new building and the demolished building. This only works in some situations. The practitioner should do a cost segregation study on the building prior to making the GAA election. This process will segregate 39-year property into 5, 7, or 15 year accelerated recovery periods. Then the planner can elect the GAA only for the 39-year portion. That way clients can immediately gain deductions by retiring the 5, 7, and 15 portions if they demolish the asset.

Two schools of thought are integrated here. The planner does a cost segregation on a building immediately, putting just the 39-year property into the GAA election because when the client does demolish it, instead of continuing have to depreciate a certain portion of that, the personal property and land improvements then can be written off immediately.

Practitioners never know what's going to happen in the future. They can only go off of what they know at the time. But if there's a high likelihood of the building being demolished after acquisition in the future, then planners and clients might want to take a look at some of these strategies.

## STUDY QUESTION

**6.** Which of the following building categories has a 15-year useful life?

    **a.** Roof

    **b.** Windows

    **c.** Irrigation

    **d.** Doors

# MODULE 3: TAX ISSUES RELATED TO PROPERTY—Chapter 7: Determining Tax Basis of Property

## ¶701 WELCOME

This chapter discusses how the tax basis of property applies to a multitude of situations when taxpayers and practitioners need to know what their tax basis in property is. The issue arises in many contexts, such as disposition of property, but also what basis to use for depreciation purposes and estate tax. Changes to depreciation rules under the *Tax Cuts and Jobs Act* (H.R. 1) that became effective starting in 2018 will affect tax basis of depreciable personal property. These changes are discussed later in the module.

## ¶702 LEARNING OBJECTIVES

Upon completion of this chapter, you will be able to:

- Recognize general tax basis rules and outcome of common "cost" basis situations
- Identify rules that apply in determining how to allocate basis or determine which basis to use when not all of a taxpayer's property is sold
- Recognize the special rules that apply to property received by gift or inheritance
- Recognize the effects of depreciation and nonrecognition exchanges on calculating basis

## ¶703 INTRODUCTION

The tax code defines "basis" as a property's cost, but in many cases it can be difficult to determine what this means. It is easily determined when it just refers to property that's purchased for cash. Then the basis is simply what a purchaser paid for the property. But it can be difficult in other scenarios to know what is meant by cost.

This course will cover what that definition of cost basis is, including the result if property is acquired in an exchange—not a cash purchase, but a property-for-property exchange. What is the basis when a client has a nonrecognition transaction, such as when property is granted in exchange for services or received by inheritance? In a lot of these situations, special basis rules apply, and the new tax law affects the thresholds and ceilings for imposition of estate and gift taxes on property.

The chapter will also cover special rules regarding allocating basis when only a part of a property is sold, and the discussion looks at the significant effects on basis of bonus depreciation under Code Sec. 168(k), which under the new tax law is now 100 percent bonus depreciation. Also, the text examines the effects of immediate expensing.

Thus, the text describes and illustrates the general tax basis rules and the definition of cost basis; special rules for basis of property received by gift or by bequest or inheritance; the rules regarding allocating basis when not all of the property is sold; the basis of property received in exchanges, including nonrecognition transactions; and the basis effects of depreciation, including what happens if someone fails to claim the allowable depreciation.

# ¶ 704 GENERAL RULES FOR "COST" BASIS

Code Sec. 1012(a) defines cost basis as follows:

> The basis of property shall be the cost of such property, except as otherwise provided in this subchapter and subchapters C (relating to corporate distributions and adjustments), K (relating to partners and partnerships), and P (relating to capital gains and losses).

Cost basis is the amount paid if an individual purchases property for cash, but what about property that is purchased using debt? Does a purchaser get basis credit for that? Cost also will include tax cost. If an individual receives some property for free, there's also tax cost associated with it because the receipt of that property is taxable, the individual would include that tax cost in basis.

## Basis of Property Acquired with Debt

If a taxpayer purchases property using debt, the law allows the taxpayer to have basis credit for the amount that the taxpayer essentially contributed, the amount "contributed" with the debt.

Why would the law give basis credit for it? Because the rules give equity buyers and debt buyers equal footing with respect to basis, particularly for depreciation purposes. If only people who are financing with equity were allowed to take depreciation and other cost recovery deductions, taxpayers would think that that was a bit unfair between equity buyers and debt buyers. The tax code does give the debt buyers credit for the fact that they're purchasing with the debt.

There is a big assumption of the tax law in general: if there is debt on property, the law assumes that the debt will be repaid. The tax code doesn't force taxpayers to take amounts into income when they borrow money, because the law assumes that the debt will be repaid. That's true whether the debt is recourse or nonrecourse. If the debt is recourse, the lender can go after the borrower personally for repayment, whereas if it's nonrecourse, the lender is limited to the security that is securing the debt. Even if the property is nonrecourse debt, the lender's sole recourse would be to go after that asset that secures the debt, but the tax code is still going to treat that as basis. Debtors are still going to get basis credit even for their nonrecourse debt.

The basis credit is true whether it's purchase money debt or not. "Purchase money debt" is essentially seller financing. Even if it's third-party borrowing from a bank, the law is going to give basis credit for it.

One interesting situation arises if the taxpayer borrows money and uses the underlying property as security.

> **EXAMPLE:** Helena Dorkas owns an appreciated building that she purchased for $500,000. Now the building has gone up in value to $1 million, and Helena wants to borrow money using that building as security, but when she borrows, she uses the debt proceeds for another purpose. She doesn't use it to improve the building or to do anything related to the building.

> In that case, those borrowing proceeds will not affect the basis of Helena's property that is used as a security. But if the security property is sold subject to that debt, or if the debt is ultimately forgiven by the lender or there's a foreclosure, then the full face amount of the debt, that full balance, will go into the amount realized, even if it's nonrecourse debt, and even though that debt may not have gone into basis because the money was used for something else.

Even if a borrower uses the property as security so the debt does not affect his or her basis, the relief of that debt would still be considered to be the amount realized when the property is ultimately sold.

## Inclusion of Tax Cost

Another special rule regarding basis is that cost basis can also include tax cost. Cost can mean tax cost when the taxpayer has taxable income from the receipt of the property. Essentially in that situation, the rules treat the transaction as though the taxpayer received the income in cash rather than receiving the property and used the cash to purchase the property for that price.

> **EXAMPLE:** Tomas Bartonas got a bonus from his law school employer, who decided to give Tomas a new car worth $40,000. That car would be taxable to Tomas. Tomas would have $40,000 of income and would have a $40,000 basis in the car. The IRS would treat it as though he got $40,000 in cash and used it to purchase the car.

This attribution of basis also can apply if the taxpayer has a bargain purchase opportunity. This is a common situation. A taxpayer has an opportunity to purchase property at a bargain price, and this arrangement is for some compensatory purpose. He or she gets a bargain purchase opportunity from an employer, so the tax law assumes it's for a compensatory purpose. The bargain purchase is the kind of thing that would not qualify as an excludable fringe benefit. In that case, whatever the discount amount is would be taxable to the taxpayer, and then the taxpayer would get a basis that would be equal to the amount actually paid plus that discount amount. If the taxpayer has the opportunity for a bargain purchase basis, it would essentially be fair market value (FMV).

> **EXAMPLE:** James MacLachlan received 5,000 shares of stock from his employer as a bonus, and the stock was worth $10 per share. What is James' basis in the stock? If the tax law looked at cost purely in the definition of the amount that he paid, it would be nothing.
>
> The law takes his tax cost into account, and because James is getting $50,000 worth of stock, James is going to have $50,000 in income. If there are restrictions on the stock, that may defer the taxation, but in this case he just gets it outright. His basis in the stock should be $50,000, which is his tax cost.
>
> On the bargain purchase opportunity, what if James gets the chance to buy a Ferrari from his employer, which is a Ferrari dealer, for $50,000 when the car usually goes for $120,000? In his case, he's getting a bargain of $70,000. This is too large to qualify for a fringe benefit, he's going to have $70,000 of income, and then his basis in the car would be made up of the $50,000 he actually paid plus the $70,000 of tax cost, for an FMV basis of $120,000.

## Options

Some rules affect when taxpayers would add on basis for using options. This does not refer to employee stock options, but just options to purchase property. The general rule is that when an individual exercises an option, the basis of the acquired property would be the exercise price—in other words, the amount he or she paid for the acquired property plus any amount that was paid for the option itself.

> **EXAMPLE:** Geoffrey Halverston pays $1,000 for an option to acquire property for $10,000. He exercises the option when the property is worth $14,000. His basis in the acquired property would be $11,000: the $10,000 he paid, and the $1,000 he paid for the option. The tax law regarding basis doesn't consider that the

property is worth $14,000. Geoffrey would not have any gain or loss on the exercise of the option even if the option is considered to be in the money, which it is here. He can buy property for $10,000 when it's worth $14,000.

## STUDY QUESTION

---

**1.** If a taxpayer borrows money using underlying property as security and then uses the debt proceeds for a purpose other than for that property, then:

    **a.** The borrowing proceeds will not affect the debt of the property acting as security.

    **b.** It is assumed that the debt will not be repaid if it is recourse debt.

    **c.** The face amount of the debt will be excluded from the amount realized.

    **d.** The taxpayer receives a basis credit for the amount contributed with the debt.

---

# ¶ 705 BASIS OF PROPERTY ACQUIRED BY GIFTS AND BEQUESTS

Some specific rules concern the situation of property acquired by gift or by bequest. These specialty rules address the fact that gifts are nonrecognition transactions, and typically so are bequests.

## Carryover Basis and Built-in Gain

With respect to gifts, there are two important rules to start off with receipt of gifts: first, there's no income inclusion. Receipt of that gift will not result in income to the recipient, but the second rule says there will be a carryover basis to the recipient. The general rule for gifts is carryover basis. One case helpful in establishing this principle is *Taft v. Bowers*. In that case, the taxpayer received a gift of stock from her father that had built-in gain at the time. He had a basis such as $1,000, and the FMV was $2,000.

She got the property with no taxable event in the transfer, and she sold the property later that year for an amount such as $5,000. She took a carryover basis of $1,000 under carryover basis rules, and then wound up with a gain of $4,000.

The daughter complained and essentially contested this carryover basis rule for gifts, saying that she was essentially stuck with the $1,000 of built-in gain that was built into the property when she got it from the father. Her position was that it wasn't fair in that receipt of a gift is supposed to be tax-free, but it wasn't not tax-free for her, because she was taxed with this $1,000 of gain that was built in at the time that she got the property. She claimed only the appreciation that was in her hands should be taxed to her. The court was not sympathetic, holding the rule just means that the receipt of the gift itself would not be taxable, but it doesn't mean that the built-in appreciation can't be shifted from the donor to the recipient. If the tax code did not have this rule with the carryover basis, all of that gain would escape taxation forever; therefore, the tax law has to have a carryover basis rule so all of the gain doesn't escape taxation permanently.

When the text discusses the rule regarding death later, in that situation all of the gain does escape taxation forever, because the tax code has a different rule about inheritances. In *Taft v. Bowers* the court decided the carryover basis rule is the only rule that works. Otherwise, that appreciation would escape tax forever. Donors can't escape the appreciation just by giving gifts. Donors can shift built-in gain to the recipient on appreciated property by making that gift.

Code Sec. 1015(a) does restrict the scope of the gift exclusion, and it only gives basis credit for the donor's original cost. The appreciation, the built-in gain, is deferred until the recipient, the donee of the gift, actually decides to sell it. Unless the law made the gift a taxable event, that's really the only way the law could go.

## Fair Market Value Less Than Basis at the Time of Gift

Code Sec. 102's provisions say gifts are excluded from income. Under Code Sec. 1015's rules, the donee will take a carryover basis in property received by gift. A special rule also applies. When the FMV of the property is less than the basis at the time the gift is made—when the property has a built-in loss—a special basis rule applies in that situation.

The tax code doesn't want people to be able to transfer built-in losses to people who could better use them by making a carryover basis gift. Generally, the laws do not want to allow the shifting of losses. This rule in Code Sec. 1015(a) provides that if the FMV is less than the basis at the time the gift is made for purposes of determining loss—and that is only for purposes of determining loss—the donee will use the FMV as the basis rather than using that carryover basis. This is limiting the individual's ability to shift a built-in loss.

When there is a situation in which the FMV is less than the basis at the time the gift is made, here's how the special rule works. Because it's only for purposes of determining loss, the dual basis is in place for a little while until the property is ultimately disposed of. This dictates whether the recipient is to use that lower FMV basis or the carryover basis.

When the donee makes a subsequent sale of the gifted property by the donee, the planner first starts by using the normal carryover basis. If, when the planner uses that carryover basis, it produces a gain, and the planning is done, and the donee would just use a regular carryover basis, it's just like any other gift.

But if, when the planner uses the carryover basis and ends up with a loss, then he or she must recalculate using that lower FMV basis at the time the gift was made as the basis instead. If that ultimately produces a loss, then the planning is finished. If it does not produce a loss, then the donee will have no gain or no loss. In a situation when the planner uses the carryover basis that produces a loss, but then when he or she uses the lower FMV basis it does not produce a loss, the basis ends up in a no-gain-or-loss situation. The purpose of this rule is to prevent the donor from shifting unrealized loss to the donee.

The reason the tax code has this rule is because realization is controlled by the taxpayer. The timing is controlled by the taxpayer, and it would essentially be elective as to who would get to take the loss and when he or she would get to take it. Because a loss is a benefit to a taxpayer, the tax code doesn't want the taxpayer to be able to transfer it to someone who did not incur that loss whenever it would be beneficial for the taxpayer to do so.

**EXAMPLE:** Amanda Richards receives a gift of income-producing property for which the FMV is less than the basis at the time the gift is made. The property has an adjusted basis of $100,000 as of the date of the gift, but its FMV at that date is $90,000. So the carryover basis is $100,000; the FMV is $90,000. Amanda later sells the property for $95,000.

Amanda's planner first tries to use the carryover basis of $100,000 because that's the normal rule for gifts. When the carryover basis of $100,000 is used, the sale will produce a loss when Amanda sells the property for $95,000. So therefore, for purposes of determining loss, the planner needs to use the lower FMV basis of

$90,000. When the planner crunches the numbers using the lower FMV basis of $90,000, Amanda doesn't end up with a loss but a gain. So this would be one of those situations in which the seller had no gain and no loss, because when the lower FMV basis is used, the sale no longer produces a loss.

The Treasury Department's regulations under Treas. Reg. 1.1015-1(a)(2) give an example of how this rule applies and shows that this is indeed how it works.

## STUDY QUESTION

---

**2.** As a general rule, when a taxpayer receives a gift:

    **a.** That gift is included in income

    **b.** The donee takes a carryover basis in property received

    **c.** The donor must make the gift a taxable event

    **d.** The donor's appreciation is permanently excluded

---

## Gift Tax

Another rule (Treas. Reg. 1.1015-5) is that the donee will increase the basis of the property by any gift tax that's ultimately paid. The basis of property received by gift will be the carryover basis of the donee, as just shown, or that lower FMV basis, increased by any gift tax that is paid.

Beginning in 2018, the new tax law altered the exemption taxpayers receive from the application of the gift tax: $11.18 million for a single filer, $22.36 million per couple. Planners are not going to see the gift tax apply as much as they used to, but they do still need to know this rule. The gift's basis cannot be increased by more than the FMV of the property at the time the gift is made. That rule is in Treasury Reg. 1.1015.

**EXAMPLE:** Sam, a father made a gift of property to Alissa, his daughter, that had an adjusted basis in Sam's hands of $60,000. At the time the gift was made, the property had a FMV of $65,000, and Sam paid a gift tax of $7,545 on the transfer.

If the transfers tax applies then the tax applies of the time of the transfer, the basis at the time of the gift in Alissa's hands would be the same as what it had in Sam's, which was the $60,000, and would then get increased by the gift tax paid, but not in excess of the FMV of the property. Her planner would only increase it by the gift tax up to the tune of $5,000 more dollars, so that the total basis would be $65,000.

## Part Gift/Part Sale

Another situation that comes up in the gift context is part gift/part sale, a situation in which the recipient had a sale at a discount, not a gift context.

**EXAMPLE:** Jean and William Winston are selling their house to their son Will at a discount because they want to give their son a lower price even though they want to sell. Instead of $400,000, they're selling it on the cheap to Will for $100,000. Does their planner need to allocate the parents' basis in the property between the gift part and the sale part of the transaction? Do they have to carve up the basis to determine whether the parents have a gain or loss?

Treas. Reg. 1.1001-(e) says that in this part gift/part sale situation, planners can actually allocate the entire basis to the sale, but they cannot end up taking a loss on the transaction. If clients have so much basis that they end up with a loss, they can't claim a loss on the transaction.

Treas. Reg. 1.1015-4 says that for the donee's basis—this part gift/part sale—the treatment to the donee would be the greater of the amount paid for the property or the donor's basis plus any increase for gift tax paid. The donee is either going to take the purchase price the donee paid for the property or the carryover basis of the donor, whichever is greater. That will be the donee's basis.

**EXAMPLE:**   Sally Lessing transfers property to her son, Stan, for $60,000. Sally's basis on the property is $30,000, and the FMV of the property is $90,000. Sally is selling the property for $60,000, even though the property is worth $90,000.

In this instance, Sally is going to have gain of $30,000. She will use her entire basis in the property of $30,000 to offset the sale to her son. She does not have to allocate. She's going to have a gain of $30,000, and she's going to be considered to be making a gift of $30,000.

Stan will take a basis of $60,000, which would be the greater of the amount that he paid or the carryover basis. In this case, the amount that he paid is $60,000, which is greater than the carryover basis of $30,000.

**NOTE:**   There cannot be a part gift/part sale in an employer/employee context because the rules assume that the bargain element is not a gift. The tax law says employers can't really have gifts between employer/employees. Instead, the IRS considers the transaction to be compensation income. If it were a discounted sale in the employer/employee context, it would be more like that Ferrari example.

The gift piece would be compensation to the employee and would result in a compensation deduction for the employer. Then the employee would, of course, take a FMV basis in that context.

The rule is slightly different when there is a part gift/part sale in a charitable context. In this case, the donor actually does not get to use the entire basis to offset the sale proceeds.

But for a partial gift to charity, the IRS says the donor must carve up basis and keep track of the amount of actual gain by allocating the basis between the gift piece and the sale piece. So Code Sec. 1011(b) says that when donors have a part gift/part sale to a charity or a bargain sale to a charity, they're required to actually allocate the basis among the sale piece and the contribution piece." The adjusted basis for determining the gain from such sales shall be that portion of the adjusted basis which bears the same ratio to the adjusted basis as the amount realized bears to the FMV of the property."

**EXAMPLE:**   Alex Ogilvie transfers property that is worth $100 to a charity for $40—letting the charity buy it on the cheap—his basis is $30. There's a gift here of $60, and a sale of $40. So 60 percent of the value of the property is being gifted and 40 percent of the value of the property is being sold. Alex has to allocate basis in a similar proportion. Thus, $30 basis is going to go 40 percent to the sale, which would be $12 of the basis would go toward the sale, and 60 percent of his basis, or $18, would go to the gift. On the sale piece for $40, Alex gets to use $12 of basis against that. He would end up with a gain of $28 on the sale. He only gets to use the proportional amount of the basis against the sale, unlike the part gift/part sale in the noncharitable context.

If for some reason Alex did need to know what the charity's basis in the property was, he would add the two parts of the basis together. The charity would get basis credit for the $40 it actually paid that was attributable to the sale piece, and then the portion of Alex's basis that had been attributable to the gift. That would be $18 that was the 60 percent of the basis. Thus, the charity's basis in the property would be a basis of the $40 actually paid plus the $18 of carryover basis that was attributable to the gift, for an aggregate basis of $58.

## STUDY QUESTION

**3.** What does a planner do first to determine the value to use in a donee's subsequent sale of a gift that had an FMV at the time of gift that was less than the donor's basis?

    **a.** Determine whether the sale produced a gain

    **b.** Determine whether the sale produced a loss

    **c.** Recalculate basis using the FMV

    **d.** Subtract the donor's original basis from the sale price

# ¶706 BEQUESTS UPON DEATH

Bequests of property upon death are really important in the tax code. Some people think that this basis rule is the greatest loophole in the tax code. There definitely are significant revenue effects of bequests because if an individual inherits property rather than receiving it by gift, that gain, that built-in gain that might be inherent in the property, will actually escape taxation forever. It's not something that gets shifted to the recipient. Like in the gift context, Congress has determined that death is not an appropriate time to tax appreciation in property transferred.

And so that has great revenue effects to the Treasury, because all of that built-in appreciation—that the taxpayer has been getting deferral on over all those years if he or she hasn't sold the property—now gets to be wiped clean.

Formerly this rule went hand in hand with the estate tax, because the idea was to avoid double taxation so property would not be subject to the estate tax and then also the capital gains tax for the heirs.

Now under the new tax law there is a very high exemption for the estate tax ($11.18 million for a single filer, $22.36 million per couple), and the step-up in basis rule applies to everyone. Even if there's no estate tax until individuals have a very large estate, even the smallest estate would get still get a step-up in basis.

The tax code could say that when an heir inherits property, even without an estate tax, the recipient of that property would have a realization event. Congress has determined that death should not be a realization event for the recipient, there isn't a rule the estate has to pay tax on the gain.

Unlike the gift context, however, there is a permanent exclusion of that apprecia-tion from tax because the donee will get a step-up in basis to the FMV. Note that this is essentially what the taxpayer was arguing for in that *Taft v. Bowers* case, that it's not fair to shift the appreciation from one taxpayer to another.

> **NOTE:** The rule is not a step-up in basis only; it just says that it's a FMV basis. If there were actually a built-in loss in the property at the time of death, the basis would be stepped down.

Individuals can't transfer a loss at death, that loss would escape taxation forever, just like a gain would. Which means if a taxpayer does have a built-in loss property and can plan accordingly, the taxpayer should sell that built-in loss property before death to actually take advantage of the loss rather than losing it forever.

## Rules Governing Bequests

Code Sec. 1014(a)(1) says that when property is acquired from a decedent, the donee will get a basis equal to the FMV of the property at the decedent's death. That explains the effect of the transfer.

Code Sec. 1014(b)(1) through (9) set forth scenarios detailing what it means to get property from a decedent:

(1) Property acquired by bequest, devise, or inheritance, or by the decedent's estate from the decedent;

(2) Property transferred by the decedent during his lifetime in trust to pay the income for life to or on the order or direction of the decedent, with the right reserved to the decedent at all times before his death to revoke the trust;

(3) In the case of decedents dying after December 31, 1951, property transferred by the decedent during his lifetime in trust to pay the income for life to or on the order or direction of the decedent with the right reserved to the decedent at all times before his death to make any change in the enjoyment thereof through the exercise of a power to alter, amend, or terminate the trust;

(4) Property passing without full and adequate consideration under a general power of appointment exercised by the decedent by will;

(5) In the case of decedents dying after August 26, 1937, and before January 1, 2005, property acquired by bequest, devise, or inheritance or by the decedent's estate from the decedent, if the property consists of stock or securities of a foreign corporation;

(6) In the case of decedents dying after December 31, 1947, property which represents the surviving spouse's one-half share of community property held by the decedent and the surviving spouse under the community property laws of any State; and

(7), (8) have been deleted

(9) In the case of decedents dying after December 31, 1953, property acquired from the decedent by reason of death, form of ownership, or other conditions (including property acquired through the exercise or nonexercise of a power of appointment).

Code Sec. 1014(b)(1) is essentially what people would think of as inheriting property. It covers situations in which heirs get property with bequests, devise, or inheritance, or by the decedent's estate from the decedent. This provision lists basic situations of inheritance. Bequest, devise, or inheritance could cover wills. It could also cover "intestate succession," in which the person who dies does not make any kind of will or trust, and so the property just passes on to the heirs according to whatever the law of that state says.

Numbers (2) and number (3) cover lifetime trusts for beneficiaries.

Number (4) deals with a situation when property is given under a power of appointment, which is assigned by a will to someone else with the power to decide where that property will go at the time of the death.

Number (5) is kind of a specialty scenario that deals with stock in foreign corporations, so it's not of too much concern here.

Code Secs. 1014(b)(6) and 1014(b)(9) are both important situations that determine that recipients are getting the property essentially by operation of law. They're not getting it by will. They're not getting it by trust. They're getting it by operation of law, yet they still get a basis step-up because they're getting the property from someone who dies.

Code Sec. 1014(b)(6) describes the case of decedents dying after December 31, 1947, for property that represents the surviving spouse's one-half share of community property held by the decedent and the surviving spouse. 1014(b)(6) is a free basis step-up for the surviving spouse when there is community property—a form of ownership in which each of the two members of the community is considered to own kind of half rights in it. If a married couple owns property as community property, and the husband dies, he could do whatever he wanted with his half. He could leave his half to his brother. He could leave his half to charity. Code Sec. 1014(b)(6) says that the surviving spouse's half, when the first spouse died, would get stepped up. The half is not being transferred because the spouse dies; it's the surviving spouse's half that continues to be held, and it will get stepped up upon the first spouse's death under Code Sec. 1014(b)(6). This only is the case if it's community property. The decedent's half will get stepped up when it is distributed out of the estate to the beneficiary. The beneficiary would get a step-up under a will that gave the property to the beneficiary. So that half would get stepped up according to 1014(b)(1). The surviving spouse's half would get stepped up according to Code Sec. 1014(b)(6).

The reason the rule's in place is because a lot of times the dying spouse will be giving his or her half to the surviving spouse. The idea is, step up the whole basis rather than the half. Note that that is not required.

Code Sec. 1014(b)(9) covers a situation in which the parties own the property as joint tenants or tenants by the entirety. Those are both forms of ownership where the property will pass automatically from one of the members of the joint tenancy or the tenancy by the entirety to the other member by operation of law. Typically, this is also held by married couples, and what this means is that when one spouse dies, his or her half passes automatically to the other spouse. No will needs to stipulate the transfer. That is going to step up the dying spouse's half. If by the form of ownership the dying spouse's half is going to pass to the surviving spouse by the form of ownership, then the dying spouse's half gets stepped up. In California, and possibly in some other states, there's also a form of ownership called "community property with right of survivorship." That combines community property with joint tenancy with right of survivorship, which has this automatic passage to the surviving spouse. The surviving spouse's half of property would get stepped up according to Code Sec. 1014(b)(6), and the decedent's half would get stepped up under Code Sec. 1014(b)(9), and the decedent's half would pass automatically to the survivor. Thus, under both (6) and (9), the entire property is stepped up.

These two situations, Code Secs.1014(b)(6) and 1014(b)(9), are the most complicated of the 1014(b) situations. Code Sec. 1014(b)(6) would be the decedent's half of the property that passes to the surviving spouse with joint tenancy. The surviving spouse will have a step-up under the community property rule even if the dying spouse does not leave his or her half to the other.

Numbers (7) and (8) were skipped because they have been deleted in the code section.

**EXAMPLE:** Mike and Mary Silverton are married, and they own property as joint tenants with right of survivorship. Community property does not apply here. They bought their home for $250,000 30 years ago. In 2018 Mike dies when the home is worth $400,000. Mary now has a basis of $325,000, because the half that transferred to her on Mike's death gets stepped up, but her half does not. When Mike dies, the half that passes to her gets stepped to $200,000. Her half remains at $125,000, which was half of the $250,000 purchase price. She's going to have half of her basis stepped up to $200,000. That's the part she inherited from Mike by this joint tenancy form of ownership. The half that she's just continuing to hold onto does not get stepped up.

If instead Mike and Mary had owned the home as community property with right of survivorship, then Mary's basis would be $400,000, because one half would get stepped up under Code Sec. 1014(b)(6), and the other half would get stepped up under Code Sec. 1014(b)(9).

If Mike and Mary owned the property as community property, and Mike decided to leave his half to his children from his first marriage by making a will that stipulated that, his children would take their half with a basis of $200,000 under Code Sec. 1014(b)(1), and Mary, the surviving spouse, would keep her half with a basis of $200,000 under Code Sec. 1014(b)(9).

## STUDY QUESTION

**4.** When is basis allocated between the sale piece and the contribution piece?

   **a.** When a decedent bequests property to a donee

   **b.** When a donor sells property to a charity at a discounted price

   **c.** When a donor sells property to a minor at a discounted price

   **d.** When an employer sells property to an employee at a discounted price

### Gifts in Anticipation of Death

Code Sec. 1014(e) deals with property that is essentially gifted in the anticipation of a death. There's no step-up in basis that normally occurs under Code Sec. 1014 if the decedent—the person dying, that is—received appreciated property as a gift from the ultimate beneficiary within one year prior to the death.

   **EXAMPLE:** Brothers Jonas and Jeff Everton know that Grandma does not seem like she's going to be around so much longer, and they both want to get a step-up in basis in the home the brothers share. They make a gift of the property to Grandma, and Grandma receives it with the carryover basis. And then when Grandma dies nine months later, she gives the property back to Jonas and Jeff via her will. Magically, they get back the home with stepped-up basis. Code Sec. 1014(e) says the brothers will not get that step-up in basis because Grandma had received that appreciated property as a gift from the beneficiaries less than one year prior to her death.

   This rule says one year prior to the death. If Grandma had survived a year and a day, the brothers would be fine. Code Sec. 1014(e) is an automatically applying rule. Instead, they would get the property back with the carryover basis.

   If she survived a little longer than a year but there's evidence that the brothers had this all planned when they made the gift to Grandma, if the IRS can prove that it was all preordained that they were going to get the property back, under substance over form the IRS might still be able to get the same result as under Code Sec. 1014(e) by claiming that the brothers' gift to the grandmother was not a real and valid gift.

Maybe the gift was transitory, which would mean that the brothers knew the home was coming back to them; it was all preordained and prearranged. Just because Grandma could make it a little bit longer than a year doesn't mean the brothers are necessarily going to be okay.

This antiabuse rule—although it sounds a little surprising to be doing all this planning, but sometimes people do—applies in situations when someone has a terminal illness, and their eventual beneficiaries are interested in and willing to do some estate planning. These are the kind of things that they would want to be thinking about. The Code Sec. 1014(e) carryover basis rule is intended to avoid "cleansing" property and getting a stepped-up basis by gifting the property to someone likely to die soon.

## STUDY QUESTION

---

**5.** Jacob and Belinda Howard purchased a home for $325,000 just 10 years ago. Upon Belinda's death in 2018, Jacob had the house appraised, and the current worth was $600,000 In which circumstance would Jacob have a step-up in basis totaling $600,000?

    **a.** Jacob and Belinda owned the home as community property and Belinda bequeathed her share to another donee

    **b.** Jacob and Belinda owned the home as community property with right of survivorship

    **c.** Jacob and Belinda were a married couple who owned the home as joints tenants with a right of survivorship

    **d.** Jacob and Belinda were siblings who owned the home as joint tenants with a right of survivorship

---

# ¶ 707  RELATIONSHIP OF FMV AND ESTATE TAX

Treas. Reg. 1.1014-3 says that the fair market value for estate tax purposes is presumed to be the fair market value for purposes of Code Sec. 1014. It is only presumptive and may be rebutted. It is intended to try to prohibit gaming the system and taking a low value for estate tax purposes and a high value for basis purposes.

If a client were trying to take a fairly low value for estate tax purposes—and that used to definitely be the case, particularly when the tax code had an estate tax that applied at much lower levels—if the client took the position that the property had a low FMV it was presumed to be the FMV for purposes of determining basis under Code Sec. 1014. Although the rule is only presumptive, it would be hard to find a situation when clients could claim that they're different.

Under the new tax law, the estate tax exemption is so high—$11.18 million per individual and $22.36 million for married couples in 2018—this situation isn't going to be relevant quite as often, and so now, rather than planning for the estate tax, many tax advisors are doing basis planning to try to get the maximum basis possible for the people who are going to be taking that property.

> **PLANNING POINTER:** Factors like minority discounts and discounts for lack of liquidity—strategies planners would do in closely held businesses to decrease the estate's value—may actually be counterproductive now that the estate tax exemption is so high. If planners use those techniques to make clients' interests worth less, then they're going to have a lower basis to the recipient. With the estate tax exemption being so high, planners may actually want to undo some of those things that were put into place when the estate tax exemption was lower.

# ¶ 708  GIFTS OF SPLIT INTERESTS

Another situation that planners may sometimes encounter are gifts of split interests. What happens if clients make gifts such as gifts of a life estate and a remainder, or gifts of a term of years plus a remainder? The *Irwin v. Gavit* case, which is a very old case, helped set up the rule for how such gifts work. The case involved a gift of a life estate to the father, and then a gift of a remainder to the son.

The father collected the rents on the life estate. He was able to use the property during his life, and so he collected the rents. He tried to claim that the receipt of a gift was tax-free. The court held it was not tax-free because if the holder of the property had collected those rents, he would have had to pay tax on them. The father still had to pay tax when he got the income for life. Code Sec. 102(b)(2) says that only principal of a gift or a bequest is excludable from the income of the donee.

The other interesting facet of the rule about gifts of split interests concerns the basis. If a client has a life estate, and the holder of that life estate is getting older every single year, the basis of the life estate and the remainder interest will change each year. Published tables show planners the percentage of that carryover basis that goes with the life estate and goes with the remainder every year. The life estate basis will go down to reflect the passage of time and reflect the fact that the life estate holder is getting older, while the basis and the remainder will go up. This will not have any impact on the life estate because, if the life estate holder is to sell his life estate by itself, he or she does not get any basis offset for it. That is covered in Code Sec. 1001(e). All of the dollars, if the client sells the life estate, would be taxable to him or her. Code Sec. 1001(e)(3) says to disregard the basis on the sale of a term interest—that includes a life estate—unless the term interest and the remainder are sold together. The only situations when the planner would care about that basis to the life estate holder that's calculated based on those tables would be if the life estate holder and the remainder-men get together and sell the entire property and share the proceeds.

Planners would need to know how much of that was gained to the life estate holder. Similarly, the remainderman might want to know what the basis is in the remainder so that he or she could know how much gain to have if he or she sells only the remainder.

# ¶ 709  ALLOCATION OF BASIS WHEN NOT ALL OF THE PROPERTY IS SOLD

Situations arise when basis must be allocated because not all of the property is sold. This resembles the handling of the part gift/part sale in the charitable context, when planners do not think it's appropriate to give a full basis credit and deduction against the sale of property because clients are not really essentially selling the entire property. If clients are not considered to be selling the entire property, then they shouldn't be allowed to use all of the basis.

How would the practitioner allocate that basis when not all of the property is sold? Treas. Reg. 1.61-6(a) covers this rule: when part of a larger property is sold, the basis of the property must be equitably apportioned among the parts. "Equitably apportioned" is important. The allocation is not arbitrary; it must be an equitable apportionment among the parts. The 1947 Tax Court case that resulted that rule is *Inaja Land.*

In *Inaja Land,* the taxpayer owned land that had a stream on it, and the land was used as a private fishing club. The city built an aqueduct near the property, and it ended up damaging the taxpayer's stream with different erosion and debris, so the stream was not as clean as it was before and could no longer be used for fishing. Inaja Land sued. The settlement was that the city ended up paying $50,000 for an easement so that the city could allow water to overflow over the taxpayer's land. The city essentially agreed to pay to do this and have this erosion and debris over the taxpayer's land. An easement is a permanent interest in land. Unlike a license or rent, it's a permanent change.

This case essentially treated the action as though the taxpayer sold an easement, because it had a permanent impact on the land. In this case, the taxpayer's basis in the entire property was $61,000. So the case hinged on what the gain or loss was on the easement.

The taxpayer reported no gain or loss and just took it as a full basis recovery. The IRS challenged this use of the entire basis. The court held there was no gain in this situation. The Tax Court said the taxpayer did get to use the entire basis to offset the easement payment. The court reasoned that it didn't have any logical way to apportion the basis, to spread the basis and give an appropriate amount toward the easement, because the court didn't know what percentage the easement represented. The easement was not really based on a certain number of acres. The court held the apportionment of the basis was required, because it wouldn't be fair to give the taxpayer no basis. The rule requires taxpayers to apportion the basis except when it's wholly impracticable or impossible to do so. In this case, the net payment from the city was $49,000 after deducting attorney fees. The Court allocated $49,000 of the $61,000 basis of the land to the sale of the easement. There is no gain or loss on this sale. When the land, now subject to an easement, is eventually sold, the remaining basis of $12,000 (61,000-49,000) should be used for the land.

This was the result in **_Inaja Land_**. Today the result might well be different, because today it could be possible to figure out how to allocate the basis in most situations. What are some situations warranting equitable apportionment? Here are some scenarios:

- _What if the taxpayer simply sells one of five acres of land?_ Easy. Apportion the basis in some manner and use that portion of basis to offset gain.

- _What if a taxpayer grants a right of way easement, but only over one of five acres?_ Divide basis among five acres, then figure out how much basis is attributable to easement on one acre (if possible).

- _What if a taxpayer grants an easement for five years, instead of in perpetuity?_ This is probably more like a dividend or rent situation of current income, with no basis offset, because taxpayer gets full value of land back at end.

- _What if instead of buying an easement for $50,000, the city in the **Inaja Land** case agreed to pay the taxpayer $2,500 in perpetuity for the damage it was causing the taxpayer's land?_ Taxable income each year with no basis offset. Strange because the easement of $50,000 is presumably just the present value of the future income stream of $2,500 per year.

It just goes to show that how an easement is structured can have very different tax consequences.

What would a practitioner be doing in the actual _**Inaja Land**_ case now? The court said there was no way to apportion the basis. However, the way the parties could apportion the basis is how that part gift/part sale in the charitable context where the apportionment was based on FMV. If the city bought an easement for $50,000, the planner would ask what the entire property was worth. If the entire property was worth $250,000, the planner would attribute one-fifth of the basis to the easement. Doing it based on FMV is always a good backup and a good way to go.

**EXAMPLE:** Donald Jameson bought riverfront land for development for which he had to pay a premium price for the nonriverfront piece to gain access to the riverfront piece. He paid the same price per acre for all of the land. The price per acre that he paid for the nonriverfront land was above market. His practitioner needs to consider what the basis is when Donald sells the riverfront piece, and presumably in that case the practitioner would allocate more basis to the riverfront piece so that when Donald sold that, there would be more basis to go with that portion of the property. Donald and his practitioner would argue that the riverfront piece has a higher basis because that's the reason for the premium, and it is the more valuable piece. The case law says that equitable apportionment, as required by Treas. Reg. 1.61-6, is based on all the facts and circumstances, but that the relative values of the various parts must be taken into account.

# ¶ 710 BASIS OF PROPERTY RECEIVED IN EXCHANGES UNDER CODE SECS. 1001 AND 1031 AND NONRECOGNITION PROVISIONS

## Code Sec. 1001 Exchange Transactions

When clients have nonrecognition transactions and property that's received in an exchange, all of this is property received in an exchange. If property is received in an exchange, an exchange transaction is going to be governed under Code Sec. 1001, just like a sale transaction is. Code Sec. 1001 states that the amount realized includes the fair market value of any property received, and the amount of any money received. If clients exchange property for other property, Code Sec. 1001 states there will be gain or loss.

In certain situations nonrecognition rules which will say that even though an individual realized that gain, he or she does not have to recognize that gain, can have nonrecognition for that gain.

What if a taxpayer does not buy property but receives it in a noncash exchange? Code Sec. 1012 in that case says that the basis should be cost, but a planner needs to consider what the cost is in that situation. Is it the fair market value of the property that was given up, or is it the fair market value of the property received? What is considered to be the cost?

On the one hand, maybe it's the FMV of the property given up, because that's what it cost to obtain the new property. What is really measured is the tax cost, so perhaps it's the FMV of the property received. Under Code Sec. 1001, the amount realized is the FMV of the property that's received. This amount measured the gain or loss in a taxable exchange. Because this is what measures gain or loss, this is what to use as the tax basis, because that tax basis needs to reflect the tax cost. Even though it's cost, it's tax cost.

Because the FMV of the property received determines the amount realized, that is what to use for the basis in terms of cost, because it's a discussion about tax cost.

Most times, the FMV of the property that's received is the same as that of the property given up. But sometimes there would be a difference. One party may have made a bad deal because that party has different subjective values on the property.

**EXAMPLE:** Stuart McClean owns a painting and Collin Devane owns a sculpture. Everybody would say the sculpture is worth more, but Collin is happy to give up the sculpture for a painting of lesser value because he just prefers the painting more. In that case, when the properties are of unequal value, the FMV of the property received—of the sculpture for Stuart and the painting for Collin—has to become the basis, because that's what is measured for gain or loss.

**EXAMPLE:**  Bob Kozloski exchanges his baseball card collection with a basis of $100 and an FMV of $200 for Carol Maloney's stamp collection with a basis of $100 and an FMV of $150. So the fair market values are different in this case, maybe because they have different subjective values.

Bob exchanged his baseball card collection, and Bob is going to have to take a basis of $150 in the stamp collection because that was the FMV of that stamp collection. Carol will take a fair market value basis of $200 in the baseball card collection because that was the FMV of what she received.

## Nonrecognition Exchange Transactions

A nonrecognition exchange transaction occurs when, even though a transaction has exchanged one type of property for another, a special nonrecognition rule applies. It says that even though an individual has realized gain, he or she does not have to recognize that gain. A nonrecognition rule, in most instances, does not say that the gain is excused forever. Instead, an individual is preserving that gain or loss for future recognition and does so with a carryover basis.

In nonrecognition transactions, typically clients use carryover basis from the property that was exchanged to make sure that they can preserve future gain for later recognition. In many nonrecognition provisions, the taxpayer does have to recognize gain to the extent that he or she received boot.

Most of the nonrecognition rules allow nonrecognition as long as clients are trading one type of property for another, and clients will provide that they only are going to have nonrecognition as long as they are trading those sorts of approved types of property. Examples of such trades could be Code Sec. 1031 and like-kind property, described next. Transactions could also be transfer of a property to a business entity in exchange for stock or partnership interests.

In those situations, clients have approved property that they can receive on a nonrecognition basis. If the clients also take any nonapproved property in the transaction, then they would have to recognize gain and the basis rules have to be adjusted to reflect the fact that the clients did recognize gain.

## Code Sec. 1031 Like-Kind Exchange Transactions

Transactions in which determining the basis can be rather complicated is a Code Sec. 1031 exchange. A Code Sec. 1031 exchange is a like-kind exchange, which allows taxpayers to exchange property of a like kind for other property of a like kind.

Code Sec. 1031 has a pretty generous definition of "like kind" with respect to real estate, which is why it arose as a provision that essentially involved like-kind exchanges with respect to real estate. The rules used to have broader applicability that would apply to all different types of property, even though such exchanges weren't used very often for personal property rather than real property. It was theoretically permissible to have like-kind exchanges for personal property.

After passage of the *Tax Cuts and Jobs Act,* Code Sec. 1031 has been limited, so it could only be used for real estate, not held for sale to customers in the ordinary course of business. In the future clients are going to be using Code Sec. 1031 only with respect to real estate. If clients trade property that was used in a trade or business or held for investment for like-kind property that will be used in a trade or business or held for investment, clients get to defer the gain. They don't have to recognize that gain. Clients need to preserve that future gain. The rule in Code Sec. 1031(d) helps planners to compute the basis, which can be very complicated.

What Code Sec. 1031(d) states is that the basis of property that is received in a like-kind exchange will be the basis of the property that is given up plus any gain recognizing minus any money received. That's the formula that's given in Code Sec. 1031(d):

Basis of property given up + Gain recognized – Money received = Basis of property received

This rule gets further complicated when there is debt involved in the Code Sec. 1031 exchange. A lot of the time in a 1031 exchange, there will be debt on the replacement property or the relinquished property, and that debt relief is treated as boot that requires gain recognition.

What planners do for a Code Sec. 1031 exchange involving debt is look at which party had the net debt relief. If clients got rid of more debt than they took on, then that excess debt is treated as boot. Clients have to recognize it as gain. Any parties who get actual cash have to recognize gain for that actual cash even if they took on more debt than they were getting relieved of.

When planners apply the basis rule of Code Sec. 1031(d) using the formula above, any cash that is transferred along with the property that was given up has to be included in the client's basis of property given up.

Planners use both the basis of the like-kind property that clients gave up plus any cash that they had to kick in to equalize the values, plus any deemed cash that the clients gave in the form of debt relief. Clients use cash given along with the property given up, and any debt that the clients took on is going to end up going into their basis of property given up, because it's treated as deemed cash that they had to kick in. Any debt relief or actual cash will be treated as money received when planners apply the formula.

**EXAMPLE:** Bob Buffet trades Blackacre land with a basis of $100,000, a fair market value of $200,000, and subject to a debt of $50,000 with Wilma Fleisch, and Wilma gives up Whiteacre land. Her basis in Whiteacre is $120,000, and it has a fair market value of $250,000, and it is subject to a debt of $75,000.

Bob's property has an FMV of $200,000 and is subject to a debt of $50,000, its net value is $150,000. Wilma's property has a FMV of $250,000 – $75,000, her net is $175,000. Bob has to give Wilma $25,000 cash also to equalize the net values of the property.

From Bob's standpoint, he has realized gain of $50,000. The basis of the property that he's given up to determine his gain is going to be the $100,000 basis he has in Blackacre plus the $25,000 cash that he is kicking in. His amount realized will be the $250,000 FMV of the new property minus that debt that it is subject to. He's getting $175,000 of value.

Bob is going to have realized gain of $50,000 and will have to recognize this gain to the extent of any boot that he is receiving. Bob got rid of $50,000 of debt, and he took on $75,000. Bob does not have any net debt relief from this transaction. He's not going to have any boot from net debt relief.

Bob is also not getting any actual real cash. If he's getting any actual real cash, that would be boot. Even though he took on $25,000 more debt than he got rid of, he did not get any actual cash here.

Bob's basis is going to be pretty easy. It's going to be the basis of the property that he's given up, $100,000 of the basis in Blackacre, plus the $25,000 of cash that he had to kick in, plus the $75,000 of debt that he had to take on. He's going to get a basis of $200,000 in Whiteacre because he had to turn over his own property with a basis of $100,000, he had to kick in $25,000 of cash and he had to take on $75,000 of debt.

Bob has a $200,000 basis in Whiteacre. Whiteacre is worth $250,000, if Bob were to sell tomorrow, he would have gain of $50,000, and that's appropriate, because that's what his realized gain was, and he didn't have to recognize any of that yet.

# ¶711 EFFECTS OF CAPITAL IMPROVEMENTS, DEPRECIATION, AND AMORTIZATION ON BASIS

Code Sec. 1016 provides that basis shall be adjusted for expenses chargeable to a capital account. Even though the rule says "chargeable to a capital account," the language means expenditures that must be capitalized. Basis is also adjusted downward for deductions that are allowed for depreciation and amortization. Those rules are contained in Code Secs. 1016(a)(1) and (a)(2).

Note that this will include both annual depreciation and amortization, which is regular allowable depreciation amortization taken each year, plus any bonus depreciation, such as the old 50 percent depreciation under Code Sec. 168(k) and the new 100 percent bonus depreciation for 2018 property purchases under Code Sec. 168(k) under the new tax law (and at the applicable percentages for periods after September 27, 2017 but before the phase-out of bonus depreciation in 2023). It also includes deductions for immediate expensing, for example, under Code Sec. 179 elections.

## Repair Regulations

Code Sec. 263A provides the repair regulations, which help try to determine whether expenditures for property have to be capitalized or may be deducted. There's been a lot of disagreement over the years between taxpayers and the IRS about this, and the distinction between things that are deductible repairs and capital improvements was largely determined through case law.

In late 2013, the IRS issued repair regs to try to give more clarity to the area. The regs became applicable for taxable years beginning in 2014. In general, the test under those regs says that if individuals have expenditures that restore the property to its operating state, that's a deductible repair. The individuals are just putting the property back in its operating state.

The restorations contrast with expenditures that provide a permanent improvement in the life or the value of the property. Those improvements are more likely to be capital, and they should be added to the basis.

These regs have a broad reach. They apply to anyone who pays or incurs amounts to acquire, produce, or improve tangible, real, or personal property. There are some *de minimis* safe harbor exceptions if they're applied to small amounts: up to $5,000 per invoice or item if the taxpayer has an applicable financial statement or $2,500 per invoice or item if not. If taxpayers have been treating items differently prior to the implementation of the regulations, the taxpayers must file Form 3115, *Change in Accounting Method,* to adopt the new and proper method.

Incidental supplies and materials get to be deducted in the year in which their costs are paid or incurred. Other supplies and materials maybe deducted when used or consumed. They do not change the requirement to capitalize inventory costs if what is analyzed is inventory type of property.

## Capitalization Requirement

Items for the betterment or adaptation of property require capitalization. Following are examples of the three terms distinguishing deductible repairs from capitalizable improvements:

- *Restoration:* Restoration of property after a casualty loss or property has deteriorated to a state of disrepair, or rebuilding of property to like-new condition;

- *Betterment:* A material addition to property, material increase in strength, or amelioration of a material defect; and

- *Adaptation:* Changes to property for a new and different use, such as converting a fishing boat to a sightseeing boat or a manufacturing building to a retail showroom.

Rebuilding property to a like-new condition, restoring it after a casualty loss or a state of utter disrepair are considered capital improvements, as well, because they are not just minor changes to the property's operating state. And adapting the property to a different use would also require capitalization.

## Basis Adjustments for Depreciation

Clients must adjust basis in depreciable property for depreciation or amortization deductions actually claimed or allowed to be claimed. The rules regarding basis say taxpayers shall decrease their basis in the property by the greater of the allowed depreciation or the allowable depreciation.

"Allowed depreciation" is the amount of depreciation that the taxpayer actually claimed. "Allowable depreciation" is the amount of depreciation that the law entitles the taxpayer to deduct regardless of whether the taxpayer did actually take the correct amount of depreciation. Clients must reduce basis by the depreciation that was allowable to them even if they did not claim it.

> **EXAMPLE:** Rick Styron purchased equipment for $50,000. He should have used 200 percent declining balance for the expense. Instead, he used a straight-line method in 2001. Rick only took $2,500, and he should have taken $7,145. His basis is reduced by the $7,145 even though he did not claim that. His planner has to be careful with this when Rick later sells the equipment, because he's going to have a basis reduction whether he got the benefit of those depreciation deductions or not. This unclaimed depreciation can also result in depreciation recapture.

Note that if someone properly elects out of allowable depreciation to use a slower method, then the allowable depreciation will be smaller, and the basis would not be reduced by the larger amount.

Planners should watch out for this allowed or allowable distinction, particularly with respect to the automatic bonus depreciation. Many types of property automatically qualify for bonus depreciation under the new tax law even if the taxpayer doesn't want the bonus depreciation.

Under the Tax Cuts and Jobs Act, qualified property is eligible for 100 percent bonus depreciation if it is acquired or placed in service after September 27, 2017 and before 2023. After 2022, the percentage is phased out year by year. Previously, only new property was eligible for 168(k) bonus depreciation. Under the *Tax Cuts and Jobs Act,* used property is also now eligible for bonus depreciation.

If clients can't use all those big depreciation deductions, the planner should ensure the clients elect out, because otherwise the basis will be reduced even if the taxpayers do not claim them. With regard to 168(k) this generally means electing out of the bonus depreciation (otherwise it will apply automatically) and taking only the applicable "regular" section 168 depreciation. However, for the tax year that includes September 27, 2017, the taxpayer may also elect to use 50 percent bonus depreciation rather than 100 percent bonus deprecation. This reduction would result in greater gain and recapture later. If the taxpayer could go back and amend returns and claim the depreciation; that's one solution. If too many years have gone by to do that, they're going to just be stuck with the lower basis.

## STUDY QUESTION

6. Which of the following would be deducted rather than capitalized?

    **a.** Expenditures that add to the betterment of a property

    **b.** Expenditures that are used to restore a property to a like-new condition

    **c.** Expenditures that change the property's use

    **d.** Expenditures that restore property to its operating state

**CPE NOTE:** When you have completed your study and review of chapters 6-7, which comprise Module 3, you may wish to take the Final Exam for this Module. Go to **cchcpelink.com/printcpe** to take this Final Exam online.

# MODULE 4: FINANCIAL AND ESTATE PLANNING—Chapter 8: Understanding the Federal Gift Tax

## ¶ 801 WELCOME

This chapter discusses issues that arise when donors make gifts to beneficiaries, including the effects on giving and related tax exclusions under the 2017 *Tax Cuts and Jobs Act*.

## ¶ 802 LEARNING OBJECTIVES

Upon completion of this chapter, you will be able to:

- Recognize the types of transfers and donors are subject to the gift tax
- Identify how to plan for exclusions for annual and lifetime gifts
- Recognize reporting requirements when gift amounts exceed the annual exclusion

## ¶ 803 INTRODUCTION

The *Tax Cuts and Jobs Act* enacted in 2017 significantly increased the lifetime exclusion for paying gift tax on giving to $11.8 million (for a married couple, more than $22 million). With appropriate decision making, donors can make such gifts, report them, and avoid payment of gift tax. Although most taxpayers will never make such significant gifts, nor will clients, this chapter discusses the major concerns for such gifts under the new tax law.

A couple of caveats apply here. One overriding concern is that this law sunsets at the end of 2025; that is, this generous exclusion will expire for subsequent tax years. Donors have the political risk that there are elections between now and then. Certainly, depending upon the outcome of those elections, that generous number might be reduced. It's important that clients file the appropriate returns and pay attention to the rules; so that if in the future the rules are less generous, clients have done all the right preparation, so that they're on record taking the appropriate action.

Some practitioners believe that if the government does reduce the amount of the exclusion, the ceiling will be grandfathered. That is, if clients have made a big exclusion during their lifetime and the government reduces it, Congress and the IRS are not going to try to figure out how to get the money back that donors don't have anymore. That's called "clawback," and the 2017 tax act has instructed the IRS to issue regulations "as may be necessary or appropriate" to address the difference between the exclusion amount at the date of death and the exclusion amount at the date of the gift; taxpayers will see. With political risk anything's possible, but that's what planners are looking for as they go forward.

This chapter delves into when the gift tax applies; when it doesn't apply; where the exclusions are; what the deductions are; how spouses could be involved; how practitioners and the government value gifts; and some special techniques to make gifting occur less often—when transactions look like gifts but are legally not gifts. Then the chapter covers requirements for filing a gift tax return so that the IRS can't come back years later, saying clients didn't handle the paperwork and financial dealings correctly. Those are all important features of the gift tax serving as the focus of the discussion.

# ¶ 804 TRANSFERS SUBJECT TO THE GIFT TAX

## Persons Subject to the Tax

The first question to address is: who is responsible for paying this tax? The person who is responsible is the person who gives away the property: the donor. The donor is the giver and he or she is responsible for filing returns and, if any tax is due, for paying the gift tax.

If somehow the donor owes tax and fails to pay it, only then does the donee, the person who receives the gift, have to step forward and become the responsible taxpayer. That technically is called "transferee liability."

As a very broad, general rule, the best way to think about the gift tax is to say that anything a person gives away, whatever it might be, is at least potentially subject to the gift tax. How do donors and recipients not have to apply the rule that says every gift is potentially subject to gift tax? There are a number of issues: valuation, the present interest exclusion, and the ordinary business exception.

There's always a chance that a gift tax could apply to clients. Practitioners should ensure clients have a very comfortable exception to use. This text focuses on where the exceptions arise.

## Basis of the Gift Tax

When the gift tax issue arises, the value of the property on the date of the gift becomes the value considered; not the cost basis of the donor.

> **EXAMPLE:** Sophie McClellan bought stock at $10 a share, gives it away when it's $60 a share, the gift is $60 a share. Unfortunately, the basis to the donee under the gift tax rules is $10 a share, and that's a taxable situation for which planning needs to take place. Sophie, like a lot of older folks, wants to be generous to her children and grandchildren and plans to give away low-basis stock. That's a mistake, because when she dies her heirs get a basis equal to fair market value at the date of Sophie's death, and it's much higher than her purchase price.

Clients and planners have to be careful in planning gifting to give recipients assets that have a high basis. Doing so avoids the issue of giving low-basis assets that force capital gain on heirs. U.S. citizens and residents are subject to the gift tax at the maximum rate of 40 percent starting with 2017 and going forward. A different rule applies to transfers by "nonresident aliens." Where is the property that donors are giving away? Is it located in the United States? Is it tangible property, such as real estate, jewelry, at works, cars, or boats? Nonresident alien clients are taxed on property in the United States. If property is located outside of the country or is intangible property such as bank accounts or securities, it is not taxable to nonresident aliens. Perhaps a client wants to make a gift of a car to a child in the United States, and with planning, purchases it outside of the country and has it shipped here at less expense than a local purchase.

> **NOTE:** A "gift" may include any transaction in which an interest in property is gratuitously passed or conferred upon another, regardless of the means or device employed. The donor receives no consideration (monies) from the transfer.

> **EXAMPLE:** When is there a situation that gets that consideration? If a client makes a transfer of property that is for consideration (i.e., receives money as payment), then the client is not going to be subject to the gift tax. If Harry

Andersen has a coat worth $100 that he sells to Gerald, who pays $100 for it, there is no "gift" involved. However, Hugh Sanders sees a car at the dealer with a $30,000 sticker price and offers the sales rep $25,000 for it, after negotiations they agree on a $25,000 price. Is the $5,000 difference a gift? The law says no; it's an ordinary business transaction at arm's length and not between related parties. If Hugh gets a "bargain," there's no gift.

A bargain sale transaction between family members is different. The situation has a gift element as well as a sale element.

**EXAMPLE:** Geoffrey Tilson's daughter Vanessa pays him $10,000 for a convertible worth $50,000. He's making a gift to her of $40,000. If she had paid $20,000, the gift amount would be $30,000. This is a gift situation even though some amount is being paid.

**EXAMPLE:** When Bertram Livingston's son Callum starts college, he asks Bertram, "If I get my degree in four years, not six or seven, will you give me a check for $25,000?" Callum does graduate in four years and receives the check. Is that consideration? Under the law, it is not consideration because what Callum provided was not money or monies worth.

## STUDY QUESTION

1. Which of the following statements about the nature of the gift tax is correct?
    a. It is imposed on the transfer of property by gift
    b. It is based on the value of the transferred property on the date the gift is offered
    c. The maximum tax rate for gifts is 35 percent for 2018
    d. The same rules apply to transfers by persons who are classified as nonresident aliens

# ¶ 805 TRANSFERS NOT SUBJECT TO THE GIFT TAX

## Direct Transfers to Political Organizations

When an individual makes a gift to a political organization, a candidate, or a political action committee (PAC) that raises money for politicians, none of those donations are considered as taxable for purposes of the gift tax.

## Direct Transfers to Educational Institutions

If a client makes a transfer to an educational institution and pays for an individual's tuition that is not considered a gift at all. It's important because for other purposes a donor can give away no more than $15,000 to a single recipient as an "annual exclusion" gift without that being called a gift either. But payments of tuition can exceed that exclusion amount. Clients might have several children or grandchildren who are going to college. So clients can write a check directly to the educational institution for more than their $15,000 annual exclusion. That's the key: *directly to the institution* for whatever the college tuition is going to be, and the clients are not considered to have made a gift on behalf of the person benefitted.

**PLANNING POINTER:** The tax-free transfer applies to K–12, private school tuition as well. The IRS issued private rulings that can enable clients to prepay the 13 years of tuition to the school (which probably runs hundreds of thousands of dollars). Grandparents can use this to avoid generation skipping transfer (GST) tax for gifts to grandchildren. The IRS ruled prepayments qualify as a Section 2503(e) transfer. Make sure the prepaid tuition is not refundable and that it guarantees enrollment in the school.

**PLANNING POINTER:** Gifts of tuition paid directly to the financial institution or direct gifts of cash to the child (direct cash support) can reduce the student's eligibility for need based financial aid. A better gift planning strategy in some cases would be to pay the $15,000 annual exclusion to the child's student loans.

## Direct Transfers to Medical Care Providers

A similar rule applies for payments of medical expenses if transfers are made directly to the provider on behalf of anyone (not necessarily a child or grandchild). Medical expenses are determined as if clients were paying for their own care; they simply can pay costs on someone else's behalf. Even if clients' children or grandchildren have medical insurance through their jobs or self-insured plans, premiums, deductibles, and copays are high for younger people and will no doubt increase. If the children and grandchildren have sudden illnesses or accidents, the clients may pay the providers the difference—directly.

**EXAMPLE:** Jeremy Martin has triplet granddaughters who need braces. Jeremy can pay the $19,500 directly to the orthodontist to cover the costs. No gift tax is imposed on the payment.

If clients are making a substantial donation to a medical provider for a nonrelative, the gift does not need to be disclosed.

Qualifying medical expenses include expenses incurred for the diagnosis, cure, mitigation, treatment, or prevention of disease; or for the purpose of affecting any structure or function of the body; or for transportation primarily for and essential to medical care; or for the direct payment of medical insurance premiums to the health insurer. This section also covers long term care services such as the cost of nursing homes or assisted living facilities if provided by a licensed healthcare provider.

Treasury Reg Section 25.2503-6(b)(3) says that if donee's medical expenses are subsequently reimbursed by insurance, the donor's payment does not qualify for the exclusion. In this case, the donee must reimburse the donor. If he or she does not, the donor's payment is treated as a taxable gift.

## Loans of Artwork

If clients lend their own artwork to a museum or other charitable organization to be used for charitable purposes, it doesn't constitute a taxable gift. Even if the clients are giving up use of the art, it's considered a loan and not a taxable gift.

A "qualified work of art" includes any archaeological, historic, or creative personal property.

## Waivers of Pension Rights

If an individual waives any survivor benefit or the right to such a benefit before the death of the plan participant under Code Sec. 401(a)(11) or 417, such a waiver is not treated as a transfer of property by gift for purposes of the gift tax. If a client's spouse is a qualified plan participant, by law the client has a right to the plan benefit. The spouse cannot leave the plan's account without the client's permission. But if the client gives up the right to that qualified pension, it is not considered making a taxable gift. Any waiver of the right to a spouse's qualified plan must be in writing.

IRAs are not qualified plans. No permission is required to change an IRA's beneficiary.

**¶805**

# ¶ 806 EXCLUSIONS FROM THE GIFT TAX

## Annual Exclusion

For 2018, the first $15,000 gift made by a donor to each donee during the calendar year is excluded in determining the total amount of gifts made by the donor during the year. A client can give a $15,000 gift to each of his or her 10 grandchildren during 2018 without incurring gift tax. The entire $15,000 can be given all at once or incrementally.

There are a couple of points to make with clients. This is an annual exclusion, it is to be used in the current year or lost. But when clients don't use it, it renews itself next year. However, clients cannot make the gift cumulative and tax free, giving a recipient $30,000 in 2019 if they miss making the gift in 2018. If clients do that, only $15,000 of that is the present interest annual exclusion gift. The other $15,000 is not an annual exclusion gift because the annual exclusion is capped per person per donor and per donee at $15,000.

One approach to giving away property that has a value that must be appraised is to obtain the appraisal in the fall, then making the maximum excludable gift in December. Then the same appraisal can be used to make another gift of the appraised property in January so that the appraisal doesn't go "stale."

The key to the annual exclusion is that it's a gift of a present interest versus a future interest. A present interest gives the recipient the immediate use of property, whether it's cash, real estate, or other valuable item. If the gift is of a future interest, no part of the annual exclusion is available.

## The Present Interest Exclusion in Transfers in Trusts

On the other hand, if clients say in a trust or in some other arrangement that upon their passing their heirs are the beneficiaries, there's no present interest there. The clients are not planning on passing immediately. The gifts to the beneficiaries are a future interest gift, and the annual exclusion does not apply in this situation. When clients create a future interest gift, it's still a gift. Clients have to value it but they can't use the annual exclusion to address $15,000 per recipient for it. The IRS focuses on this issue and will figure this move out.

> **EXAMPLE:** A leading case on this issue is ***Hackl.*** Hackl set up a tree farm limited liability company (LLC) and said he was the manager of the tree farm and no one was to get any income or sell anything without his approval. The IRS stance was that there was no present interest to members there. When the case went to court, the IRS won.
>
> How does a practitioner fix that? If Hackl didn't want the beneficiaries of such generosity to get all the income, what the practitioner can say is beneficiaries have to get enough income to pay any tax that might be due on their share of the income. If their share of the income were $50,000 and their tax was $10,000, the trust would have to allocate a corresponding $10,000. The trust would not have to give beneficiaries the whole $50,000, but the fact that the donor has to give them some current income is a present interest. Also, if beneficiaries had a right to sell, a present interest was created even if Hackl had a right of first refusal. If a supposed donee said he or she wanted to sell an interest in the farm and he would either have to buy it himself or let the donee sell it, that's a present interest because the donee is not barred from selling.

Sometimes these issues are addressed in more sophisticated tax planning, with arrangements using grantor-retained annuity trusts (GRATs) and plans of that more complicated nature, in which there are both a defined current interest and a defined remainder interest. The remainder interest is a future interest and a donor doesn't get the annual exclusion in that situation.

Clients try to get creative and establish multiple, separate trusts for the same donee. But under the law, multiple trusts for the same person "look through" the trusts.

> **EXAMPLE:** Henry Tennison wants to establish five trusts for each of his children, believing he should get six exclusions: one for his child and one for each of the five trusts that he created because they're all separate taxpayers. Under the law, if Henry sets up trusts for the same person, he is looking through the trusts. If he has five trusts for a child and gives the child $15,000 and give each of the trusts $15,000, he should get one present interest exclusion. Clients can't use trusts in other vehicles—LLCs or other arrangements—to get around the present interest rule.

The IRS looks through trusts of LLCs, S corporations, and so on to who is the beneficial owner: the donee in that situation. Also, many trusts are written to have a present interest, the income, and maybe a remainder interest. A trust could grant the donor's children income for life and the remainder to the donor's grandchildren. If that's the story, then the grandchildren certainly have no present interest because the children are alive and they're getting the income. The donor's gift tax exclusion would be limited to just $15,000 for his or her actual children. The value of the remainder interest in these trusts is valuable. Practitioners have to do an actuarial calculation that says: if the child is 20 years old, 30 years old, or 40 years old, the gift to the child is different based on his or her age. The remainder interest gift to grandchildren is also different based on their ages.

# ¶ 807 SPECIAL TRUSTS FOR MINORS AND THE PRESENT INTEREST EXCLUSION

The general rule: The entire value of property transferred in trust for the benefit of a minor will not be treated as a gift of a future interest if the requirements of Code Sec. 2503(c) are satisfied.

Often clients wish to make gifts to their grandchildren, to set up an arrangement for their grandchildren. What are the choices for such gifts?

## UTMA Accounts

In addition to a trust, another option is a *Uniform Transfers to Minor Act* (UTMA) account. Most states have adopted the UTMA law and such accounts are available at banks and brokerages. Clients make the gift to the newborn or child before the age of adulthood. When the child turns age 18 or 21, depending upon state law, that child is entitled to the money. The practitioner sitting with a client should explain that when today's gift of $15,000 to the child grows to $300,000 over the years, eventually that 21-year-old child could just cash out the entire balance. Most clients would realize that that's a lot of money for a young person to handle; they might do something really foolish with it.

If a client's going to put $1,000 or $5,000 in an UTMA and that's it, it may double in 10 years and double again in 10 more. Maybe there's $20,000 or so in the account. At age 21, 20 years from now, what will $20,000 buy? Who knows? Maybe that's not going to scare someone from doing it. But for big numbers, the idea of providing an 18- or 21-year-old with hundreds of thousands of dollars may scare people.

There are special rules for withdrawal from these accounts by the custodian before the age of majority of the child. The withdrawals must benefit the child.

## STUDY QUESTION

2. Which type of transfer would be subject to the gift tax?

   a. A follower donating $20,000 to a political organization

   b. A direct transfer donating $20,000 for certain educational expenses to a qualifying education organization

   c. A transfer of $20,000 to a granddaughter's UTMA account

   d. A direct transfer to a medical specialist for certain medical expenses

## Section 2503(c) Trusts

What else can clients do? There's a trust allowed under Code Sec. 2503 referred to as a Section 2503(c) trust. This trust is for the benefit of a minor, but the law of this code section states that a donor can make gifts for a child who is 2, 3, or 4 years old and he or she can't take the money out until age 21; plus, the law says this is a present interest gift. Such a trust still meets the federal gift tax exclusion and generation-skipping transfer tax (GSTT) exemption amounts for the donor. Parents, grandparents, and other donors can make tax-free gifts to the trust up to the annual gift tax exclusion amounts.

Three terms make these trusts unique:

- Up until the child reaches age 21 if the money is needed for the child, it can be used because the trustee must have the discretion to distribute the trust's income and principal;

- If the child should pass on before reaching 21, the property is included in the child's estate, which shouldn't be very large given that the child is a minor; and

- At age 21 the child must be allowed to withdraw the money and the trust ends.

If the donor wants the gifted assets to be excluded from his or her gross estate for estate tax purposes, that donor may not serve as the trust's trustee. The age of majority (whether 18 or 21 years old) is still an issue for protecting funds from misuse by a young beneficiary, despite the fact that the donor has more control in the trust compared with an UTMA account, but the young person still can get the money at age 21. A lot of clients still are not comfortable with that type of trust because 21 is still 21. The funds may grow to hundreds of thousands of dollars over 20 years, and clients don't want the 21-year-old to be in that position. Many clients look for a third option.

## *Crummey* Trust for Gift Tax Exclusion and Life Insurance Planning

The *Crummey* trust is based on a case called ***Crummey v. Commission.*** The law for the *Crummey* trust says: If a donor gives someone a right of withdrawal for assets that were put into the trust, that's a present interest.

> **EXAMPLE:** A client, Genevieve Martin, has a son George who is 35 years old. George has a two-year-old child Alex that's her grandchild. Genevieve says to little Alex, "I'm putting $15,000 into a trust for you. You have 30 days to withdraw it." Obviously, Alex is not legally capable of taking withdrawal. George who is Alex's legal guardian says, "Thanks mom, but we're not taking the money out. Leave it there." Genevieve gets a present interest for the $15,000.

The *Crummey* trust is a kind of a legal fiction. The IRS has challenged this for years, and the courts consistently hold that if the IRS doesn't like this rule, the Treasury must get Congress to change it. And since 1968 when the *Crummey* case was decided, Congress has not changed it. 50 years of history says donors can set up trusts this way. This is how donors get around the age 21 issue; the *Crummey* trust doesn't ever have to end. The donor can draft a *Crummey* trust that provides income for life to the beneficiary once he or she turns 21, 25, or 30 or some other age. Principal is managed at the trustee's discretion, or the trust can say the trustee has total discretion and doesn't have to give out income or principal. While the donor is putting money this year and subsequent years into the trust for the right of withdrawal, that's the donor's present interest.

The child turns 18 or 21—of age to exercise the right of withdrawal. Maybe the donor doesn't trust the child anymore to use good judgment, so he or she doesn't put any more gifts in the trust. The donor put 18 or 21 years' of gifts in and now stops, and the child has no right to take anything out. It's all up to the trustee who is hopefully looking out for the child's best interest. This is how clients can get around the problem of age 21 and still get the present interest exclusion for this. The donor puts a right of withdrawal in the trust agreement and that creates the present interest. To handle it correctly the donor has to give notice to the person who has the right of withdrawal. The recipient has to have a reasonable time to exercise the right. The recipient has to either choose not to exercise the right and let it lapse or sign off a document relinquishing the right of withdrawal each time the donor makes a gift to the trust.

A *Crummey* trust is irrevocable; the donor cannot change the beneficiary or get back property already gifted to the trust. The donor should decide the amount of control he or she wishes to exercise over the gifts (i.e., whether the minor's guardian agree with the donor's wishes for the funds). Also of concern is the donor's total tax picture for income, estate, gift, and generation-skipping transfer taxes.

## STUDY QUESTION

3. Which of the following statements is correct regarding exclusions from the gift tax?
    a. The first $16,000 made by a donor in 2018 is excluded in determining the donor's gift tax.
    b. Outright transfers to individual skip persons that qualify for the present interest exclusion from gift tax are also exempt from the generation-skipping transfer tax rules.
    c. In order for the annual exclusion to be available, the gift must constitute a gift of a future interest.
    d. The entire value of property transferred in trust for the benefit of a minor will be treated as a gift of a future interest if the requirements of Code Sec. 2503(c) are satisfied.

## ¶ 808  THE LIFETIME GIFT TAX EXEMPTION

Perhaps wealthier clients are more generous in their gifts than $15,000 per donee per year. Now they deal with the lifetime gift exclusion. In 2018 under the *Tax Cuts and Jobs Act,* the lifetime gift exclusion per donor became $11.18 million. That ceiling for the exclusion starts in 2018 and sunsets at the end of 2025, when it returns to the $5.49 million number indexed for inflation. Professionals guess that the lifetime exclusion is going to change sometime between now and then, either if there's political change following the 2020 election and the whole administration changes or that the administration continues and will try to make the lifetime exclusion permanent so it never goes down. Then there's another election in 2024. These different possibilities are in play.

This $11.8 million is the lifetime exclusion (twice that for married couples). All the gifts they made beyond their annual exclusion gifts factor into their lifetime exclusion.

> **EXAMPLE:** Raj Patel gifts his children amounts that have no present interest at all. He makes a gift to his children that states that when they turn 35 years old, they can have some money. In 2018 none of his children is 35 years old yet. That's a future interest gift. Every dollar of that gift is a future interest.

> **EXAMPLE:** Alistair Dugan sets up a trust for his child that states she can get all the income currently. And he funds that gift with $100,000, so it's a present interest gift, but Alistair is aware that the present interest exclusion is $15,000, not $100,000. He has used up his annual $15,000 present interest gift exclusion and has an $85,000 excess, which still constitutes a present interest, but he ran out of his $15,000 exclusion for that child. Accordingly, Alistair also used up $85,000 of his lifetime gift exclusion.

The important thing to know here is that the lifetime gift exemption is a *cumulative* calculation. That's why on a gift tax return (Form 709), the IRS always asks the practitioner to describe all the prior gifts made by the taxpayer. And add up all those prior gifts and add them to the current gift to arrive at the cumulative total of gifting by that person. The present interest gift does not count toward that cumulative total. It's only the gifts above and beyond the present interest exclusion of $15,000 per annum per donee that would be part of the cumulative lifetime total gifts. The cumulative lifetime total goes back to all the gifts the client has made since 1977.

That's why practitioners advise clients to never throw out a gift tax return but to retain each one; when clients die the IRS wants to see each of the returns. The IRS wants to know what each taxpayer's cumulative total is. So that's what practitioners want to focus on when they think of the lifetime gift exemption. The imposition of the tax is not just for a current year's gift.

> **EXAMPLE:** Elain Gaston gave away $100,000 to one person in 2018, so she used up $85,000 of her lifetime exclusion. Does she start again at zero the following year? No, she starts at $85,000 next year. If Elain gives another $100,000 away next year, it's the same story: She's now used up $85,000 times two or $170,000 over the two years. If she ever gets to the full amount of the lifetime exclusion—the $11.18 million under present law—then she owes tax. If Elain never reaches that number, she never owes the gift tax. This is important to note.

If a practitioner has clients who should have filed gift tax returns in the past and didn't get around to it, the planner should not despair. He or she can file it now. There is no penalty for filing a late gift tax return, assuming there's no tax due.

> **EXAMPLE:** Michele Stewart has a client, Ben Strasse, who says, "Someone told me I should deal with the gift tax. I've given away $100,000 for each of the last 10 years to my children." Michele files 10 years of back tax returns for Ben with the IRS. He doesn't get a penalty. He also doesn't get interest because he owes nothing. That is allowed by law. Now Ben can sleep better at night because he is complying with the law and doesn't have to dread what might happen when an examiner shows up and accuses Ben of violating his obligations of tax filing.

A client might have an extra exemption. That is, the client can claim the $11.18 million exclusion for herself/himself but also is a surviving spouse. He or she may have had a deceased spouse who died in 2011 or later. If that's the case, that's a question a practitioner should always ask of a client. Prior to 2011, portability of assets was not available; nothing the planner can do will change any issues here.

But if the client cites the year of death of the spouse as 2011 or later, when the "portability rule" took effect, the next question is: was Form 706, *United States Estate (and Generation-Skipping Transfer) Tax Return,* filed for that predeceased spouse? If the answer is yes, then the surviving spouse might have what's called a "deceased spouse's unused exclusion" (DSUE).

>    **EXAMPLE:**   Bennie Harrison died in 2015 and left wife Beth all of his property. The marital deduction applied, so no estate taxes were due and no lifetime exclusion was used. The full amount of the 2015 exclusion of $5 million is now available to Beth. She has not only his or her $11.18 million exclusion but also has Bennie's $5 million. The DSUE estate tax exclusion is not indexed for further inflation. The current exclusion in the year of death is what the survivor gets.

A client might have his or her own exclusion and the available exclusion of a deceased spouse. The good news is if the client is making gifts, the surviving spouse can and should use the unused exclusion of his or her deceased spouse first. Because if the survivor remarries, that individual has a new spouse, and if that spouse dies, the survivor loses the DSUE of the last deceased spouse.

>    **EXAMPLE:**   Peggy and Bill McFee are married. Peggy dies, leaving everything to Bill. Bill has his own lifetime gift exclusion, plus Peggy's exclusion because she hadn't used it before her death. Bill marries Cathy. Bill can still use Peggy's exclusion. But if Cathy dies, Cathy is now Bill's last deceased spouse. Peggy's DSUE goes away. Bill can use Cathy's DSUE if she had a remaining balance. But maybe Cathy left all of her property to her children, using up all the exclusion. So there's no DSUE from either wife for Bill. He only had his exclusion left. This is the planning that a practitioner and client should address.

The portability rule's pretty important to understand. If a client's spouse died after 2010, he or she can use it. Portability of the $11.18 million applies if Form 706, *United States Estate (and Generation-Skipping Transfer) Tax Return,* was filed and if the decedent didn't use up all of the exclusion. If a client hasn't filed Form 706 yet and his or her spouse died within the last two years, the client should file the form now. A deceased spouse's amount is used first when the survivor makes gifts, that is, before the surviving spouse's own transfer tax exclusion is applied. The IRS allows two years from date of death to file, even if the client did not get an extension of time to file the 706. He or she can file the 706 now for purposes of claiming the DSUE. There might not be any tax due. That's fine. The client should file the return!

The IRS simplified the procedure of completing the 706, so in all cases when a client's spouse dies, there should be a 706 filed just in case somehow, some way, however unexpectedly, the surviving spouse becomes wealthy. Maybe the surviving spouse wins the lottery, hits a casino jackpot, or unexpectedly inherits a ton of money from a relative. Maybe the surviving spouse remarries a very wealthy person who wants to be generous and make gifts and use the previous decedent's DSUE. Or maybe if none of those things happens because the client can say none of those is going to happen in his or her family, maybe that surviving spouse is injured horrifically but not killed. A plaintiff lawyer gets a massive settlement for the surviving spouse's injuries, and now the surviving spouse is rich. Did the client have a portability opportunity from the first death to be able to give more away tax free? This possibility is why the Form 706 should always be filed and the portability remain an open possibility.

# ¶ 809 GIFT SPLITTING BY SPOUSES

"Gift splitting by spouses" is the opportunity to double up on all the gifts that a married couple wants to make. Code Sec. 2513 allows spouses to make double the amount of tax-free gifts per year per donee. Each spouse can make a gift (of up to $15,000 in 2018) to the same donee and can split that $30,000 total gift.

> **EXAMPLE:** Diana and Philip Duncan are spouses. All the $30,000 gift they plan to give granddaughter Melissa can come from Diana or all of it can come from Philip. It can be 50-50 from Diana and Philip. It can be 60-40, 70-30—it doesn't matter. They can split the gift. One of them can give the $30,000, because they're married; the other can give nothing. They can split it; it doesn't matter. Spouses can split gifts. That becomes a nice way to double up. Instead of $15,000 annually per donee, they can make $30,000. Instead of $11.18 million in total lifetime gifting, they can think $22.36 million in lifetime gifting. This is obviously a massive opportunity to be incredibly generous, even in blended (but wealthy) families.

In order for gift splitting to work, both spouses must be U.S. citizens or residents when the gift is made. The spouses have to consent to split all the gifts. They can't cherry pick here. One of the couple can't say, "Well, I don't like this person; so I'll only split certain gifts." Either they split all or split none.

Spouses can't split gifts to each other. But gifts to their children or anybody else, can be split. If a person dies during the year, the donor has to be careful how that gift-splitting takes place.

> **EXAMPLE:** Antoine Denay dies in March and wife Sofie survives. In February Antoine made a gift shortly before he died. In August, Sofie makes a gift. She is alive but Antoine is not.

The way her tax planner would treat those gifts is to split the gift made in February between the spouses. Antoine has died but was alive at the time of making the gift. Antoine's estate executor, which might be Sofie or might be someone else, can consent to split the February gift with her. The gift that Sofie made in August can't be split with Antoine because they weren't married at the time; he had died. Those are the rules estate planners have to keep in mind. Planners can split the gifts made by a decedent prior to death but can't split gifts made by the survivor subsequent to death.

A planner should make sure if the parties are getting divorced and they plan to make a gift to a third party, they do so and split the gift while they're married. If the divorce becomes final and then the gift is made, the donor doesn't have a spouse anymore and there's no person with whom to split the gift. If it's a big number, that's a mistake. If clients are a married couple that don't like each other but like their children, the planner should ensure they make all the gifts to the children before the divorce is final. That way those gifts can be split. Otherwise, only one spouse becomes the donor.

Gift splitting is very valuable. If clients live in the community property state, such as California, then what happens is all the gifts of community property that a couple makes are deemed automatically split if it's community property (that is, not acquired before marriage and kept separate from the community property pot). If it's separate property, that's a different discussion. To gift separate property the gift would have to be split. When the couple files a gift tax return, there is a section where a consent is required; so the couple must consent to gift splitting.

> **EXAMPLE:** A couple lives in a noncommunity property state and the husband, Skip Haroldson, gives away his classic car worth $100,000 to his son Skip Jr., and spouse Debbie is willing and happy to split the value of the gift. Debbie has

to sign the return—not as the donor; Skip is the donor. Debbie is the consenting spouse. She signs that return as the consenting spouse. And now each person gets a $15,000 exclusion. Each person is deemed to have made half the gift. They also give $30,000 cash to Skip, Jr.

In the past Skip and Debbie have not made too many gifts so there's still $100,000 left after this present interest exclusion; each person has now used $50,000 of the lifetime gift and each person has used $15,000 of the annual gift. They give their child $130,000. Skip splits it with Debbie, with each giving $65,000; $15,000 of that is each spouse's $15,000 annual exclusion, and $50,000 is using up some lifetime exclusion.

# ¶ 810 AVAILABLE GIFT TAX DEDUCTIONS

The marital deduction is an unlimited transfer tax deduction, which is a major point planners stress with married couples. There is no limit or taxation on a gift to a spouse, whether it's an outright gift or a gift in a special kind of trust, QTIP, discussed later. No gift tax applies to a spousal gift.

## Nondeductible Terminable Interests

There are deductible interests and nondeductible interests for spousal gifts. Spouses may encounter a "nondeductible terminal interest" in gifts given with conditions.

**EXAMPLE:** Sherri Kostner plans to give husband Walter some of her jewelry worth $100,000. "But," she says, "if you ever remarry, it comes back to me or my children. If I'm dead, it comes back to my estate or goes to my kids." Sherri is making a nondeductible gift because she is conditioning it on something that can terminate. Walter's interest is good only if he doesn't remarry. If he remarries, he loses the jewelry to their children. That is a nondeductible terminable interest.

## QTIP Trusts

But certain "terminable interests," interests that terminate, are deductible. Deductible terminable interests state that a spouse has the benefit of property and at some point the spouse may lose that benefit, but the law allows this type of interest without tax. The best example of that is a "qualified terminable interest property" (QTIP) trust. Terminable interest property allows for a spouse's interest to terminate at some point without taxation as long as the interest is qualified.

With a QTIP trust, a spouse sets up a trust for his or her spouse that says the spouse has to get all the income for life. Nobody else can get the trust principal during the spouse's lifetime but that spouse. The spouse doesn't have to claim the property but nobody else can get it. The donor can be very generous and say that the trustee can pay it to the spouse for whatever needs he or she has, or be more narrow in the trust agreement and state a purpose for accessing the funds, such as the spouse's health, support, and maintenance. So, a QTIP trust allows access to principal if needed.

The trust agreement can also provide that when the donor's spouse dies, the trust controls where the remaining property should go. This trust provides a terminable interest for the spouse because his or her interest terminates upon death. The unlimited marital deduction still applies even though the spouse's interest will terminate at death. The death of the surviving spouse triggers the distribution of the remaining principal to the ultimate heirs..

Practitioners use these trusts in estate planning all the time as ways to get the marital deduction for the transfer to the spouse but still control the ultimate disposition of the property by the first decedent. Clients like that because the planner can say to clients, "This is your first marriage, your only marriage. But what if you die and your spouse marries somebody else? Do you want that person to get your property?" Most clients have reservations about that; clients may also want the remaining assets to go to their children. The issue often arises in blended families, in which at least one of the spouses was married previously.

> **EXAMPLE:**  Elaine and William Buress are already a blended family. Both were married and had children previously. Elaine's first husband died, and William divorced his previous wife. Does William want Elaine's children to get the property when he dies? If Elaine leaves the property outright to William, her children may never get it. William may leave the remainder to his kids. This is when the planning and the QTIP trust become useful and the tax law cooperates by saying the marital deduction applies and Elaine can still control the destiny of her own property.

## The Gift Tax Charitable Deduction

The other big deduction is the charitable deduction. If clients make gifts to charity, they have an unlimited charitable transfer tax deduction for estate purposes. These gifts don't have all the rules that are in play for income taxes. The income tax deduction for charitable giving is 60 percent of AGI now for cash donations under *Tax Cuts and Jobs Act*. 30 percent applies for gifts of capital gain property if assets are held over one year. The charitable deduction is still taken as part of itemized deductions in 2018. None of these rules apply when clients make a gift at death. When clients make a gift to a charitable organization, the entire gift is subject to zero gift tax.

The issue becomes whether clients have to file a gift tax return when they make a gift to charity. Generally, no. But the IRS in its instructions for Form 709, *United States Gift (and Generation-Skipping Transfer) Tax Return,* adds some complexity. If clients make a gift to no one else but charity, they don't have to file a Form 709. But if they make a gift to people that is reportable, then clients have to list all their charitable gifts.

A lot of practitioners don't follow that rule. When a client gives a child $25,000 and files a gift tax return to show it's more than the $15,000 threshold and that client also makes a hundred gifts of $25 each to a long list of charities, the client doesn't file a return showing all those $25 gifts. Some practitioners find that a reasonable approach. Other practitioners advise erring on the side of caution because if the client is worried about a future tax liability, the IRS might come back and claim the client didn't file a "complete return" because those small charitable deductions were omitted.

# ¶ 811  VALUATION OF GIFTS

The gift tax is based upon the value of the property on the date the gift is completed— the fair market value on that date. For estate returns, an alternate valuation date is available: six months after the person's date of death. It's not the case for gift tax purposes. Everything is valued on the date of the gift. That's the issue for gift tax purposes.

## Valuation of Publicly Traded Securities

How does a practitioner value property? What's the fair market value of property? It depends on what that property is. If it's publicly traded securities, they're the easiest thing to value. The practitioner simply looks at the high and low share price on the date of the gift and takes the median number. A client gave away Apple shares when the price on the date of the gift was 160 low, 170 high; thus, 165's the value per share. That's the easy case. What if it's a publicly traded stock but infrequently traded? Then the practitioner tries to take a weighted average.

The fair market value definition is:

> The price at which the property would change hands between a willing buyer and a willing seller when the former is not under any compulsion to buy and the latter is not under any compulsion to sell, both parties having reasonable knowledge of relevant facts.

## Valuation of Gifts in Closely Held Businesses

If it's stock in a closely held business, that's where things get complicated. And this is where the most disputes occur between the IRS and the taxpayer about the fair market value of stock that isn't publicly traded. Because what is the value of the shares if the stock is not publicly traded? It depends on a variety of factors. Valuation principles come into play. Rev. Rul. 59-60, an old ruling from 1959, lists eight factors the IRS is going to look at when it values a business:

- Sec. 4.01—All available financial data, as well as all relevant factors affecting the fair market value
- Sec. 4.02(a)—The nature of the business and the history of the enterprise from its inception;
- Sec. 4.02(b)—The economic outlook in general and the conditions and outlook of the specific industry in particular;
- Sec. 4.02(c)—The book value of the stock and the financial condition of the business;
- Sec. 4.02(d)—The earning capacity of the company;
- Sec. 4.02(e)—The dividend-paying capacity;
- Sec. 4.02(f)—Whether or not the enterprise has goodwill or other intangible value;
- Sec. 4.02(g)—Sales or the stock and the size of the block of stock to be valued;
- Sec. 4.02(h)—The market price of stocks of corporations engaged in the same or similar line of business having their stocks activity traded in a free and open market either on an exchange or over-the-counter.

## Valuation Discounts in Transfer Planning

A discount of 20 to 40 percent can be applicable to the share value of a closely held ownership position to lower its value for gift and estate tax purposes. The discount applies to corporate stock, limited liability companies, partnership interests, and sole proprietorships.

The importance of Rev. Rul. 93-12 (issued in 1993) is that the IRS recognized in that ruling that family members are not necessarily of one mind, that family members can see things differently. If clients make a gift to a family member, they can claim a discount for minority interest, for lack of marketability. Clients' children may not see things the way the clients do. It's not one unified opinion situation. Clients may control the majority and certainly their control will be significant. But the point is that Rev. Rul. 93-12 allows discounting by recognizing that minority interests are different from 100 percent of the value of the business.

Clients can claim discounts when they value the transfer of a closely held business for gift tax purposes. The major types of valuation discounts are for minority interest, as just described, and lack of marketability. They're separate discounts. The minority interest means that clients gift their children a percent less than controlling interest of the business. That's not passing along control, but it is worth the children getting a small percent of the income or of the losses. It's valuable but discountable because no control is involved in the transfer.

Lack of marketability means that a business isn't that easily saleable, even if a client controls most of it. If it's a closely held business, it's not as though the client can go on the New York Stock Exchange and in a nanosecond sell the shares and have someone buy them. Lack of marketability creates a discount.

A somewhat less claimed discount is the key person discount. This is a situation that arises when the primary motivating, leading member of the business has died or has retired and given away stock or given away an LLC interest. The discount is attributable to the fact that the business is not as valuable because the key person is no longer running it. Sometimes the IRS is skeptical of this discount and claims the key person wasn't so key after all. The business may well have done better after the key person left. When the key person retires or dies, maybe the business is better off because that salary is gone or the key person was hurting the business with his or her old-fashioned ways.

The built-in capital gain discount is more for a C corporation if the company is going to be double-taxed. If the owner is selling the assets, he or she pays corporate tax—now 21 percent on C corps under the new tax law. If the owner distributes the assets to the shareholders, they're going to have to pay capital gain tax on the distribution of the assets. Long term capital gains rates in 2018 are 15 or 20 percent, depending upon the taxable income of those taxpayers. In addition, there are state taxes. That's another discount that the family business owner should consider.

On August 4, 2016, the IRS proposed Code Sec. 2704 regulations that were very harsh. They eliminated most discounting in family business transactions. Those Regs were never adopted. They were proposed and withdrawn as being burdensome. For now clients and planners don't need to worry about those limitations on valuation discounting.

When a donor makes a gift of a minority interest, the idea is that every gift is valued separately. If a client gives away 10 percent a year to children, after four years it amounts to 40 percent. Then the owner gives away 9 percent the next year. Now the gifts total 49 percent of the business. Each gift is separately valued. Each gift is a minority interest. If the owner gives away 2 percent to make the children majority owners, that's only a 2 percent gift. The law does not say when an owner crosses the line of control and interest somehow and has given away something different. Practitioners often adopt that plan for wealthier clients who are giving away their business in pieces to get the valuation discount every step of the way.

## Valuation of Life Insurance Policies, Annuities, and Life Estates

What is the value of a life insurance policy? Clients give family members a policy with half a million dollars of proceeds in the future. Is that a $500,000 gift? No, the donors are alive. For a life insurance policy on which no further payments are to be made (a "paid-up" policy), the "replacement cost" standard applies or what a life insurance company would charge for a single premium contract of the same specified amount on the life of a person the same age as the insured. For a life insurance policy that has been in force for some time and requires further premium payments, the value is called the "interpolated terminal reserve"—fancy words. Planners get that number from the insurance company, which hopefully sends back a number. That becomes the value for gift tax purposes. For newly issued policies, say up to one year after issue, the fair market value of the policy is the cost of that policy.

What if planners are valuing an annuity, a life estate, or something like that? A planner has to look at the IRS monthly interest rate. The IRS issues the applicable federal rate every month. The rate varies based upon inflation and life and all those factors. In May of 2018, it was 3.2 percent. Use the Rev Rul 2018-12 Table 5 for this purpose. The interest rate is adjusted around the 20th of every month for the next month. Code Sec. 7520 has become the source of valuation guidance for valuing partial interests in property transferred.

The lower the value, the more attractive an annuity interest usually is for tax planning. If clients are doing a grantor-retained annuity trust (GRAT), the low interest rates mean the value of the annuity interest is bigger. The value of the gifted portion, the remainder interest, is smaller. That's good for planning. If it goes the other way, if interest rates go up, that will make the annuity interest less valuable, and the remainder interest more valuable. That means the gift is larger. Donors and planners should just watch where the interest rates are going.

### Penalties for Incorrect Valuations

Planners should be wary of valuations, because the government does have penalties. If clients get improperly valued property, the government will hit them with a penalty. If clients value property at 65 percent or less than the correct value, the IRS will hit them with a 20 percent penalty. If clients value the property at 40 percent or less, the IRS will hit them with a 40 percent penalty.

# ¶ 812 AVOIDING GIFT TREATMENT BY USING DISCLAIMERS

A problem commonly occurs with disclaimers for gifts that wind up affecting gifting exclusions. A disclaimer is an act by a beneficiary whereby the beneficiary declines, refuses, and renounces any interest in property otherwise bequeathed to him or her.

> **EXAMPLE:**  Henry Worsley makes a gift to Rutherford. Rutherford may not want the gift, saying: he's rich enough; he doesn't need the gift. If Rutherford turns around and takes it and gives it to Candy, Henry's made a gift to Rutherford; Rutherford's made a gift to Candy. The transactions have used two people's gifting exclusions. A wise planner can fix that. The planner can have Rutherford make a disclaimer. He rejects the gift. Well, is there a pathway to another beneficiary?
>
> Good planning would say: Yes, there should be a pathway. Often a person adds a clause to his or her will; in this cause Henry can state that he's leaving his property to Rutherford. If Rutherford doesn't survive Henry or disclaims the gift, then it passes to granddaughter Bethany. In this example, Rutherford doesn't need or want the property, so he disclaims the gift and now it goes to Bethany. The transfer is from the decedent to Bethany. Rutherford made no gift. Why would anybody do that? The majority of the time, Rutherford is the child of the decedent and Bethany is the grandchild of the decedent, Rutherford's child.
>
> In this case Rutherford says that he doesn't need the money, but if he takes it and gives it to Bethany, Rutherford has made a gift to her. He realizes he can avoid the dent to his gifting exclusion by just stepping aside and letting Bethany get the property. He's made no gift. Code Sec. 2518 has a list of requirements for a qualified disclaimer. Rutherford would have to make it within nine months of the transfer of the property. If it's a lifetime transfer, if it was made today, the clock starts today. If it's a transfer at death and the person died today, the nine-month clock starts with the person's date of death.
>
> Such transfers have to occur within nine months. There is no extension. It's nine months. Whenever planners have clients when there's been a death and a will or a trust describes the property, at least the planners should determine whether everyone is

happy with the way it works. Is anyone getting more than necessary? Is anyone thinking of a disclaimer?

Recipients have to be careful with certain things in a disclaimer. They can't accept the property. They can't collect rent checks for six months from rental real estate and then disclaim the property. If the recipient disclaims after accepting the property, he or she has made a gift. Or if the recipient decides to gift that property to another recipient, that's a gift because the first recipient chose the beneficiary. Individuals can't name a successor recipient once they make a disclaimer. If someone disclaims the property to name grandchildren of the donor, for example, and those children have addiction or divorce problems, the funds may wind up in the wrong hands. A wiser strategy is to disclaim into a trust, in which the trustee has discretion over distributions.

## STUDY QUESTION

4. Each of the following statements regarding valuation of gifts is correct *except:*

   a. Gifts of publicly traded stock is valued using the mean between the highest and lowest quoted selling price of the date of the gift

   b. For life insurance, the gift tax value depends on the type of policy being gifted

   c. There is a penalty incurred for certain understatement of gifts

   d. Taxpayers can elect an alternative value date for gift tax purposes

# ¶ 813 SPECIAL RULES AND SITUATIONS INVOLVING GIFT TRANSACTIONS

## Power of Attorney

The IRS has taken the position that transfers pursuant to a durable power of attorney that do not specifically refer to the authority of the attorney-in-fact to make gifts were revocable transfers at the time of the principal's death and includible in the decedent/principal's estate. So, if the durable power does not grant the attorney that authority, the gifts don't count.

> **EXAMPLE:** Dorothy Wells is wealthy, and her estate may be taxable. She has 10 family members that she cares about, and before she dies all of them receive $15,000 checks. By so doing the client and planner remove $150,000 from Dorothy's estate prior to her death. At up to a 40 percent tax rate for transfer tax, this transaction saved the family $60,000.

Thus, having a durable power that permits gifts from a person who might be otherwise incapacitated makes sense. Some states, like New York and Florida, require a special document attached to the power of attorney authorizing the gifts to be made. It's a separate approval because they've had some problems in Florida and particularly in New York in which people with powers of attorney have caused elder abuse against their relatives.

Planners must be careful in these situations. It's wise to create a gifting power of attorney limiting the gifting to family members so that the powerholder can't give it to some third party that no one knows or doesn't care about or care for. It's also smart to prescribe the amount not to exceed the annual exclusion. That way, a client with failing capacity can't give away $1 million to a favorite person while the other heirs get nothing. Such terms may also include charities but usually only charities that have been benefited by the person who granted the power.

Donations made to charities become complete gifts the day the check is delivered to the charity. The donor may die in the interim before the charity gets to the bank. If the gift is going to the charity, there's no problem. If the recipient is an individual, there's a problem. The individual has to negotiate the check before the decedent dies.

**EXAMPLE:** Grandma Helene Rostram is dying. Everybody in her family gets a check written from Grandma's account. Recipients must run to the bank and deposit it or negotiate it, endorse it, do something so that the recipients can claim that that money has now been distributed and disbursed before Grandma dies. If heirs wait until after Grandma dies, it's too late and it's includible in Grandma's estate. Is her estate worth more than $11.18 million? If so, Grandma's estate owes the transfer tax. If the estate is not more than $11.18 million, donees need not rush to get a share. With lower exclusion amounts, this used to be a much bigger deal. It's not so much now under the new tax law's higher exclusion. But don't forget some states still have gift taxes.

## Transfers in Contemplation of Marriage

If a client's getting married, the client may sign a prenuptial agreement. It may promise to transfer a certain amount of money or property under the arrangement he or she has agreed to. The client should not make the gift until the marriage is concluded because prior to that the client is not a spouse.

**EXAMPLE:** Client Robby Mayer transfers half-a-million dollars to Joanne, a fiancé he intends to marry. Even if Robby marries Joanne, if the gift was made before marriage, there is law saying it is a taxable gift because the marital deduction doesn't apply.

In other words, premarital agreements or antenuptial agreements that may provide for the transfer of property from one person to another in exchange for the release or relinquishment by the recipient of property of his or her marital rights are treated as taxable gifts.

What transpires in these cases when a couple has a prenuptial agreement? The agreement gets signed. Money is held by the attorneys for the parties in escrow. When the marriage is official and done, then the property gets transferred out of the escrow account. If for some reason the marriage doesn't happen, the gift doesn't get completed; the property goes back to the person who placed it in the escrow account and that all works very nicely.

## Transfers of Property in Connection with Divorces

The whole world of divorce is going to be upside down in the next year or two because the new tax law denies the alimony deduction to the payor and permits the payee not to include the payments in his or her income. Many interesting negotiations will occur going forward. This only applies to divorces after 2018.

**PLANNING POINTER:** If clients are going to be the payors, they should expedite the proceeding to be complete in 2018. If they're going to be the payees, they should take time for the agreement to occur after 2018.

What happens with transfers of property in divorce? Code Sec. 2516 provides that when property is transferred in settlement of marital or property rights or to provide a reasonable allowance for the support of minor children, such transfers are deemed to be made for full and adequate consideration, and are not subject to the gift tax

Often the divorce is over before the property transfers are settled. Sometimes a person can't wait to get out of the marriage relationship, so the matrimonial relationship is done with the understanding that the settlement agreement on property follows. Ex-spouses should be careful here. There are certain rules beyond the scope of this course, on how long after the dissolution of marriage the property transfer can take place.

## STUDY QUESTION

**5.** Which of the following code sections provides that when property is transferred in settlement of marital or property rights or to provide a reasonable allowance for the support of minor children, such transfers are deemed to be made for full and adequate consideration, and are not subject to the gift tax?

    **a.** Code Sec. 2516

    **b.** Code Sec. 2517

    **c.** Code Sec. 2519

    **d.** Code Sec. 2520

# ¶ 814 STATUTES OF LIMITATIONS ON GIFT TAX VALUATION AND ASSESSMENT

## Filing Requirement

Planners come to address the adequate disclosure rules. What's going on here? All planners want the statute of limitations to run. The general statute of limitations applied for gift tax returns is three years, but no statute runs if no gift tax return is filed.

What starts it running? The client files a gift tax return. People get very clever and they file an inadequate gift tax return that basically says they're giving away property with such-and-such a value. That's not an adequate return. Clients must have a return that makes adequate disclosure to get the statute of limitations running.

This became a major matter for gifting. On line four of Form 706 for filing an estate tax return is an item for "adjusted taxable gifts." The law requires in filing Form 706, the preparer adds up the value of the property the client owned on date of death and adds that to the value of the gifts made since 1976 beyond the amount of the annual exclusion. All those gifts made from 1977 forward that were above and beyond the annual exclusion amount, plus what the decedent owned at death, become the amount on which death tax is paid.

## Adequate Disclosure

Section 25.2504-2(b) says that for gift tax purposes, the value of a gift made after August 5, 1997, may not be adjusted after the statute of limitations has run if the transfer was adequately disclosed on a gift tax return.

Before this rule, the IRS position was that it didn't care when the decedent made a gift; upon the individual's death the IRS could go back and revalue anything the decedent ever gave away. Taxpayers' position was that the IRS approach was ridiculous. If a client made a gift in 1987, his or her family shouldn't need to worry in 2018 that the gift may be revalued. Who's going to have records? If the IRS disputes the value as too low, what is the client going to do? Who's going to testify? The taxpayer that filed the tax return is dead. The accountants and attorneys might be retired or dead as well. The records might be gone.

It was really unfair for the IRS to take that position. The law changed. In 1997 the IRS changed its position so that if a filer adequately disclosed the valuation on a tax return, the IRS will respect it. The client has a three-year statute during which time the IRS may audit the return. If no audit occurs during that period, along with adequate disclosures, the valuation stands.

Planners can advise clients not to play fast and loose and put their family at risk by filing a return that is clearly inadequate. The preferable alternative is to get an appraisal or do what the IRS states constitutes adequate disclosure and thus limit the period of risk to three years.

What's adequate disclosure? There are two ways to go about it. One way, if the gift comes from a publicly traded company, the donor just relies on the value of the company—say, for Apple or Netflix shares. That's easy. But what if it's a closely held business? That's where the issues arise. To give away an interest in a closely held business, what does the client have to attach to that tax return? Documentation includes:

- Five years of financials
- A list of all the donees
- The relationship between the donor and the donees
- The history of the business that justifies why the donor is claiming the value
- If the donor is claiming a discount what the basis is for that discount

The second way is to get an appraisal, and the appraisal does everything. It includes all the information about the client's history and value of the property, but it includes the opinion of a professional appraiser. Such a professional has certifications and appropriate credentials and states his or her take on the value of the business and a justifiable discount. This statement is attached to the return along with the financial records. Thus, adequate disclosure is quite important to launching the run of the statute of limitations. Of course, having an appraisal puts the burden of proof back on the IRS.

# ¶ 815 SPECIAL VALUATION RULES IN CODE SECS. 2701 THROUGH 2704

In 1990, Congress and the IRS agreed that the whole gift tax valuation process involved too many loopholes and too many abuses of the gift tax. They tightened up the rules and they passed four new sections in Chapter 14 of the tax code. Code Sec. 2701 is exceptionally complicated and talks about a "preferred stock bailout." Donors used to plan to keep all the preferred stock of a family company and give all the common stock to the children. All the growth is in the common stock. Donors would opt for a preferred dividend. Many donors never got around to receiving it. Code Sec. 2701 struck down that practice. The dividend must be cumulative and contain guaranteed payments. If not, the dividend is valued at zero. All the value is in the common stock gifted to the children. Donors now must file a gift tax return and use of a portion of this lifetime exclusion or owe a tax, depending on the gift's value. Currently it's harder to remove value from the family's business without at least showing the gift tax. Code 2701 applies only to transfers to or for the benefit of a member of the transferor's family.

Code Sec. 2702 describes how property may be transferred by using trusts: grantor retained annuity trusts (GRATs), grantor retained unitrusts (GRUTs), and qualified person residence trusts (QPRTs). Under Code Sec. 2702 for clients who transfer property and retain an interest in the property, the interest has to be "qualified." If it's a qualified interest, then clients can value it and subtract the value of the qualified interest from the fair market value of the property; so that the gift is the remainder interest.

**EXAMPLE:** Allison MacDuff puts $1 million into a trust and says she's to get all the income for 20 years. The value of her retained interest in that case is zero. It's not a qualified interest. The value of her gift is all the money she put into the trust.

Alternatively, for the next 20 years she will get a 6 percent annuity based upon her $1 million investment and gets $60,000 a year. That's a qualified interest. She can take the actuarial value of that annuity, subtract the value of the property, and say the remainder interest is the amount of her gift and only have to report that as her taxable gift.

In the QPRT, the qualified personal residence trust, the donor does the same thing for a home. Clients use their personal residence for a period of years, and the value of their use in those years—another actuarial calculation—is a retained interest from which the value of the transfer is subtracted, so only the remainder interest is a gift.

Under Code Sec. 2702, if trusts do it the right way with qualified interests, a portion of the value as a gift is eliminated. The hope is for GRATs and QPRTs that the donors outlive the term.

**EXAMPLE:** Jamile Davis puts $1 million in trust but only has to call it a $600,000 gift because she retains an interest worth $400,000. The term of the trust is 10 years; after that the value is now $2 million. The trust is over and Jamile's children have an asset worth $2 million. How much gift tax exclusion did Jamile use up to get them something worth $2 million? Just $600,000. Not bad.

What if Jamile had done nothing and kept the property for the rest of her life? When she dies, it's worth $2 million. Now the children have an asset worth $2 million. But Jamile uses up $2 million of her exclusion—the $11.18 million.

A GRAT is a fixed annuity. A GRUT is a fixed percentage of an annually determined fair market value. In a GRUT, if the grantor does not outlive the term of the trust, all of the property is brought back into the grantor's estate. For estate planning, practitioners use GRATs, not GRUTs, because planners don't want the grantor to get back more property. The goal is to make the grantor's estate smaller.

In the QPRT, the qualified personal residence trust, donors put their home into a trust. If the donors outlive the trust's term, the value is not part of their estate. The only inclusion in the estate is the adjusted taxable gift; the portion of the gift when the donors made the transfer in the initial trust creation. If donors outlive the term, they're happy that their heirs got appreciation. The interesting issue is basis. If donors outlive the term of one of these trusts, their children as beneficiaries get the donors' cost, not the current market value of the residence, as their basis.

**EXAMPLE:** Herb and Elise Davis paid $100,000 for their house. It's now worth $700,000, and both of the spouses die after the term. The QPRT worked. The couple gave their children the house. They own the house with a basis of $100,000.

However, that's not really what the couple wanted to have happen now. When they were worried about estate tax, they were happy. Now they're worried about income tax and not so happy. Planners are seeing people violate the terms of the QPRT and not leave the house. Mom and Dad stay, the children don't complain. Mom and Dad die. The children state that Mom and Dad had a retained life estate, includable in their estates at fair market value. At the second death, if their estate is less than $11.18 million, they don't even have to file an estate tax return; the government will never really know what it was worth.

Code Sec. 2703 is the section that says: if clients have a buy-sell agreement between family members, the IRS does not have to respect the clients' value for the property. The IRS wants to view comparable sales, which of course is exceptionally difficult in the context of a closely held business. It doesn't mean clients can't go this route. It just means they can't expect that the number they come up with among family members is a guaranteed, respected number.

If clients have limitations on the sale while they're alive and have a price at death, the IRS can still say it's a deal between family members. The IRS doesn't have to respect it. Code Sec. 2703 gives the IRS that right. Clients should either be very fair or not have the expectation that the number is going to bind the IRS.

Code Sec. 2704 is less often used. Remember that some of Code Sec 2704 proposed regulations limiting valuation discounts were repealed in 2017. Code Sec. 2704 says that if clients have a right and somehow don't exercise that right and thus someone in line behind the clients gets a better deal, the result is that the clients made a gift.

> **EXAMPLE:** Jonas Johnston has a right to collect $1 million because his company liquidates. Jonas decides he doesn't want it. So now the $1 million goes to his children. Code Sec. 2704 says that's a gift to the children because Jonas had a right and didn't take it. Code Sec 2704 applies because immediately before the transfer, Jonas held control of the company. It's not like a disclaimer. This scenario reflects when a valuable right somehow gets transferred. In the Code Sec. 2704 fact patterns, specific lapses of rights are not disclaimers, they're considered gifts.

# ¶ 816 UPSTREAM PLANNING FOR THE GIFT TAX

The last strategy is the following point. Planners should think about gifting and think about basis. If clients give Grandma a low-basis asset, Grandma has the assets. When Grandma dies, if she's held the property for more than one year and the clients get it back, they get a basis at her fair market value at death. If she's not going to be a taxpayer at death, the clients win and get a higher basis. She paid no tax; the clients used up some of their gift exclusion to give it to her. But if the clients are not worth $22 million as a couple, who cares?

The last issue is that the instructions require charitable gifts to be reported, and a Form 709 must be filed. Is there any risk to not claiming these charitable gifts? Some practitioners will say that even if clients have a gift of $25 that they left out, could the IRS in the future hold they did not file a complete return and so the statute of limitations does not run? The argument against the IRS states it's terms like those that are not in the statute or regulations. It's in the form's instructions and the instructions do not have the force of law. That said, if clients are concerned about that, are making some big gifts, and then also have gifts to charity, the planner include the list of the charitable gifts. If a client is giving away a $1 million business with an appraisal attached to Form 709 and wants that statute to run plus gives $5,000 to charity, the planner should include the charitable gift. No harm in including it.

If clients making cash gifts to their children and the planner leaves out that kind of charitable gift, the likelihood is that's never going to be an issue. But again, to be very careful, planners should follow the instructions.

## STUDY QUESTION

**6.** Which of the following statements is correct regarding the special valuation rules of Chapter 14?

    **a.** Chapter 14 of the tax code was enacted to eliminate certain divorce-related gift tax issues.

    **b.** Code Sec. 2705 applies only to transfers to or for the benefit of a member of the transferor's family.

    **c.** A popular gifting technique that falls outside of the rules of Code Sec. 2702 is the qualified personal residence trust.

    **d.** The value of a qualified retained interest is added to the fair market value of the transferred property in determining the amount of any gift.

# MODULE 4: FINANCIAL AND ESTATE PLANNING—Chapter 9: *Tax Cuts and Jobs Act*: Impact on Financial and Estate Planning

## ¶ 901 WELCOME

This chapter discusses the effects of the new tax law (*Tax Cuts and Jobs Act*, H.R. 1) specific to its impact on financial and estate planning. Many of the rules in the law pertain to wealthy individuals. Only taxpayers who have more than $11.2 million in assets will now be subject to the transfer tax, gift tax, estate tax, and generation-skipping transfer (GST) tax. This chapter explains to practitioners and estate planners that they should not stop planning for this client base, because the higher exclusions are due to sunset after 2025.

## ¶ 902 LEARNING OBJECTIVES

Upon completion of this chapter, you will be able to:

- Recognize how existing assets are affected by and should transition to terms of the new law
- Identify ways the law opens favorable opportunities for taxpayers subject to transfer taxes
- Recognize how planners and wealthier clients can use financial and estate planning tools to minimize tax liabilities in the post-tax cuts environment

## ¶ 903 INTRODUCTION

The good news of the *Tax Cuts and Jobs Act* is that most of us aren't going to be taxpayers for estate and gift taxes. Less than one-tenth of 1 percent of individuals will be considered "taxpayers" under the new law. But the more important news for practitioners and planners is that they shouldn't stop planning for themselves and certainly clients. Because, what does this law really say? This law says that these higher exclusion numbers sunset after 2025. The law says tax provisions for individuals are going back to where they were in 2017, influenced by inflation since 2017, and using this new chained Consumer Price Index (CPI), so the inflation indexing is going to be at a slower rate than previously. That's what the chained CPI is designed to do. However, before 2025 or 2026, when this law sunsets of its own provision, the political risk means that the political and tax realms can change in our country, and what we think is permanent for eight years may be changed a lot sooner than that. If the political pendulum swings to the other side of where it is now, practitioners and clients may find themselves going back to lower numbers to trigger transfer taxes.

Spouses will continue to benefit from "portability" under the new tax law. The advantage of portability is if one spouse dies and does not use his or her transfer tax exclusion, the unused DSUE—the deceased spouse's unused exclusion or unused exemption—passes to the surviving spouse. If spouse A dies and leaves whatever he or she has to spouse B, spouse B under current law will have approximately $22 million of free transferability of assets with no tax, at least for the eight years or until this provision is changed. Obviously, portability is important. Obviously, most married people—if they're careful—will not be taxpayers.

**COMMENT:** Issues arising for practitioners and planners from the new tax law include considering whether clients who no longer have transfer taxes imposed will be willing to embrace the complex planning and professional fees often associated with the complexity. Will they decide to opt for the simplest and least expensive plan? Many taxpayers may take a "do it yourself" approach to planning, but they should consider issues that may arise when individual tax benefits sunset in 2025—or earlier, under some political circumstances.

# ¶ 904 A NEW EMPHASIS IN PLANNING

Practitioners are going to see planning taking into account the fact that people still need to plan and so now the focus isn't how to save the individual taxes but how to ensure that a plan makes sense, that clients are doing the important financial measures for their family as well as saving as much income tax now and later as possible.

## Refocused Planning

Look at the client's assets. Is the individual at risk of liabilities to creditors (because of debt or business liabilities)? Practitioners can set up arrangements—typically trust arrangements—to protect assets from creditor claims. Additionally, a client might get divorced, involving matrimonial creditors or alimony. A practitioner would be wise to save those assets from the reach of creditors.

Under the new tax law, clients in some states have even more reason to reduce income tax: the new state and local tax (SALT) limitation that caps deduction of such taxes at $10,000 on the itemized deduction schedule of the individual return. However, with the increase in the standard deduction for joint-filing couples to $24,000, many less wealthy clients might not even itemize, so reducing both their state and local taxes is very important.

The major planning focus for individuals having assets worth less than $11.2 million ($22.4 million for couples) is "core dispositive planning," in which practitioners recommend clients make significant asset transfers while the law's exclusions and standard deduction are high. Clients may fear "clawback," in which in later years the government claims the exclusion is too generous and reclaims some of the assets. The *Tax Cuts and Jobs Act* states that "The Secretary (IRS) shall prescribe such regulations as may be necessary or appropriate to carry out this section with respect to any difference between (A) the basic exclusion amount at time of the decedent's death, and (B) the basic exclusion amount under such section applicable with respect to any gifts made by the decedent." These regulations have not been written as of the date of this course.

**PLANNING POINTER:** Core dispositive planning by practitioner and client should begin with a meeting to review the taxpayer's current personal and financial situation, estate plan, and list of beneficiaries. Under the new tax law, certain trusts and beneficiary designations may change or be unnecessary. Provisions of the client's will should be checked to ensure that enough of the estate's assets will remain to support the surviving spouse for his or her lifetime, especially when stepchildren are involved. At that meeting the planner and client should check assets that will pass outside of his or her will, such as bank accounts, investment plan benefits, and retirement plan balances.

Other planning concerns income tax planning for the fair market value of property as of the decedent's date of death, and how to preserve assets and manage them properly. If a taxpayer lives in a "decoupled state," one that has retained a state estate tax such as New York, Oregon, or Illinois, the state's estate tax rate does not automatically match that of the new federal exclusion. The planner and client may wish to ensure that the state's exclusion is used at both spouses' deaths.

      **EXAMPLE:** If client Rosie Macduff dies in Illinois and leaves $4 million (all of her assets) to her spouse, she doesn't use her $4 million exclusion. Now Johnny, her surviving spouse, has his $4 million exclusion, but the couple has only excluded $4 million of the family's wealth. They could have excluded $8 million of the family's wealth from Illinois tax instead of paying tax on $4 million with poor planning.

      Even if a client's state does not have a state death tax and it is not a concern at the moment, given the large federal exclusion, it would not shock planners if some states desperately in need of revenue look around and note that not all wealthy residents will be paying federal death tax and thus enact a law to collect tax at the state level.

## Spousal Lifetime Access Trusts and Use of Life Insurance

Spousal trusts (abbreviated as SLATs) are available to married couples and receive gifts or sales transfers to use the transfer tax exclusion now. In 2018, a donee may be gifted up to $15,000 without triggering gift tax. The SLAT protects a spouse's entitlement to lifetime income and thereafter gives the remainder to children or other heirs without the surviving spouse having to claim the marital deduction. Then when the survivor dies, the heirs' trust property is not taxed. The income is protected.

      If the spouse predeceases the donor creating the SLAT, the way to avoid loss of income for the individual is to have a life insurance policy on the donee spouse. Practitioners can suggest holding the policy in an irrevocable trust so that no one will pay any transfer tax.

      In addition to SLATs, taxpayers may still manage asset transfers without using the lifetime gifting exclusion by:

- Maxing out the annual present interest gift tax exclusion of $15,000 per donee ($30,000 for married couples);
- Making gifts directly to educational institutions to pay tuition (even greater than the $15,000 cap for gift tax);
- Making gifts to medical care providers to pay someone's medical deductibles, premiums, and expenses.

# ¶ 905  AREAS FOR WHICH ESTATE PLANNING IS STILL REQUIRED

When should the planner and client still want to talk about estate planning? There are all kinds of reasons in addition to taxes.

## Inheritance of Property

Whom does the client want to inherit property: the spouse, children, grandchildren, a favorite charity? And to what extent should each of those beneficiaries be rewarded or left out?

## Protection of Assets from Creditors

Planners and clients worry about asset protection. American society is exceptionally litigious. What can they do? Seventeen states permit domestic asset protection trusts (DAPTs). Such a trust makes it much more difficult for creditors to access a client's assets. These trusts are especially protective for clients with high liabilities who have the potential for substantial recovery for negligence—for example, surgeons, architects, and engineers.

## Care of Special Needs Beneficiaries

Clients who have family members who are or may become disabled or legally incompetent also require special estate plans. These plans may create a special needs trust instead of giving the heirs their inheritance outright. Such a trust provides that public assistance is not available to the heir until the inheritance is exhausted or one that requires public assistance to be effective because trust funds are unusable for any expense public assistance would cover.

Trusts may be created for the donor who anticipates heirs may have issues like substance abuse problems, gambling addiction, or other objectionable lifestyle issues. The trustee is authorized to hold onto this property in trust until there's either some sign of "improvement" or perhaps use the money to provide for rehabilitation costs.

## Succession Planning

What about business succession planning? What if a client is the sole owner of a company, such as an entrepreneur? Does the client have a plan? Has the client identified family members who are competent to take over the business? If the succession is not well planned or does not identify third parties who might be purchasers of the business, the client's family will get little or no value for what the client owned.

## Divorce

Another planning issue occurs when a client contemplates divorce. The law is changing with respect to the taxation of assets following divorce. For agreements signed after 2018, alimony is not deductible by the payor and not includable in the income of the person who receives it. If a client is contemplating divorce and is likely to be the payor, the planner should recommend expediting the procedure for 2018, because the personal exemption for alimony paid is gone beginning in 2019. If the client is likely to be the payee, the opposite applies.

A client with children usually negotiates which spouse will claim them as dependents. Under the new tax law, personal exemptions are eliminated, so dependent issues are up in the air.

A client may have a child who is getting divorced. How can an estate plan protect the client's assets from inheritance by the former spouse? The plan should avoid allocating a portion of the assets directly to the child upon the client's death, which might allow the former spouse to get a piece of that money. And a court can certainly take into account that the client's child has inherited a lot of money and is in a better position to give up more assets.

The remedy is to have a client whose child is thinking of a divorce set up a trust that says that the trust can't be touched by the person unless the trustee agrees. That way the plan makes it harder for the former spouse to get at this client's child's wealth.

## Charitable Giving

Charitable giving hasn't changed under the new law. People still want to be charitable, so where does the practitioner build that into the plan? A gift may be designated in the client's will, for example, $1 million from a total estate of $8 or $9 million. How much tax benefit will the client get for that? Zero, because the donor wouldn't have been an estate tax taxpayer anyway.

Wouldn't it have been smarter to leave that money to the client's children, if he or she trusts them to satisfy the charitable goal? The client's heir could make the gift to the charity while getting an income tax deduction for that gift to charity. Whether the child's tax bracket is under 22 percent or as much as 37 percent, it's worth something to that child to make that gift, whereas the decedent gets no tax benefit.

## Dynastic Planning

The client's children might be spendthrifts who can't save a nickel. In that case, the practitioner and client should create a trust containing a spendthrift clause stating that the assets can't be pledged as collateral. The children can't access the inheritance unless the trustee gives it to them.

For dynastic planning, a trust is set up that involves the generation skipping tax (GST) exclusion. That's $11.2 million, and the trust's terms can provide that trust to last for dozens or hundreds of years or forever, depending upon constraints of some jurisdictions. And the advantage, at least under current law, is that each time a generation dies out, there's no transfer tax to pay because all the assets are in a trust of which the beneficiary is not the owner, so the client passing away doesn't make the beneficiary a taxpayer.

Money that goes through three or four generations without being taxed—even if the trust starts with a modest funding level—is worth a multiple of the balance if beneficiaries paid tax each time a generation member died. The new law allows $11.2 million a person to give heirs through such a trust. Mitigating tax makes sense.

## Real Estate in Multiple Jurisdictions

A trust also minimizes complications for a client who owns real estate in more than one jurisdiction. If property passes by means of a will, beneficiaries have to probate the will and deal with transfer tax separately in each state. And if property is held in other countries, additional wills might be required for all the foreign jurisdictions and subject to the exclusion level of transfer tax in each country. On the other hand, the client may be a nonresident alien who has property in the United States but who has a much lower transfer tax exclusion than that of the $11.2 million level, or only $60,000 in 2018. One approach to mitigate tax in such a case is to make gifts of property to U.S. residents.

Alternatively, the client can place ownership of all that property in a trust whose title stays just as it was prior to the death of the client, avoiding probate complications. The client and planner should keep in mind, however, the possible sunset of the $11.2 million exclusion in the long term—after the 2020 and 2024 presidential elections.

## Guardianship of Minors and Elders

Often one of the most contentious issues in a family is who will be the guardian for any surviving minor children. If the parents pass, who's in line—siblings, grandparents? Often family members don't agree about the guardianship, so the estate plan should include terms of some arrangement.

Another issue is elder care planning, not only for the client but other family members that are elderly who need some help. Trusts may be established for mom and dad when they may not be able to care for themselves. There are financial issues just as there were before the passage of the new tax law. The client should ensure that the transfer tax is minimized for the elderly family members; not doing so could jeopardize the client's own estate assets.

## STUDY QUESTION

---

**1.** The major focus for estate planning for persons having assets less than $11.2 million and married couples with assets less than $22.4 million will turn to each of the following *except:*

- **a.** Core dispositive planning
- **b.** Charitable contributions
- **c.** Preservation of assets
- **d.** Income tax planning

---

# ¶ 906 PORTABILITY OF THE ESTATE TAX EXEMPTION

Portability, or the "death tax insurance," is the next issue. Portability says that when a married person dies, any unused transfer tax exclusion passes to his or her surviving spouse. The $11.2 million exclusion to a spouse could become $22.4 million, and the decedent's spouse can now make gifts of that money or keep it until death, and the couple still has a $22.4 million exclusion under current law.

The way to declare the exclusion is to file Form 706, *United States Estate (and Generation-Skipping Transfer) Tax Return,* due nine months after the decedent's death. Another challenge for planners is that clients may say, "Why should I pay for a Form 706 to be filed when my assets are a couple million dollars or less, and the likelihood that I'm ever going to get to $22 million is so slight I don't even want to think about it?"

Is that wrong? It might be shortsighted because something may happen in the future of the client's life that makes him or her a wealthy person: winning the lottery, hitting a jackpot in the casino, or inheriting money unexpectedly. What happens if the surviving spouse client never filed Form 706 when the first spouse died? Or maybe the surviving spouse remarries a really wealthy person who states he or she will be generous to the client because, after all, he or she filed the deceased spousal unused exemption (DSUE) from a previous spouse and so may give away $11.2 million.

If the surviving previous spouse never filed Form 706, becomes injured, and receives a settlement, having filed Form 706 offers protection. Portability of the death tax exclusion makes sense, just like having health care or auto insurance. The client has two years from the spouse's time of death to obtain portability, with a six-month automatic filing extension. Filing Form 706 offers protection through simply filing the completed form listing the assets with estimated values. Beyond a two-year period, the IRS must grant permission to file a late Form 706 and the estate must submit a user fee of $10,000. The recommendation is for every estate of a deceased married client to make a timely portability election to obtain an $11.2 million free pass of assets.

If a client makes a gift as the survivor with a DSUE from his or her first decedent spouse, that DSUE is used first, but the surviving spouse and a second spouse may combine their exclusions. The recommendation is to make the portability election in every case, especially for clients whose assets are well below $11 million.

# STUDY QUESTION

**2.** The primary motive for enacting portability of the federal estate tax exemption was to:

    **a.** Simplify estate planning for married couples

    **b.** Simplify trust planning for single filers

    **c.** Encourage married couples to file jointly

    **d.** Increase federal tax revenue

## Simple Wills and Bypass Trusts

Should planners recommend that clients go with simple wills? Married people are probably more willing to just simply say, "I'll leave everything to my spouse" in an "I Love You" will. It's not terrible to do that because if the client files a Form 706, he or she will get portability and get a basis step-up at both deaths. That's the income tax side. The 2017 act did not change the rule that says fair market value at death is the basis used for an heir. That's an exceptionally important retained provision in the 2017 tax act.

    **EXAMPLE:** When Henry Hudson dies, the value of his assets at date of death is the basis to spouse Emily Hudson. When she dies, the value of the property at her date of death is the value to Emily's heirs. Is this stipulation enough, or should Emily and the planner create a bypass trust?

    Prior to the portability coming into the law beginning in 2011, planners always wanted to use a bypass trust because the bypass trust was designed to say at the death of the first of a married couple, it was important to use the available exclusion because terms stated use it or lose it. If a spouse died and left everything to the surviving spouse, none of the available exemption or exclusion was used. No tax was due because the marital deduction applied.

    But when the surviving spouse died, that estate got to use his or her one exclusion. However, two exclusions would be available if the couple had set up a bypass trust. And so, prior to portability, planners were very aggressively addressing bypass trusts.

    Under current law, these trusts are not as important because most individuals don't have the issue of losing the exclusion. But there are still some possible advantages because if a bypass trust exists, the property in that trust will not be included in the estate of the survivor when he or she dies. The advantage to that is that the survivor perhaps accrues a lot of appreciation and no tax when the survivor dies because he or she is not the owner of the bypass trust.

    **EXAMPLE:** Go back to the situation for Emily. Henry dies at age 86 and Emily dies at age 90. She's had 30 years of appreciation. What will the law be in 30 years? Who knows? If the property appreciates significantly and the tax law is very unfavorable, when Emily dies, her estate may owe a lot of tax because the appreciation may have exceeded any exemption. Perhaps it is advisable to use the bypass trust at Henry's death to lock in any future appreciation from being taxed at Emily's death.

    But now the other side of that is the basis issue. The assets get a basis increase at the first death, the date of death value. If the estate passes the property per the marital deduction to Emily, the property gets a basis increase when she dies. But if the estate uses the bypass trust, there's no basis adjustment when she dies. What that suggests is an up-front discussion of the assets that are likely to be placed in this trust.

    **EXAMPLE:** Henry's assets consist of stocks and bonds and property that does appreciate in value and is easily sold. Then Emily does not want bypass trust to lock in the appreciation because she won't get a basis adjustment at the second death.

Alternatively, what if Henry's asset consists of a family business or a vacation home that are being used to fund the bypass trust? How likely is it that that asset will be readily sold by Emily's heirs? Maybe they want to run the business. Maybe they want to enjoy the vacation home. If that's the case, who cares what the basis is if no one is ever going to be a seller that Henry or the planner can reasonably anticipate?

This is why planning is important, why discussing these issues with clients is important. They're not going to be worried about the basis to heirs in 20 or 30 years without the practitioner being the thought leader that brings up some of these issues.

## Nonportability of the GST Exclusion

Portability of the decedent's unused exclusion, while allowed for federal tax purposes, is not recognized in any of the states that continue to have a state estate tax, with the exception of Hawaii which does allow portability with respect to its state estate tax. What does that mean? If the client has a wealthy family and really wants to make substantial transfers to grandchildren or more distant heirs, the planner should make sure each person uses a GST exclusion. Each one needs to use that GST exclusion to make this planning work.

**EXAMPLE:** Grandpa and Grandma Bliston leave everything to their survivor, with no tax marital deduction, but the GST was not used at grandpa's death, so at grandma's death, their survivor may use the GST exclusion, but only grandma's GST exclusion, unlike the estate tax rules that allow portability in full when the DSUE (Deceased Spouse's Unused Estate tax deduction), applies. There is no DSUE for the GST, for such wealthy clients, the planner should at least think about ensuring somehow that the GST exclusion is used by the first decedent rather than assuming it's all going to be available at the second person's death.

There is an unlimited statute of limitations when an estate has a DSUE situation. Maybe a planner is "getting away with" a really favorable low valuation at the first death of a married person, and the planner doesn't want to take a chance that when the second one dies, the IRS can reopen the first decedent's estate. That would be the case if an estate claimed portability because of creating a DSUE situation.

Maybe the planner just uses the bypass trust to take advantage of that significantly low value. Maybe the estate claims aggressive discounting and doesn't want the government too interested in exactly how the estate is handled. That would be another reason to use the bypass trust.

Perhaps the estate has hard-to-value assets with aggressive discounts. The nasty rules that were proposed in 2016 under Code Sec. 2704 to severely limit valuation discounts for family business transfers, have been withdrawn, but they're still sitting in the IRS computer somewhere, and with a change of presidential administration, could come back. Seizing these advantages while they're available might be a worthwhile thing to do.

## Prevention Provisions of Trusts

These planning scenarios compare different choices. Thinking that the client wants everything to be held in trust so the only option is the bypass trust would be an incorrect conclusion. Another option is the qualified terminable interest property (QTIP) trust, in which a client leaves property in trust for the surviving spouse. The spouse must get all the income; nobody else can get the principal while the spouse is alive, but the first decedent controls where the property goes.

The QTIP trust is distinguished from the bypass trust. In the bypass trust there is no inclusion of the trust property in the surviving spouse's estate. With the QTIP trust, there is inclusion in the surviving spouse's estate. The survivor gets an inclusion, but if he or she is not taxable, so what? The advantage of the inclusion at the second death is the basis adjustment. The fair market value of property at the second death is the property value to the heirs.

Even if the estate is using a simple will that just leaves everything to a spouse, how does that setup leave it? Using trusts doesn't mean that the beneficiary is restricted or limited, assuming the beneficiary is appropriately mature, deserving, etc. What the planner is creating with the trust is the asset protection for the family, the management by a trustee, someone who is appropriately organized, hopefully competent to do that, who if necessary can restrict the surviving spouse's transfer of assets.

Clients should consider whether their children are protected if the surviving spouse remarries and leaves everything to the second spouse. That could be a concern, so clients may prefer to put property into a trust to ensure the surviving spouse doesn't leave the assets to third parties.

Trust terms can consider how to prevent the surviving spouse who gets dementia from giving assets away to undeserving third parties. It doesn't mean the spouse may not use the income and the property and benefits, etc., but the trust serves as protection in this situation.

Because no one knows future eventualities, it's a good idea to build that protective structure, just in case beneficiaries go off the track (whether because of dementia, remarriage, or reckless spending).

Not every asset belongs in a trust. Perhaps a client does not want to put residential property or certain other assets in the trust and have to share them with children.

**EXAMPLE:** Clyde and Teri Bosworth have four children. They each get a 25 percent interest in a piece of property that has maintenance fees and expenses. Three of the children kick in their share, but the fourth child says, "Oh, I'm a little short of money this month. I can't add my share." Well, what are the children going to do? The municipality doesn't want to get three-quarters of the property tax and the contractor doesn't want to get three-quarters of the repair fees. So these issues become a concern. If Clyde and Teri have a trust and fund it, it can address some of these issues.

# ¶ 907 INCOME TAX PLANNING

For taxpayers whose assets do not exceed the $11.2 million threshold, income tax planning is more vital than transfer tax planning. Although most individuals will never be subject to transfer taxes (under the current tax law), everyone wants to pay the least possible federal and state income tax. Planners and less wealthy clients want to address basis adjustments and fair market value of assets. Key for these clients will be preserving a stepped-up basis of assets at the death of each spouse.

## Basis Adjustments

The maximum capital gains rate is 20 percent, and the net investment income tax rate is 3.8 percent. The net investment income tax thresholds are not indexed for inflation, its maximum is $250,000 of AGI for married taxpayers filing jointly, $200,000 for a single filer, or $125,000 for a married person filing separately. Those numbers are not indexed. Where the 20 percent rate kicks in is indexed, and that's more than $470,000 for a married person.

Taxpayers in most states have state taxes as well. If individuals are going to pay the 15 percent capital gains tax and the state income tax, or the 23.8 percent capital gains and the state income tax, clients might be paying a lot of income tax on assets' gains. Also involved are qualified dividends and ordinary income. What planners want to accomplish are basis adjustments at every possible place.

The simple will gives heirs a basis adjustment. The QTIP trust provides for a basis adjustment at both spouses' deaths as long as an asset is includable in the estate of the first to die, left to the surviving spouse, and includable in that person's estate.

What about lifetime gifts? In the past many planners encouraged clients who had property with appreciation potential to make lifetime gifts. That was good planning. Is it still good planning under the new tax law? Maybe not, if planners take into account basis. For a low-basis stock clients give away during their lives, what is the basis to their heirs? It's a carryover basis when clients make a gift.

If clients die, basis is the value at the date of death. Clients may not want to be so quick to give away low-basis stock or other low-basis assets. There's an upside-down plan. If the property is going to appreciate, fine, clients' estates are not going to be taxed when clients die unless the value exceeds these new higher thresholds. Unless clients' assets exceed $11.2 million or, as a surviving spouse, exceed $22.4 million, clients are not going to be taxed when they die. The advice here is to let the property appreciate rather than give it away when it has a low basis.

Even more aggressive is "upstream planning" for gifting assets to older heirs, especially for assets worth less than the $11.2 million exclusion.

**EXAMPLE:** Yoshi Tanaka is a 60-year-old client. His parents, Yamika and Kana, are 90 years old and healthy. Yoshi gifts them low-basis assets. Actuarially, the parents are going to die before Yoshi. If they return the assets to Yoshi when they die, the value to him is the fair market value at death, as long as they live one year from the time Yoshi gives the assets to them.

If they don't live longer than a year and Yoshi gets the property back within the year, he receives it with the same basis he had before. Not the end of the world. So the parents hold a couple of million dollars. Yoshi thereby gives some of his exclusion amount away to mom and dad, gets it back with a higher basis, and can sell it or depreciate it all over again with the higher basis, with no gains to be paid, no tax to be paid.

Alternatively, Yamika and Kana are not particularly healthy but able to sign a will including disposition of the assets. They can state that some of the assets can be bequests to Yoshi's children. Because the grandchildren are not the donors, the basis to them is the fair market value at the time of the grandparents' death. This plan moves low-basis assets to create higher-basis property during the parent's and grandparents' lifetimes.

If clients have loser stocks with a decline in value, those are the worst assets to leave the family. If clients paid $100 per share and the stock is now selling at $20, clients should sell that stock, realize the $80,000 capital loss, and use that loss to offset some gain elsewhere. That makes more sense than dying and giving heirs a stock worth $20 per share, which becomes their basis. Also, clients have lost the ability to claim that tax loss.

## Valuation Discounts

How aggressive should a plan be to claim valuation discounts, particularly when the client dies? When a client dies and the practitioner states the value of the illiquid business assets or real estate as $5 million, then that's the fair market value. However, because it's a closely held asset, the plan is leaving minority interest shares to various family members, so the valuation includes a 30 percent discount.

Now the property is worth $3.5 million to the heirs—their basis. The plan just deprived them of the significant basis adjustment. Plans should not provide for valuation discounts at death when clients are not going to be transfer tax taxpayers; clients want the highest value that is appropriately justifiable.

Will the IRS force estates to claim discounts? Possibly, but the estate may not even have to be filed if it's the surviving spouse's estate and it's not anywhere near $11.2 million. Then estates don't even have to file Form 706. It's not filed to gain portability if the survivor is not married.

So what have heirs got? Nothing. The estate doesn't have to file anything. There is no need to be aggressive for discounting when clients don't have a taxable estate.

## Working with Appraisers

Similarly, if practitioners are dealing with an appraiser, typically he or she would ask, "What's this for? Are you selling your business or are you doing it for a death situation?" Planners will answer appropriately and not dictate to the appraiser how to do the valuation. However, planners may explain to what use the appraisal will be applied.

> **EXAMPLE:** Jason Wilson is working with an appraiser for his client. When asked about the purpose of the valuation, Jason states, "Look, if you have a range of high to low, we'd appreciate it if you're a little more aggressive on the low side because we're going to pay estate tax." If Jason's client is not going to be paying estate tax, is it improper for him to say within his professional responsibility, "If you have a range from low to high, the high number is better for us." That may influence the appraiser somewhat appropriately. Jason avoids anything that's unethical, but what he says to the appraiser is, "We need this for a federal estate tax number. We are not paying the federal estate tax." The appraiser understands what Jason is saying, so the appraisal may come back with a more aggressive number. That's what Jason wants in that situation.

## State Estate and Income Taxes

What if the beneficiary is going to be a state estate tax payer, not a federal one? Now that is more complicated, because the planner may want the valuation discount to avoid the state death tax. The beneficiary may want the lower appraisal to avoid the state death tax or at least pay as little as possible.

The state tax issue raises another concern. If the plan is to obtain a low basis to the heirs because they are taking a lower value of the state death tax, what is the tax rate that states charge? The highest rate is 16 percent, except for the state of Washington, which has a 20 percent tax rate, but even that rate does not apply to 100 percent of the assets; it's a graduated tax rate structure.

At the worst case, the state's tax hit is 16 percent to 20 percent. If the estate has a low basis in assets, what's the tax rate heirs are going to pay on capital gains? Well, maybe 20 percent if their federal taxable income is high enough, plus perhaps the 3.8 percent net investment income tax, for a total rate of 23.8 percent. Do the heirs live in a state that has a state income tax?

Maybe the clients decide to have the estate pay the estate tax or perhaps leave everything to a surviving spouse who is going to move away after that first death. If all the heirs live in Florida or California or another locale that doesn't have a death tax, the plan can give the higher basis to the spouse, or the spouse may move to a state like Florida or California or Texas or Nevada or one of the states that don't have state death taxes.

Another new rule for itemizing deductions allows a maximum $10,000 deduction for state, local income, property, etc. (SALT), taxes going forward. Well, how can a planner minimize state income tax? If clients live in a state that does have one, there is a technique that is being used around the country, referred to as a NING, a DING, or a WING trust.

These are incomplete, nongrantor trusts, that's the "ING" part. The NING, WING, and DING would represent Nevada, Wyoming, and Delaware—states that have encouraged individuals to create trusts in their states using a trustee in one of those states, and claiming intangible assets (e.g., portfolio assets, and the interest/dividends/capital gains generated by those investments) are now located in this type of trust. Because these states have no state income tax, taxpayers don't owe any income tax on this trust. And if clients live in a state like New Jersey or California or another high income tax state, they saved their state income tax, unless the state decides to not let them do that.

New York has made that decision. New York says regardless of having a NING, DING, WING, or whatever, the state is going to tax the trust as a grantor trust. New York still wants to collect tax from the trust income. Will other high income tax states pass similar statutes? It's certainly possible.

Planners should try to spread the income tax liability among other people. Clients in states like New Jersey annually have $30,000 or $40,000 property tax bills. How can this tax be mitigated?

Planners suggest giving a percentage interest in the property to each of the clients' three or four children in a revocable trust. The trust then owns, for example, a 20 percent interest in the home. The trust has its own tax liability, with property taxes to pay. However, the trust can deduct that share of the property tax. Obviously, the trust has to have some income to offset the payment of the property tax, but clients can generate income by making gifts, all the while having the trust for their children and earning income. The trust pays the property tax, and it gets a deduction. This effort is designed to defeat the SALT limitation.

## STUDY QUESTIONS

**3.** Which of the following states allows portability of its exemption amount?

    **a.** Texas

    **b.** California

    **c.** Hawaii

    **d.** Oklahoma

**4.** Which of the following statements regarding the new planning considerations is correct?

    **a.** Avoidance of both capital gains taxes and net investment income taxes and passing assets with a stepped-up basis becomes a secondary concern.

    **b.** Traditional estate planning techniques used to reduce the value of assets on death continues to be the most advantageous.

    **c.** Planners should consider downstream planning.

    **d.** Planners should consider whether there are provisions in the governing documents of an entity that were crafted to allow or encourage discounting.

## Pass-Through Entity Deduction and Lower Corporate Rate

The new pass-through deduction offers the opportunity to claim a 20 percent income tax deduction for individuals in a pass-through entity. Trusts and estates can claim that deduction.

Is a client in a service business? If so, he or she should ensure that income is less than $315,000 (if married filing jointly), or $157,500 if a single filer. So planners want to try to take advantage of these benefits under the new law or help clients reorganize a business to qualify.

Should everybody convert to a C corporation entity because it now has a 21 percent tax rate? Not everybody. If a client is only accumulating capital and doesn't need withdrawals for salary and dividends, the C corp makes a lot of sense. But beware of the personal holding company tax and the accumulated earnings tax rules. If the client needs money to be withdrawn, whether it be salary or dividends, and here planners have to be mindful of reasonable compensation, C corporation status doesn't make sense, because the 21 percent corporate rate along with the tax to the individual on a dividend or on a salary might not be saving much money. Planners should consider entity choice on a case-by-case basis.

In the optimal situation for a C corporation, all the entity is doing is accumulating capital because the owner doesn't need the money (has other income sources to live on). The corporation pays the 21 percent tax, continues in business for at least five years, and then the owner sells the stock. What is the tax rate in that case? Zero. The company profits, the company closes after at least five years, and the owner sells the stock. Code Sec. 1202 (Qualified Small Business Stock) says the tax rate is zero as long as the corporation is not in certain service businesses or other nonqualifying business and acquired the stock between September 27, 2010 (certain other rules also apply). There's a lot of opportunity here for planning.

Planners and clients should examine the business structure. Is a client's entity a sole proprietorship, a limited liability company (LLC), a partnership, an S corp, or a C corp? How do these new rules about pass-through deductions apply to them? Simply put, at the low levels of income, entity owners would rather be a proprietorship; at the high levels of income, owners would rather be an S corp. And at some levels, a C corp works best. The new tax law will keep accountants and lawyers busy from its implementation in 2018 until it changes down the road.

## Code Sec. 754 Election

If a client's entity is taxed as a partnership (that is, a partnership or an LLC taxed as a partnership), a Code Sec. 754 election is available. If a partner dies, the election enables the inside basis of the partnership assets to increase only for that heir, not for everybody, to equal the outside basis, the value of the partnership interest inherited from a decedent.

Without the 754 election, the heir's basis in the partnership interest is the fair market value when the decedent died, but the inside basis doesn't change. Then, if the partnership sells assets, the heir is taxed on his or her share of the profit on those assets. The 754 election can make that not happen. The downside of the 754 is if the entity has lots of partners and lots of assets, every person could have a different basis; keeping track of that is very difficult and this election may even be prohibited by the partnership agreement in large partnerships

## Trust Income

Should the client leave all the property in a trust? Trust income is taxed at terribly compressed tax rates. At $12,500 of trust income, a client would be in the top 37 percent tax bracket. Although a planner wants to use trusts to be protective of a client, the trustee should also be at least able and willing to distribute the income to the beneficiary to get the income taxed at the beneficiary's bracket.

This setup should not be automatic, because sometimes, as discussed earlier, the beneficiary is a person who shouldn't be getting income. It may be better to pay a higher tax and protect the beneficiary from problems than it is to pay the lower tax: give the money to the beneficiary, and exacerbate the beneficiary's problems.

Giving the trustee discretion for distributions is a major reason to use trusts. If a client just left all assets outright to the beneficiary, there would be no chance for asset protection, special needs protection, active asset management, etc. If, on the other hand the trustee makes no distributions, then heirs are probably going to pay more tax than necessary. But discretion gives trustees the appropriate opportunity and flexibility to make these important decisions.

It's important in a new trust to ensure that the trustee has the ability to distribute capital gains. Dividends are typically low, and interest is even lower. If a trust is well invested and there are capital gains involved, it is smarter to permit distributions of those gains as appropriate. Because if a trust is paying tax on the gains at the trust level at a very low level, tax is hitting the 20 percent bracket, plus the 3.8 percent net investment income tax. Heirs, on the other hand, would not pay such a rate unless they earned hundreds of thousands of dollars.

The new law affects the kiddie trust tax rules. Children younger than the age of 19 (or 24 for full-time students) will no longer have their unearned income taxed at mom and dad's rates but at the trust's rates. The parents' rate is not going to be applicable. That may save money in a few cases, probably cost more in others.

Tax preparers will have to do a separate return now for every child with unearned income. Individuals may have to pay estimated taxes on the child's income. It might be a good idea to have a bunch of trusts—one for every child—so each trust will have its own income and its own income tax responsibility. Well, the SALT deduction is now spread among the family. Clients might be able to deduct a little higher percentage of their own state and local tax if they've moved some of the tax-generating assets to family members.

Should clients use a separate share for each beneficiary or a sprinkling trust? The advantage, and the disadvantage, of the separate share trust is that everybody is treated the same. It may be smarter in some families to have a sprinkling trust that empowers the trustee to decide who gets the income. That way the lower-bracket folks might get more of the income to balance out the overall family tax bill.

That may create some resentment if clients don't have separate shares. One recipient may get more than another. That's why clients have a discussion with family members once they establish what they want. To minimize resentments, it's much better to inform beneficiaries in advance of the clients' reasoning for a sprinkling trust with uneven distributions.

Another planning technique that clients can certainly use to address the compressed rates of trusts is the 65-day rule. A checkbox on the bottom of page 2 of Form 1041 asks whether the trust is making a Section 663(b) election. The election enables a trust to make a distribution 65 days into the next tax year but treat that distribution of income as occurring in the previous year. That means the trust will get a deduction for making the transfer, and the beneficiaries will pick it up as income in the previous tax year. The trust has 65 days from the end of the calendar year to do that (in a non-leap year with the calendar year taxpayer, March 6). The 65-day rule can help with taxation of mutual fund distributions occurring in late December for which clients are unaware until January's statements are received. The election can adjust where the income is taxed as well as allowing adjustments to the amount of distributions made to the lower-bracket beneficiaries. The disadvantage of the election, of course, is that beneficiaries have more income to report. However, the family as a whole saves tax.

# ¶ 908 FINANCIAL PLANNING USING LIFE INSURANCE

Generally, clients have bought life insurance for all the traditional reasons: protecting the lifestyle of family members, making sure that if the clients die young, their spouse is protected, and their children can be educated. The insured clients needed liquidity to pay a home mortgage before there was a chance to save money to cover that mortgage or get it paid off. The core reasons for requiring life insurance were nontax reasons.

Should clients keep their life insurance policies now? Perhaps they are not useful under the new, current federal law, but might be under future law. What about state law? Where do the clients live—in one of the decoupled states? These may be reasons to keep their insurance. Even if everyone thinks the transfer tax exclusion is going to stay high, will it stay this high? We don't know.

## Insurance to Provide for Children Under Divorce Agreements

What about a situation in which a divorce agreement requires a client to provide funds to children from the marriage? Life insurance can be used to provide direct bequests to children from a prior marriage without having to address the blended family concerns of trusts or dividing assets between the current spouse and the children of an earlier marriage. Sometimes the agreement states that upon the client's death, the children are to receive X dollars. Life insurance is a good way to cover that, so that way the client doesn't have to worry that if he or she is remarried or starts a new family, upon death assets will be taken away from the new spouse or new family. Having a life insurance policy to address the issue makes sense.

## Investment Strategies Using Insurance

Some planners say that as the wealth of clients increase, they should buy more whole life insurance, because the buildup of the cash value of the policy is not taxable to clients, and if they withdraw it, the funds are only taxable if they exceed the premiums paid. Whole life insurance can be a useful way to build up money. In some policies, the internal buildup is a higher percentage than it is in the bank, in which accounts offer minimal interest, which is subject to income tax. If clients increase the cash value of insurance even by 2 percent or so, they're not paying any income tax on the funds. Thus, whole life insurance may serve as a vehicle for asset growth.

## Insurance Policies Held in Trust

There are several advantages to holding life insurance in an irrevocable trust. If the insured creates the trust, puts the policy into the trust and lives beyond three years, the proceeds of the policy will not be part of the insured's estate. Similarly, if the beneficiary is a spouse or a child, who is not given a right to own the policy or own the proceeds, but rather gets life insurance, the client may get the income for life as well as access to principal if needed. When the client passes on, policy funds go to the next people in line.

If that's the situation, that irrevocable life insurance trust will keep the insurance policy from being taxed in any heir's estate unless he or she inherits the property outright. Keeping the policy in trust for multiple beneficiaries and multiple generations makes sense.

## Insurance to Protect Inheritances

If a client is going to leave a business interest to his or her children, for example, and the proceeds will be taxable at the client's death (if the interest is worth that much money), having life insurance to cover taxes is worthwhile.

There are a number of protections offered by life insurance, an important one being that a policy left to family members keeps creditors from having access to it. State law protects policies in those situations. The policy may also serve as an easy means of gifting (because the insured won't be using the proceeds after death).

Because the new law repeals the corporate alternative minimum tax (AMT), having buy-sell agreements funded by corporate-owned life insurance is a better idea than it was before the repeal. Before the repeal of the corporate AMT, life insurance payable to the corporation was a tax preference. A corporation used to be required to pay a 15 percent tax on life insurance proceeds it received. That's gone now, which provides a planning opportunity for corporate holdings of clients.

What should clients do with a life insurance trust? If they have a survivorship policy, do they want to keep it? A practitioner should ask why clients got such a policy in the first place. A common reason for the survivorship policy, which only pays off at the second spouse's death, is the plan to cover death taxes, because that's when the death taxes are typically due.

Before the new law, plans deferred death tax from death of one spouse to the death of the surviving spouse, paid the tax at death two. The survivorship policy would ensure that the family didn't have to sell real estate, business, or other assets to cover taxes.

Do clients still want to keep such a policy, given the higher exclusion under the new law? Perhaps, but maybe clients should consider another investment for the value of the policy. Clients may consider making a tax-free swap of the policy for an annuity. An annuity actually provides payments to clients rather than leaving more money to their heirs. If clients prefer to leave the money to their children, they may decide to keep the survivorship policy going. Otherwise, clients may either convert the insurance policy to an annuity or maybe just stop paying any more premiums, making the policy a paid-up policy with whatever death benefit it includes.

Many planners deal with all the *Crummey* notices over the years—the notice issued to ensure that when clients pay the life insurance premium, it's treated as a present interest for gift tax purposes. That's the point of these *Crummey* notices. If clients cover a policy's premiums and don't have a *Crummey* withdrawal power in the hands of the beneficiary, then the IRS considers the payments to be made as a future interest gift, which uses up some of the clients' lifetime gift exclusion.

When the exclusion was $1 million, a lot of clients were reluctant to use up the exclusion so fast and used the *Crummey* withdrawal to get the present interest exclusion. But that meant every year clients and planners would have to give a notice to beneficiaries, who would have to sign off receipt of the notice.

The new law raises the exclusion from $1 million to $11.2 million, so many clients may be less concerned about the *Crummey* issue now. Or beneficiaries may decide not to receive notices, saying rather that they withdraw their right of withdrawal.

# ¶ 909 FINANCIAL PLANNING USING RETIREMENT BENEFITS

## Updating Beneficiaries

How should clients reconsider retirement plan accounts with their planners? First, planners should examine client retirement beneficiary designations, because the law is that retirement plan assets are passed by the terms of their designation, not the terms of the account holders will and not the terms of a marital agreement. Whose name is on the plan is who gets the money. End of discussion.

The U.S. Supreme Court case, **Kennedy v. DuPont Savings Plan**, involved a married couple who had a divorce. The wife signed off saying, "I relinquish all my rights to my husband's plan," and her husband never changed the beneficiary. When the husband, Kennedy, died, the divorced wife stepped forward to take the funds.

Her stepchildren objected, and the case went to the U.S. Supreme Court, which ruled that whoever's name was on the plan should inherit the money. The lesson for planners and their clients is that clients' designations should be comfortable with how they assign benefits to their beneficiaries.

The general implementation is to name the spouse as the beneficiary of the plan. He or she can roll assets over to an IRA, not paying any income tax and not paying any estate tax until the second spouse dies. That gives the spouse the ability to wait until age 70½, if desired, to start taking minimum required distributions (RMDs), and then name a designated beneficiary of his or her own choosing to get the money.

By doing so, the planner hasn't used up any of the decedent's exclusion to get the retirement plan to the spouse, so all the portability opportunity remains. This solves the former problem of some folks with retirement plan balances to fund or partially fund the bypass trust. Those issues remain with the high exclusion now, so clients can leave plan accounts to a spouse and let the surviving spouse control them.

What if clients have that blended family situation? The family includes spouse A with his or her children, plus spouse B with his or her children. What should the planner do in that case? Perhaps in that case the estate should use a QTIP trust to ensure the surviving spouse doesn't exercise all of the control.

Keep in mind that retirement plan benefits are income in respect to the decedent. There is no basis adjustment when the decedent dies. The beneficiary is going to pay income tax on 100 percent of the money he or she receives unless the funds are in a Roth IRA.

## Charitable Gifts of IRA Funds

If a client is older than age 70½, there is a wonderful planning opportunity if he or she is charitably inclined. The client can give up to $100,000 per year to a charity as a trustee-to-trustee transfer; the retirement plan directly gives the $100,000 to the charity (not with a check to the donor; it's form over substance). The plan gives the money to the charity and the funds are not included in the client's income, they're not part of his or her adjusted gross income (AGI).

Very significantly, the gift to charity counts as meeting the client's RMD. If the RMD is, say, $30,000 a year and the client gives $30,000 to charity, he or she has been generous to charity, plus the year's RMD is satisfied. Also, the client pays zero income tax on that withdrawal from the retirement plan.

And if the client has to take out $90,000 and gives $30,000 to charity, fine. Then he or she has given to charity toward the RMD and will pay income tax on the $60,000 difference. This is a way to satisfy charitable goals and RMD requirements at the same time.

## Roth Conversions

The 2017 act changed some rules regarding Roth IRAs. Until 2018 a client could convert a traditional IRA to a Roth, be responsible for paying the income tax, but would have the ability up until October 15 of the next tax year to recharacterize the conversion. If the stock market tanked in the year the client converted a traditional IRA to the Roth and didn't want to pay income tax on money he or she doesn't have anymore, the client could recharacterize the converted funds. No harm, no foul.

That option is gone beginning with 2018 conversions. The IRS issued a notice saying that 2017 Roth conversions can be recharacterized in 2018, but that's the last time taxpayers can do that. Clients can still use what is called a "backdoor Roth," using a nondeductible IRA (because the client's income is too high to use a traditional deductible IRA). The clients can convert that type of IRA to a Roth. There is no income tax unless clients had some small gain or a return on the nondeductible IRA when they do the conversion.

## STUDY QUESTIONS

**5.** Which of the following identifies a special planning concern when trusts are used?

a. Taking advantage of the 65-day rule for complex trusts

b. Retaining income within a trust as a favorable planning decision

c. Comparing the compressed rate threshold for trusts distributions to thresholds for married taxpayers

d. Considering a bypass trust to maximize income shifting opportunities

**6.** Which of the following is a correct statement regarding the considerations around retirement plan benefits?

a. Examining and updating the client's beneficiary designations.

b. The surviving spouse has not always been the favored beneficiary of a decedent's retirement plans.

c. Distributions from a retirement plan are not considered income in respect of a decedent.

d. The new tax law eliminated the option to convert traditional IRAs to Roth IRAs.

# ¶ 910   DESIGNATING TITLES OF PROPERTY

How do married people typically record property titles? Up until the portability rules, one needed to use it or lose it for the exclusion. At some point, title designations became either uncomfortable or impossible—say, for a medical or accounting practice or family business.

Now that discussion is unnecessary. Couples do not need to separately title assets unless they reside in a decoupled state. Portability for federal law allows a couple to keep all assets in spouse A's name. When A dies, he or she leaves property either outright or in trust for spouse B. The marital deduction applies and the entire exclusion ports to the survivor. There is no need to have separate title. However, in the decoupled state, to use the exclusion upon the passing of the first spouse, a couple still needs separate property to be held. Joint property can be disclaimed, so that might yield some benefit.

As part of their review in terms of the new tax law, clients and planners should look at existing titling of property. If a couple split everything up 10 years ago, because that was the right call in 2008 or 2009 before the law changed, now might be the time to rethink the terms. Planners should ensure title is in the person's name who has the least exposure to creditors (such as when client couples are a surgeon and spouse). The first step is to get the property out of the surgeon's name. Clients and planners can do that without worrying about future tax planning.

> **EXAMPLE:** JoAnn and Emory Jacobi retitle JoAnn's surgical practice in 2018. The retitling is considered a marital gift; there's no gift tax issue. The marital deduction, of course, covers these situations.

If clients reside in one of the community property states, all the property that involves community property is deemed owned 50–50. Each spouse owns a half-interest in the community property—end of discussion. But if they do not live in a community property state—a common-law state—the planner must figure out titling.

In the community property state, if one spouse dies, both halves of the community property get a basis equal to the fair market value of the property at death. It doesn't matter if only one of the spouses died.

However, in a joint property situation, that's not the law. In a joint property jurisdiction, the joint property for the survivor, his or her basis, is one-half of the value at the first decedent's death plus one-half of the original cost. The basis in joint property may be a lot lower than the full fair market value at the first death.

If property is owned by the survivor, there is no basis adjustment at the first death. That would suggest planners may try to figure out which spouse is likely to die first and to get most of the property into that person's name. Complicated planning!

An interesting issue is whether a couple created a qualified personal residence trust (QPRT), let's say as a 10-year trust. The advantage of doing a QPRT was that the couple got a reduced gift tax involvement, because by retaining the right to use and enjoy their home for some number of years, the estate subtracted that actuarial value from the value of the home, leaving only the remainder interest as the gift.

And so, if an individual outlives the term, there is no inclusion in the estate and heirs take the individual's basis in the home. That's where the problem now comes from. If the client did this in 2008 when the exclusion was just a couple million dollars, it wasn't a crazy idea; it was a good idea. Now, where the exclusion is so much higher, how happy is the individual that the $700,000 or $800,000 home won't be included in the estate, meaning that heirs get the individual's basis?

How does the planner fix this? In some cases the estate is violating the terms of the QPRT. Mom and dad are still alive. Technically, the children should own the property. Mom and dad continue to live in the home, and the heirs claim mom and dad had a retained life estate in their house under Code Sec. 2036, which is taxable in their estate. Heirs get a basis equal to the fair market value at date of death.

# ¶ 911 STATUS OF AN LLC, FLP, OR SALE TO DEFECTIVE GRANTOR TRUST

A limited liability company (LLC) or family limited partnership (FLP) is set up to claim a significant valuation discount and minimize the federal estate tax of the owner. Does the client still need to minimize the federal estate tax? The answer, at least for now, might be no. Some planners will advise clients to get rid of all those bells and whistles, amend the operating or partnership agreement. Then the planner can ensure that when the principal owners die, the heirs get a higher basis in the entity. If there's no estate tax, that's what the planner wants to do.

What if future law does not provide such a generous exclusion? Does the planner then go back and put all those bells and whistles back? How many clients are going to pay for all that work? The planner should examine every case, client by client. How important is the basis? If the family is going to get a low basis but never going to sell the entity, what good is a low basis? But if the heirs plan to sell the entity, a high basis becomes more important.

Did a planner use an intentionally defective grantor trust so the grantor pays all the income tax? Well, that was (is) a great plan for wealthier clients, but maybe is not as important now. Perhaps the planner advises ending the grantor trust status, relinquishing the power that gave the grantor the requirement to pay the income tax. Now clients may prefer to spread the tax among the family members, because maybe there are state and local income taxes involved in that taxation. Rather than have the grantor be the only one paying tax and capped at a $10,000 state tax deduction, the planner can get the four or five other family members to share the tax burden so some of that state and local tax actually gets deducted on someone's tax return.

If clients have a sale to a defective grantor trust with a big note still outstanding, maybe they can make a gift of a couple million dollars and pay off the note. If clients are in that position and have that gift that is theirs to make and they pay off the note, now planning is simplified, and that $2 or $3 million gift is nowhere near the clients' $11.2 million (or, if married, $22.4 million) exclusion.

# ¶912 PLANNING FOR CLIENTS IN DECOUPLED STATES

The most difficult estate planning issues are for people in decoupled states. They may be taxpayers on the state level, not on the federal level. Should they leave everything to their spouse to try to get the high basis and only get one exclusion over two deaths, or do they use some type of a bypass trust? Or maybe what a planner should do is create a very flexible plan that says, "I leave all my property to my spouse but my spouse may disclaim some of what I'm leaving my spouse and the disclaimed property shall be used to fund the state death tax exclusion."

And maybe the planner caps the amount of the disclaimer at the then-applicable state death tax exclusion. Perhaps the state where clients reside will enact an estate tax; maybe it will repeal an existing estate tax. The best path is hard to know going forward, but this type of planning for an estate death tax situation between the bypass trust and the marital trust should be kept flexible. The planner should not force a funding of a bypass trust because maybe a surviving spouse will move. Maybe a spouse will die as a resident of a different state. Maybe the state will change the law.

# ¶913 ADDITIONAL ESTATE PLANNING TECHNIQUES UNDER THE NEW LAW

But all these maybes suggest flexible planning. A plan should either have a disclaimer opportunity for the surviving spouse or have a fiduciary given the authority to allocate between a bypass trust and a marital deduction trust. The law allows that. A federal case called *Clayton* allows that. The IRS regulations allow that, so that might be another way to go.

For wealthier clients, one outcome essential to plan is basis adjustments upon death. Maybe a client has been given a trust. The client is a beneficiary of a trust, a trust for life that won't be included in the client's estate. But when that client dies, will he or she have a big enough estate to be taxable? If so, that trust should not be in the estate. But if not, maybe it's preferable to hold that trust in the estate.

## General Power of Appointment

How does a planner make it work? One way to do it is in the client's will, in the trust, in which a person is named—either the trustee or a separate trust protector—who is the authority to grant the beneficiary of the trust a general power of appointment over the trust property. Now when the beneficiary dies possessing that general power of appointment, the trust property is in his or her estate. That provision gives his or her heirs a stepped-up basis.

Is the planner concerned the trustee or protector will exercise the power in a way to defeat the interests of the heirs? If so, the plan should not give the person a general power that is the broadest general power, including the ability to name him- or herself or the subsequent estate as the beneficiary. Instead, the plan should limit the general power of appointment to allow creditors to be beneficiaries of the general power.

If the trustee doesn't have any creditors, that makes sense. If the trustee does have creditors, the plan should not give them a general power. But such an arrangement does offer an opportunity. The trust could be a several-million-dollar trust and the basis could be what it was 30 or 40 years earlier because the basis doesn't get an adjustment when a non-power holder dies. The plan should create the power late in the person's life, hoping he or she doesn't exercise it. If clients trust the trustee not to exercise it, their heirs get a stepped-up basis.

Another opportunity to do that is possible when an estate is much more complicated and requires a lot of sophisticated planning: a Delaware tax trap. In this situation a person who is a trust beneficiary is given the power to extend the term of the trust under Code Sec. 2041(a)(3). That power is enough to force inclusion of the trust property in the decedent's estate. If the beneficiary is not going to be a federal taxpayer but was including trust property in his or her estate, no taxes are due. But the basis is now fair market value at death to the children or the other heirs.

## Grantor Retained Annuity Trust

If the law is going to sunset in eight years, what about a grantor retained annuity trust (GRAT) that ends in eight years? That way, if the client dies within the eight years, the estate inclusion is equal to the amount of the property necessary to pay a remaining annuity. If the client lives beyond the eight years, then the property is out of the estate and the planner got the benefit of all the subsequent actions during that eight years. And now if the law sunsets and it's a whole lot worse, the GRAT is over. The planner doesn't have to worry about where the law is going afterward.

A more complicated and sophisticated technique is called an "upstream GRAT," in which clients name their parents as the beneficiaries. The parents inherit the money and then leave it to the clients' children. In this grandchildren situation; clients give their parents, who may have minimal assets, use of a generation-skipping transfer to enhance the fair market value of property to the clients' children.

## Charitable Gifts with Tax Benefits

What about charity? As mentioned at the very outset, if an estate is not going to be taxable, clients should make the charitable gifts for people who can get an income tax deduction, whether they're the clients' parents themselves, the senior members of the family, or children who then can make the gifts. In other words, plans should ensure that someone gets a tax benefit from the gift to charity. If it's a death tax benefit because the clients are wealthy, great. Otherwise, an income tax benefit for the heirs is the way to go.

Wealthy families want to maximize the generation-skipping exclusions. Planners must remember the rule: the exclusion is not portable. Each person has to use the GST exclusion.

If clients have created generation-skipping trusts in the past and failed to allocate GST exclusion to those trusts, planners should allocate it now while clients have the $11.2 million GST exclusion. They can avoid GST tax forever. If clients come as close to that number as their wealth allows, there won't be any GST tax to pay in the future.

---

**CPE NOTE:** When you have completed your study and review of chapters 8-9, which comprise Module 4, you may wish to take the Final Exam for this Module. Go to **cchcpelink.com/printcpe** to take this Final Exam online.

---

# ¶ 10,100 Answers to Study Questions
## ¶ 10,101 MODULE 1—CHAPTER 1

**1. a. *Incorrect.*** This is not the new tax bracket for those joint filers making more than $600,000. Instead, this represents the new tax bracket for joint filers making more than $315,000 but less than $400,000.

**b. *Incorrect.*** This is not the new tax bracket for those joint filers making more than $600,000. Instead, this represents the new tax bracket for joint filers making more than $400,000 but less than $600,000.

**c. *Correct.* This is the new tax bracket for joint filers making more than $600,000. Joint filers in 2017 making this level of taxable income were subject to a 39.6 percent tax rate. This rate has been reduced based on the new tax legislation.**

**d. *Incorrect.*** This is not the new tax bracket for those joint filers making more than $600,000. Instead, this represents the existing 2017 tax bracket for the highest income earners. This rate was reduced based on the new tax legislation.

**2. a. *Incorrect.*** This is not the new standard deduction for heads of household. Instead, this amount represents the new standard deduction for single filers, which is a significant increase from the prior year.

**b. *Incorrect.*** This is not the new standard deduction for heads of household. Instead, this amount represents the previous standard deduction for those individuals who are married and filing jointly.

**c. *Correct.* This is the new standard deduction for heads of household. This is nearly a doubling of the previous standard deduction, which for 2017 was $9,350. This near doubling was also the case for other tax filing statuses.**

**d. *Incorrect.*** This is not the new standard deduction for heads of household. Instead, this amount represents the new standard deduction for those individuals who are married and filing jointly.

**3. a. *Correct.* Under the new tax legislation, most education tax breaks remain the same. In one change, 529 plans can distribute up to $10,000 per year per student for elementary and secondary school expenses.**

**b. *Incorrect.*** The child tax credit under the new tax legislation did not remain the same. Instead, the child tax credit was increased to $2,000, with new rules relating to Social Security number requirements.

**c. *Incorrect.*** The state and local tax deduction for those filers who itemize did not remain the same under the new tax legislation. The deduction was not entirely eliminated, but there is a cap of $10,000 (or $5,000 for married couples filing separately).

**d. *Incorrect.*** The personal exemption claimed by taxpayers did not remain the same under the new tax legislation. It was eliminated. In fact, even though the standard deduction is doubling, this may not fully offset the loss of personal exemptions for some taxpayers.

**4. a. *Incorrect.*** This statement is incorrect. The new tax legislation as it relates to disaster zone relief is only applicable to federal disaster areas. Accordingly, those disasters that are at the state or local level and are not classified as federal disasters are ineligible for certain new tax relief.

**b. *Incorrect.*** This statement is incorrect. The new tax legislation as it relates to disaster zone relief no longer carries a 10 percent of AGI limit. This provision was eliminated.

**c. *Incorrect.*** This statement is incorrect. Although there is certain relief afforded to taxpayers for early withdrawals from certain retirement plans, these amounts can be paid back over three years (not two) before they are included in the income of the taxpayer.

**d. *Correct.* This statement is correct with respect to the new tax legislation related to federal disaster zones. There is no penalty for amounts up to $100,000 if the amount was withdrawn by January 1, 2018.**

**5. a. *Correct.* This statement is correct with respect to business provision changes. Other changes include an expansion of the 50 percent deduction for food when it is *de minimis* and for the convenience of the employer.**

**b. *Incorrect.*** This statement is incorrect regarding business provision changes. The 50 percent deduction for food has actually been expanded when it is *de minimis* and for the convenience of the employer.

**c. *Incorrect.*** This statement is incorrect with respect to business provision changes. There is no a five-year (not four-year) amortization period for research and development expenditures.

**d. *Incorrect.*** This statement is incorrect with respect to business provision changes. The research and development amortization has been preserved as part of the new tax legislation but has not been increased for qualifying small businesses.

**6. a. *Incorrect.*** This is not the new corporate tax rate after 2017. Instead, this percent represents the tax on the repatriation of accumulated foreign earnings not classified as cash or cash equivalents.

**b. *Incorrect.*** This is not the new corporate tax rate after 2017. Instead, the percent represents the tax on the repatriation of accumulated foreign earnings in the form of cash or cash equivalents. There is a different tax applied on repatriation of other earnings not classified a cash or cash equivalents.

**c. *Correct.* This is the new corporate tax rate after 2017. In addition to lowering the rate, the new law made special rules for normalization of method of accounting. Additionally, the 80 and 70 percent dividends received deduction has been reduced to 65 and 50 percent, respectively.**

**d. *Incorrect.*** This is not the new corporate tax rate after 2017. Instead, this percent represents the proposed estate tax rate (as proposed by the House of Representatives) for amounts of more than $2,250 and less than $9,150.

# ¶ 10,102 MODULE 1—CHAPTER 2

**1. a. *Correct.* This represents the rate of tax on old-age, survivors and disability insurance. This is in addition to the 2.9 percent Medicare tax as well as the 0.9 percent additional Medicare tax for certain income levels.**

**b. *Incorrect.*** This is not the rate of tax on old-age, survivors and disability insurance. Instead, this is the rate of tax with respect to Medicare tax.

**c. *Incorrect.*** This is not the rate of tax on old-age, survivors and disability insurance. Instead, this is the rate of tax with respect to additional Medicare tax for certain higher income levels.

**d. *Incorrect.*** This is not the rate of tax on old-age, survivors and disability insurance. Instead, this is the new tax on corporations enacted in December 2017 through the Tax Cuts and Jobs Act.

**2. a. *Incorrect.*** The threshold triggering the 0.9 percent additional Medicare tax is $200,000 for single taxpayers' income.

**b. *Incorrect.*** The additional Medicare tax applies to heads of households who have an annual income of more than $200,000.

**c. *Correct.* Married couples who file separately must pay the additional Medicare tax if a spouse's income is more than $125,000.**

**d. *Incorrect.*** The $200,000 threshold applies to a qualifying widow or widower.

**3. a. *Correct.* Self-employed individuals earning less than $400 are generally not required to pay self-employment tax. Instead, if the self-employed individual earned in excess of this amount, they would be generally required to pay self-employment tax.**

**b. *Incorrect.*** Real estate agents and direct sellers are subject to self-employment tax. Additionally, rental income from farming by a landlord if they materially participated in production or management of the production of farm products would also be subject to self-employment tax.

**c. *Incorrect.*** Certain employees of churches and church organizations are subject to self-employment tax. Additionally, real estate rentals if substantial services are rendered to tenants are also subject to self-employment tax.

**d. *Incorrect.*** Independent contractors are subject to self-employment tax. Additionally, statutory non-employees with certain income levels are also subject to self-employment tax.

**4. a. *Incorrect.*** Earnings being subject to self-employment tax is not a characteristic of a hobby as it relates to self-employment tax rules. Instead, this is a characteristic of business income subject to self-employment tax.

**b. *Incorrect.*** Expenses being deducted above the line is not a characteristic of a hobby as it relates to self-employment tax rules. Instead, this is a characteristic of business income for self-employment tax purposes.

**c. *Correct.* A business is an activity regularly carried on and engaged in for profit. In contrast, a hobby, may lack a profit motive, have no business plan, and be inconsistently carried on. Any hobby income is not subject to self-employment tax.**

**d. *Incorrect.*** The need to consider Code Sec. 469 and material participation tests are not characteristics of a hobby as it relates to self-employment tax rules. Instead, this is a characteristic of a business subject to self-employment tax.

**5. a. *Correct.* In this case, the court found that the blogger's ad revenue represented self-employment income. This was due to the fact that the individual worked at it full-time with the intent to make profit from the regular and continuous activity.**

**b. *Incorrect.*** This case involved a real estate agent with one commission reported on Schedule C with no self-employment form. The court found that self-employment tax was due from the individual.

**c. Incorrect.** This case involved a payment related to tax shelter activity. The defendant asserted that he provided no meaningful services and just signed a lot of documents. The court ruled that it represented continuous and regular work and that self-employment tax was in fact owed.

**d. Incorrect.** In this case, the Tax Court held that the federal payments were subject to self-employment tax. However, the 5th Circuit noted that land conservation payments to non-farmers were real estate rentals so no self-employment tax was owed.

**6. a. Incorrect.** Ryther was an occasional seller, not exhibiting a factor of self-employment.

**b. Correct. The sales of the scrap metal—$317,000—were substantial, but the court ruled this factor as neutral rather than an indicator of self-employment.**

**c. Incorrect.** Unlike a business owner who would sell the metal as soon as possible, Ryther sold the scrap over a seven-year period.

**d. Incorrect.** Unlike a business owner subject to self-employment tax, Ryther did not use the profits from the sales to purchase more inventory.

# ¶ 10,103 MODULE 1—CHAPTER 3

**1. a. Correct. The Tax Cuts and Jobs Act passed on December 22, 2017. Although the corporate provisions were generally permanent, individual and trust provisions are generally temporary between January 1, 2018, and December 31, 2025.**

**b. Incorrect.** It was not signed into law on January 3, 2018. Instead, it was passed and signed into law on December 22, 2017.

**c. Incorrect.** Many of the corporate provisions remain permanent, not temporary.

**d. Incorrect.** The payroll provisions brought about by the Tax Cuts and Jobs Act are not effective January 1, 2019. Instead, they are effective a year earlier, on January 1, 2018.

**2. a. Incorrect.** There is not a planned increase in the number of itemizers given the change to the state and local tax deduction. Instead, there will likely be a decrease given the limit of $10,000 for state and local taxes.

**b. Incorrect.** There was not an increase in the AGI limit to 75 percent on charitable contributions. Instead, as a result of the Tax Cuts and Jobs Act, there was an increase in the AGI limit from 50 percent to 60 percent with respect to charitable contributions.

**c. Correct. This is a provision of the new Tax Cuts and Jobs Act. Additionally, the exclusion is adjusted for inflation. Because of this change, it may lead to a disincentive for charitable giving to reduce estate and gift taxes.**

**d. Incorrect.** This tax benefit was not preserved as a result of the Tax Cuts and Jobs Act. Instead, there was a repeal of the contribution deduction for the value of the contributions to secure better seats at college sporting events.

**3. a. Incorrect.** This is not the 2018 standard deduction for married filing jointly taxpayers. Instead, this amount represents the 2017 standard deduction for heads of households.

**b. Incorrect.** This is not the 2018 standard deduction for married filing jointly taxpayers. Instead, this amount represents the 2017 standard deduction for married filing jointly taxpayers.

**c.** *Incorrect.* This is not the 2018 standard deduction for married filing jointly taxpayers. Instead, this amount represents the combination of the standard deduction and personal exemptions for heads of households for 2017.

**d.** *Correct.* **This is the 2018 standard deduction for married filing jointly taxpayers. This is an increase from the 2017 amount which was $12,700. However, personal exemptions under the *Tax Cuts and Jobs Act* have been eliminated.**

**4. a.** *Incorrect.* The changes to highly compensated employees generally apply to the top five employees. The compensation includes amounts paid by the filing organization and all related organizations.

**b.** *Incorrect.* Exempt organizations paying compensation of more than $1 million beginning January 1, 2018 are subject to a 21 percent excise tax on the excess compensation to certain individuals. However, individuals in a certain profession will be exempt from these requirements.

**c.** *Incorrect.* Parachute payments are included in this compensation. There are questions about whether these requirements apply to organizations exempt under Code Sec. 115(1).

**d.** *Correct.* **Certain licensed medical professionals are excluded from these requirements. However, for other nonmedical professionals, exempt organizations paying compensation of more than $1 million are subject to a 21 percent excise on the excess compensation.**

**5. a.** *Incorrect.* This case did not result in the denial of the deduction due to the CWA date being after the taxpayer filed the return. Instead, this case related to the deduction of a 40-year old aircraft donation being denied due to Form 1098-C and issues with CWA.

**b.** *Incorrect.* This case did not result in the denial of the deduction due to the CWA date being after the taxpayer filed the return. Instead, this case related to the deduction being denied over "good or services" language and adequate description.

**c.** *Correct.* **In this case, the IRS denied a charitable deduction due to the CWA date being after the taxpayer filed the return. The *Tax Cuts and Jobs Act* eliminates the confusing language in Code Sec. 170(f)(8) suggesting charities can provide some other documentation or form other than the contemporaneous donor acknowledgment letter.**

**d.** *Incorrect.* This case did not result in the denial of the deduction due to the CWA date being after the taxpayer filed the return. Instead, this case related to a $64.5 million deduction being denied due to no CWA and an amended Form 990 did not fix the issue.

**6. a.** *Incorrect.* This is not a characteristic of Section 3. Instead, this relates to Section 4 of the notice relating to satisfying a personal pledge out of a donor advised fund. This action is permissible but is pending additional guidance.

**b.** *Incorrect.* This is not a characteristic of Section 3. Instead, this relates to Section 5 of the notice relating to changing the way Code Sec. 509(a)(1) and (2) public charities calculate public support when they receive certain funds from a donor advised fund.

**c.** *Correct.* **This is a characteristic of Section 3 of Notice 2017-73. Additionally, Section 3 mirrors PLR 9021066 applicable to private foundations controlled by corporations in that it may be inappropriate as donor advised funds are required to give written notice to donors in no uncertain terms that the gifts are a complete gift.**

**d.** *Incorrect.* This is not a characteristic of Section 3. Instead, this relates to Section 5 of the notice relating to changing the way Code Sec. 509(a)(1) and (2) public charities calculate public support when they receive certain funds from a donor advised fund. Furthermore, if the contribution is truly a completed gift and the donor only has advisory privileges, Section 5 does not seem to be a reasonable change to the public support test.

# ¶ 10,104 MODULE 2—CHAPTER 4

**1. a.** *Incorrect.* The deduction limitation applies to taxable income before, not after, any net capital gain.

**b.** *Incorrect.* The deduction is not available to C corporations; it is a tax benefit for businesses operated in a non-C corporation form.

**c.** *Correct.* **The general 20 percent deduction applies to the taxpayer's "combined" qualified business income; therefore, a loss from one business offsets income from another.**

**d.** *Incorrect.* Code Sec. 199A excludes guaranteed payments for services rendered by a partner from qualified business income.

**2. a.** *Incorrect.* Code Sec. 199A excludes guaranteed payments for services rendered by a partner from qualified business income.

**b.** *Incorrect.* Reasonable compensation is not considered qualified business income under Code Sec. 199A.

**c.** *Correct.* **Under Code Sec. 199A, qualified REIT dividends are qualified business income and eligible for the 20 percent deduction.**

**d.** *Incorrect.* Interest income is included if it relates to the trade or business; interest not allocable to a trade or business is not considered qualified business income under Code Sec. 199A.

**3. a.** *Correct.* **The income limitation is $157,500 of taxable income for single taxpayers.**

**b.** *Incorrect.* The deduction is phased out for single filers with an income of more than $207,500.

**c.** *Incorrect.* This amount is the income limitation for married taxpayers filing jointly.

**d.** *Incorrect.* This is the income amount at which the deduction is phased out for married taxpayers who file joint returns.

**4. a.** *Incorrect.* The unadjusted basis is not reduced by Code Sec. 179 depreciation, or by bonus depreciation or regular depreciation.

**b.** *Correct.* **The unadjusted basis is eliminated if the asset is no longer used in the qualifying business; the property is only counted if it is held at year end.**

**c.** *Incorrect.* The unadjusted basis is used for the recovery period or for 10 years, whichever is greater.

**d.** *Incorrect.* The unadjusted basis of depreciable property used in a trade or business is taken into account when calculating a taxpayer's qualified business income deduction.

**5. a.** *Incorrect.* Physical therapy and other health services are considered a specified service trade or business under the new law.

**b.** *Correct.* **The new legislation specifically excludes engineering businesses from the definition of a specified service trade or business.**

**c.** *Incorrect.* Businesses that perform services such as financial consulting and accounting are service businesses for purposes of the new law.

**d.** *Incorrect.* According to IRS guidance, veterinary services constitute a specified service under the *Tax Cuts and Jobs Act.*

**6. a.** *Incorrect.* This is true of a nonservice business (e.g., architects and engineers), not a service business.

**b.** *Incorrect.* The reduction computation for the qualified business income deduction depends on whether a business is a service or a nonservice business.

**c.** *Correct.* **When a service business's taxable income exceeds the threshold amount, the deduction limitation can reach zero. There is no floor on the allowed deduction.**

**d.** *Incorrect.* Law firms are considered service business under the code section, as they are businesses whose principal asset is the skill or reputation of one or more of their employees.

**7. a.** *Incorrect.* This amount results from multiplying the threshold amount for a single taxpayer ($157,500) by 20 percent. Peter is a married taxpayer filing jointly, and this is not the correct method for calculating the QBI deduction.

**b.** *Correct.* **Peter's taxable income of $250,000 does not exceed the threshold of $315,000. Therefore, his QBI deduction is 20 percent of $200,000, or $40,000.**

**c.** *Incorrect.* This amount is the result of multiplying Peter's taxable income by 20 percent. This is not the correct way to determine his QBI deduction.

**d.** *Incorrect.* This amount results from multiplying the threshold amount for a married taxpayer filing jointly ($315,000) by 20 percent. The QBI deduction is not calculated this way.

**8. a.** *Incorrect.* The taxable income limit applies to Suzanne's case.

**b.** *Correct.* **Suzanne's QBI deduction is $20,000.**

**c.** *Incorrect.* Suzanne's QBI deduction is $30,000.

**d.** *Incorrect.* Code Sec. 199A does not apply to Suzanne's situation.

**9. a.** *Correct.* **The taxable income limit applies because the 20 percent of QBI limit ($40,000) is more than the wage or wage/capital limit ($30,000).**

**b.** *Incorrect.* Because taxable income is greater than $415,000, the deduction is limited to $30,000 (full reduction to wage limit).

**c.** *Incorrect.* The deduction is reduced by 100 percent (from $40,000 to $30,000).

**d.** *Incorrect.* The threshold limit for married taxpayers filing jointly is $315,000; Taxpayer Q's taxable income is over this limit.

**10. a.** Incorrect. Code Sec. 199A outlines provisions related to qualified business income but does not directly address whether a rental property is a trade or business.

**b.** *Correct.* **A single rental property falls under the category of a trade or business within the meaning of Code Sec. 162.**

**c. Incorrect.** The Code Sec. 355 divisive reorganization test sets a higher hurdle for real estate to be a business.

**d. Incorrect.** Code Sec. 1231 addresses the tax treatment of gains and losses on the sale or exchange of real property.

**11. a. Incorrect.** Although in theory this type of allocation would be correct, in practice it might not be.

**b. Incorrect.** Allocating W—2 wages among the four partners based on how the wage deduction is allocated can pose some issues.

**c. Incorrect.** The W-2 wages should be allocated in some way.

**d. Correct. The answer is not explicit in the new law, and therefore IRS guidance is needed. Until the IRS issues regulations on this issue, practitioners may need to adopt a reasonable position.**

**12. a. Correct. The proposed regulations say that these adjustment do not affect the UBIA for Code Sec. 199A purposes.**

**b. Incorrect.** Code Sec. 199A is silent on whether Code Sec. 734 or Code Sec. 743 adjustments can be used.

**c. Incorrect.** Both Code Sec. 734 and Code Sec. 743 affect the capital base.

**d. Incorrect.** This is not necessarily true. Unadjusted basis might not be impacted by negative Code Sec. 743 or Code Sec. 734 adjustments.

# ¶ 10,105 MODULE 2—CHAPTER 5

**1. a. Correct. The fact that distributions of cash are generally not taxed is an advantage of an S corporation. An additional advantage is that basis adjustments for undistributed profits and losses are similar to rules for other pass-through entities.**

**b. Incorrect.** This is a disadvantage of forming an S corporation. A corporation for state law purposes elects to be treated as an S corp under the Internal Revenue Code. An S corp is no different than a C corp for legal purposes.

**c. Incorrect.** This is a disadvantage for forming an S corp. If the election for treatment as an S corp is made at the outset, the corporation will generally be treated as a pass-through entity for tax purposes.

**d. Incorrect.** Basis adjustments for undistributed profits are similar to the rules for other pass-through entities (not C corps) and are a disadvantage of forming an S corp.

**2. a. Incorrect.** In order to elect S corp status, there can only be one class of stock.

**b. Incorrect.** In order to elect S corp status, the corporation can only be owned by individuals and certain trusts.

**c. Correct. A maximum of 100 shareholders applies to S corporations.**

**d. Incorrect.** In order to elect S corp status, the corporation can only be owned by U.S. citizens or residents. Foreign persons are not allowed to own stock in an S corp.

**3. a. Incorrect.** Under the ordering rules, a reduction for nondividend distributions is not the first step but the second.

**b. Incorrect.** Under the ordering rules, a reduction for nondeductible expenses is the third step in the process.

**c.** *Incorrect.* Under the ordering rules, a reduction for losses and separately stated deductions is the last (fourth) step in the process.

**d.** *Correct.* **A required increase to basis is the first step in the ordering rules, before the step related to reductions for nondividend distributions.**

**4. a.** *Incorrect.* The S corp rules are different (inconsistent) with partnership rules. Additionally, if a shareholder's interest in the corporation is terminated during the year, the basis reduction is applied with respect to the indebtedness held immediately before the termination.

**b.** *Correct.* **A loan from a shareholder to an S corporation gives the shareholder basis in the debt. This debt may be used to "absorb" losses but *not* tax-free distributions.**

**c.** *Incorrect.* Personal guarantees by a shareholder do not create a shareholder basis. The basis of stock is reduced by distributions not includible in income; in contrast, the basis of indebtedness is not reduced by the amount of such items.

**d.** *Incorrect.* For a shareholder to receive debt basis, the shareholder must make a direct loan to the corporation—one owed by the corporation to the shareholder.

**5. a.** *Incorrect.* A shareholder that owns at least 1 percent is not required to include the value of fringe benefits in income; the ownership percentage is higher.

**b.** *Correct.* **A shareholder that owns at least 2 percent is required to include the value of fringe benefits in income. Also, officers are paid a salary that is subject to employment taxes.**

**c.** *Incorrect.* This is not the minimum percent a shareholder owns in order to report the fringe benefits in income.

**d.** *Incorrect.* A shareholder that owns 10 percent of the S corp is required to include the value of fringe benefits in income, but the minimum percent of ownership for such reporting is less.

**6. a.** *Incorrect.* Memorialization of past actions is an acceptable reason for backdating, such as when minutes from a meeting are prepared subsequent to the meeting.

**b.** *Incorrect.* Ratifying past actions is an acceptable reason for backdating, such as when final terms of an LLC are reached subsequently.

**c.** *Correct.* **Backdating an invoice to reflect an earlier period is not an acceptable reason for the practice.**

**d.** *Incorrect.* Clarification of terms is an acceptable reason for backdating, such as whether a distribution is from salary, profits, or a loan.

# ¶ 10,106 MODULE 3—CHAPTER 6

**1. a.** *Incorrect.* New or used property is considered qualified property with respect to bonus depreciation. Additional qualified property is MACRS property with a GDS recovery period of 20 or fewer years.

**b.** *Incorrect.* Water utility property is considered qualified property with respect to bonus depreciation. Additional qualified property is computer software (except for software covered by Code Sec. 197 purchased as part of a business).

**c.** *Correct.* **Qualified restaurant and retail improvements (as defined in the regulations) are not qualified property if placed in service after 2017, even if the improvement meets the requirements of qualified improvement property.**

**d.** *Incorrect.* Long production period property is considered qualified property with respect to bonus depreciation. Additionally, 100 percent bonus depreciation is applicable for assets acquired after September 27, 2017, through the year 2022.

**2. a.** *Correct.* **The bonus depreciation rate for the year 2026 is 20 percent. This compares to 40 percent for the year 2025 and 60 percent for the year 2024.**

**b.** *Incorrect.* 40 percent is the bonus depreciation rate for the year 2025, not 2026.

**c.** *Incorrect.* 60 percent is the bonus depreciation rate for the year 2024, not 2026.

**d.** *Incorrect.* 80 percent is the bonus depreciation rate for the year 2023, not 2026.

**3. a.** *Correct.* **Qualified improvement property placed in service after 2017 is now depreciated over 15 years (versus the prior 39-year life) and remains eligible for bonus depreciation. The new law provides 20-year ADS life (versus the prior 40-year life).**

**b.** *Incorrect.* Qualified leasehold improvement property is any Section 1250 property that is an improvement to nonresidential real property. It is depreciated over 15 years with half year convention and qualifies for bonus depreciation.

**c.** *Incorrect.* Qualified restaurant property was any Section 1250 property that was a building or an improvement to the building. Additionally, at least 50 percent of the building's square footage must have been devoted to the preparation of, and seating for on-premises consumption of, prepared meals.

**d.** *Incorrect.* Qualified retail property is similar to restaurant property in that it had a 15-year depreciable life that was permanently extended. This type of property shall not include any improvement for which the expenditure was attributable to (1) the enlargement of the building, (2) any elevator or escalator, (3) any structural component benefitting a common area, or (4) the internal structural framework of the building.

**4. a.** *Incorrect.* Costs for the enlargement of a building are not classified as QIP. Based on the PATH Act, there are no more separate definitions for qualified leasehold improvements, qualified restaurant property, and qualified retail property.

**b.** *Correct.* **Nonstructural interior common area improvements are an example of QIP. In this situation, these would be depreciated over 39 years but would be bonus depreciation eligible.**

**c.** *Incorrect.* Elevators or escalators are not classified as QIP. QIP placed in service after 2017 is now depreciated over 15 years (versus the prior 39-year life) and remains eligible for bonus depreciation.

**d.** *Incorrect.* Costs related to the internal structural framework of a building are not classified as QIP. For restaurants, only interior improvements made after the building was originally placed in service are depreciated over 15 years.

**5. a.** *Incorrect.* A client signing a contract to acquire the property before construction begins is not a characteristic of acquired property. Instead, this is a characteristic of self-constructed property.

**b.** *Incorrect.* The date of a contract not being relevant to bonus depreciation eligibility is not a characteristic of acquired property. Instead, this is a characteristic of self-constructed property.

**c.** *Correct.* **This is a characteristic of acquired property. An additional characteristic of acquired property is that the client signs a contract to acquire property after construction begins.**

¶10,106

**d.** *Incorrect.* The consideration of when construction began and a 100 percent safe harbor is not a characteristic of acquired property. Instead, this is a characteristic of self-constructed property.

**6. a.** *Incorrect.* A roof carries a 39-year useful life, not 15. An example of an asset with a 15-year useful life is paving.

**b.** *Incorrect.* Windows carry a 39-year useful life, not 15. An example of an asset with a 15-year useful life is landscaping.

**c.** *Correct.* **Irrigation carries a 15-year useful life. Other examples of building categories that have a 15-year useful life include paving, landscaping, site lighting, fencing, walkways, drainage, and decking.**

**d.** *Incorrect.* Doors carry a 39-year useful life, not 15. An example of an asset with a 15-year useful life is site lighting.

# ¶ 10,107 MODULE 3—CHAPTER 7

**1. a.** *Correct.* **The debt of the property acting as security will not be affected if a taxpayer borrows using property as security but uses the debt proceeds for some other purpose. The amount of debt owed will remain the same.**

**b.** *Incorrect.* It is assumed that the debt used to purchase property will be repaid whether the debt is recourse or nonrecourse, and whether or not it is purchase money debt.

**c.** *Incorrect.* If the security property acquired with nonrecourse debt is sold subject to the debt or the debt is forgiven, the face amount of the debt will be included in the amount realized even if the debt did not go into basis.

**d.** *Incorrect.* When a property is acquired with debt, the taxpayer is allowed a basis credit for the amount "contributed" with the debt. This is an "accession to wealth." If the taxpayer then borrows again using this property as security, and then uses the proceeds for another purpose, the basis of the property remains the same.

**2. a.** *Incorrect.* Generally speaking, gifts are excluded from income under Code Sec. 102.

**b.** *Correct.* **Under Code Sec. 1015, the donee takes the carryover basis in property received by gift. This means that any appreciation of property before the transfer (in the hands of the donor) is deferred until the sale of that property by the donee.**

**c.** *Incorrect.* It is possible to make the gift a taxable event, which would allow for the deferment of appreciation. But there is no requirement that the gift be made a taxable event.

**d.** *Incorrect.* Code Sec. 1015(a) restricts the scope of the gift exclusion from income because it only permanently excludes the donor's original cost, not appreciation, from the donee's income.

**3. a.** *Correct.* **The first step in determining what value to use in a subsequent sale of a gift that had an FMV that was less than the donor's basis is to use the carryover basis to see whether it produced a gain. If a gain is produced, then the taxpayer uses regular carryover basis.**

**b.** *Incorrect.* The planner wants to determine whether the subsequent sale produces a loss using the carryover basis second.

**c. *Incorrect.*** After determining that there is a loss using the carryover basis, the planner must recalculate using FMV at the time of gift as basis to determine whether there is a loss or a gain.

**d. *Incorrect.*** The donor's original basis of the property that was gifted is not used to determine whether there is a gain or loss for the subsequent sale of the property by the donee. Instead, the carryover basis is first subtracted from the adjusted basis of the gift.

**4. a. *Incorrect.*** Generally a donee who receives property through bequest gets a basis equal to FMV of property at the decedent's death.

**b. *Correct.* When a donor sells property to a charity at a discounted price, Code Sec. 1011(b) states that the basis must be allocated between the sale piece and the contribution piece. The charity would take the basis of the sale price plus the portion of the carryover basis that is allocated to the property.**

**c. *Incorrect.*** The entire basis of a property is allocated to the sale of a property that a child receives from a parent. No portion of the basis must be split.

**d. *Incorrect.*** When an employer sells a property to an employee at a discount, the transaction is not considered a partial gift. Instead, the "gift" piece is treated as compensation to the employee and results in a compensation deduction for the employer.

**5. a. *Incorrect.*** If Jacob and Belinda, spouses, own property as community property, according to Code Sec. 1014(b)(6), Jacob's one-half share of the property would have a stepped-up basis of $300,000. The other half of the property, which was bequeathed by Belinda to another donee, also receives a stepped-up basis to $300,000. Jacob's basis is $300,000.

**b. *Correct.* Because Jacob and Belinda owned the property as community property with right of survivorship, Jacob received the other half of the property at Belinda's death. The entire property, which now completely belongs to Jacob, has a step up in basis to $600,000 based on Code Sec. 1014(b)(6).**

**c. *Incorrect.*** Jacob and Belinda, spouses, owned the home as joint tenants with a right of survivorship, which would mean that the entire property would belong to Jacob at Belinda's death. However, because the property is owned in this way, according to Code Sec. 1014(b)(9), only Belinda's portion receives a step up in basis. Jacob's basis in the property would be $300,000 + ($325,000 ÷ 2) = $462,500.

**d. *Incorrect.*** Because Jacob and Belinda are siblings, they cannot own property as community property like married couples or registered domestic partners may. Although Jacob cannot get a step up in his basis of $162,500, he will benefit from a step up in basis to $300,000 on Belinda's share of the home.

**6. a. *Incorrect.*** Expenditures that add to the "betterment" of a property would be capitalized. Material additions to a property, material increases in strength of a property, and amelioration of a material defect of a property are all examples of betterment.

**b. *Incorrect.*** Expenditures related to the restoration of a property must be capitalized, rather than deducted. Restoration could include the rebuilding of a property to a like-new condition or restoring a property after casualty loss or after a property has deteriorated to a state of disrepair.

**c. *Incorrect.*** Under the repair regulations of Code Sec. 263A, expenditures related to adaptation of a property shall be capitalized. Adaptation of a property means that a property is changed to a new and different use.

**d.** *Correct.* Under the repair regulations issued in late 2013, generally, expenditures that restore the property to its operating state are deductible repairs. These regulations apply to anyone who pays or incurs amounts to acquire, produce, or improve tangible, real, or personal property. Incidental supplies and materials may be deducted in the year in which they were purchased or incurred, whereas other supplies and materials may be deducted when used or consumed.

# ¶ 10,108  MODULE 4—CHAPTER 8

**1. a.** *Correct.* The federal gift tax is imposed on the transfer of property by gift. In addition the tax is based on the value of the transferred property on the date the gift is complete.

**b.** *Incorrect.* The gift tax is not based on the value of the transferred property of the date the gift is offered but rather the date the gift is complete.

**c.** *Incorrect.* The maximum gift tax rate is 40 percent for 2018 and subsequent years' gifts.

**d.** *Incorrect.* The gift tax is imposed on individuals who are citizens or residents of the United States. A different rule applies to transfers by persons who are classified as "nonresident aliens."

**2. a.** *Incorrect.* The gift tax is not imposed on the transfer of money or other property to a political organization for the use of such organization.

**b.** *Incorrect.* A qualifying educational organization is one that normally maintains a regular faculty and curriculum and normally has a regularly enrolled body of students in attendance at the place where its educational activities are regularly carried on. In these situations, the gift tax is not imposed.

**c.** *Correct.* A transfer to a close relative would be subject to gift tax. A gift may include any transaction in which an interest in property is gratuitously passed or conferred upon another, regardless of the means or device employed.

**d.** *Incorrect.* Qualifying medical expenses include expenses incurred for the diagnosis, cure, mitigation, treatment or prevention of disease; or for the purpose of affecting any structure or function of the body, or for transportation primarily for and essential to medical care. In these situations, the gift tax is not imposed on the donor.

**3. a.** *Incorrect.* In 2018 he first $15,000 gift a donor makes per donee during the calendar year is excluded in determining the total amounts of gifts for the year.

**b.** *Correct.* Outright transfers to individual skip persons that qualify for the present interest exclusion from gift tax are also exempt from the GSTT rules, which have their own $15,000 exclusion for 2018.

**c.** *Incorrect.* In order for the annual exclusion to be available, the gift must constitute a gift of a present (not future) interest.

**d.** *Incorrect.* The entire value of property transferred in trust for the benefit of a minor will *not* be treated as a gift of a future interest if the requirements of Code Sec. 2503(c) are satisfied.

**4. a.** *Incorrect.* This is a correct statement. The fair market value of a publicly traded stock or bond is the mean between the highest and lowest quoted selling price on the date of the gift.

**b.** *Incorrect.* This is a correct statement. Code Sec. 7520 offers valuation guidance for partial interests in property transferred.

**c. Incorrect.** This is a correct statement. A substantial valuation understatement exists when the value of property on a gift tax return is 65 percent or less of the amount determined to be the correct value.

**d. Correct. There is no "alternate valuation date" for gift tax purposes. The value of a gift of property is the fair market value of that property of the date the gift is considered complete.**

**5. a. Correct. Code Sec. 2516 outlines the requirements for such property transfers, primarily addressing the transfers of property in connection with divorces.**

**b. Incorrect.** This section does not relate to property transfers in connection with divorces but instead has been repealed.

**c. Incorrect.** This section does not relate to property transfers in connection with divorces but instead the disposition of certain life estates.

**d. Incorrect.** This section does not relate to property transfers in connection with divorces.

**6. a. Incorrect.** Chapter 14 deals with special valuation rules.

**b. Incorrect.** Code Sec. 2701, not Code Sec. 2705, applies only to transfers to or for the benefit of a member of the transferor's family.

**c. Correct. This involves a trust in which the grantor transfers a personal residence to a trust, reserving the use and enjoyment of the property for a fixed period of years.**

**d. Incorrect.** The value of a qualified retained interest is subtracted, not added, from the fair market value of the transferred property in determining the amount of any gift.

# ¶ 10,109 MODULE 4—CHAPTER 9

**1. a. Incorrect.** Core dispositive planning is a major focus for estate planning for persons having assets under $11.2 million and married couples with assets under $22.4 million. Ensuring that the available exclusions are used while still available is another focus area.

**b. Correct. Charitable contributions is not identified as a major focus for estate planning for persons having assets under $11.2 million and married couples with assets under $22.4 million. Instead, ensuring that the available exclusions are used while still available is a major focus.**

**c. Incorrect.** Preservation of assets is a major focus for estate planning for persons having assets of less than $11.2 million and married couples with assets not exceeding $22.4 million. Additionally, the management of asset is another key focus area.

**d. Incorrect.** Income tax planning is a major focus for estate planning for persons having assets under $11.2 million and married couples with assets under $22.4 million. It's also important to consider potential clawbacks should the exclusions be reduced in the future.

**2. a. Correct. The primary motive for enacting portability of the federal estate tax exemption was simplifying estate planning for married couples. Furthermore, an issue all married clients will face at all levels of wealth is whether to make the portability election at the death of the first spouse.**

**b.** *Incorrect.* Simplifying trust planning for single filers was not the primary motive for enacting portability of the federal estate tax exemption. However, it's important to note that if an estate tax return is not filed to make the portability election, the planner will want to obtain a waiver letter signed by the executor.

**c.** *Incorrect.* Encouraging married couples to file jointly was not the primary motive for enacting portability of the federal estate tax exemption. The law allows portability of any unused applicable exclusion amount for a surviving spouse of a decedent who dies after 2010.

**d.** *Incorrect.* Increasing federal tax revenue was not the primary motive for enacting portability of the federal estate tax exemption. It's important to note that it is suggested that every estate of a deceased married person should make a portability election.

**3. a.** *Incorrect.* Texas is not a state that allows for portability of the exemption amount related to bypass trusts. With respect to bypass trusts, there is an unlimited statute of limitations on values for purposes of determining the DSUE.

**b.** *Incorrect.* California is not a state that allows for portability of the exemption amount related to bypass trusts. With respect to bypass trusts, the statute of limitations does run on values if a bypass trust is funded at the first spouse's death.

**c.** *Correct.* **In general, the state exemption amount is not portable related to bypass trusts. This is not the case for Hawaii. It's also important to note that growth in the assets in a bypass trust is excluded from the estate of the survivor.**

**d.** *Incorrect.* Oklahoma is not a state that allows for portability of the exemption amount related to bypass trusts. With respect to by-pass trusts, the unused DSUE of the first spouse is lost if the surviving spouse remarries and the new spouse predeceases the surviving spouse and leaves behind little or no unused exclusion.

**4. a.** *Incorrect.* Avoidance of both capital gain taxes and net investment income taxes and passing assets with a stepped-up basis becomes a primary concern, not a secondary concern.

**b.** *Incorrect.* Traditional estate planning techniques used to reduce the value of assets on death may in fact be counter-productive to planning. In a sense, estate planning is upside down from what has been traditionally favored.

**c.** *Incorrect.* Planners should consider "upstream planning," which gifts low-basis assets to older family members, who then leave them at death to the donor. This gives the donor a fair market value basis when the donee dies.

**d.** *Correct.* **In this situation, planners should consider amending the governing document to minimize or eliminate the discounting opportunity.**

**5. a.** *Correct.* **This is a special planning concern where trusts are used. This election can be used in a number of helpful planning situations including, but not limited to, shifting income to a lower bracket taxpayer and shifting income to avoid an underpayment of estimated taxes by the trust.**

**b.** *Incorrect.* This is not a special planning concern when trusts are used. Instead, income within a trust is not a favorable planning decision. This is due to the highly compressed income tax rates for trusts.

**c.** *Incorrect.* This is not a special planning concern when trusts are used. Instead, planners should compare the compressed rate threshold for trust distributions to thresholds for individual taxpayers.

**d. *Incorrect.*** This is not a special planning concern when trusts are used. Planners and clients should consider a "sprinkling trust" to maximize income shifting opportunities. Planners should include a broad list of current or at least permitted beneficiaries.

**6. a. *Correct.*** It's important to note that the surviving spouse has always been the favored beneficiary of a decedent's retirement plans. In the planning world under the new tax law, a recommended planning strategy would be to leave the retirement and IRA benefits directly to the surviving spouse to gain the advantages of income and estate tax deferral at the first death.

**b. *Incorrect.*** The surviving spouse has always been the favored beneficiary of a decedent's retirement plans. This is because of the fact that a rollover of the decedent's qualified plan or IRA to a surviving spouse enjoys the marital deduction to avoid the estate tax and special rules to defer the income tax on the rollover.

**c. *Incorrect.*** Distributions from a retirement plan are income in respect of a decedent. Additionally, there is no basis step-up when the decedent dies and the distributions are not considered net investment income.

**d. *Incorrect.*** The new tax law continues to allow IRAs to be converted to Roth IRAs, but after for 2018 and later conversions, the law eliminates the opportunity to recharacterize the conversion once it has been done.

# Index

*References are to paragraph (¶) numbers.*

# ¶ 10,200 Glossary

**Additional Medicare tax**—a tax applied to the amount of wages, self-employment income, and railroad retirement (RRTA) compensation that is more than a threshold amount.

**Alternative depreciation system**—a system the IRS requires to be used in special circumstances to calculate depreciation on certain business assets.

**Alternative minimum tax**—a supplemental income tax imposed by the federal government in addition to baseline income tax for certain individuals, estates, and trusts that have exemptions or special circumstances allowing for lower payments of standard income tax.

**Backdating**—assigning an event to a date prior to that of the actual occurrence.

**Basis**—a cost of a property; the amount paid when property is purchased for cash.

**Basis of acquired property**—the exercise price plus any amount paid for the option itself.

**Bequeath**—to leave (a personal estate or one's body) to a person other than a beneficiary by a will.

**Bonus depreciation**—an additional amount of deductible "depreciation" on the purchase of eligible business property that is awarded above and beyond what would normally be available based on current tax code regulations.

**Bypass trust**—an irrevocable trust into which the settlor deposits assets and that is designed to pay trust income and principal to the settlor's spouse for the duration of the spouse's life.

**C corporation**—any corporation that is taxed separately from its owners and is distinguished from an S corporation, which generally is not taxed separately at the corporate level.

**Capital gains tax**—a type of tax levied on capital gains that are profits an investor realizes when he or she sells a capital asset for a price that is higher than the purchase price.

**Carried interest**—a share of the profits of an investment paid to the investment manager in excess of the amount that the manager contributes to the partnership, specifically in alternative investments (private equity and hedge funds).

**Contemporaneous written acknowledgment**—a receipt received when the value of a single charitable contribution is $250 or greater.

**Cost basis**—the basis of a property plus the tax cost.

**Cost segregation**—the process of identifying personal property assets that are grouped with real property assets and separating out personal assets for tax reporting purposes.

***Crummey* trust**—a trust that allows families to transfer lifetime gifts to children while taking advantage of the gift tax exclusion.

**Disclaimer**—an act by a beneficiary whereby the beneficiary declines, refuses, and renounces any interest in property otherwise bequeathed to the beneficiary.

**Domestic asset protection trust**—an irrevocable self-settled trust in which the grantor is designated a permissible beneficiary and allowed access to the funds in the trust account.

**Fringe benefit**—an extra benefit supplementing an employee's salary, for example, a company car, subsidized meals, or health insurance.

**Gift**—any transaction in which an interest in property is gratuitously passed or conferred upon another, regardless of the means or device employed.

**Guaranteed payment**—a payment determined "without regard to the income of the partnership" under Code Sec. 707(c); it is not dependent on entrepreneurial risk.

**Itemized deductions**—eligible expenses that individual taxpayers can claim on federal income tax returns that decrease their taxable income, and that are claimable in place of a standard deduction, if available.

**Life insurance**—a contract between an insurance policy holder and an insurer or assurer in which the insurer promises to pay a designated beneficiary a sum of money (the benefit) in exchange for a premium, upon the death of an insured person.

**Like-kind exchange**—a transaction or series of transactions that allows for the disposition of an asset and the acquisition of another replacement asset without generating current tax liability from the sale of the first asset.

**Modified accelerated cost recovery system**—the current system allowed in the United States to calculate tax deductions on account of depreciation for depreciable assets (other than intangible assets).

**Net capital gain**—for purposes of Code Sec. 199A, the excess of the net long-term capital gain for the taxable year over the net short-term capital loss for such year.

**Net earnings from self-employment**—the gross income derived by an individual from any trade or business carried on by such individual, less the deductions allowed by Code Sec. 1402 that are attributable to such trade or business, plus his or her distributive share (whether or not distributed) of income or loss described in Code Sec. 702(a)(8) from any trade or business carried on by a partnership of which he or she is a member.

**Net operating loss**—a "loss" (tax credit) taken in a period in which a company's allowable tax deductions are greater than its taxable income, creating negative taxable income for tax purposes.

**Nonrecourse debt**—a secured loan that is secured by a pledge of collateral, but for which the borrower is not personally liable.

**Not for profit**—a type of organization that does not earn profits for its owners.

**Old age, survivors, and disability insurance tax**—the money that employers collect that goes to the federal government to fund the Social Security program.

**Partnership**—the relationship between two or more persons who joint through an agreement to carry on a trade or business.

**Personal exemption**—an amount received to deduct from income for every taxpayer and most dependents claimed on the tax return; the new tax law combines that and the standard deduction into one larger standard deduction for 2018.

**Portability**—an estate tax feature that allows a surviving spouse to use a deceased spouse's estate tax exclusion.

**Preferred stock**—a class of ownership shares in a corporation that has a higher claim on its assets than common stock.

***Protecting Americans from Tax Hikes Act***—the law created in order to protect taxpayers and their families against fraud and permanently extend many expiring tax laws.

**Qualified business income**—the net amount of qualified items of income, gain, deduction, and loss for a taxpayer's qualified trade or business; it does not include wages.

**Qualified business income deduction**—a deduction allows by Code Sec. 199A that is based on the combined income from qualifying trade or business operations; the QBI deduction is subject to several limitations and does not include wages.

**Qualified interest**—an interest in a qualified annuity, qualified unitrust, or qualified remainder.

**Qualified trade or business**—for purposes of Code Sec. 199A, any trade or business other than a specified service trade or business, or a trade or business of performing services as an employee.

**Qualified work of art**—any archaeological, historic, or creative tangible personal property.

**Qualifying educational organization**—an institution that normally maintains a regular faculty and curriculum and normally has a regularly enrolled body of students in attendance at the place where its educational activities are regularly carried on.

**Qualifying medical expenses**—costs incurred for the diagnosis, cure, mitigation, treatment, or prevention of disease, or for the purpose of affecting any structure or function of the body, or for transportation primarily for and essential to medical care.

**Real estate investment trust**—a business that invests in real estate.

**Recourse debt**—debt that holds the borrower personally liable and is backed by collateral from the borrower; the lender may collect from the debtor.

**Roth IRA**—a special retirement account that is funded with posttax income (contributions are currently nondeductible from income); all subsequent future withdrawals that follow Roth IRA regulations are tax-free.

**S corporation**—a closely held corporation (or, in some cases, a limited liability company [LLC] or a partnership) that makes a valid election to be taxed under Subchapter S of Chapter 1 of the Internal Revenue Code.

**Section 199A**—a new Internal Revenue Code section added by the *Tax Cuts and Jobs Act* enacted in 2017 that provides for a deduction for qualified business income.

**Self-employment income**—net earnings from self-employment derived by an individual (other than a nonresident alien individual, except as provided by an agreement under Section 233 of the *Social Security Act*) during any taxable year.

**Self-employment tax**—the self-employed person's version of the tax paid by employers and employees for Social Security and Medicare, calculated for net earnings from self-employment.

**Service business**—a business that is subject to special limitations on the 20 percent qualified business income deduction; it includes businesses in health, law, accounting, actuarial science, performing arts, consulting, athletics, financial services, brokerage services, investing or investment management, business trading, or dealing in securities, partnership interests, or commodities.

**Spousal lifetime access trust (SLAT)**—An irrevocable trust benefiting the donor's spouse and children in which a donor may reduce a spouse's exposure to estate taxes at death by taking advantage of the gift tax exemption.

**Sprinkling trust**—a trust in which the trustee has the discretion to either accumulate or distribute income.

**Standard deduction**—a dollar amount that nonitemizing taxpayers may subtract from their income before income tax is applied; the new tax law increases the deduction amount and combines it with personal exemptions.

**Subordinate debt**—debt that ranks after other debts if a company falls into liquidation or bankruptcy.

**Tax cost**—the value of the property on which the taxpayer will have to pay taxes.

***Tax Cuts and Jobs Act* (H.R. 1)**—the law enacted on December 22, 2017, that makes widespread changes to the Internal Revenue Code affecting tax rates, exemptions, and deductions, with most provisions having an effective date of January 1, 2018.

**Tax distribution**—provision of cash to pay the tax that may be due on such income.

**Threshold amount**—for purposes of the qualified business income deduction allowed under Code Sec.199A, an amount at or exceeding $315,000 for a married couple filing jointly or $157,500 for other filers.

# ¶ 10,300 Final Exam Instructions

To complete your Final Exam go to **cchcpelink.com/printcpe,** click on the title of the exam you wish to complete and add it to your shopping cart (you will need to register with CCH CPELink if you have not already). Click **Proceed to Checkout** and enter your credit card information. Click **Place Order** to complete your purchase of the final exam. The final exam will be available in **My Dashboard** under **My Account.**

This Final Exam is divided into four Modules. There is a grading fee for each Final Exam submission.

| Online Processing Fee: | Recommended CPE: |
|---|---|
| $113.95 for Module 1 | 6 hours for Module 1 |
| $113.95 for Module 2 | 6 hours for Module 2 |
| $75.95 for Module 3 | 4 hours for Module 3 |
| $75.95 for Module 4 | 4 hours for Module 4 |
| $379.80 for all Modules | 20 hours for all Modules |
| **IRS Program Number:** | **Federal Tax Law Hours:** |
| Module 1: 4VRWB-T-03161-18-S | 6 hours for Module 1 |
| Module 2: 4VRWB-T-03171-18-S | 6 hours for Module 2 |
| Module 3: 4VRWB-T-03162-18-S | 4 hours for Module 3 |
| Module 4: 4VRWB-T-03163-18-S | 4 hours for Module 4 |
| | 20 hours for all Modules |
| **CTEC Program Numbers:** | |
| Module 1: 1075-CE-1381 | |
| Module 2: 1075-CE-1391 | |
| Module 3: 1075-CE-1382 | |
| Module 4: 1075-CE-1383 | |

Instructions for purchasing your CPE Tests and accessing them after purchase are provided on the **cchcpelink.com/printcpe** website. **Please note, manual grading is no longer available for Top Federal Tax Issues. All answer sheets must be submitted online for grading and processing.**

---

Recommended CPE credit is based on a 50-minute hour. Because CPE requirements vary from state to state and among different licensing agencies, please contact your CPE governing body for information on your CPE requirements and the applicability of a particular course for your requirements.

---

**Expiration Date:** December 31, 2019

**Evaluation:** To help us provide you with the best possible products, please take a moment to fill out the course Evaluation located after your Final Exam.

# ¶ 10,401 Final Exam: Module 1

**1.** Which of the following identifies the new tax rate for single filers with taxable income greater than $200,000 but less than $500,000?

    **a.** 22 percent

    **b.** 24 percent

    **c.** 32 percent

    **d.** 35 percent

**2.** Which of the following identifies the new capital gains tax for joint filers with taxable income greater than $479,000?

    **a.** 0 percent

    **b.** 12 percent

    **c.** 15 percent

    **d.** 20 percent

**3.** Which of the following tax breaks or credits were eliminated with respect to the *Tax Cuts and Jobs Act*?

    **a.** Personal exemptions

    **b.** Charitable contributions

    **c.** Retirement contributions

    **d.** Mortgage interest deduction

**4.** The tax on stock compensation of insiders of expatriated corporations has been increased to what amount under the new tax legislation?

    **a.** 15 percent

    **b.** 20 percent

    **c.** 25 percent

    **d.** 35 percent

**5.** Although the individual alternative minimum tax was preserved through 2025 in the new tax legislation, the new exemption amount for joint filers is what amount?

    **a.** $70,300

    **b.** $85,600

    **c.** $103,300

    **d.** $109,400

**6.** Based on the new tax legislation, through 2025 there is no longer a deduction for moving expenses except for which of the following individuals?

    **a.** Armed Forces

    **b.** Teachers

    **c.** Social workers

    **d.** Disabled veterans

**7.** Code Sec. 179 small business expensing has been increased to what amount in the new tax legislation?

   **a.** $500,000

   **b.** $750,000

   **c.** $1 million

   **d.** $2 million

**8.** Based on the other business provisions included in the new tax legislation, the cash method of accounting has been expanded when average gross receipts do not exceed what amount over three years?

   **a.** $25 million

   **b.** $50 million

   **c.** $75 million

   **d.** $100 million

**9.** Which of the following identifies the new repatriation tax on accumulated foreign earnings that are in the form of cash or cash equivalents?

   **a.** 8.0 percent

   **b.** 11.1 percent

   **c.** 15.5 percent

   **d.** 20.5 percent

**10.** Based on the new tax legislation, the individual mandate as prescribed for the *Affordable Care Act* has been repealed after what date?

   **a.** 2017

   **b.** 2018

   **c.** 2019

   **d.** 2020

**11.** Which of the following chapters of the Internal Revenue Code relates to tax on self-employment income?

   **a.** Chapter 1

   **b.** Chapter 2

   **c.** Chapter 3

   **d.** Chapter 4

**12.** Additional Medicare tax is due on self-employment income in excess of what amount if a couple is married and filing jointly?

   **a.** $100,000

   **b.** $150,000

   **c.** $200,000

   **d.** $250,000

**13.** Which of the following identifies the 2018 wage income or self-employment income cap for 2018 for Social Security?

   **a.** $127,200

   **b.** $128,400

   **c.** $128,900

   **d.** $129,500

**14.** All of the following are not allowed under the new tax law as deductions from self-employment tax *except:*

    **a.** Self-employment tax deduction

    **b.** Personal exemption

    **c.** Foreign earned income exclusion

    **d.** Section 199 deduction for domestic production activities

**15.** "Net earnings from self-employment" is defined in which section of the tax code?

    **a.** Code Sec. 1401

    **b.** Code Sec. 1402

    **c.** Code Sec. 1403

    **d.** Code Sec. 1404

**16.** In general, self-employment tax is due when income from self-employment in a year exceeds:

    **a.** $100

    **b.** $200

    **c.** $300

    **d.** $400

**17.** Which of the following is a characteristic of a business (as opposed to a hobby) under the self-employment tax rules?

    **a.** Expenses are deducted above the line

    **b.** Expenses deducted are limited to income earned

    **c.** There is no deduction for alternative minimum tax

    **d.** Expenses are only deductible on Schedule A

**18.** Which of the following court cases related to self-employment tax dealt with payments related to a tax shelter activity?

    **a.** *Wang,* TC Memo 2016-123

    **b.** *Chai,* TC Memo 2015-42

    **c.** *Methvin,* TC Memo 2015-81

    **d.** *Martin,* 149 TC No. 12

**19.** Which of the following factors was determined to be neutral in the eight-factor analysis related to the *Ryther* court case?

    **a.** Substantiality of sales

    **b.** Frequency and regularity of sales

    **c.** Length of time the property was held

    **d.** How the sales proceeds were used

**20.** Each of the following identifies one of the key due diligence considerations for practitioners *except:*

    **a.** Appropriately assessing whether the client is self-employed in a trade or business

    **b.** Understanding whether the client is an active partner in an LLC

    **c.** Calculating estimated self-employment tax payments for employees of C corporations

    **d.** Ensuring proper calculations for married couples

**21.** Payroll provisions of the *Tax Cuts and Jobs Act* are effective:

    **a.** January 1, 2018

    **b.** January 1, 2019

    **c.** January 1, 2020

    **d.** January 1, 2021

**22.** Uniform basic income changes should follow a not-for-profit's _____.

    **a.** Calendar year

    **b.** Fiscal year

    **c.** Tax year

    **d.** Reporting year

**23.** Which of the following changes made by the *Tax Cuts and Jobs Act* may result in a positive impact (i.e., increase) on charitable contributions?

    **a.** Increase in the adjusted gross income limit on charitable contributions

    **b.** Repeal of the contribution deduction related to college sporting events

    **c.** Limit of $10,000 for deduction of state and local income taxes

    **d.** Limit of interest from new mortgage debt to $750,000

**24.** A disincentive for charitable giving in order to reduce estate and gift taxes may result from an increase in the estate and gift tax exclusion to what amount (not indexed for inflation)?

    **a.** $1 million

    **b.** $5 million

    **c.** $8 million

    **d.** $10 million

**25.** Prior to the passage of the *Tax Cuts and Jobs Act,* economists estimated under the proposed legislation that less than what percentage of all taxpayers will itemize on personal income tax returns?

    **a.** 5 percent

    **b.** 10 percent

    **c.** 15 percent

    **d.** 20 percent

**26.** Exempt organizations paying compensation of more than $1 million beginning January 1, 2018, will be subject to an excise tax on the excess compensation of what percent?

    **a.** 21 percent

    **b.** 27 percent

    **c.** 31 percent

    **d.** 34 percent

**27.** Which of the following types of professions are excluded from the highly compensated employees' excise tax on excess compensation?

    **a.** Lawyers

    **b.** CPAs who practice publicly

    **c.** Certain license medical professionals

    **d.** Venture capitalists

**28.** Under the *Tax Cuts and Jobs Act,* net operating losses may be carried forward for how many years to offset income from the same business line in future periods?

    **a.** 2 years

    **b.** 10 years

    **c.** 20 years

    **d.** Indefinitely

**29.** Which of the following cases resulted in charitable deductions being denied because Form 8283 was not properly completed?

    **a.** *Mecox Partners, LP v. U.S.* (2016, SDNY)

    **b.** *Izen, Joe Jr. No 5* (2017) 148 TC

    **c.** *Reri Holdings I, LLC v. Comm'r* 149 T.C. No. 1

    **d.** *Big River Development LP v. Commissioner,* T.C. Memo 2017-66

**30.** Which of the following sections of Notice 2017-73 prescribe that ticket purchases having a quid pro quo value to the donor advised fund contributor are impermissible?

    **a.** Section 3

    **b.** Section 4

    **c.** Section 5

    **d.** Section 6

# ¶ 10,402 Final Exam: Module 2

**1.** Anton Duvall, a married taxpayer who files a joint return, has $200,000 of qualified business income. His taxable income is $300,000, which includes $50,000 of net capital gain income. What is Anton's qualified business income (QBI) deduction?

    **a.** $40,000

    **b.** $50,000

    **c.** $60,000

    **d.** $70,000

**2.** Under Code Sec. 199A, "threshold income" is based on:

    **a.** Capital gains

    **b.** Taxable income

    **c.** Adjusted gross income

    **d.** W-2 wages

**3.** For taxpayers with income beyond the "threshold amount," the qualified business income deduction may be reduced to the greater of 50 percent of the W-2 wages from the qualifying business or:

    **a.** 20 percent of the taxpayer's combined business income from qualified business activities

    **b.** 25 percent of W-2 wages

    **c.** 50 percent of W-2 wages

    **d.** The sum of 25 percent of the W-2 wages and 2.5 percent of the unadjusted basis of depreciable property used in the business

**4.** Cynthia Villanueva's qualified business income equals $100,000. She may claim the 20 percent QBI deduction on her personal tax return. Cynthia's individual tax rate is 37 percent. Which of the following represents Cynthia's tax savings as a result of the *Tax Cuts and Jobs Act*?

    **a.** $3,700

    **b.** $7,400

    **c.** $10,000

    **d.** $20,000

**5.** Under Code Sec. 199A, the threshold amount for a married taxpayer filing jointly is:

    **a.** $157,500

    **b.** $207,500

    **c.** $315,000

    **d.** $415,000

**6.** An owner of an S corporation engaged in service business whose income does *not* exceed the threshold amount is entitled to:

    **a.** The full Code Sec. 199A deduction

    **b.** A reduced Code Sec. 199A deduction

    **c.** No Code Sec. 199A deduction

    **d.** 25 percent of the S corporation's paid wages

**7.** For purposes of Code Sec. 199A, a service business includes all of the following businesses *except:*

    **a.** Engineering

    **b.** Financial services

    **c.** Real estate

    **d.** Tax preparation

**8.** A married taxpayer filing jointly who has taxable income of $415,000 or more will have a qualified business income deduction for a non-service business equal to the lesser of 20 percent of combined business income or the _____.

    **a.** Wage limit

    **b.** Wage/capital limit

    **c.** Greater of the wage or wage/capital limit

    **d.** Lesser of the wage or wage/capital limit

**9.** Which of the following is a "gray area" of Code Sec. 199A?

    **a.** The phaseout of the threshold income limitations

    **b.** The "skill and reputation" issue in determining whether a business is a service business

    **c.** The definition of W-2 wages

    **d.** The code section's effective date

**10.** Which code section is *most* likely to apply in determining whether real estate is considered a business?

    **a.** Code Sec. 162

    **b.** Code Sec. 179

    **c.** Code Sec. 199A

    **d.** Code Sec. 1231

**11.** If a single taxpayer's taxable income is less than _____, the W-2 limitations and the specified service business disqualification do *not* apply.

    **a.** $157,500

    **b.** $207,500

    **c.** $315,000

    **d.** $415,000

**12.** Assume a taxpayer has $1 million of taxable income subject to the 37 percent top marginal rate. Assuming all of the income is qualified business income from a non-service business, and the amount of the deduction is not reduced by the W-2 and capital limitation, his qualified business income deduction would reduce the taxpayer's taxable income to:

    **a.** $296,000

    **b.** $370,000

    **c.** $740,000

    **d.** $800,000

**13.** Code Sec. 199A imposes more stringent limitations on:

    **a.** Specified service trades or businesses

    **b.** Nonservice trades or businesses

    **c.** S corporations

    **d.** Sole proprietorships

**14.** Helen Straka, a married taxpayer who files a joint return, has taxable income of $410,000. Which of the following is true?

    **a.** Helen can deduct 20 percent of QBI income properly allocable to her, regardless of the W-2 wage and capital investment limitations

    **b.** Helen's QBI deduction is not subject to any limitations

    **c.** Helen's QBI deduction is subject to limitations based on capital investments and W-2 wages

    **d.** Helen's taxable income is well below the threshold amount for married taxpayers filing jointly

**15.** Which of the following statements is true regarding Code Sec. 199A deductions?

    **a.** The Code Sec. 199A deduction reduces a taxpayer's adjusted gross income

    **b.** The Code Sec. 199A deduction is taken before adjusted gross income is determined

    **c.** The taxable income limitation is determined before the Code Sec. 199A deduction

    **d.** Nonqualified business income deductions can help reduce the Code Sec. 199A deductions

**16.** The 20 percent QBI deduction is based on:

    **a.** Gross income

    **b.** Adjusted gross income

    **c.** Taxable income

    **d.** W-2 wages

**17.** W-2 wages are:

    **a.** Wages reported to the Social Security Administration

    **b.** Wages plus property held

    **c.** Wages plus payments to independent contractors

    **d.** Guaranteed payments

**18.** The W-2 limitation comes into play when:

    **a.** Taxable income is under the threshold amount

    **b.** Taxable income is above the threshold amount

    **c.** The taxpayer has depreciable business assets

    **d.** The taxpayer is a nonservice business

**19.** Which of the following is true regarding the new Code Sec. 199A?

    **a.** Treasury regulations have been issued to clarify some of its provisions

    **b.** It only applies to "pass-through" entities such as S-corporations and partnerships

    **c.** Taxpayers with service businesses are not eligible for the deduction

    **d.** Income from real estate business is ineligible for the deduction

**20.** A taxpayer who has taxable income between the lower and higher thresholds is subject to

   **a.** The full wage/capital limitation

   **b.** No wage/capital limitation

   **c.** A phase-in of the wage/capital limitation

   **d.** A penalty

**21.** Which of the following is a disadvantage of an S corporation related to the entity restrictions on the ability to make and maintain S corp status?

   **a.** Ownership is limited to only 50 individuals

   **b.** Estates and trusts are not allowed to own stock in an S corp

   **c.** S corporations that were formerly C corporations must keep track of built-in gains at the time of conversion

   **d.** S corps are only allowed to have two classes of stock

**22.** In order to form an S corporation, there must not be more than how many shareholders?

   **a.** 50

   **b.** 75

   **c.** 90

   **d.** 100

**23.** A stockholder's basis in an S corp increases from a:

   **a.** Separately stated item of income

   **b.** Nontaxable distribution

   **c.** Separately stated loss

   **d.** Nondeductible expense

**24.** Which of the following identifies the last item in the order of adjustments?

   **a.** Required increases to basis

   **b.** Reductions for nondividend distributions

   **c.** Reductions for nondeductible expenses

   **d.** Reduction for losses and separately stated deductions

**25.** The _____ keeps track of previously taxed undistributed earnings earned while the entity is an S corp.

   **a.** Accumulated earnings account

   **b.** Accumulated adjustment account

   **c.** Accumulated undistributed earnings account

   **d.** Accumulated income account

**26.** If a shareholder's interest in the corporation is terminated during the year, the basis reduction is applied with respect to the indebtedness held immediately _____ the termination of the interest. In this case, any indebtedness acquired by the shareholder after such last day _____ be considered.

   **a.** Before; may not

   **b.** Before; may

   **c.** After; may not

   **d.** After; may

**27.** Although certain amounts are nontaxable (such as rental and dividend income), most earnings of an S corp are taxable at what percent for Social Security tax?

a. 7.5 percent

b. 7.9 percent

c. 12.4 percent

d. 12.8 percent

**28.** Which of the following revenue rules provides that the IRS may recharacterize as wages a corporate distribution to a shareholder in lieu of wages and thus assess FICA and FUTA taxes that would have been due?

a. Rev. Rule 74-44

b. Rev. Rule 75-44

c. Rev. Rule 74-55

d. Rev. Rule 75-55

**29.** In a July 2002 Treasury Inspector General Report, data summarizing the average shareholder wages and distribution of 84 S corps that were under audit indicated that the average shareholder wage of those S corps was approximately _____ whereas the average distribution was nearly_____.

a. $5,300; $350,000

b. $45,000; $230,000

c. $5,300; $150,000

d. $45,000; $75,000

**30.** Which of the following provides a means for S corporation shareholders to pay the tax liabilities resulting from allocations of income?

a. Salaries

b. Tax distributions

c. Return of basis

d. Payment of equity

# ¶ 10,403  Final Exam: Module 3

**1.** MACRS property with a GDS recovery period of _____ or less is considered qualified property with respect to bonus depreciation.

    **a.** 10 years

    **b.** 20 years

    **c.** 25 years

    **d.** 39 years

**2.** Which of the following identifies the bonus depreciation rate for the year 2025?

    **a.** 20 percent

    **b.** 40 percent

    **c.** 60 percent

    **d.** 100 percent

**3.** Based on the new tax law, property constructed or acquired after _____ qualifies for the 100 percent bonus depreciation.

    **a.** August 27, 2015

    **b.** October 27, 2015

    **c.** September 27, 2016

    **d.** September 27, 2017

**4.** Code Sec. _____ allows businesses to deduct the purchase of qualifying equipment and qualifying software and carries a $1 million deduction limit for 2018.

    **a.** 179

    **b.** 181

    **c.** 193

    **d.** 195

**5.** Which of the following identifies the primary goal for cost segregation?

    **a.** Identify all property-related costs that can be depreciated faster

    **b.** Establish the depreciable tax value for each major building component that is likely to be replaced in the future

    **c.** Assign longer useful lives to those assets that are considered improvement property

    **d.** Apply Code Sec. 179 expensing to qualified leasehold improvement property

**6.** Which of the following techniques allows an individual to use income or losses between two related entities to offset one another?

    **a.** Offsetting

    **b.** Grouping

    **c.** Netting

    **d.** Grossing

**7.** For assets placed in service before January 1, 2018, qualified leasehold improvement property is depreciated over _____.

    **a.** 10 years

    **b.** 15 years

    **c.** 20 years

    **d.** 25 years

**8.** Which of the following building categories has a 39-year useful life?

    **a.** Ceilings

    **b.** Paving

    **c.** Landscaping

    **d.** Decking

**9.** When making a GAA election for a demolished building, an individual should do which of the following:

    **a.** Elect GAA only for 7-year property

    **b.** Do a cost segregation study on the building prior to making the GAA election

    **c.** Immediately deduct 39-year property upon demolition

    **d.** Discontinue depreciating basis in an old building

**10.** Which of the following identifies the Code Sec. 179 deduction limit for 2018?

    **a.** $1 million

    **b.** $1.1 million

    **c.** $1.34 million

    **d.** $1.79 million

**11.** Generally, how does the tax code define "basis"?

    **a.** The amount of gain in the value of property at transfer

    **b.** The cost of property

    **c.** The cost of property plus the tax cost

    **d.** The fair market value of the property received

**12.** If a taxpayer has an opportunity to purchase an item at a bargain rate for some compensatory purpose, the basis in the property would be the property's _____.

    **a.** Carryover basis

    **b.** Fair market value

    **c.** Intrinsic value

    **d.** Present value

**13.** When does a donee use the fair market value rather than the carryover basis of property received by a gift?

    **a.** When the donee is a child of the donor

    **b.** When the donee is an employee of the donor

    **c.** When the fair market value is less than the basis at the time the gift is made

    **d.** When the property has built-in appreciation at the time the gift is made

**14.** Nannette LeBeau purchased property for $100,000 in 2000. She gave her son Andre a gift of the property that had an adjusted basis in her hands of $150,000. At the time of the gift, the property had a fair market value of $165,000 with respect to which Nannette paid a gift tax in the amount of $16,500. What is the basis of the property in Andre's hands immediately after the gift?

    **a.** $116,500

    **b.** $150,000

    **c.** $165,000

    **d.** $166,500

**15.** What is a tax consequence of selling a property at a discount in a gift context?
   **a.** The donee's basis is the amount paid for the property
   **b.** The donee's basis is the donor's basis plus any increase for gift tax paid
   **c.** The entire basis is allocated to the sale
   **d.** There may be a loss on the transaction

**16.** Under Code Sec. 102(b)(2), what is excludable from the income of the donee?
   **a.** Only the principal of a gift or bequest
   **b.** The principal of and any interest derived from a gift or bequest
   **c.** The principal of and earnings from a gift or bequest
   **d.** The principal of a gift or bequest and income for life

**17.** When part of a larger property is sold, the basis of the property must be:
   **a.** Based on the entire basis of the larger property
   **b.** Based on half of the basis of the larger property
   **c.** Based on the relative value of the entire property
   **d.** Equitably apportioned among the parts

**18.** What is the "cost" of other property (boot) that is received in a two-party noncash exchange?
   **a.** Half of the sum of the fair market values divided by two
   **b.** The fair market value of the property given up
   **c.** The fair market value of the property received
   **d.** The carryover basis

**19.** After the *Tax Cuts and Jobs Act,* like-kind exchanges under Code Sec. 1031 can be used for exchanges of:
   **a.** Debt
   **b.** Personal property
   **c.** Real estate
   **d.** Stocks

**20.** What is the basis of a like-kind exchange under Code Sec. 1031(d) when debt is not involved?
   **a.** Actual cash, plus basis of property given up, plus gain recognized, plus any deemed cash
   **b.** Basis of property given up, plus gain recognized, minus any money received
   **c.** Fair market value of the property received
   **d.** The basis of the property given up minus the greater of the allowed depreciation or allowable depreciation

# ¶ 10,404 Final Exam: Module 4

**1.** Which of the following identifies the maximum gift tax rate for 2018?

    **a.** 25 percent

    **b.** 35 percent

    **c.** 40 percent

    **d.** 45 percent

**2.** The first $_____ for 2018 made by a donor to each donee during a calendar years is excluded in determining the total amount of gifts made by the donor during the year.

    **a.** $15,000

    **b.** $16,000

    **c.** $17,000

    **d.** $20,000

**3.** In order for the annual exclusion to be available, the gift must constitute a gift of a _____ interest.

    **a.** Future

    **b.** Present

    **c.** Determinable

    **d.** Realizable

**4.** The entire value of property transferred in trust for the benefit of a minor will not be treated as a gift of a future interest if the requirements of which of the following are made?

    **a.** Code Sec. 2503(c)

    **b.** Code Sec. 2728(d)

    **c.** Code Sec. 3489(e)

    **d.** Code Sec. 4477(b)

**5.** Which of the following identifies the lifetime gift tax exemption for 2018 as amended by the *Tax Cuts and Jobs Act*?

    **a.** $5,490,000

    **b.** $6,789,000

    **c.** $9,445,000

    **d.** 11,180,000

**6.** Which of the following is available to a surviving spouse of a decedent who died after 2010 and who did not use all of his or her exclusion amount during lifetime or at death?

    **a.** Portability

    **b.** Transferability

    **c.** Deductibility

    **d.** Retract ability

**7.** The marital deduction is available for gifts to a donee spouse if the spouses are married to each other:

    **a.** For at least 2 years

    **b.** For at least 5 years

    **c.** During the previous year of the gift

    **d.** At the time of the gift

**8.** The value of a gift of property is the _____ of that property on the date the gift is considered complete.

    **a.** Thrift shop value

    **b.** Fair market value

    **c.** Net realizable value

    **d.** Net book value

**9.** A substantial valuation understatement exists when the value of property reported on a gift tax return is what percent or less of the amount determined to be the correct value?

    **a.** 65 percent

    **b.** 70 percent

    **c.** 75 percent

    **d.** 80 percent

**10.** In general, the statute of limitations that applies with respect to gift tax returns is:

    **a.** Two years

    **b.** Three years

    **c.** Five years

    **d.** Seven years

**11.** In 2018 the applicable exclusion from federal transfer taxes is approximately how much per person?

    **a.** $11.2 million

    **b.** $14.6 million

    **c.** $18.3 million

    **d.** $19.8 million

**12.** With respect to refocused planning, married clients should consider forming which of the following?

    **a.** Traditional IRAs

    **b.** Spousal lifetime access trusts

    **c.** Bypass trusts

    **d.** Simple trusts

**13.** Regarding planning for nonresident aliens with assets in the United States or who plan to move to the United States, the estate tax exemption for nonresident aliens remains at:

    **a.** $60,000

    **b.** $75,000

    **c.** $80,000

    **d.** $95,000

**14.** The primary motive for enacting portability of the federal estate tax exemption was simplifying estate planning for:

    **a.** Single filers

    **b.** Heads of households

    **c.** Married couples

    **d.** Trustees

**15.** The use of a bypass trust can avoid unequal treatment that might otherwise occur in a _____ family situation.

    **a.** Foreign

    **b.** Blended

    **c.** Domestic

    **d.** Large

**16.** In order to get the basis adjustment to the donor on return of the asset, a donor must hold the asset at least how long to get it?

    **a.** One year

    **b.** Two years

    **c.** Three years

    **d.** Five years

**17.** Which of the following types of trusts should be used to maximize income shifting opportunities?

    **a.** Bypass trust

    **b.** Sprinkling trust

    **c.** Simple trust

    **d.** Complex trust

**18.** Life insurance can be used to provide direct _____ to children from a prior marriage without having to address the blended family concerns of _____.

    **a.** Bequests, trusts

    **b.** Benefits, taxes

    **c.** Bequests, taxes

    **d.** Benefits, portability

**19.** If clients are age _____ or older, they may take advantage of the transfer of IRA funds directly to charity.

    **a.** 50½

    **b.** 60

    **c.** 65

    **d.** 70½

**20.** When trusts are used, plans should consider giving the beneficiary a/an _____ general power of appointment to achieve a basis step-up at the beneficiary's death.

    **a.** Testamentary

    **b.** Portable

    **c.** Exclusive

    **d.** Unrestricted

# ¶ 10,500 Answer Sheets

## ¶ 10,501 Top Federal Tax Issues for 2019 CPE Course: MODULE 1

(10014583-0007)

Go to **cchcpelink.com/printcpe** to complete your Final Exam online for instant results.

A $113.95 processing fee will be charged for each user submitting Module 1 to **cchcpelink.com/printcpe** for online grading.

## Module 1: Answer Sheet

(10014583-0007)

Please answer the questions by indicating the appropriate letter next to the corresponding number.

| | | | |
|---|---|---|---|
| 1. \_\_\_ | 9. \_\_\_ | 17. \_\_\_ | 25. \_\_\_ |
| 2. \_\_\_ | 10. \_\_\_ | 18. \_\_\_ | 26. \_\_\_ |
| 3. \_\_\_ | 11. \_\_\_ | 19. \_\_\_ | 27. \_\_\_ |
| 4. \_\_\_ | 12. \_\_\_ | 20. \_\_\_ | 28. \_\_\_ |
| 5. \_\_\_ | 13. \_\_\_ | 21. \_\_\_ | 29. \_\_\_ |
| 6. \_\_\_ | 14. \_\_\_ | 22. \_\_\_ | 30. \_\_\_ |
| 7. \_\_\_ | 15. \_\_\_ | 23. \_\_\_ | |
| 8. \_\_\_ | 16. \_\_\_ | 24. \_\_\_ | |

**Please complete the Evaluation Form (located after the Module 4 Answer Sheet). Thank you.**

# ¶ 10,502 Top Federal Tax Issues for 2019 CPE Course: MODULE 2

## (10014584-0007)

Go to **cchcpelink.com/printcpe** to complete your Final Exam online for instant results.

A $113.95 processing fee will be charged for each user submitting Module 2 to **cchcpelink.com/printcpe** for online grading.

## Module 2: Answer Sheet

(10014584-0007)

Please answer the questions by indicating the appropriate letter next to the corresponding number.

| | | | |
|---|---|---|---|
| 1. ___ | 9. ___ | 17. ___ | 25. ___ |
| 2. ___ | 10. ___ | 18. ___ | 26. ___ |
| 3. ___ | 11. ___ | 19. ___ | 27. ___ |
| 4. ___ | 12. ___ | 20. ___ | 28. ___ |
| 5. ___ | 13. ___ | 21. ___ | 29. ___ |
| 6. ___ | 14. ___ | 22. ___ | 30. ___ |
| 7. ___ | 15. ___ | 23. ___ | |
| 8. ___ | 16. ___ | 24. ___ | |

**Please complete the Evaluation Form (located after the Module 4 Answer Sheet).
Thank you.**

# ¶ 10,503 Top Federal Tax Issues for 2019 CPE Course: MODULE 3

## (10014585-0007)

Go to **cchcpelink.com/printcpe** to complete your Final Exam online for instant results.

A $75.95 processing fee will be charged for each user submitting Module 3 to **cchcpelink.com/printcpe** for online grading.

## Module 3: Answer Sheet

(10014585-0007)

Please answer the questions by indicating the appropriate letter next to the corresponding number.

1. ____        8. ____        15. ____

2. ____        9. ____        16. ____

3. ____        10. ____       17. ____

4. ____        11. ____       18. ____

5. ____        12. ____       19. ____

6. ____        13. ____       20. ____

7. ____        14. ____

**Please complete the Evaluation Form (located after the Module 4 Answer Sheet). Thank you.**

# ¶ 10,504 Top Federal Tax Issues for 2019 CPE Course: MODULE 4

## (10066307-0001)

Go to **cchcpelink.com/printcpe** to complete your Final Exam online for instant results.

A $75.95 processing fee will be charged for each user submitting Module 4 to **cchcpelink.com/printcpe** for online grading.

## Module 4: Answer Sheet

(10066307-0001)

Please answer the questions by indicating the appropriate letter next to the corresponding number.

| | | |
|---|---|---|
| 1. _____ | 8. _____ | 15. _____ |
| 2. _____ | 9. _____ | 16. _____ |
| 3. _____ | 10. _____ | 17. _____ |
| 4. _____ | 11. _____ | 18. _____ |
| 5. _____ | 12. _____ | 19. _____ |
| 6. _____ | 13. _____ | 20. _____ |
| 7. _____ | 14. _____ | |

**Please complete the Evaluation Form (located after the Module 4 Answer Sheet). Thank you.**

# ¶ 10,600 Top Federal Tax Issues for 2019 CPE Course: Evaluation Form

(10024491-0006)

Please take a few moments to fill out and submit this evaluation to Wolters Kluwer so that we can better provide you with the type of self-study programs you want and need. Thank you.

## About This Program

1. Please circle the number that best reflects the extent of your agreement with the following statements:

|   |   | Strongly Agree | | | | Strongly Disagree |
|---|---|---|---|---|---|---|
| a. | The Course objectives were met. | 5 | 4 | 3 | 2 | 1 |
| b. | This Course was comprehensive and organized. | 5 | 4 | 3 | 2 | 1 |
| c. | The content was current and technically accurate. | 5 | 4 | 3 | 2 | 1 |
| d. | This Course content was relevant and contributed to achievement of the learning objectives. | 5 | 4 | 3 | 2 | 1 |
| e. | The prerequisite requirements were appropriate. | 5 | 4 | 3 | 2 | 1 |
| f. | This Course was a valuable learning experience. | 5 | 4 | 3 | 2 | 1 |
| g. | The Course completion time was appropriate. | 5 | 4 | 3 | 2 | 1 |

2. What do you consider to be the strong points of this Course?

3. What improvements can we make to this Course?

**THANK YOU FOR TAKING THE TIME TO COMPLETE THIS SURVEY!**